Applied Guide for Event Study Research in Supply Chain Management

Lincoln C. Wood
University of Otago, New Zealand & Curtin University, Australia

A volume in the Advances in Logistics,
Operations, and Management Science (ALOMS)
Book Series

Published in the United States of America by
    IGI Global
    Information Science Reference (an imprint of IGI Global)
    701 E. Chocolate Avenue
    Hershey PA, USA 17033
    Tel: 717-533-8845
    Fax: 717-533-8661
    E-mail: cust@igi-global.com
    Web site: http://www.igi-global.com

Library of Congress Cataloging-in-Publication Data

Names: Wood, Lincoln C., author.
Title: Applied guide for event study research in supply chain management /
  by Lincoln Wood.
Description: Hershey, PA : Business Science Research, [2022] | Includes
  bibliographical references and index. | Summary: "The primary objective
  of this book is to support readers in understanding how to develop,
  execute, and publish an event study specifically in the area of supply
  chain management, with valuable support for wider management studies"--
  Provided by publisher.
Identifiers: LCCN 2022008745 (print) | LCCN 2022008746 (ebook) | ISBN
  9781799889694 (hardback) | ISBN 9781799889700 (library binding) | ISBN
  9781799889717 (ebook)
Subjects: LCSH: Business logistics--Mathematical models.
Classification: LCC HD38.5 .W665 2022 (print) | LCC HD38.5 (ebook) | DDC
  658.7--dc23/eng/20220224
LC record available at https://lccn.loc.gov/2022008745
LC ebook record available at https://lccn.loc.gov/2022008746

This book is published in the IGI Global book series Advances in Logistics, Operations, and Management Science (ALOMS) (ISSN: 2327-350X; eISSN: 2327-3518)

British Cataloguing in Publication Data
A Cataloguing in Publication record for this book is available from the British Library.

For electronic access to this publication, please contact: eresources@igi-global.com.

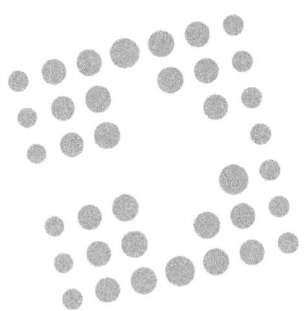

Advances in Logistics, Operations, and Management Science (ALOMS) Book Series

John Wang
Montclair State University, USA

ISSN:2327-350X
EISSN:2327-3518

MISSION

Operations research and management science continue to influence business processes, administration, and management information systems, particularly in covering the application methods for decision-making processes. New case studies and applications on management science, operations management, social sciences, and other behavioral sciences have been incorporated into business and organizations real-world objectives.

The **Advances in Logistics, Operations, and Management Science** (ALOMS) Book Series provides a collection of reference publications on the current trends, applications, theories, and practices in the management science field. Providing relevant and current research, this series and its individual publications would be useful for academics, researchers, scholars, and practitioners interested in improving decision making models and business functions.

COVERAGE

- Computing and information technologies
- Organizational Behavior
- Finance
- Services management
- Production Management
- Marketing engineering
- Risk Management
- Networks
- Information Management
- Operations Management

IGI Global is currently accepting manuscripts for publication within this series. To submit a proposal for a volume in this series, please contact our Acquisition Editors at acquisitions@igi-global.com or visit: https://www.igi-global.com/publish/.

Titles in this Series

For a list of additional titles in this series, please visit: www.igi-global.com/book-series/advances-logistics-operations-management-science/37170

Handbook of Research on Global Networking Post-COVID-19
Ana Pego (Nova University of Lisbon, Portugal)
Business Science Reference • © 2022 • 400pp • H/C (ISBN: 9781799888567) • US $295.00

Increasing Supply Chain Performance in Digital Society
Ramona Diana Leon (Universitat Politecnica de Valencia, Spain) Raul Rodriguez (Universitat Politecnica de Valencia, Spain) and Juan Jose Alfaro Saiz (Universitat Politecnica de Valencia, Spain)
Business Science Reference • © 2022 • 315pp • H/C (ISBN: 9781799897156) • US $250.00

Sales Management for Improved Organizational Competitiveness and Performance
José Duarte Santos (Instituto Superior Politécnico Gaya, Portugal)
Business Science Reference • © 2022 • 325pp • H/C (ISBN: 9781668434307) • US $240.00

Handbook of Research on Post-Pandemic Talent Management Models in Knowledge Organizations
Mohammad Rafiqul Islam Talukdar (American International University-Bangladesh, Bangladesh) Carmen z. Lamagna (American International University-Bangladesh, Bangladesh) Charles Carillo Villanueva (American International University-Bangladesh, Bangladesh) Rezbin Nahar (American International University-Bangladesh, Bangladesh) and Farheen Hassan (American International University-Bangladesh, Bangladesh)
Business Science Reference • © 2022 • 415pp • H/C (ISBN: 9781668438947) • US $295.00

Global Air Transport Management and Reshaping Business Models for the New Era
Kannapat Kankaew (Suan Sunandha Rajabhat University, Thailand)
Business Science Reference • © 2022 • 300pp • H/C (ISBN: 9781668446157) • US $250.00

International Perspectives on Value Creation and Sustainability Through Social Entrepreneurship
Hesham Magd (Modern College of Business and Science, Oman) Dharmendra Singh (Modern College of Business and Science, Oman) Raihan Taqui Syed (Modern College of Business and Science, Oman) and David Spicer (Bradford University, UK)
Business Science Reference • © 2022 • 300pp • H/C (ISBN: 9781668446669) • US $250.00

Examining the Vital Financial Role of SMEs in Achieving the Sustainable Development Goals
Dalila Taleb (A. Belkaid University, Algeria) Mohammed El Amine Abdelli (University Of Brest, France) Afef Khalil (University Of Tunis Carthage, Tunisia) and Asma Sghaier (University Of Sousse, Tunisia)
Business Science Reference • © 2022 • 325pp • H/C (ISBN: 9781668448342) • US $250.00

701 East Chocolate Avenue, Hershey, PA 17033, USA
Tel: 717-533-8845 x100 • Fax: 717-533-8661
E-Mail: cust@igi-global.com • www.igi-global.com

This volume is dedicated to our new son, Fionnlagh.
  My boy, we know you have quite the journey ahead.
  We will always work hard every day, in every way, to support and help you.
  You have our love forever.

Table of Contents

Preface

The concepts and ideas in this book have been drawn, and frustration that the volumes and with a paucity of background information about how event studies are often conducted. While we have commonly used event studies in other research areas, the use in management and supply chain research is more limited but growing. However, there remain several important research design considerations we need to account for over the process of planning, executing, and writing up event studies. While discussing this with the students on their supervised projects, many issues and sources of uncertainty emerged. Consequently, I found myself repeating the same explanations for students time and time again. I generated a written document with some of the common issues and how to address them. Many of these ideas delve into nuances and steps to take; often, students wonder whether these might be acceptable, how other researchers do it, and what is practical. Most times, I refer my students to other sources, such as well-established textbooks, if they need to understand some of the key ideas behind regression analysis. However, despite this, there are still elements of the particular type of approach and data that will cause consistent issues that will not be well addressed in more general treatments of, for example, regression analysis.

Out of frustration, I gathered and collected my notes on these issues. I used email discussions and commentaries exchanged with my students and comments from the margins of their work where I scribble or annotate using the word processor. Some insight has been drawn from particular conversations with students, feedback from my presentations to departments and colleagues, and editors and anonymous reviewers working through the manuscript publication process. In each case, I have learned a great deal. In addition, many questions and feedback during the process caused me to reflect on some of the core issues, questioning the assumptions that I was holding.

While I firmly believe that the event study method has wide applications and broader management and supply chain research, the projects must be carefully planned, designed, and conducted. For example, the approach will interest all management or splotchy management researchers, as it can address only a small subset of the many interesting and important questions that we need to address in our research. This manuscript is not designed to be a bible for all researchers but to complement other existing standard treatments of the common research methods. Nevertheless, the volume provides insight into how those with a management background can approach this type of method with more confidence, particularly as they begin to deal with some of the nitty-gritty of the elements. In particular, students often ask questions about how to generate a sample for use in the analysis, which is often not well addressed in other literature. I have been surprised about the lack of questions about sample generation during the publication process, either from editors or reviewers.

I intend this volume as an applied guide; it addresses core issues but is not overly prescriptive. This is important, as an enormous range of different circumstances might be addressed during any particular study. It focuses less on the theory and the statistics in the modeling in the study; instead, it focuses on fundamental design decisions and the activities that must occur during the project. We have not delved into the software and how to use software, simply due to the wide variation software availability and the different approaches to using the software.

Similarly, I focus on the other activities and process steps rather than get bogged down in the details of the equations. In some ways, the equations are of limited interest to many readers in management departments, as we often use the software to run the calculations. However, as always, I have included a wide range of citations throughout the work so that interested readers can enjoy more extensive treatments of the topics. Some of these are addressed in passing or parenthetically within the main body of the text within text citations; in other cases, I have included a range of valuable additional readings. By looking through the list of additional readings, readers should identify key seminal and methodological texts that might enable them to go further or deeper in some of these issues.

In many cases, while completing a project and compiling a manuscript, readers must acknowledge there are often no strict answers to some of the questions that may come up. Where this is the case, I have tried to indicate my thinking about what might be most appropriate and explain why or under what circumstances. In many cases, research decisions are judgment decisions, and they will often create interesting limitations to the research while also remaining open to new avenues for future explorations of the issues.

I believe the event study method is an interesting and important method for wider management research. It allows us to make inferences about particular events and say something about the overall importance of the event's magnitude, which will interest senior managers. In the search for research relevance, it is much easier to engage with a senior manager when discussing how an event might influence the company's overall value. Talking about the change in value indicates that it is not just, for example, minor or insignificant operational detail but rather the event that was talking about can have a meaningful or outsized impact on the value of the firm, the underlying shareholder value, and even potentially the executive bonuses if they are connected to the market value of the firm.

It is also worth noting that while the event study uses stock returns and analyzes the stock market reactions in response to events, the results are still going to be meaningful for those who operate and run privately-held companies. Even if we can see the event causes an abnormal stock market reaction, just because a firm is not publicly listed does not mean that this is meaningless. Instead, if there is a creation of shareholder wealth or destruction of shareholder wealth as evidenced by the outcomes and insights from the event study, a private company should also consider that the same results would hold for their situation. Just because they are not publicly listed does not mean that there is no shareholder value, and similarly, we can expect the events we are studying to have a comparable impact on the shareholder value, although this is more difficult to assess due to the lack of trading of the stock on the market.

Ultimately, there is more use of the event study method and management and supply chain research. While the number of studies has been extending in recent years, the complexity and difficulty of presenting meaningful studies in leading journals are increasing. Throughout this volume, we treat some challenges and issues that can help a researcher new to this method understand what might be required to publish in leading journals and how they might extend the preliminary analysis to provide additional insight.

Through this volume, I hope to change the perception that the event study is simple, straightforward, and quick. While some calculations in the modeling work are relatively fast and easy to undertake, the actual design and consideration often involve substantial work. In particular, the development of the sample, the search for relevant announcements, the screening process of announcements, the search for confounding events can all take substantial time. Also important is how these can be crucial steps to undertake and undertake with great focus and rigor.

Finally, this work builds on many other researchers' insights, anonymous reviewers, and many generous editors who have provided insight and asked tough questions. I would also like to acknowledge the insight of Professor Vinod Singhal, who provided me with the original impetus and motivation to explore this method further over dinner at a small regional conference in Australasia. Finally, I am indebted to my many students who have used this approach and other related approaches and for all the questions that are provided me with challenging opportunities to expand my knowledge and insight, there being able to give them more comprehensive answers and reassurances about what they are doing and why they are doing it that way. In particular, I am pleased to acknowledge two past students, Dr Jason X. Wang (Huddersfield University, U.K.) and Dr Hari Srivastava (Auckland University of Technology, New Zealand) for their feedback and helpful remarks over the years as we have collaborated on event study projects.

Ultimately, I hope this book will expand the capacity of management and supply to management researchers to undertake event studies and empirical research. In addition, I hope this volume opens up the opportunity for management and supply chain researchers to include event studies in their repertoire. Finally, I appreciate any feedback, remarks, and suggestions on this volume. There is always the opportunity to improve, enhance, and add value to my readers, so any insight is always gratefully received.

I structured the book to walk through a project from start-to-finish and provide support, and address issues that occur throughout a project.

We first look at some of the theoretical underpinnings of the method in Chapter 2. Then, we address the core finance study assumptions and some of the practical questions you may face when introducing this approach to your colleagues. Finally, this chapter also addresses some implications possible from this type of study.

Chapter 3 summarizes the method, from start to finish. This sets the scene as we progressively move through the nuances of each of the research design and execution steps in the later chapters.

In Chapter 4, I discuss selecting a suitable topic and how you might approach this initial issue. This will be a make-or-break issue for many, as only a tightly defined set of topics will be of interest that can be addressed with this method.

Chapter 5 develops expertise on the sample construction. This is, likely, the most crucial chapter, as without a good sample, the rest of the study is entirely pointless. Poor data inputted into the analyzes means you will get poor results out from the method.

We then cover the archival and literature searches in Chapter 6. This includes techniques that may apply to both searching for a sample (e.g., news announcements) and searching research databases.

Chapter 7 recaps and extends discussions on the research design considerations. At this point, the project should be further along, and some issues will become apparent and will need to be addressed.

Chapter 8 discusses the financial and accounting data and some issues that need to be considered when collecting and using these data. We discuss the management of data and the efforts that should be made to ensure your data are kept safely and securely.

Chapter 9 discusses the data analysis using the event study method. Then, we dig deep into the calculation of the event study's abnormal return calculations.

In Chapter 10, we pause and allow for problem solving as problems and real-world issues creep into the project.

Chapter 11 extends the analysis by discussing the cross-sectional regression. The analytic steps are crucial to publishing and developing effective results. While many readers will be familiar with multivariate analyzes, this chapter contains nuances specific to this method and issues that will need to be accounted for because of the use of the data. Such issues are unlikely to have been as crucial in past studies for management scholars using, for example, survey data.

Chapter 13 discusses the importance of writing up and making sense of your results. The focus is on crafting a compelling manuscript, with lessons for both the writing or research articles and dissertations/theses.

Chapter 14 discusses and introduces other types of event studies, using long-term studies and operational data. While these are becoming more common in SCM studies, it is essential to be familiar with them and their similarities and differences.

Finally, Chapter 15 presents some case studies and examples of studies published in SCM areas, addressing interesting topics of wide interest. We look at their methods, research design decisions, the results, and how they are interpreted and explained.

Lincoln C. Wood
University of Otago, New Zealand & Curtin University, Australia

Chapter 1
Introduction to the Event Study Method in Management and Supply Chain Management Research

ABSTRACT

In management studies, the event study method has seen some use and much misuse and misunderstanding. Nevertheless, it remains a valuable and powerful technique to study the impact of various management events and can be used over a range of sub-disciplines in the management area. Used in the way the author examines in this book, he undertakes an event study to determine whether there is a stock market reaction to a management event, showing the overall positive or negative nature of the event. A subsequent cross-sectional regression can be undertaken to dive into the factors that influence or drive this result. This chapter introduces the approach, the history, and use of the approach, and some key factors that determine the suitability for management research. Next, he explores the boundaries for when this approach can be used and the type of issues and questions that the approach may not be gainfully used to explore. Finally, he presents an overview of the volume structure and how the topics will be addressed.

INTRODUCTION

When we consider the interest of most researchers in the areas of operations, supply chains, and general management, we often find that we want to improve things. However, to achieve these outcomes, we often need to know whether a change makes a difference. Consequently, we often look for causal relationships between managerial implementations and initiatives and meaningful outcomes for the company or organization.

In this light, it is interesting to consider the event study method, which has been widely used in the finance area. This has become one of the major approaches to conducting modern corporate finance research and forms the basis for a growing body of research. In finance, the focus is often on the an-

DOI: 10.4018/978-1-7998-8969-4.ch001

nouncement of dividends, stock splits, mergers and is less associated with many of the day-to-day management activities in which we are interested. However, the approach is also valuable to investigate activities and events that will interest general management and operations and supply chain management researchers and practitioners.

This book intends to introduce general management and supply chain management researchers and postgraduate students to the event study method. I am framing this as an applied guide that focuses on the method and many core assumptions, required to design and execute an effective and meaningful study. As such, we do not deeply examine the mechanics of specific tools or software packages to run the calculations, but on the steps to get you there and interpret what you get out of the software.

Therefore, this book guides the reader through the required steps in completing a study. For example, considering the type of event that may be useful, finding appropriate announcements and use that will help create the list of events for the study, developing hypotheses, identifying issues and problems. Finally, we look at running the analysis to calculate the abnormal returns in a subsequent cross-sectional regression and how to interpret and make sense of the results before writing up the studies.

This introductory chapter summarizes the widespread nature of the method and how the approach may be interesting to readers in a range of management and supply chain research journals. We also explore how it may interest many departments and examiners of dissertations.

Through the volume, we will also look at many examples with excerpts from different studies that highlight some of the critical issues and how you might address them. In addition, I provide commentary and explanation in additional detail about how you might overcome some of these problems and challenges to develop a unique and powerful study based on the event study method. Through doing this, I have taken a non-mathematical treatment, assuming that many readers will use established software and are more interested in designing a compelling study while using well-established analytical techniques. Therefore, while we do not address the state-of-the-art in terms of statistical advances in this area, we do look at some of the consequences and meaning of the different models that might be used in the estimation procedures and ensure that you follow best practice. By doing this, I aim to enable the readers to overcome obstacles and the uncertainty around many fundamental design steps and activities before and after calculations and estimation procedures that are often the focus of event study works.

Background

Most management scholars and supply chain researchers want to make a difference in the world of practice – we strive to understand what a manager may influence and change to change outcomes. What variables we can manipulate to cause the final change we want to see in a simple sense? What 'independent variables' can be changed to drive a desired outcome in the 'dependent variables'?

The event study method ultimately does not answer these questions, but it answers the broad question about whether a management event creates a discernible outcome, one that an investor (as reflected by stock market changes) would care about. It does not answer the how or why this happens, just whether there is an observable shift in outcomes. As an approach, it helps a researcher understand the different approaches and gives us a yardstick to understand the relative impact of each by decanting all changes in outcomes into stock prices. We measure and evaluate a given event in terms of whether there is a change in the stock returns that is 'abnormal' or beyond what we may otherwise expect to see in the day-to-day fluctuations. If there is a consistent pattern of these abnormal returns, we can assess the overall direction and infer whether this was a valuable 'event' for the firm. For instance, there are studies on product recalls showing that they reduce shareholder value (as assessed by the negative stock market reaction) and indicating factors that managers may control to lessen the damage from recalls (Kumar & Budin, 2006; Wood, Wang, et al., 2017; Zhao et al., 2013). Other studies show an impact from operational successes from quality programs influencing positive stock returns (Hendricks & Singhal, 2001; Nicolau & Sellers, 2002) or from winning awards for excellence in logistics (Eroglu et al., 2016).

Is this important? It depends on your perspective. This has limited utility if you are primarily concerned with operational details and what a day-to-day manager might influence. However, if you are concerned about whether a broad program of change may be beneficial, if this category of event usually produces positive abnormal returns, then we may say that it is indeed valuable. On the other hand, if we associate an event with negative abnormal returns, understanding this magnitude may allow a senior management team conversation about the value of avoiding this event. Framed this way, given an adverse event (such as a product recall) may negatively influence the firm's value by a given amount, there may be an incentive to invest up to this amount to reduce or mitigate the chance of this occurring.

The method is not something I learned about as a student in our quantitative and qualitative research methods classes. This does not mean it is not an accepted method; no number of classes could cover more than a rudimentary selection of core methods in a single area of study. Researchers in accounting and finance have more extensively used the method itself. However, it does not suggest that event studies have not seen widespread adoption and use in particular management problems. It has been, for instance, used to understand a range of different scenarios that include the impact of executives joining the senior management team (Hendricks et al., 2014), sustainable construction practices (Kajander et al., 2012), benefits of becoming sustainable (Cheung, 2011), food safety (Dai et al., 2013; Hammoudi et al., 2009; Mazzocchi et al., 2009), signing new construction contracts (Choi, 2014), managing business process outsourcing (Duan et al., 2014), and product recalls and safety failures (Chen et al., 2009; Ni et al., 2014; Wood et al., 2017).

Given the wide range of applications – how can event studies be useful in a particular area such as supply chain management research? First, a major focus will always be whether an approach can provide a substantial and demonstrable benefit to the firm. Early studies in a stream of research may look at a case study approach (saying, in essence, that a particular company did this and derived benefit) to explore the phenomenon of interest. A few firms can be used, given the early adoption, which can be acceptable in exploratory research. However, as the technology or approach becomes more commonplace, surveys may be undertaken and a sample of hundreds of responses allows an analysis to see what factors are causally related to improved higher performance, as reported by the respondents. Surveys are often challenging to run in a way that extracts reliable and objective data about outcomes. For example, do we ask respondents whether something made a substantial change and have them evaluate this on a five-point scale (strongly disagree, disagree, neutral, agree, strongly agree)? Or do we ask them to input real-world data from their management system? While this would be preferred, many respondents may not have ready access to those data and may not be willing or able to share it in a survey.

While researchers in different disciplines naturally examine different options for managers and addressing different issues, the end impact of the changes should influence company performance. We expect a shift in stock returns for the (publicly listed) firm as it recognizes the changed company performance and long-term influences. Granted, a supply chain manager will probably not be interested in stock returns,[1] and instead may be more focused on the day-to-day and operational outcomes of interest. They may focus their attention on their usual reported data and KPIs on pressing operational metrics (e.g., 'stock turns' or inventory levels). However, long-term changes in operations or supply chain initiatives should flow through to a more successful firm. Consequentially, positive changes should flow through to long-term changes in the company's stock returns.

Such causality is implied but rarely contemplated. The mere fact that there are multiple links in the causal chain between cause and stock-return-as-an-effect suggests that the influence will have to be strong and the effect a powerful one. If we are using other methods, we may evaluate a change, such as an improved quality system,

Operations managers may also be interested in long-run studies of stock returns and operations performance (introduced in chapter 14). Operational data is more common in these studies, and the measures are more likely to interest operations and supply chain managers. Examples include Huey-Lian and Tang (2000) and Holder-Webb, Lopez, and Regier (2005). In examining changes in operating performance, Huey-Lian and Tang attempt to explain the commonly observed stock market reaction to mergers by analyzing operating performance changes as a source of gains during the merger. The corporate and operational restructuring study presented by Holder-Webb et al. reports changes in the return on equity and operating margins. Further, the approach can be used to examine the impact of an event on other factors, such as growth trends in transport use (X. Zhang, 2021).

However, the short-run studies in this book use the changes in stock returns over a short period (ideally, one or two days) to measure the event's overall impact on the firms involved. Examples in the supply chain topics area include, for example, Park, Park, and Zhang (2003) and Gong, Firth, and Cullinane (2008). Clearly, when we consider stock returns, we are talking about publicly listed companies. However, the fact that the studies are conducted using publicly listed companies does not mean the results are solely generalizable to other behemoths of the corporate world. The impact is just as true for other firms, even if the changes would not be immediately apparent in stock returns (as they are not listed). For example, product recalls are generally negative, as we see from many event studies(Ni et al., 2014; Rupp, 2001) and as is regarded as important in the SCM literature where there is also a focus on internal factors, more difficult to study with event studies, that influence recall success(Wowak et al., 2016; Wowak & Boone, 2015). On the other hand, quality is encouraged, and we see from event studies it has a positive impact on companies (Hendricks & Singhal, 2001; Nicolau & Sellers, 2002; Pinar & Ozgur, 2007; Terziovski & Guerrero, 2014) and this is mirrored in other operations management literature with different methods ((Wang et al., 2012; M. Zhang et al., 2020).

A substantial benefit from using the event study method approach is that we are using secondary data that is less biased than survey data. As we are using financial and accounting data, there is less likely to be the social desirability bias that we may find in survey research about sustainability (Carter & Easton, 2011; Walker et al., 2012). Such bias can be acute when focusing on topics such as sustainability (Walker et al., 2012) and other measures of sensitive topics (such as project success). In addition, surveys can suffer from mis-worded (or carefully and cynically worded) survey questions, ordering of questions, scales used in questions, and how respondents may not make much mental effort in answering the question (Bertrand & Mullainathan, 2001). These factors can all combine to ensure that respondents' perceptions of improvements may be more rosy and positive than they are, suggesting a much stronger effect size than exists. Using operational or financial performance changes should support researchers to identify better and measure the outcomes of interest.

THE WIDESPREAD USE OF THE METHOD IN THE ACADEMIC COMMUNITY

Many people in management or supply chain departments come from a background of social science-oriented research methods. As such, they may not have been exposed or be familiar with the event study method. In itself, this is not a problem if we look through many of the top journals, they publish a range of research using methods that would not be covered in a traditional research methods class. Even Advanced Research methods classes can only cover a small subset of possible ways of addressing pertinent research questions of interest in that discipline.

The event study method itself comes from the finance department slash background but despite this, it has found wide application over a range of different topics and subjects, addressing that core research question: how does the stock market react to a particular event? We see the research used in a range of different disciplines and areas to address the impact of an event and different contexts. If you are not sure whether the method will be acceptable to the editor or your advisory team, you can certainly explain a bit about the background and note where this method has been used in the past. In many cases, you might see a short section and the introduction of articles explaining that this method has been used to study a range of different scenarios such as food recalls (Salin & Hooker, 2001), the impact of excellence in product design as evidenced by winning awards (Xia et al., 2016), benefits from quality programs (Hendricks & Singhal, 2001), innovation launches of products such as green vehicles (Ba et al., 2013), or the negative impact caused by quality problems such as the Toyota accelerator pedal recall issues (Gokhale et al., 2014). By including such examples, you show the validity of this method, the wide-spread acceptance, and a range of circumstances in which it has been used.

As we might expect, an event study that has published in a leading journal has probably been conducted rigorously and correctly, with attention paid to many important assumptions or nuances of the method. This is not to say that a doctoral student's project that has rejected from a top journal is not good enough. A rejection may be due to the journal editor not accepting this type of method, a lack of novelty (i.e., you have studied something already well understood with few essential contributions), or there could be fundamental errors or an inability to assert why this is important research, or an error that would not be possible to address in a short time during a revision..

In many cases, there will be journals or editors with fundamental (but often not articulated) opposition to the event study method. These might include journals that emphasize qualitative research, for example. However, many management or supply chain and operations management journals welcome a range of established qualitative and quantitative research methods. It's up to you to be familiar with the stated methods that a journal might accept and be familiar with their past publications of events studies. This also helps you to note in the covering letter while this may be an uncommon research method in your area, it remains an accepted research method as seen in their past publications at their own journal or perhaps by being able to cite other event studies published in other leading journals in this area.

IS THIS A REAL METHOD THAT WILL BE ACCEPTABLE TO MY SUPERVISORS AND DEPARTMENT?

There are some other advantages to using this method, particularly pedagogical advantages. Students with a limited time or access to external resources and organizations may find this a particular tractive approach. It enables an emerging postgraduate student to conduct a research project from start to finish in a way that can be done relatively quickly to understand the research process without being tied up with data collection issues when dealing with, for example, surveys or interviews. Further, most management-related departments will have members who work with secondary data, such as the event study method used. It has been used to study a range of topics of interest to management researchers, such as CEO retirement and succession plans (Bilgili et al., 2017), innovation and sustainable product designs (Duong et al., 2021), and sustainability and environmental practices (Chen et al., 2021).

I found that there is more benefit from having engaged in a project from start to finish and an event study project enables them to get to grips with that thinking about research, doing research and then learning more through doing and going through the process. In particular, the doctoral students, an event study project early on, can also help them understand why I make and stress the importance of journaling and keeping records about the research process and the need to understand and manage the data set in the project. While we complete a full-blown playgroup project together, I am often in a position where I ask specific questions, diving right down into the details of the data they have used with their approach. This process forces them to reflect on the records they have kept, whether these would be satisfactory to address an examiner query or a reviewer query that is received months, or perhaps years, after the initial analysis and writing.

Is not to say that this is the best method, nor does this method invalidate or conflict with other methods. It certainly will have different axiological assumptions (Collis & Hussey, 2003; Gray, 2014) than some of the other methods that might be used in management research, but it can sit alongside other methods to provide evidence and data and insight into many of the phenomenon of interest and management. We are reminded of the need to challenge the methods and perspectives we adopt by some of the leading supply chain scholars, who note that as:

quality outputs require a well-designed, constantly improved production process. One of the biggest challenges companies face is falling into the routine of doing things the way they have always done them. Such behavior is particularly dangerous in a dynamic world where the competitive rules may change at any time. (Fawcett & Waller, 2011, p. 4)

CONTEMPORARY RESEARCH QUESTIONS THAT MIGHT BE ANSWERED WITH AN EVENT STUDY

As has been previously noted, the type of issue that an event study project can address is very limited because of the study's nature. In the broad sense, we merely examining the impact of an event and this could take on any range of data or any type of topic where there's a specific and well-defined event that can be studied. However, most studies take a stock market-based approach and look at changes in the stock market or asset prices in reaction to the event. When you think about the implications, the event must be suitably large and significant, that is of impact to the company's value. In addition, the event must be one that is sudden and unexpected, so there is no prior warning that this will happen; The news should hit the market suddenly and force that instantaneous reaction.

As a result, we can study a very fleetingly small subset of projects and topics with event studies. For instance, the introduction of a product or service could be an event. The disruption caused by a disaster could be an event. There are other ways of approaching these topics, though. For instance, there can be an event that takes place at a certain point in time that relates to past achievements. For instance, studies on the impact of quality can use an event study approach to examine the impact of an award on the company's value. In this way, the recipient of the award should see a positive change in the firm's market value even though the underlying work has been in place for many years prior. However, all that development works in lifting the quality, such as through a TQM or six Sigma process, has been creating value for the company which the investors have just recognized through the investiture of the award.

So the implementation of an approach can be studied. We can also use an event study to estimate the value or benefit from implementations. For instance, we know that big data analytics are broadly helpful (Bag et al., 2020; Wood, Reiners, et al., 2017); an event study can be used to estimate the financial value of these types of software implementations, much as how the value of ERP packages have been studied (Hendricks et al., 2007).

It is also important to recognize that there are many potential research questions, issues, and topics that may not be pertinent or relevant or able to be answered with the event study method. For instance, even if we know there is a benefit from taking an approach, we may not know or understand how or why there is a benefit. Under these circumstances, we might want to understand more about the process, while other factors or issues may enhance the outcome of interest. An event study method and the following cross-sectional regression only provide outcomes and correlations. It does not give us any insight into the process or sequencing that may be relevant, particularly to managers. Therefore, when we want insight into the process of change, an implementation event study method may have limited utility. However, it may still be of value relatively early in the research process or later. It can provide some insight into the costs of consequences of the outcome of interest, just not providing any insight into how to get to the outcome. As such, this is one method on the methodological continuum (Meredith, 1998) that may be appropriate, given the issues facing the researcher and the phenomenon they wish to study. These issues surrounding the selection of appropriate methodological selection tools reflect the cautionary note from Fawcett and Waller, who state:

We should occasionally challenge the appropriateness of our methodological tools. As we do so, we may realize that the way we collect and analyze data constrains our vision, hiding from view alternative contexts, phenomena, and explanations. We need to periodically ask ourselves, "Are we using the best research strategies to cultivate meaningful understanding?" (Fawcett & Waller, 2011, p. 3)

Considering the Event Study Method in Relation to Other Methods

It may be useful to consider how this method can fit in with other methods in a wider program of study and what the contribution might be relative to other methods.

There are several benefits of coupling the method with other methods in management research. First, but uses objective data and takes a more positivistic stance. This can remove bias found in other methods when studying sustainability (Carter & Easton, 2011; Walker et al., 2012). Second, it may be a method that can be more comprehensible and meaningful to senior management teams and leaders as it relates directly to stock market reactions providing clear evidence of the benefits and drawbacks to management actions.

When we consider a broader focus of management research, we often identify an intervention program that we can initiate that we believe will make a positive difference to the company or the wider community and stakeholders. The usual approach for many management research projects at this point is to identify the initiative and then evaluate the initiative's effectiveness by either collecting low-level operational data (such as changes to stock levels for a supply chain initiative) or using management and survey response perceptions of whether there was a positive or negative impact from the initiative.

Considered another way, a positive management initiative should not only improve operational data outcomes, but these outcomes measured with operational data should also subsequently improve firm operational performance and therefore firm financial performance.

While this is outside the scope of many management studies, positive initiative should yield positive operational outcomes that should flow through to positive firm financial outcomes. We considered this way, the event study essentially takes the initiative or event of interest and then determines whether there is a stock market reaction. There must be improvements transmitted from the successful initiative to improvements in operations in the event study method when management assumes all this happens so that market participants drive the stock market reaction accordingly.

We considered that, depending on the effect size that we are studying, the outcome of many events may only be determined when looking at changes in operational data to evaluate whether there was a successful change. It is perhaps only the more substantial and consequential events are initiatives that can be studied with the event study because there are more chains of transmission before we can identify those positive benefits in the stock market reaction.

PURPOSE OF THE BOOK

In writing this book, I wanted to overview the event study method for management and supply chain management researchers. It should enable postgraduate students or research is new to the approach to gain an overview of the method and what they need to know to make this happen. More experienced researchers may dive into specific chapters to address particular issues, such as the mechanics of running the study or how to troubleshoot problems. Emerging research is, such as postgraduate research students, may benefit from reading the entire book is also captures many other useful tips and tricks for studying the subject. By reading and following the book, researchers should be positioned to craft their articles. As Fawcett et al. (2014, p. 2) note, when writing up your research, you must "[m]ake sure your method is appropriate for addressing your research question. Explain your methods clearly and in sufficient detail. Follow established procedures and make it easy for reviewers to see what you've done." Through this book, I hope to support new researchers in achieving these outcomes.

In addition, I have included much relevant material about writing and structuring writing that may be valid, relevant, and valuable to other research students, which gives some insight into how to increase productivity and overcome common difficulties and challenges when writing. In this way, there is some general material within the book in particular chapters that focus on the 'thinking about' doing research that will be generalizable to other methods. As such, some of the content should be relevant for both event study topics and other management and supply chain management research topics.

Research Methods Reading Prior to This Book

It is important to note that this volume is not intended as a stand-alone volume to support a class on research methods. It has been prepared with the assumption that a reader has a particular level of understanding of the general quantitative research methods process. Readers should be at least familiar with the research processes described in an undergraduate or postgraduate research instruction book, such as Collis and Hussey (2021), Creswell and Creswell (2018), or Saunders et al. (2015). By listing these resources, I am not endorsing them, but I am at least passingly familiar with them. An understanding of key elements of the research process for supply chain focused research can be found in the trail guide to publishing success by Fawcett et al. (2014), which can be used to help understand crucial research design decisions in the supply chain discipline.

If a reader requires additional support with the research process, the *Academy of Management Journal* has an exceptional sequence of articles that may be of interest (Bansal & Corley, 2012; Bono & McNamara, 2011; Colquitt, 2008; Colquitt & George, 2011; Geletkanycz & Tepper, 2012; Grant & Pollock, 2011; Sparrowe & Mayer, 2011). The series details many issues, design factors and considerations, challenges, and opportunities for conducting and writing about management research.

I encourage all readers to read this book with a purpose. If you are an emerging postgraduate research student, it is important to first work through a volume on research methods, design, and process first (Collis & Hussey, 2021; Creswell & Creswell, 2018; Saunders et al., 2015). Then it may be useful for you to read through the chapters sequentially even if you go through quickly, before coming back to some of the key issues are working through some ideas in more depth and detail later.

How to Use This Book

If you are an experienced researcher searching for particular help, it may be useful for you to focus on the chapters that will be most relevant to the issue at hand. For example, a quick overview of the hall method or jumping into the specifics of the analysis.

The book has been written as a series of chapters; we can use each of which as a reference for a particular topic issue. There is some overlap in the content and the explanation provided over the topics where a particular issue may span those issues addressed in several chapters. Reading the book from start to finish should hopefully support and reinforcement of some of the key ideas and concepts that are important in the event study method. On the other hand, while reading individual chapters as required, this approach should enable a complete treatment of the topic and the core issues at hand.

Through the book, the reader should also develop a sense of how the method can provide senior managers and business leaders with:

- A sense of the benefit of positive initiatives, such as new enterprise resource planning (ERP) systems and other similar systems (Hendricks et al., 2007). Understanding the positive benefits of management-focused changes on shareholder value or the total value of the firm, it gives managers an understanding of the benefits that may accrue from what are often substantial investments.
- An evaluation of the costs of mis-management and poor performance, such as the issues associated with supply chain glitches (Hendricks & Singhal, 2003). By being able to assess the overall cost to the company as reflected in a negative impact on shareholder value, the managers are more able to see the benefits of investments that may mitigate or reduce the likelihood of these consequences.

Working through the book will provide a reader with an overview of the steps and activities required in starting and completing an event study analysis project. This starts with the planning stages, the review of literature and development of hypotheses, the collection of a sample and other data, the analysis, the determination of results, and the final write-up and publication. This is not a linear nor straight-forward

Figure 1. A flow of the steps and activities within an event study analysis project. These are usually not linear and there are often situations where there is backtracking or re-visiting earlier steps to check, correct, or re-do work.

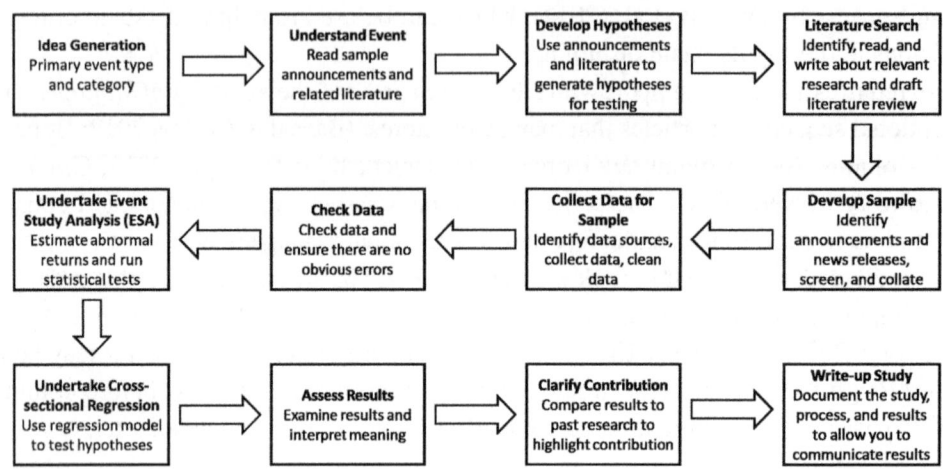

list and there will be some deviances, but an overview of the steps and how they are connected is provided in Figure 1. In practice, in many cases there will be times where the researcher backtracks or revisits an earlier stage. For instance, the literature review, hypothesis development, and sample development may all occur simultaneously in an iterative process.

My hope is that this volume helps new researchers feel comfortable learning a method, to provide them with a head start, and help them identify additional resources. As someone reading the book gets stuck, they should be able to identify appropriate chapters which contain support and help. If someone reading the book is still stuck, then they should get in touch and let me know how things are going.

REFERENCES

Ba, S., Lisic, L. L., Liu, Q., & Stallaert, J. (2013). Stock market reaction to green vehicle innovation. *Production and Operations Management, 22*(4), 976–990. doi:10.1111/j.1937-5956.2012.01387.x

Bansal, P., & Corley, K. (2012). Publishing in AMJ—Part 7: What's different about qualitative research? Academy of Management Journal, 509–513.

Bertrand, M., & Mullainathan, S. (2001). Do people mean what they say? Implications for subjective survey data. *The American Economic Review, 91*(2), 67–72. doi:10.1257/aer.91.2.67

Bilgili, H., Tochman Campbell, J., Ellstrand, A. E., & Johnson, J. L. (2017). Riding off into the sunset: Organizational sensegiving, shareholder sensemaking, and reactions to CEO retirement. *Journal of Management Studies, 54*(7), 1019–1049. doi:10.1111/joms.12264

Bono, J. E., & McNamara, G. (2011). Publishing in AMJ—Part 2: Research design. *Academy of Management Journal, 54*(4), 657–660. doi:10.5465/amj.2011.64869103

Carter, C. R., & Easton, P. L. (2011). Sustainable supply chain management: Evolution and future directions. *International Journal of Physical Distribution & Logistics Management*, *41*(1), 46–62. doi:10.1108/09600031111101420

Chen, Y., Ganesan, S., & Liu, Y. (2009). Does a firm's product-recall strategy affect its financial value? An examination of strategic alternatives during product-harm crises. *Journal of Marketing*, *73*(6), 214–226. doi:10.1509/jmkg.73.6.214

Chen, Y., Singhal, V., & Zhu, Q. (2021). Environmental policies and financial performance: Stock market reaction to firms for their proactive environmental practices recognized by governmental programs. *Business Strategy and the Environment*, *30*(4), 1548–1562. doi:10.1002/bse.2693

Cheung, A. W. K. (2011). Do stock investors value corporate sustainability? Evidence from an event study. *Journal of Business Ethics*, *99*(2), 145–165. doi:10.100710551-010-0646-3

Choi, J. (2014). Effects of contract announcements on the value of construction firms. *Journal of Management Engineering*, *30*(1), 86–96. doi:10.1061/(ASCE)ME.1943-5479.0000178

Collis, J., & Hussey, R. (2003). *Business Research: A Practical Guide for Undergraduate and Postgraduate Students*. Palgrave Macmillan.

Collis, J., & Hussey, R. (2021). *Business research: A practical guide for students* (5th ed.). Red Globe Press.

Colquitt, J. A. (2008). Publishing laboratory research in AMJ: A question of when, not if. *Academy of Management Journal*, *51*(4), 616–620. doi:10.5465/AMJ.2008.33664717

Colquitt, J. A., & George, G. (2011). Publishing in AMJ—Part 1: Topic choice. *Academy of Management Journal*, *54*(3), 432–435. doi:10.5465/amj.2011.61965960

Creswell, J. W., & Creswell, J. D. (2018). *Research design: Qualitative, quantitative, and mixed methods approaches* (5th ed.). SAGE Publications, Inc.

Dai, Y., Kong, D., & Wang, M. (2013). Investor reactions to food safety incidents: Evidence from the Chinese milk industry. *Food Policy*, *43*, 23–31. doi:10.1016/j.foodpol.2013.08.004

Duan, C., Grover, V., Roberts, N., & Balakrishnan, N. (2014). Firm valuation effects of the decision to adopt relationally governed business process outsourcing arrangements. *International Journal of Production Research*, *52*(15), 4673–4694. doi:10.1080/00207543.2014.884289

Duong, L. N. K., Wang, J. X., Wood, L. C., Reiners, T., & Koushan, M. (2021). The value of incremental environmental sustainability innovation in the construction industry: An event study. *Construction Management and Economics*, *39*(5), 398–418. doi:10.1080/01446193.2021.1901950

Eroglu, C., Kurt, A. C., & Elwakil, O. S. (2016). Stock market reaction to quality, safety, and sustainability awards in logistics. *Journal of Business Logistics*, *37*(4), 329–345. doi:10.1111/jbl.12145

Fawcett, S. E., & Waller, M. A. (2011). Making sense out of chaos: Why theory is relevant to supply chain research. *Journal of Business Logistics*, *32*(1), 1–5. doi:10.1111/j.2158-1592.2011.01000.x

Fawcett, S. E., Waller, M. A., Miller, J. W., Schwieterman, M. A., Hazen, B. T., & Overstreet, R. E. (2014). A trail guide to publishing success: Tips on writing influential conceptual, qualitative, and survey research. *Journal of Business Logistics*, *35*(1), 1–16. doi:10.1111/jbl.12039

Geletkanycz, M., & Tepper, B. J. (2012). Publishing in AMJ—Part 6: Discussing the implications. *Academy of Management Journal*, *55*(2), 256–260. doi:10.5465/amj.2012.4002

Gokhale, J., Brooks, R. M., & Tremblay, V. J. (2014). The effect on stockholder wealth of product recalls and government action: The case of Toyota's accelerator pedal recall. *The Quarterly Review of Economics and Finance*, *54*(4), 521–528. doi:10.1016/j.qref.2014.06.004

Gong, S. X. H., Firth, M., & Cullinane, K. (2008). International oligopoly and stock market linkages: The case of global airlines. *Transportation Research Part E, Logistics and Transportation Review*, *44*(4), 621–636. doi:10.1016/j.tre.2007.05.008

Grant, A. M., & Pollock, T. G. (2011). Publishing in AMJ—Part 3: Setting the Hook. *Academy of Management Journal*, *54*(5), 873–879. doi:10.5465/amj.2011.4000

Gray, D. E. (2014). *Doing research in the real world* (3rd ed.). Sage.

Hammoudi, A., Hoffmann, R., & Surry, Y. (2009). Food safety standards and agri-food supply chains: An introductory overview. *European Review of Agriculture Economics*, *36*(4), 469–478. doi:10.1093/erae/jbp044

Hendricks, K. B., Hora, M., & Singhal, V. R. (2014). An empirical investigation on the appointments of supply chain and operations management executives. *Management Science*, *61*(7), 1562–1583. doi:10.1287/mnsc.2014.1987

Hendricks, K. B., & Singhal, V. R. (2001). The long-run stock price performance of firms with effective TQM programs. *Management Science*, *47*(3), 359–368. doi:10.1287/mnsc.47.3.359.9773

Hendricks, K. B., & Singhal, V. R. (2003). The effect of supply chain glitches on shareholder wealth. *Journal of Operations Management*, *21*(5), 501–522. doi:10.1016/j.jom.2003.02.003

Hendricks, K. B., Singhal, V. R., & Stratman, J. K. (2007). The impact of enterprise systems on corporate performance: A study of ERP, SCM, and CRM system implementations. *Journal of Operations Management*, *25*(1), 65–82. doi:10.1016/j.jom.2006.02.002

Holder-Webb, L., Lopez, T. J., & Regier, P. R. (2005). The performance consequences of operational restructurings. *Review of Quantitative Finance and Accounting*, *25*(4), 319–339. doi:10.100711156-005-5458-7

Huey-Lian, S., & Tang, A. P. (2000). The sources of railroad merger gains: Evidence from stock price reaction and operating performance. *Transportation Journal*, *39*(4), 14–26.

Kajander, J.-K., Sivunen, M., Vimpari, J., Pulkka, L., & Junnila, S. (2012). Market value of sustainability business innovations in the construction sector. *Building Research and Information*, *40*(6), 665–678. doi:10.1080/09613218.2012.703893

Kumar, S., & Budin, E. M. (2006). Prevention and management of product recalls in the processed food industry: A case study based on an exporter's perspective. *Technovation, 26*(5–6), 739–750. doi:10.1016/j.technovation.2005.05.006

Mazzocchi, M., Ragona, M., & Fritz, M. (2009). Stock market response to food safety regulations. *European Review of Agriculture Economics, 36*(4), jbp043. Advance online publication. doi:10.1093/erae/jbp043

Meredith, J. (1998). Building operations management theory through case and field research. *Journal of Operations Management, 16*(4), 441–454. doi:10.1016/S0272-6963(98)00023-0

Ni, J. Z., Flynn, B. B., & Jacobs, F. R. (2014). Impact of product recall announcements on retailers' financial value. *International Journal of Production Economics, 153*, 309–322. doi:10.1016/j.ijpe.2014.03.014

Nicolau, J. L., & Sellers, R. (2002). The stock market's reaction to quality certification: Empirical evidence from Spain. *European Journal of Operational Research, 142*(3), 632–641. doi:10.1016/S0377-2217(01)00312-5

Park, J.-H., Park, N. K., & Zhang, A. (2003). The impact of international alliances on rival firm value: A study of the British Airways/USAir Alliance. *Transportation Research Part E, Logistics and Transportation Review, 39*(1), 1–18. doi:10.1016/S1366-5545(02)00023-6

Pinar, M., & Ozgur, C. (2007). The long-term impact of ISO 9000 certification on business performance: A longitudinal study using Turkish stock market returns. *The Quality Management Journal, 14*(4), 21–40. doi:10.1080/10686967.2007.11918044

Rupp, N. G. (2001). Are government initiated recalls more damaging for shareholders? Evidence from automotive recalls, 1973–1998. *Economics Letters, 71*(2), 265–270. doi:10.1016/S0165-1765(01)00379-2

Salin, V., & Hooker, N. H. (2001). Stock market reaction to food recalls. *Review of Agricultural Economics, 23*(1), 33–46. doi:10.1111/1058-7195.00044

Saunders, M. N. K., Lewis, P., & Thornhill, A. (2015). *Research methods for business students* (7th ed.). Pearson.

Sparrowe, R. T., & Mayer, K. J. (2011). Publishing in AMJ—Part 4: Grounding hypotheses. *Academy of Management Journal, 54*(6), 1098–1102. doi:10.5465/amj.2011.4001

Terziovski, M., & Guerrero, J.-L. (2014). ISO 9000 quality system certification and its impact on product and process innovation performance. *International Journal of Production Economics, 158*, 197–207. doi:10.1016/j.ijpe.2014.08.011

Walker, H., Miemczyk, J., Johnsen, T., & Spencer, R. (2012). Sustainable procurement: Past, present and future. *Journal of Purchasing and Supply Management, 18*(4), 201–206. doi:10.1016/j.pursup.2012.11.003

Wang, C.-H., Chen, K.-Y., & Chen, S.-C. (2012). Total quality management, market orientation and hotel performance: The moderating effects of external environmental factors. *International Journal of Hospitality Management, 31*(1), 119–129. doi:10.1016/j.ijhm.2011.03.013

Wood, L. C., Wang, J. X., Olesen, K., & Reiners, T. (2017). The effect of slack, diversification, and time to recall on stock market reaction to toy recalls. *International Journal of Production Economics*, *193*, 244–258. doi:10.1016/j.ijpe.2017.07.021

Wowak, K. D., & Boone, C. A. (2015). So many recalls, so little research: A review of the literature and road map for future research. *The Journal of Supply Chain Management*, *51*(4), 54–72. doi:10.1111/jscm.12079

Wowak, K. D., Craighead, C. W., & Ketchen, D. J. Jr. (2016). Tracing bad products in supply chains: The roles of temporality, supply chain permeation, and product information ambiguity. *Journal of Business Logistics*, *37*(2), 132–151. doi:10.1111/jbl.12125

Xia, Y., Singhal, V. R., & Peter Zhang, G. (2016). Product design awards and the market value of the firm. *Production and Operations Management*, *25*(6), 1038–1055. doi:10.1111/poms.12525

Zhang, M., Hu, H., & Zhao, X. (2020). Developing product recall capability through supply chain quality management. *International Journal of Production Economics*, *229*, 107795. doi:10.1016/j.ijpe.2020.107795

Zhang, X. (2021). Does high-speed railway strengthen the ties among nearby regions? Evidence from China. *Asian Transport Studies*, *7*, 100039. doi:10.1016/j.eastsj.2021.100039

Zhao, X., Li, Y., & Flynn, B. B. (2013). The financial impact of product recall announcements in China. *International Journal of Production Economics*, *142*(1), 115–123. doi:10.1016/j.ijpe.2012.10.018

ADDITIONAL READING

Brown, K. C., Harlow, W. V., & Tinic, S. M. (1988). Risk aversion, uncertain information, and market efficiency. *Journal of Financial Economics*, *22*(2), 355–385. doi:10.1016/0304-405X(88)90075-X

Brown, S. J., & Warner, J. B. (1980). Measuring security price performance. *Journal of Financial Economics*, *8*(3), 205–258. doi:10.1016/0304-405X(80)90002-1

Brown, S. J., & Warner, J. B. (1985). Using daily stock returns: The case of event studies. *Journal of Financial Economics*, *14*(1), 3–31. doi:10.1016/0304-405X(85)90042-X

Chen, Y., Singhal, V., & Zhu, Q. (2021). Environmental policies and financial performance: Stock market reaction to firms for their proactive environmental practices recognized by governmental programs. *Business Strategy and the Environment*, *30*(4), 1548–1562. doi:10.1002/bse.2693

Duong, L. N. K., Wang, J. X., Wood, L. C., Reiners, T., & Koushan, M. (2021). The value of incremental environmental sustainability innovation in the construction industry: An event study. *Construction Management and Economics*, *39*(5), 398–418. doi:10.1080/01446193.2021.1901950

Hendricks, K. B., & Singhal, V. R. (2001). Firm characteristics, total quality management, and financial performance. *Journal of Operations Management*, *19*(3), 269–285. doi:10.1016/S0272-6963(00)00049-8

Jacobs, B. W., & Singhal, V. R. (2014). The effect of product development restructuring on shareholder value. *Production and Operations Management, 23*(5), 728–743. doi:10.1111/poms.12074

Jacobs, B. W., & Singhal, V. R. (2017). The effect of the Rana Plaza disaster on shareholder wealth of retailers: Implications for sourcing strategies and supply chain governance. *Journal of Operations Management, 49–51*(1), 52–66. doi:10.1016/j.jom.2017.01.002

Jacobs, B. W., & Singhal, V. R. (2020). Shareholder value effects of the Volkswagen emissions scandal on the automotive ecosystem. *Production and Operations Management, 29*(10), 2230–2251. doi:10.1111/poms.13228

Jacobs, B. W., Singhal, V. R., & Subramanian, R. (2010). An empirical investigation of environmental performance and the market value of the firm. *Journal of Operations Management, 28*(5), 430–441. doi:10.1016/j.jom.2010.01.001

Kothari, S. P., & Warner, J. B. (2007). Econometrics of event studies. In B. E. Eckbo (Ed.), *Handbook of Corporate Finance: Empirical Corporate Finance* (Vol. 1, pp. 3–36). North-Holland/Elsevier. doi:10.1016/B978-0-444-53265-7.50015-9

Singhal, K., & Singhal, J. (2012a). Imperatives of the science of operations and supply-chain management. *Journal of Operations Management, 30*(3), 237–244. doi:10.1016/j.jom.2011.11.003

Singhal, K., & Singhal, J. (2012b). Opportunities for developing the science of operations and supply-chain management. *Journal of Operations Management, 30*(3), 245–252. doi:10.1016/j.jom.2011.11.002

Wood, L. C., Wang, J. X., Duong, L. N. K., Reiners, T., & Smith, R. (2018). Stock market reactions to auto manufacturers' environmental failures. *Journal of Macromarketing, 38*(4), 364–382. doi:10.1177/0276146718781915

Zhan, X., Mu, Y., Hora, M., & Singhal, V. R. (2021). Service excellence and market value of a firm: An empirical investigation of winning service awards and stock market reaction. *International Journal of Production Research, 59*(14), 4188–4204. doi:10.1080/00207543.2020.1759837

Zhan, X., Mu, Y., Nishant, R., & Singhal, V. R. (2020). When do appointments of Chief Digital or Data Officers (CDOs) affect stock prices? *IEEE Transactions on Engineering Management, 1*–14. doi:10.1109/TEM.2020.2984619

KEY TERMS AND DEFINITIONS

Abnormal Return: The difference between an observed movement in stock returns that is clearly different or greater than an expected normal or expected return.

Cross-Sectional Regression: The analysis of how multiple variables, drawn from the theoretical model, influence the outcome of the dependent variable usually modelled as abnormal returns in event study projects.

Effect Size: How large the effect is in the wider population; in the event study, the strength of the relationship between the event and the magnitude of the abnormal returns.

Event Study: The study of how an event, situation, circumstance influences the performance of a firm, usually evaluated with short-term changes in the stock returns, long-term changes, or changes in operating performance.

Inference: The act of drawing conclusions about the wider population based on the estimations made in the particular model.

Stock Market Reaction: A sudden and fast change in the stock prices in reaction to the event, capturing the unbiased estimate of the consequences of the news on the stock's long-term prospects. The stock market reaction, measured by the abnormal returns, is usually the focus of the main hypothesis in the event study project.

ENDNOTE

[1] Unless, of course they are incentivized using a reward structure that is based on such metrics.

Chapter 2
Event Study Assumptions

ABSTRACT

This chapter focuses on the event study assumptions. We should carefully consider these at the start and mainly when writing up the study. While the author also addressed the assumptions in other chapters, it is helpful to identify several key assumptions early on to ensure that they are fully understood and built into the design. He discusses the primary assumption of stock market efficiency, unanticipated nature of events, independence, and how this is relevant. Examples are provided of some of the key points. Finally, he introduces several measures that can consider these assumptions and discuss how the study design can be adjusted if we violate the assumptions.

INTRODUCTION

All research methods have a range of assumptions that they rest on. These assumptions must be met if the study is to work with the intended design. For example, the event study methodology has the following key assumptions: market efficiency, the sudden release of information about the event, there are no other events at the same time, and independence of events (not strictly an assumption, but a key to recognize).

Alternative study designs can be considered by considering these factors early in the study design. "Regardless of your choice of technique, you need to assure the reader that it is appropriate. Know the technique's assumptions and verify that your data fits" (Fawcett et al., 2014, p. 13). One of the key elements in this chapter is a clear development of the how and why a particular event makes or drives a stock market reaction. Through careful explanation, as articulated this chapter, it should be easier to assure the reader that this is an appropriate technique and that the assumptions of this technique match well with the topic of interest and the data you have collected.

When considering research methods, we often talk about a clear division between positivistic or more quantitative studies and those that are more phenomenologically oriented (Collis & Hussey, 2003; Morgan & Smircich, 1980). When considered this way, the event study method sits on the more positivistic side of the spectrum. We claim a level of removal from what we are studying; we are a disinterested observer and our observation does not influence the stock returns we are studying. What we study is,

DOI: 10.4018/978-1-7998-8969-4.ch002

we claim, objective then if two people are looking at the same stock return data they should arrive at the same conclusions.

The event study method is in what can be defined as the empirical class of research, which "is primarily interested in creating a model that adequately describes the causal relationships that may exist in reality, which leads to understanding the processes going on" (Bertrand & Fransoo, 2002, p. 250). That is, we gain insight into the causal relationships, giving us insight into the impact of an event and, through the cross-sectional regression, understanding of how managers may address the issues to mitigate or buffer their firm from adverse situations.

THEORY

It is not enough to observe and describe what has happened. While the operations and supply chain management disciplines have a rich history, there has been a historical focus on practice and outcomes-driven research. Increasingly, however, there have been calls for building and developing theory. This is important as it allows us to tackle, with success, larger and more significant problems;

Nowhere is the outcome of this research-versus-practice debate more important than in the supply chain realm. Logistics research has its roots firmly planted in rubber meets-the-road practicality. Yet, today's supply chain challenges such as collaboration, global network design, sustainability, and value creation reach strategic heights where organizational competitiveness and societal well-being are greatly influenced. (Fawcett et al., 2014, p. 1)

Roth (2007) suggests that theory is a fundamental component of effective research and developing knowledge. It helps us create hypotheses that explain or rationale for what is going on in the world around us. From these, managers and other researchers can make predictions and provide prescriptions for what 'should' be done in practice to achieve desired outcomes. These outcomes can be refined, modified, and verified to provide additional insight drawn from subsequent observations and descriptions of what happens as a consequence. From this, the theory-building cycle continues.

Therefore, connected to this is the assumption that theory is vital in the design and development of the event study process. While there is a historic, underlying focus on practice outcomes and empirical observation in operations management research, other areas in management have more broadly welcomed theory for years. Consequently, when conducting an event study, the theory-driven study should provide more assurance to the researchers that they will identify a result of interest and capture an estimate of the importance or magnitude of the event of interest. For example, Duan et al. (2009) draw on the theory of production economics (TPE), transaction cost economics (TCE), and the resource-based view (RBV) while Riley et al. (2017) draw on human capital theory.

MAIN FOCUS OF THE CHAPTER

The Primary Assumption of Market Efficiency

One of the principal assumptions made in the event study is market efficiency (Fama, 1991). This chapter will not labor over this assumption, as it has been examined within a significant body of work (Fama, 1991).

The principal market efficiency suggests that stock prices adjust virtually instantaneously when information becomes available to market traders and investors. When an announcement is made about the event, then that information is new. Investors evaluate and judge how this information may affect both the current and future costs and revenues for the firm. As a consequence, buying and selling rapidly occurs to adjust the current stock prices based on the overall assessment of how this news affects the company, all priced in the current price.

Like any hypothesis, there will be those who argue and disagree with that. However, Malkiel (2003) has provided a comprehensive review of some of the efficient market hypothesis criticisms. The primary conclusion is that "our stock markets are far more efficient and far less predictable than some recent academic papers would have us believe" (Malkiel, 2003, p. 60).

Within this framework, news about an event is simply unanticipated and unforeseen data that investors then take and re-evaluate their estimates of the future fortunes of the firm. This process occurs nearly instantaneously.

Event studies often have a short horizon for the study (i.e., those measuring immediate reactions over a very short event window; this is the type primarily addressed within this volume). In contrast, an event study could use a longer horizon, such as the buy-and-hold abnormal return (BHAR) calculations addressed in a following chapter. While it has been noted that long event windows are poorly justified, as it would suggest that investors have failed to incorporate the news and their estimations of what the stock price should be (McWilliams et al., 1999; McWilliams & Siegel, 1997). Is not always the case, and sometimes pertinent information is released slowly; therefore, investors assess that further information will come to light. For example, an investigation of corporate wrongdoing may play out over months as more whistle-blowers come forward. In essence, the efficient market hypothesis focuses on the price conduct of stock prices.

Three primary forms have been proposed (Fama, 1970):

- The weak form suggests that stock prices simply reflect information that had already been embedded within the past prices.
- The strong form states that the prices instead reflect all information available, even if much of this information might be private and less available to other investors and traders.
- The semi-Strong form states that the stock prices not only reflect information embedded in past prices but also all publicly and widely available information. In this way, the market prices do not reflect confidential information held by investors who are market insiders.

The strong form of efficient market hypothesis is usually not a serious consideration of most research (Jensen, 1978). That is, rather, an extreme condition required that is required for a complete set of theoretical possibilities and is used as a benchmark for deviations from the market efficiency (Fama, 1970).

Instead, most studies rely on semi-Strong form, suggesting that investors and traders identify and use all publicly available information. Consequently, the market prices are constantly adjusting to reflect the available information at every moment. As news arrives and is made available to market participants, the immediate market reaction must occur. In contrast, if there is no discernible meaningful stock market reaction to the news, then it suggests that either the information has been expected by the investors or perhaps that it has no impact on the estimation of the firm's future successes, costs, or benefits (Kothari & Warner, 2007).

The reaction to news releases to the market creates a situation where there is an abnormal stock market reaction. However, the terminology here suggests that there are normal market reactions and movements that we need to define before defining what is abnormal. Consider it this way: event studies must assess not only the abnormal returns but also the normally expected returns within the market. Consequently, several benchmark models have been developed over the decades, and we address these in the following chapter.

Unanticipated Events

One of the primary assumptions is from the early discussion of the efficient market hypothesis, that the new information available to market participants is unexpected. It is not previously known and therefore already reflected in stock prices. Therefore, the new information to the market will be absorbed and considered by investors. Through their collective actions and assumptions, an unbiased estimate is based on the overall assessment of the consequences for the stock and the firm based on the news released. Therefore, this new information leads traders and investors to react, generating abnormal returns where the information is pertinent, meaningful, and relevant to the company's ongoing success.

There are also situations where information can find its way into the market before formal notifications. Such information leakages can make the event study method difficult to apply. It is often going unclear whether market participants were aware of the information ahead of published updates to the market. Therefore, in the management literature is important to consider whether some market participants may have advance information, or even an awareness, of a particular event before the release of public information. Most times, market participants might anticipate or judge there to be a very reasonable expectation that a future release of information will be pertinent.

The Event Leads to the Stock Market Reaction

One of the primary assumptions is that we can detect a stock market reaction to an event of interest. To do this, we must be able to isolate the events so that we can isolate and observe the stock market reactions. The curve for research design and several tests we can ensure that the sample used in the study means that we can attribute any observed stock market reaction to the events under study.

While we cover confounding events in future chapters, it is useful to consider now what happens if there are two different announcements on the one day. If we observe the stock market reaction on that day, we cannot easily determine whether we can attribute an observed reaction to either of those events. If we measure a stock market reaction over a larger number of days, it becomes increasingly likely that that larger window contains other contemporaneous events that may influence the stock market reactions.

The most basic approach which is commonly used is to take a short window for estimating the stock market reactions were abnormal returns, and to check for any other events that are likely to influence the stock market reaction, and where our particular observation has two or more events in that window to isolate and remove that from the sample for analysis.

Many event studies, as a matter of practicality, use end-of-day data. However, if intraday data were available, there are suggestions that multiple and very clearly defined releases of information to the market at different times of the day might be incorporated in a more sophisticated event study design. For instance, in the U.S., there are early suggestions that there was an impact within 15 minutes of a news release about a company (Dann et al., 1977). Investors are also able to assess broader information about a sector or market even if it is not about a specific firm and has not named that specific firm with a reaction within 90 minutes (M. L. Mitchell & Netter, 1989). Similar results have been found, such as the market in Germany, where stock returns adjust within 30 minutes of news (Muntermann & Guettler, 2007).

A Conceptual Model Linking the Event to the stock Market Reaction

While the critical assumption is that we can connect the event to the stock market reaction, it is also useful to reflect on some of the underlying causal connections. This will sometimes be published in research articles explicitly, while at other times, it may be more than implicit argument or couched in several paragraphs of explanation. There should always be some connection, usually in the development and explanation of the first hypothesis, between the event (or managerial initiative) and the outcome, consisting of the stock market reaction.

When we consider the events of interest, where usually talking about managerial changes that can be made that will enhance performance that we expect to lead to a more positive stock market reaction. In contrast, event studies and operations and other management research are sometimes used to examine negative events where an external event affects the company and causes a negative stock market reaction.

Considered in this way, the phenomenon that we are interested in and will properly impact either the long-term revenues, cash flows, or on the costs and risks for the firm. These will feed into financial performance expectations, such as profitability, return on assets, or sales growths. Ultimately, if these elements are going to be positively benefited by the event in question, we expect to see a positive stock market reaction because there is an increase in the underlying value of the company's shareholders. In contrast, if we expect the event to deteriorate the firm's financial performance, it will deplete shareholder value and we expect a negative stock-market reaction.

Jacobs and Singhal (2014, p. 734) provide a good example and explanation for these relationships. Their conceptual model explains how the product development restructuring is expected to enhance the performance of the product element process and how this will increase revenues and decrease costs to enhance financial performance and increase shareholder value to generate a stock market reaction. A modified version is presented in Figure 1. This figure shows how the senior management team might conceive of this type of plan for product development restructuring projects as a mechanism to improve performance and drive shareholder value.

A comparable conceptual model is presented in Figure 1 of Jacobs et al. (2010, p. 432). The same basic relationships hold true in Figure 1, as in the conceptual model presented in Jacobs et al. (2010). What they do not show is the managerial change or initiative (what is represented in the far left box of Figure 1 here), instead their model jumps straight to an enhanced environmental performance. The performance drives reputations, new markets, and revenue gains, which enhance financial performance. On the other hand, environmental performance also leads to cost reductions such as enhancements and

Figure 1. A conceptual model for how the managerial initiative may lead to a positive stock market reaction (Based on Figure 1, Jacobs et al. (2014, p. 734))

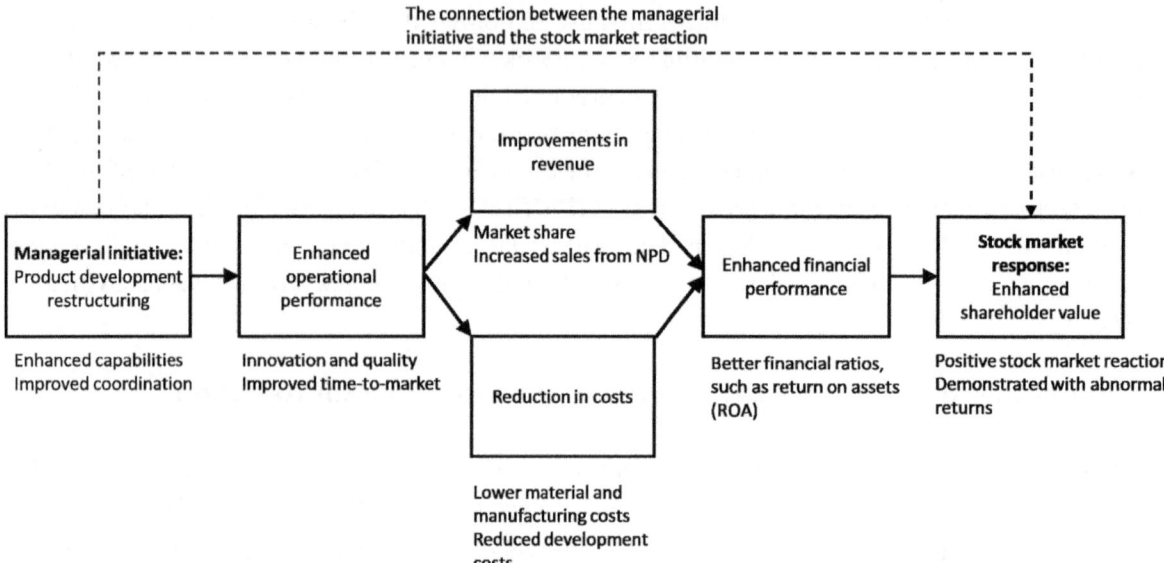

production and distribution and avoidance of penalties, which flow on to enhanced financial performance. Also not shown on their model is how the financial performance creates or leads to the market reaction, such as shown in the far-right box of our Figure 1.

In preparing a dissertation, including a chart of figures showing a similar conceptual model, may be useful for organizing your thoughts while developing the hypotheses and presenting a simple framework that you can use in departmental seminars or perhaps in the final publications in journals.

We can apply the argumentation in the section that develops the first, primary hypothesis that we expect a stock market reaction to the event of interest. For example, Jacobs et al. present three key paragraphs in their second section to develop the first hypothesis. The first argues for environmental performance, enhancing revenue growth. The second argues for the development and access to new markets. The third argues that enhanced environmental performance will reduce costs, as:

environmental performance can impact costs in a variety of ways. Environmental practices reduce the amount of waste, the consumption of various production inputs including energy and materials (Rothenberg et al., 2001; Sroufe, 2003), and the number of components in products (Ashley, 1993). Both inbound and outbound logistics benefit from reduced product weights and packaging (Rao and Holt, 2005). Pollution prevention may not only reduce disposal and mitigation costs but may also avoid the cost of installing and operating pollution control devices (Hart, 1995; Hart and Ahuja, 1996). Other cost avoidance benefits of effective environmental management include mitigation of risks of losses from crises or regulation (Reinhardt, 1999), and preventing expenses associated with lawsuits and legal settlements (Karpoff et al., 2005). Dowell et al. (2000) note that stringent environmental standards can lower the cost to develop, maintain, and enforce policies and procedures, thus allowing easy transfer of accrued knowledge and increasing employee morale and productivity. Similarly, von Paumgartten

(2003) argues that LEED-certified buildings can improve worker productivity and retention. (Jacobs et al., 2010, p. 432).

From the argumentation, we can see that it should reduce the waste, inputs, and lower costs. Logistics should be less expensive due to lower product weights. Pollution mitigation costs will be reduced, and pollution prevention and monitoring will be less costly. One element that is included is the reputational and risk elements of losses from crises or compliance with regulatory changes or legal settlement; the reduction of potentially large, future risks is likely to be perceived favorably by the stock market investors.

Risk aversion is essential, as lawsuits can be substantial. As a current example, 3M has been implicated in a long-running suit relating to the failure of earplugs supplied to the U.S. military to prevent hearing loss, representing "the largest verdict yet to result from hundreds of thousands of lawsuits over the product" (Raymond, 2022). Why would this result in skittish and uncertain stock market participants? The risk aversion comes as this is a $110m award to two veterans, "among the nearly 300,000 service members and others who have sued 3M claiming they suffered hearing damage as a result of using the earplugs in what has become the largest federal mass tort litigation in U.S. history" (Raymond, 2022). The issues are likely to be litigated for years to come, and 3M notes they had won the immediately prior two trials, with this present trial the 11th, with plaintiffs winning six and 3M the other five. Given the number of service members involved and the value of the award, risk-averse stock market participants may drive lower stock returns.

Independence and No Clustering in the Sample, so there is no Similarity of Industry and Time

Many management researchers will remember from an earlier statistics classes that independence usually has a vital role in many test statistics used in studies. While many management research designs are based on surveys, we rarely consider independence on a day-to-day basis, as we are almost always assured of having a level of independence in our samples due to (for example) the sampling used in survey projects. However, there are many practical cases for event study projects where a single event might affect multiple firms in a single industry or many firms across industries simultaneously. Consequently, they can become difficult to ignore the assumptions of independence with an event study analysis and the multiple tests used.

When there's been a clustering of observations at a particular time, it essentially reduces the level of independence in our sample of observations. Consequently, studies have shown that there is a significant positive correlation and that the statistical tests (using independence as a critical assumption) have a lower power (S. J. Brown & Warner, 1980). As such clustering occurs, we can severely underestimate standard deviations calculated during the process. Consequently, any test statistics calculated (used to judge the statistical significance of the event) are overestimated. Careful consideration shows that if we consider the impact of clustering, we can reduce the impact on test statistic calculations using a clustered version as outlined in Brown and Warner (1985)

The challenges of independence go beyond simply estimating the abnormal returns. In management projects, regression analysis follows most estimations of abnormal returns where the abnormal returns are used as a dependent variable regressed against independent variables). Therefore, it is important for studies that involve some type of clustering (whether it is a clustering of firms in the similar industry or over a similar period) to consider a range of different approaches, such as:

1. first, a multifactor model can reduce the impact of the correlation of abnormal returns that can be because of industry commonalities (Carhart, 1997)
2. there are different techniques, such as the generalized T-square, that might be used rather than cross-sectional regression. (MacKinlay, 1997)
3. cross-sectional data can also be aggregated using portfolios. In this way, using portfolio returns reduces the impact of correlation on the abnormal returns (D. T. Brown et al., 2009; Fee & Thomas, 2004)

In practice, many software packages that researchers in management may be using may have some test statistics but not a comprehensive range. Further, they have poor support for support using portfolio returns. Consequentially, interested readers should carefully consider some challenges of these approaches by reading the overview provided by Bernard (1987). Examples of studies that have observations affected by clustering:

- Homan (Homan, 2006, 2009a) studies the impact of 9/11 (calendar clustering) on returns in a sector (marine firms)
- When considering how the 2011 Great east Japan earthquake creates supply chain disruptions, Hendricks et al. (2020) have a calendar clustering affect and may need to consider sector clustering.
- Homan (Homan, 2007, 2009b) provides a further study of how the introduction of the Maritime Transportation Security Act (MTSA) influences marine firms. As this suggests, an introduction will create calendar clustering and the examination is for firms in a single sector (marine firms).
- Similarly, the Rana Plaza collapse studied by Jacobs and Singhal (2017) is based on a single disaster, representing calendar clustering and a clear focus on garment supply chains, suggesting sector clustering.

THE NATURE OF THE DATA

Many of the calculations for the abnormal returns and the follow use of test statistics to determine the statistical significance of the abnormal return calculations will require a range of assumptions. We address these in Chapter 9. They are more involved and there are usually a range of different approaches that can be used, based on the assumptions of each test and the nature of the data that you are using. In these cases, it is imperative to understand your data and, for example, if abnormal returns are skewed or the volatility increases.

Short- and Long-Horizon Studies

As noted earlier, the assumption of market efficiency suggests that there should be an immediate stock market reaction to the news as market participants learn of what is relevant to the company's successes and fortunes in the future. However, this instant evaluation reaction occurs over a very short horizon. Consequently, it assumes that no abnormal returns persist beyond this short horizon. Therefore, this change in the stock prices reflects the publicly available information with a complete response to the announcement.

However, if there is systematic mis-pricing of the equity, it may change in performance over a longer time. Long-term horizon study evaluates this performance over a period of months, even years. While this is intuitively attractive, there are several challenges to regulating expected returns over such a long horizon (Dionysiou, 2015). Even using more sophisticated models, such as the three-factor model (Fama & French, 1993) or a four-factor model (Carhart, 1997), measurement errors will compound needed challenges with statistical inference. In addition, many other events took her over the same period, making it difficult to determine whether any observed effect was because of the event that we are interested in other contemporaneous events.

While this book focuses on the short horizon event study approach is worth considering these long-horizon approaches. There are two primary approaches are used to estimate abnormal performance over longer horizons. We address these in following chapters in more detail.

The buy-and-hold abnormal returns (BHAR) approach matches the firm affected by the event with a non-event firm (Barber & Lyon, 1997; M. Mitchell & Stafford, 2000). In essence, there is a treatment firm and a control firm. The firms are matched by key characteristics. By matching a firm with comparable characteristics to firms, we assume firms to be similar and we should therefore expect comparable stock returns between the control and the treatment firm if there is no impact from the event. However, the two firms could still differ systematically as events themselves may not be random occurrences and could reflect other, deeper differences between the firms. Matching to other firms has been used several times and supply chain research (Hendricks et al., 2007; Hendricks & Singhal, 2005).

An alternative second approach is the calendar time portfolio approach, which is sometimes referred to as the Jensen alpha approach. The event portfolios are created with firms involved in the event and is rebalanced every month to include returns and the firm is affected by the event over the last period. (The unit of investigation is not the event so much as the calendar month.) While this may generate more reliable abnormal return value (Fama, 1998) and reduces cross-sectional dependence issue as returns are averaged in the single portfolio (Dionysiou, 2015), it is sensitive to the bad model problem still (Fama, 1998).

Such a long horizon event study will probably suffer from specification problems even using these two most commonly used approaches (Dionysiou, 2015). Therefore, careful research design considerations must be considered when conducting a long horizon event study.

CONCLUSION

All studies come with their own set of assumptions. Event studies are no different; however, many of the assumptions considered almost standard and commonly and easily addressed in other management research methods may prove to be troubling in event studies. A primary example of this is independence, which will be violated in many event studies where multiple firms are affected by a single shock to the market (Hendricks et al., 2020; Jacobs & Singhal, 2017).

In this chapter, we have looked at some of the core assumptions of the event study method and some examples of what the assumptions mean in practice, how you can understand them, and how you can use this in your writing. In particular, we have looked at the connection between the event and the stock market reaction, which is of interest to many researchers and readers in the management of space. One way in which they sometimes demonstrate this importance is with the explanation and development of the first hypothesis that postulates that the event an interest will cause the stock market reaction. Authors can couple this with a clear visual, conceptual model that summarizes these relationships.

The challenges do not invalidate the event study approach, but mean that researchers must be careful with their application in the research study design. We elaborate on many of these issues in the following chapters to provide insight into how issues can be addressed and managed in practice.

REFERENCES

Barber, B. M., & Lyon, J. D. (1997). Detecting long-run abnormal stock returns: The empirical power and specification of test statistics. *Journal of Financial Economics*, *43*(3), 341–372. doi:10.1016/S0304-405X(96)00890-2

Bernard, V. L. (1987). Cross-sectional dependence and problems in inference in market-based accounting research. *Journal of Accounting Research*, *25*(1), 1–48. doi:10.2307/2491257

Bertrand, J. W. M., & Fransoo, J. C. (2002). Operations management research methodologies using quantitative modeling. *International Journal of Operations & Production Management*, *22*(2), 241–264. doi:10.1108/01443570210414338

Brown, D. T., Fee, C. E., & Thomas, S. E. (2009). Financial leverage and bargaining power with suppliers: Evidence from leveraged buyouts. *Journal of Corporate Finance*, *15*(2), 196–211. doi:10.1016/j.jcorpfin.2008.10.004

Brown, S. J., & Warner, J. B. (1980). Measuring security price performance. *Journal of Financial Economics*, *8*(3), 205–258. doi:10.1016/0304-405X(80)90002-1

Brown, S. J., & Warner, J. B. (1985). Using daily stock returns: The case of event studies. *Journal of Financial Economics*, *14*(1), 3–31. doi:10.1016/0304-405X(85)90042-X

Carhart, M. M. (1997). On persistence in mutual fund performance. *The Journal of Finance*, *52*(1), 57–82. doi:10.1111/j.1540-6261.1997.tb03808.x

Collis, J., & Hussey, R. (2003). *Business Research: A Practical Guide for Undergraduate and Postgraduate Students*. Palgrave Macmillan.

Dann, L. Y., Mayers, D., & Raab, R. J. Jr. (1977). Trading rules, large blocks and the speed of price adjustment. *Journal of Financial Economics*, *4*(1), 3–22. doi:10.1016/0304-405X(77)90034-4

Dionysiou, D. (2015). Choosing among alternative long-run event-study techniques. *Journal of Economic Surveys*, *29*(1), 158–198. doi:10.1111/j.1467-6419.2012.00742.x

Duan, C., Grover, V., & Balakrishnan, N. (2009). Business process outsourcing: An event study on the nature of processes and firm valuation. *European Journal of Information Systems*, *18*(5), 442–457. doi:10.1057/ejis.2009.38

Fama, E. F. (1970). Efficient capital markets: A review of theory and empirical work. *The Journal of Finance*, *25*(2), 383–417. doi:10.2307/2325486

Fama, E. F. (1991). Efficient capital markets: II. *The Journal of Finance, 46*(5), 1575–1617. doi:10.1111/j.1540-6261.1991.tb04636.x

Fama, E. F. (1998). Market efficiency, long-term returns, and behavioral finance. *Journal of Financial Economics, 49*(3), 283–306. doi:10.1016/S0304-405X(98)00026-9

Fawcett, S. E., Waller, M. A., Miller, J. W., Schwieterman, M. A., Hazen, B. T., & Overstreet, R. E. (2014). A trail guide to publishing success: Tips on writing influential conceptual, qualitative, and survey research. *Journal of Business Logistics, 35*(1), 1–16. doi:10.1111/jbl.12039

Fee, C. E., & Thomas, S. (2004). Sources of gains in horizontal mergers: Evidence from customer, supplier, and rival firms. *Journal of Financial Economics, 74*(3), 423–460. doi:10.1016/j.jfineco.2003.10.002

Hendricks, K. B., Jacobs, B. W., & Singhal, V. R. (2020). Stock market reaction to supply chain disruptions from the 2011 great east Japan earthquake. *Manufacturing & Service Operations Management, 22*(4), 645–867. doi:10.1287/msom.2019.0777

Hendricks, K. B., & Singhal, V. R. (2005). An empirical analysis of the effect of supply chain disruptions on long-run stock price performance and equity risk of the firm. *Production and Operations Management, 14*(1), 35–52. doi:10.1111/j.1937-5956.2005.tb00008.x

Hendricks, K. B., Singhal, V. R., & Stratman, J. K. (2007). The impact of enterprise systems on corporate performance: A study of ERP, SCM, and CRM system implementations. *Journal of Operations Management, 25*(1), 65–82. doi:10.1016/j.jom.2006.02.002

Homan, A. C. (2006). The impact of 9/11 on financial risk, volatility and returns of marine firms. *Maritime Economics & Logistics, 8*(4), 387–401. doi:10.1057/palgrave.mel.9100165

Homan, A. C. (2007). The impact of MTSA on financial risk and volatility of marine firms. *Maritime Policy & Management, 34*(1), 69–79. doi:10.1080/03088830601103459

Homan, A. C. (2009a). The impact of 9/11 on the persistence of financial return volatility of marine firms. *Eastern Economic Journal, 35*(1), 71–83. doi:10.1057/palgrave.eej.9050044

Homan, A. C. (2009b). The impact of MTSA on investment uncertainty and the persistence of financial return volatility of marine firms. *Maritime Policy & Management, 36*(2), 105–115. doi:10.1080/03088830902868008

Jacobs, B. W., & Singhal, V. R. (2014). The effect of product development restructuring on shareholder value. *Production and Operations Management, 23*(5), 728–743. doi:10.1111/poms.12074

Jacobs, B. W., & Singhal, V. R. (2017). The effect of the Rana Plaza disaster on shareholder wealth of retailers: Implications for sourcing strategies and supply chain governance. *Journal of Operations Management, 49–51*(1), 52–66. doi:10.1016/j.jom.2017.01.002

Jacobs, B. W., Singhal, V. R., & Subramanian, R. (2010). An empirical investigation of environmental performance and the market value of the firm. *Journal of Operations Management, 28*(5), 430–441. doi:10.1016/j.jom.2010.01.001

Jensen, M. C. (1978). Some anomalous evidence regarding market efficiency. *Journal of Financial Economics, 6*(2), 95–101. doi:10.1016/0304-405X(78)90025-9

Kothari, S. P., & Warner, J. B. (2007). Econometrics of event studies. In B. E. Eckbo (Ed.), *Handbook of Corporate Finance: Empirical Corporate Finance* (Vol. 1, pp. 3–36). North-Holland/Elsevier. doi:10.1016/B978-0-444-53265-7.50015-9

MacKinlay, A. C. (1997). Event studies in economics and finance. *Journal of Economic Literature, 35*(1), 13–39.

Malkiel, B. G. (2003). The efficient market hypothesis and its critics. *The Journal of Economic Perspectives, 17*(1), 59–82. doi:10.1257/089533003321164958

McWilliams, A., & Siegel, D. (1997). Event studies in management research: Theoretical and empirical issues. *Academy of Management Journal, 40*(3), 626–657. doi:10.2307/257056

McWilliams, A., Siegel, D., & Teoh, S. H. (1999). Issues in the use of the event study methodology: A critical analysis of corporate social responsibility studies. *Organizational Research Methods, 2*(4), 340–365. doi:10.1177/109442819924002

Mitchell, M., & Stafford, E. (2000). Managerial decisions and long-term stock price performance. *The Journal of Business, 73*(3), 287–329. doi:10.1086/209645

Mitchell, M. L., & Netter, J. M. (1989). Triggering the 1987 stock market crash. *Journal of Financial Economics, 24*(1), 37–68. doi:10.1016/0304-405X(89)90071-8

Morgan, G., & Smircich, L. (1980). The case for qualitative research. *Academy of Management Review, 5*(4), 491–500. doi:10.2307/257453

Muntermann, J., & Guettler, A. (2007). Intraday stock price effects of ad hoc disclosures: The German case. *Journal of International Financial Markets, Institutions and Money, 17*(1), 1–24. doi:10.1016/j.intfin.2005.08.003

Raymond, N. (2022, January 28). 3M hit with $110 million verdict in latest U.S. military earplug trial. *Reuters.* https://www.reuters.com/business/aerospace-defense/3m-hit-with-110-million-verdict-latest-us-military-earplug-trial-2022-01-27/

Riley, S. M., Michael, S. C., & Mahoney, J. T. (2017). Human capital matters: Market valuation of firm investments in training and the role of complementary assets. *Strategic Management Journal, 38*(9), 1895–1914. doi:10.1002mj.2631

Roth, A. V. (2007). Applications of empirical science in manufacturing and service operations. *Manufacturing & Service Operations Management, 9*(4), 353–367. doi:10.1287/msom.1070.0197

ADDITIONAL READING

Dam, L., & Petkova, B. N. (2014). The impact of environmental supply chain sustainability programs on shareholder wealth. *International Journal of Operations & Production Management*, *34*(5), 586–609. doi:10.1108/IJOPM-10-2012-0482

Hendricks, K. B., Hora, M., & Singhal, V. R. (2014). An empirical investigation on the appointments of supply chain and operations management executives. *Management Science*, *61*(7), 1562–1583. doi:10.1287/mnsc.2014.1987

Jacobs, B. W., & Singhal, V. R. (2020). Shareholder value effects of the Volkswagen emissions scandal on the automotive ecosystem. *Production and Operations Management*, *29*(10), 2230–2251. doi:10.1111/poms.13228

Kadirov, D. (2011). Macro-systems role of marketing: Do we trade environment for welfare? *Journal of Macromarketing*, *31*(4), 359–375. doi:10.1177/0276146711409944

Liu, Y.-C., & Yeh, I.-C. (2014). Which drives abnormal returns, over- or under-reaction? Studies applying longitudinal analysis. *Applied Economics*, *46*(26), 3224–3235. doi:10.1080/00036846.2014.925081

Mahr, T. G., Nowak, E., & Rott, R. (2016). The (ir)relevance of disclosure of compliance with corporate governance codes: Empirical evidence from the German stock market. *Journal of Institutional and Theoretical Economics*, *172*(3), 475–520. doi:10.1628/093245616X14605537965067

Merikas, A., Gounopoulos, D., & Nounis, C. (2009). Global shipping IPOs performance. *Maritime Policy & Management*, *36*(6), 481–505. doi:10.1080/03088830903346053

Wood, L. C., Wang, J. X., Duong, L. N. K., Reiners, T., & Smith, R. (2018). Stock market reactions to auto manufacturers' environmental failures. *Journal of Macromarketing*, *38*(4), 364–382. doi:10.1177/0276146718781915

Wood, L. C., Wang, J. X., Olesen, K., & Reiners, T. (2017). The effect of slack, diversification, and time to recall on stock market reaction to toy recalls. *International Journal of Production Economics*, *193*, 244–258. doi:10.1016/j.ijpe.2017.07.021

Xia, Y., Singhal, V. R., & Peter Zhang, G. (2016). Product design awards and the market value of the firm. *Production and Operations Management*, *25*(6), 1038–1055. doi:10.1111/poms.12525

Zhan, X., Mu, Y., Hora, M., & Singhal, V. R. (2021). Service excellence and market value of a firm: An empirical investigation of winning service awards and stock market reaction. *International Journal of Production Research*, *59*(14), 4188–4204. doi:10.1080/00207543.2020.1759837

Zhan, X., Mu, Y., Nishant, R., & Singhal, V. R. (2020). When do appointments of Chief Digital or Data Officers (CDOs) affect stock prices? *IEEE Transactions on Engineering Management*, 1–14. doi:10.1109/TEM.2020.2984619

Zhang, G. P., Yu, J., & Xia, Y. (2014). The payback of effective innovation programs: Empirical evidence from firms that have won innovation awards. *Production and Operations Management*, *23*(8), 1401–1420. doi:10.1111/j.1937-5956.2012.01368.x

KEY TERMS AND DEFINITIONS

Efficient Market Hypothesis: The primary and long-standing assumption that the markets are efficient and instantly incorporate all new news into the stock prices.

Jensen's Alpha: Also known as Jensen's Performance Index is used to evaluate the abnormal return over the theoretical expected return and is useful when there is calendar clustering.

Long-Horizon Event Study: A study over a longer horizon that will be months, quarters, or years. It follows the changes and, with a long-horizon study of stock returns, can capture actual returns from a buy-and-hold investment strategy and provide more confirmation.

Risk Aversion: The likelihood that investors and market participants will elect to preserve their capital rather than invest in a stock with a volatile or uncertain future outcome, such as driven by large legal challenges that extend over many years.

Short-Horizon Event Study: A study that uses changes in abnormal returns over a horizon of days rather than months or years. The change reflects an unbiased market participant estimation of the event and the consequences for the company over time, reflected in the current prices.

Unanticipated Event: An event that the market participants (e.g., investors) do not anticipate. The information about the event, therefore, represents a new release of information that the participants respond to instantaneously.

Chapter 3
The Event Study Method in Brief

ABSTRACT

This chapter looks at the entire event study project from start to finish. It looks behind the scenes of some of the research design decisions and discussions behind the research article on toy recalls and talks about the process and some challenges faced. This provides, briefly, an overview of an event study project. The overview provides some insight into how it is easier than some other methods and shows how it can be challenging in several ways. The chapter provides insight into some of the design considerations and reasons why the study looks the way it does. It gives insight into the 'what' of the actions required in an event study and the sequence of steps taken.

INTRODUCTION

I had some friends asked me once where I got some ideas from that find their way into my articles. As always, a range of answers depending on the actual project. I derived some ideas over beer at barbecues with work friends and colleagues. Other project ideas grew from interesting observations and findings in some of my student projects. I source many of ideas from other research in the literature or professional issues that remain unresolved by research.

In contrast, this chapter walks us through a study I worked on where we examined the stock market reaction to toy recalls. The motivation and genesis for this project is embarrassing as it was not originally motivated so the standard reasons for doing a project. Rather, I had been at a conference where I met some people who said (and I paraphrase liberally): "Gosh, operations management how dull and boring. We like our subject of psychology because we can apply this and learn from it in everyday life." Later, when a friend knew we are expecting our first child, he joked with me that I could not make operations management relevant to parenthood. Taken together, I construed these as a challenge to do a project that would have some relevance to everyday life, was personally relevant to me as a soon-to-be parent, and used operations management concepts.

I settled on the idea of toy recalls, as this was of relevance to my (developing, parentally-focused!) shopping habits and I was sure that it would generate an abnormal return for several reasons. First, there is already considerable research on recalls showing a negative stock market reaction. That is, investors

DOI: 10.4018/978-1-7998-8969-4.ch003

are market participants believe that recalls negatively affect the company. Second, from discussions with my wife and with other parents, I know the parents place high importance on safety and are, thus, very careful in the selection of the products that they buy and use relating to the children. Therefore, a company that produced poor quality, dangerous, and substandard products and exposed children to these products would therefore experience recalls. Recalls and reputation would mean the firm struggles to continue to obtain strong future sales. That is, parents will perceive a strong negative reputational effect from recalls that would lead to decreased sales in the future. Product safety and the underlying standards are crucial (Liu et al., 2016; Rausand & Utne, 2009; Speier et al., 2011; Suhanyiova et al., 2016; Zhu et al., 2018). Conformity with standards and certification and recalls as a method to address observe quality issues is crucial (Beamish & Bapuji, 2008; Hora et al., 2011). There are several approaches to ensure quality toys are sold. Manufacturers must follow quality standards and government bodies often have requirements for particular types of products, such as food (Hammoudi et al., 2009), or a range of consumer-focusing products (CPSC, 2015).

From this, I identified the major topic for the paper. However, as we can see from the following chapter, the journey was not a simple nor straightforward one and my first daughter was about two and a half years old before the study was accepted and published. While the coverage is brief, the chapter provides some insight into some thinking behind the research design and some parameter selection decisions that were used inside of the project.

DATA SOURCES AND EVENTS

One of the first questions that we worked to answer was how we would create the event list, capturing a range of different recalls of toys over the years. We could identify press releases and announcements on recalls. However, on further investigation, it became apparent that there was an organization established that already captured much of this information: the U.S. Consumer Product Safety Commission (CPSC). Clearly, the focus is on U.S. data and there are often similar databases in other countries, although some differences in regulatory requirements that will cause different data being captured or different classifications made for each observation in the database. For the purpose of the study, however, this provided us with a starting point. At the time, the database was difficult to use and extract meaningful data from. It was difficult for us to tell, for example, whether a company mentioned was one that was publicly listed or privately listed. Obviously, with an event study, we were creating a sample of listed companies only. Starting with this is a specialized database approach, we went through carefully and isolated a sample. we had a database that provided us with fertile material. The CPSC database is valuable as:

In the U.S., toy recalls are managed by the CPSC and firms may be required to commence a recall of toys if there is an injury associated with the product. Recall announcements are published by the CPSC and added to their database. (Wood et al., 2017, p. 249)

These are available with the "[p]ublic database export of all recalls and unsafe product reports on SaferProducts.gov" (CPSC, 2022). Even here, there are several small challenges. Such as, for example, whether the toy was the major product of interest and, therefore, whether the damage or the consequences of the recall was meaningful. We carefully read through and agreed as a team on which cases the toy was the primary product.

At the end of the process, we were left with what we felt was a surprisingly small sample size. My gut reaction was that this was not an accurate reflection of what we should have found and, furthermore, it was also going to be too small for subsequent cross-sectional regression.

When we carefully examined our announcements, we noticed how we had screened for recalls from publicly listed firms. However, we quickly realized that we had not addressed recalls of brands that were owned by a subsidiary of a holding company. As noted in the article, "[w]e also searched for key brands or subsidiaries, e.g., in addition to searching for Mattel we also sought announcements regarding the Mattel-owned Fisher-Price brand" (Wood et al., 2017, p. 249). At this point, I realized that what I thought was going to be a relatively straightforward and linear process already meant going back to more carefully establish the sample of events.

CONSTRUCTING VARIABLES AND THE HYPOTHESES

In this section, we turn from the overall conceptualization of the study to examine the 'core' foundation of the research by first examining the hypotheses. We discuss those used in the study and the genesis of these and how they compare to other studies. Following this, an overview is provided of the design decisions relating to the construction of the variables and decisions such as the establishment of the estimation windows.

DEVELOPING THE HYPOTHESES

Developing the hypotheses was an interesting challenge, and we drew on a range of background reading and literature. Again, while hypotheses might be easy to develop, it was not always straightforward on how we were going to provide the data for the interesting hypotheses in the research project. Some of these are relatively simple, such as measures of slack and available resources that might help the firm accommodate and address issues of the recall. Many of these data could be easily extracted from the database, compiled, and transformed for analysis. One of the other variables, however, was the time taken for the recall. As we read more research and considered it more deeply, it became apparent that there could be a range of different measures.

The primary, leading, or first hypothesis in the study is similar to that found in most contemporaneous event study analysis research. We hypothesized that the event being studied is causally connected to an abnormal return. The terminologies used will differ between studies and some researchers may use 'stock market reaction' (Zhan et al., 2021) or the 'market will react' (Xia et al., 2016).

Beyond the primary hypothesis, most studies contain between two or three to five or six additional hypotheses that are evaluated in cross-sectional regression analysis. The development of the hypotheses here were based on several recent studies that had begun to explore several factors that managers could influence in their management of recalls:

- the level of proactivity in responding to the issues (a time-based strategy)
- how 'slack' resources could buffer to the problem and reduce the negative impact,
- and how the negative consequences could be reduced if there were a wider portfolio of other activities that would provide a buffer; how diversification reduces the impact of a negative event.

Through evaluating various factors in the literature, we were able to identify the broad factors above while also beginning to target specific measures or metrics within each that would be appropriate within the project. Note that this was not necessarily 'adopting blindly' measures; for instance, we did not adopt all 'operational slack' forms as one conceptually overlapped with another slack resource we evaluated (details are discussed below).

In most cases, we were looking at current literature to understand the current thinking on these factors, while also looking for factors where there was a divergence of opinions or a lack of clarity about the relationship or strength of the relationship. This enabled us to add evidence to the growing body of literature in each case.

Time to Recall and How Managers May Proactively Manage the Recall Strategy

Roth et al. (2008) conceptually studied how time was relevant to food recalls. They suggested that a time-based strategy might effect on stock market reactions. Studies have identified different time-based measures in response to recalls (Hora et al., 2011; Magno, 2012; Roth et al., 2008). Finally, the argument was made for the particular window (based on product launch and recall announcement) and the reason for the recall as:

a longer time between product launch and recall announcement is likely to have a less negative stock market reaction. This is for two reasons. First, a late recall indicates the product has been on sale for a longer time. A severe or hazardous defect is more likely rapidly discovered; therefore, a longer time to recall may be associated with a lower severity of hazard associated with the defects and a limit to the financial cost of the recall and reputational damage to the firm. Second, a firm which initiates a late recall is likely to have increased time to ensure flexibility of resources to buffer the financial costs associated with the recall event. These resources are accumulated by the profits and operational capabilities from greater sales level. In contrast, a firm conducting an earlier recall may have to disrupt their cash flow and operations to cover the recall costs. Additionally, as we noted, the toy industry is characterized by short product life cycles and low prices (Wong et al., 2005); a long recall time increases the possibility that the defective items (sold earlier near the time of first release) have already been disposed of, reducing the cost of managing the recall and application of an appropriate remedy. (Wood et al., 2017, pp. 248-249)

Slack Resources

A firm that has resources available to weather a storm is more likely to successfully get through the adversity with fewer challenges. As such, an investor in a firm that has plenty of available resources to manage and accommodate disruptive situations may be confident in the firm's ability to overcome adverse conditions associated with a recall. As a consequence, three hypotheses were proposed based on different forms of these 'slack' or underutilized resources. In these cases, therefore, these additional resources can be a buffer against a shock and help a firm to maintain a stable financial and operational performance in the face of an adverse event (Hendricks & Singhal, 2009; Kovach et al., 2015). Three key elements were identified in prior research: financial slack (Moses, 1992) and various forms of operational slack of which inventory and capacity slack were selected (Hendricks & Singhal, 2009; Kovach et al., 2015; Voss et al., 2008). While there is another form of operational slack (the form of supply chain slack using the cash-to-cash cycle), it was not used due to the similarity of duplicated components that would similarly be found in the financial slack (Kovach et al., 2015).

In general, while slack resources have been well-understood, the empirical evidence connecting them to enhanced (or maintained) performance was scarce and was still emerging. As a consequence, while there is now stronger understanding of the various forms of slack and how they support a firm facing adverse circumstances, this was not understood at the time and the research outcomes helped to inform the wider examination of slack resources.

Diversification

While there are multiple forms of diversification, such as over different business lines, we opted for the measure of geographic diversification as a 'hedge' or a protection against disasters and risks in one region (Hendricks & Singhal, 2009; Kovach et al., 2015). Firms with activities spread over many regions can overcome disruptions and difficulties in one area, by, for example, running plants in others to maintain overall operational flexibility over their supply network (Allayannis et al., 2001). Any given recall should, therefore, be considered to be less significant for a geographically diverse firm than one that is less diversified. As a consequence, this was seen to be an important factor.

Together, we believed that evidence about these hypotheses and how each factor influenced the stock market reaction to the recall event would further management understanding of how to design and invest for a robust and versatile organization.

DATA, CONSTRUCTING VARIABLES, AND ESTIMATION WINDOWS

Where do these data come from? The recall announcement is tied to the date from the database. Most of the announcements also include information about how long the product has been available, giving us a launch date. While a little manual work was required, we were able to engineer an appropriate variable for the recall time.

We looked at a range of estimation windows of the project that would allow us to provide an estimate for the normal returns so that we could estimate the abnormal returns in reaction to the event (McWilliams & Siegel, 1997). There is no clear guidance on this factor, and so we opted for 120 days, as used in prior research (Zhao et al., 2013); we recognized that commonly used values extended for 100 to several hundred days. We tested several estimation windows and saw few meaningful differences. We provided a 10-day buffer between the estimation window and the two-day event window (Wood et al., 2017, p. 249, 2017).

We used the market model, based on the CRSP value-weighted index as the market, to calculate the abnormal returns, noting this was commonly used (Brown & Warner, 1985; MacKinlay, 1997). If we submitted the manuscript today, I would expect to use a three- or four-factor model to calculate abnormal returns and provide the market model estimation of abnormal returns to show our calculation is not sensitive to the model selection. When calculating the abnormal returns, as well as the two-day window, we reported on several other periods. The two-day window provided the strongest evidence of an abnormal return ticket as opposed to a single day period or even the wider 11-day period measured by (-5,+5).

We prepared a range of variables that would allow us to test the hypotheses proposed in the paper. We extracted these from the database, ran some calculations in Excel, and then exported into R for analysis.

During the revision process, one variable construction was questioned by a reviewer (as we had explained how we constructed it); we went back and adjusted the calculation to accommodate their concerns and found that it had no meaningful impact on the outcomes. We constructed some of the variables using data from the announcement themselves, such as the time to recall. Further, several control variables were used, including the size of the company as measured by net sales, their position in the supply chain based on the SIC code extracted from Datastream with a conversion of SIC codes that were two digits to a simple manufacturer versus retailer (Bose & Pal, 2012). Interpretation of the announcements was required for evaluation of the recall strategy being used, as well as the mechanism of either refunding or applying another remedy to address the problem.

Initially, our submission did not include any descriptive statistics about the sample and the reviewers were quick to point out that this would provide the reader with additional insight, and it was more commonly used in the operations management area. The subsequent revisions included some key insight into the type of firms in the sample in section 4.5.

RESULTS AND REPORTING

Within the manuscript, we talked about the calculation of abnormal returns using the market model, construction of the variables using different data, and included a table of descriptive statistics providing insight into both the companies involved in the toy recalls and some data about the firms in the sample. We included a table of correlations between the variables used in the cross-sectional regression. A table was presented, showing that the abnormal returns were statistically significant from zero with test results using a range of different tests. During the revision process, we expanded this section to show the results over several periods, providing more evidence that a selection of the event window was reasonable.

We presented the regression model equation highlighting the model for which we presented the results in section 5. With the regression modeling, we first set up a model that comprised the control variables. The second model comprised both the control variables and variables of interest that would allow us to test the hypotheses. We presented the VIF values for the complete (second) model only.

While undertaking the analysis, we identified also necessary to manage heteroscedasticity with the studentized Breusch-Pagan test (Breusch & Pagan, 1979) and therefore we used HC1 estimators which worked well with smaller sample sizes as we were using the study (Kleiber, 2008; MacKinnon & White, 1985). Therefore, Table 4 (Wood et al., 2017, p. 254) uses and reports robust standard errors (White, 1982).

Finally, we were left with insight from Table 4 about whether there is evidence to support hypotheses. As with many projects, not all hypotheses have sufficient statistical evidence against the null hypothesis; we did not find material support for all of what we had hypothesized. This is particularly interesting as we had inventory, capacity, and financial slack in the model and the relative importance of each suggests that additional research is required to understand under what circumstances each form slack might be beneficial to companies facing product recalls and quality problems.

The results enabled us to report on whether there was evidence to support each of the hypotheses, and evidence of the overall abnormal return. We used many of the key research articles from the early review of the literature and development of the hypotheses and re-cited them in the discussion of the results. Doing this enabled us to explain our results in comparison with other research.

Conclusions and Journal Submission

Finally, we were ready to report on the study results and send the manuscript to a journal. The manuscript went through many revisions after receiving some negative feedback from several other journals. (At one point, we put the project aside for several months after some particularly bruising feedback.) We had originally had a separate discussions section and then a separate conclusion section. One reviewer correctly pointed out that this had resulted in some duplication of material discussion and suggested that we merely write it up as a conclusion and discussions section. We followed the suggestion and were pleased to shorten the manuscript.

As an insight into the study results, the first paragraph of the final section (discussion, summary, and future research) was used to summarize the results, where we reported:

This analysis provides empirical evidence on the effect of operational strategies to mitigate the economic impact of a toy recall. Based on a sample of 135 toy recall announcements during 1979–2016, we found evidence that the greater levels of business diversification, inventory slack, and a longer time to recall are associated with less negative financial performance to recalling firms; however, we found that greater capacity slack is associated with more negative shareholder values, whereas we hypothesized that greater slack would be beneficial to the firm as it would buffer the recalling firms' losses. We found no evidence that geographic diversification, financial slack, or the year of the recall influences the stock market reaction to the recalls. Moreover, while the literature suggested significant relationships between proactive recall strategy, the retailer or distributor status, and remedy and the stock market reaction to product recalls, we found no significant effects in our study. (Wood et al., 2017, p. 254)

Following this, we provided more insight into how the study extended past research. The results from the cross-sectional regression were used to provide insight into our results and how they confirmed and extended past studies.

Issues, Controversies, Problems

Before starting an event study, it is sensible to assess your ability to access suitable databases that will contain appropriate archival data. You should have access to databases with data for the calculation of the abnormal returns using the event study process and also for conducting the cross-sectional regression with information about the companies. It is not common for many researchers or students in supply chain or management departments to have extensive have experience or exposure to databases such as Compustat or CRSP; therefore, it may be valuable to discuss with colleagues in a finance department who can provide assistance. Furthermore, sometimes a particular database might be required, such as for the development of environmental, social, and governance (ESG) scores for inclusion into a model. If this is the case, then it may be necessary to secure funding for a database subscription (please note that the costs can be quite significant most times). Use your advisors for advice on access to funding or resources, or explore partnering with a coauthor at another institution which has access to the required database. In some cases, you may have met someone at a conference and they may help. Other times, a simple Google search will often show what databases are available at a university and then you can check the department listings.

As a result, if this event study method is of interest, it is very important to ensure that you will have access to appropriate resources. For example, you will need access to sufficient search capability, such as with the Factiva database, to find news announcements. You will also need some way of doing the calculations. There are many software packages available, and we will not examine the benefits of drawbacks of each of these. The free options include the R platform (R Core Team, 2012) and other paid and more expensive options such as Eventus. It is also possible to code and run the tests yourself, although this will open you up to making considerable mistakes and errors that would need to be checked carefully. It also means that it will be challenging to calculate more comprehensive test statistics later to ensure statistical significance.

Soon after completing the study reported in Wood et al. (2017), we were starting another study that would use a set of announcements drawn from the Factiva database. Unbeknownst to us, a decision had been made to stop the subscription to the database, driven by perceived low levels of usage. In this case, we had ascertained from the outset that we had the required resources to continue the project and then realized (with horror) that those resources disappeared part way through the project.

A final note is the need for research data management (Briney, 2015; Clare et al., 2019; Cox, 2018). This project involved colleagues at different institutions; by the time it had been published, I had changed institutions twice. Therefore, we needed careful management of the core data and effective archiving techniques. These steps take a little time but, for a few hours invested while the project is fresh in your memory, it will pay dividends later and reduce headaches.

CONCLUSIONS AND FUTURE DIRECTIONS

In this chapter, we have looked through a specific example, examining some of the key analytic and research steps used. This gives an overview and an understanding of how the event study method works and operates, in may give you some insight into the similarities and differences between this method and other methods. The intention is not to do an event study method after reading the chapter but to provide a context as we step through the following chapters, each focusing on a particular element of the event study method and design considerations. Sometimes, there is little insight in this chapter on how or why a particular decision was made; reading the following chapters will give some insight into how and why a particular design decision was made in the study, and how you might need to consider when making these decisions, and how to clarify, explain, or justify why the decision was made.

The following chapters discuss the selection of a topic and how and why your phenomenon of interest may or may not be a good candidate for an event study. We talk about developing your sample of events that will be used in the analysis and how this might differ over a range of project types. We talk about completing archival and literature searches, providing additional insight into identifying the correct literature. We talk about some of the key research design decisions and how to use and manage different data types and the analysis. We also discuss the event study analysis in the calculation of abnormal returns and the subsequent cross-sectional regression as well as introducing other possible combinations of approaches such as qualitative comparative analysis (QCA) (Wood et al., 2022). Finally, we provide insight into how you can write up the results as well as completing the write-up of the manuscript.

REFERENCES

Allayannis, G., Ihrig, J., & Weston, J. P. (2001). Exchange-rate hedging: Financial versus operational strategies. *The American Economic Review*, *91*(2), 391–395. doi:10.1257/aer.91.2.391

Beamish, P. W., & Bapuji, H. (2008). Toy recalls and China: Emotion vs. Evidence. *Management and Organization Review*, *4*(2), 197–209. doi:10.1111/j.1740-8784.2008.00105.x

Bose, I., & Pal, R. (2012). Do green supply chain management initiatives impact stock prices of firms? *Decision Support Systems*, *52*(3), 624–634. doi:10.1016/j.dss.2011.10.020

Breusch, T. S., & Pagan, A. R. (1979). A simple test for heteroscedasticity and random coefficient variation. *Econometrica*, *47*(5), 1287–1294. doi:10.2307/1911963

Briney, K. (2015). *Data management for researchers: Organize, maintain and share your data for research success*. Pelagic Publishing.

Brown, S. J., & Warner, J. B. (1985). Using daily stock returns: The case of event studies. *Journal of Financial Economics*, *14*(1), 3–31. doi:10.1016/0304-405X(85)90042-X

Clare, C., Cruz, M., Papadopoulou, E., Savage, J., Teperek, M., Wang, Y., Witkowska, I., & Yeomans, J. (2019). *Engaging researchers with data management: The cookbook*. Open Book Publishers. doi:10.11647/OBP.0185

Cox, A. (2018). *Exploring research data management*. Facet Publishing. doi:10.29085/9781783302802

CPSC. (2015). *Regulations, mandatory standards and bans*. U.S. Consumer Product Safety Commission. https://www.cpsc.gov/en/Regulations-Laws--Standards/Regulations-Mandatory-Standards-Bans/

CPSC. (2022). *CPSC Data*. U.S. Consumer Product Safety Commission. https://www.cpsc.gov/Data

Hammoudi, A., Hoffmann, R., & Surry, Y. (2009). Food safety standards and agri-food supply chains: An introductory overview. *European Review of Agriculture Economics*, *36*(4), 469–478. doi:10.1093/erae/jbp044

Hendricks, K. B., & Singhal, V. R. (2009). Demand-supply mismatches and stock market reaction: Evidence from excess inventory announcements. *Manufacturing & Service Operations Management*, *11*(3), 509–524. doi:10.1287/msom.1080.0237

Hora, M., Bapuji, H., & Roth, A. V. (2011). Safety hazard and time to recall: The role of recall strategy, product defect type, and supply chain player in the U.S. toy industry. *Journal of Operations Management*, *29*(7–8), 766–777. doi:10.1016/j.jom.2011.06.006

Kleiber, C. (2008). *Applied econometrics with R*. Springer New York. doi:10.1007/978-0-387-77318-6

Kovach, J. J., Hora, M., Manikas, A., & Patel, P. C. (2015). Firm performance in dynamic environments: The role of operational slack and operational scope. *Journal of Operations Management*, *37*(1), 1–12. doi:10.1016/j.jom.2015.04.002

Liu, A. X., Liu, Y., & Luo, T. (2016). What drives a firm's choice of product recall remedy? The impact remedy cost, product hazard, and the CEO. *Journal of Marketing*, *80*(3), 79–95. doi:10.1509/jm.14.0382

MacKinlay, A. C. (1997). Event studies in economics and finance. *Journal of Economic Literature*, *35*(1), 13–39.

MacKinnon, J. G., & White, H. (1985). Some heteroskedasticity-consistent covariance matrix estimators with improved finite sample properties. *Journal of Econometrics*, *29*(3), 305–325. doi:10.1016/0304-4076(85)90158-7

Magno, F. (2012). Managing product recalls: The effects of time, responsible vs. opportunistic recall management and blame on consumers' attitudes. *Procedia: Social and Behavioral Sciences*, *58*, 1309–1315. doi:10.1016/j.sbspro.2012.09.1114

McWilliams, A., & Siegel, D. (1997). Event studies in management research: Theoretical and empirical issues. *Academy of Management Journal*, *40*(3), 626–657. doi:10.2307/257056

Moses, O. D. (1992). Organizational slack and risk-taking behaviour: Tests of product pricing strategy. *Journal of Organizational Change Management*, *5*(3), 38–54. doi:10.1108/09534819210018045

R Core Team. (2012). *R: A language and environment for statistical computing.* http://www.R-project.org/

Rausand, M., & Utne, I. B. (2009). Product safety – Principles and practices in a life cycle perspective. *Safety Science*, *47*(7), 939–947. doi:10.1016/j.ssci.2008.10.004

Roth, A. V., Tsay, A. A., Pullman, M. E., & Gray, J. V. (2008). Unraveling the food supply chain: Strategic insights from China and the 2007 recalls. *The Journal of Supply Chain Management*, *44*(1), 22–39. doi:10.1111/j.1745-493X.2008.00043.x

Speier, C., Whipple, J. M., Closs, D. J., & Voss, M. D. (2011). Global supply chain design considerations: Mitigating product safety and security risks. *Journal of Operations Management*, *29*(7–8), 721–736. doi:10.1016/j.jom.2011.06.003

Suhanyiova, L., Flin, R., & Irwin, A. (2016). Safety systems in product safety culture. In L. Walls, M. Revie, & T. Bedford (Eds.), *Risk, Reliability and Safety: Innovating Theory and Practice: Proceedings of ESREL 2016* (pp. 1803–1808). CRC Press. https://www.crcpress.com/Risk-Reliability-and-Safety-Innovating-Theory-and-Practice-Proceedings/Walls-Revie-Bedford/p/book/9781138029972

Voss, G. B., Sirdeshmukh, D., & Voss, Z. G. (2008). The effects of slack resources and environmental threat on product exploration and exploitation. *Academy of Management Journal*, *51*(1), 147–164. doi:10.5465/amj.2008.30767373

White, H. (1982). Maximum likelihood estimation of misspecified models. *Econometrica*, *50*(1), 1–25. doi:10.2307/1912526

Wood, L. C., Duong, L. N. K., & Wang, J. X. (2022). Business Process Improvement for Sustainable Technologies Investments in Construction: A Configurational Approach. *Sustainability*, *14*(9), 5697. doi:10.3390u14095697

Wood, L. C., Wang, J. X., Olesen, K., & Reiners, T. (2017). The effect of slack, diversification, and time to recall on stock market reaction to toy recalls. *International Journal of Production Economics*, *193*, 244–258. doi:10.1016/j.ijpe.2017.07.021

Xia, Y., Singhal, V. R., & Peter Zhang, G. (2016). Product design awards and the market value of the firm. *Production and Operations Management*, *25*(6), 1038–1055. doi:10.1111/poms.12525

Zhan, X., Mu, Y., Hora, M., & Singhal, V. R. (2021). Service excellence and market value of a firm: An empirical investigation of winning service awards and stock market reaction. *International Journal of Production Research*, *59*(14), 4188–4204. doi:10.1080/00207543.2020.1759837

Zhao, X., Li, Y., & Flynn, B. B. (2013). The financial impact of product recall announcements in China. *International Journal of Production Economics*, *142*(1), 115–123. doi:10.1016/j.ijpe.2012.10.018

Zhu, A. Y., von Zedtwitz, M., & Assimakopoulos, D. (2018). *Responsible product innovation: Putting safety first*. Springer International Publishing. //www.springer.com/gb/book/9783319684505

ADDITIONAL READING

Ahern, K. R. (2009). Sample selection and event study estimation. *Journal of Empirical Finance*, *16*(3), 466–482. doi:10.1016/j.jempfin.2009.01.003

Ba, S., Lisic, L. L., Liu, Q., & Stallaert, J. (2013). Stock market reaction to green vehicle innovation. *Production and Operations Management*, *22*(4), 976–990. doi:10.1111/j.1937-5956.2012.01387.x

Bilgili, H., Tochman Campbell, J., Ellstrand, A. E., & Johnson, J. L. (2017). Riding off into the sunset: Organizational sensegiving, shareholder sensemaking, and reactions to CEO retirement. *Journal of Management Studies*, *54*(7), 1019–1049. doi:10.1111/joms.12264

Bogart, D., & Chaudhary, L. (2012). Regulation, ownership, and costs: A historical perspective from Indian railways. *American Economic Journal: Economic Policy, 4*(1), 28–57. http://dx.doi.org.ezproxy.otago.ac.nz/10.1257/pol.4.1.28

Bose, I., & Leung, A. C. M. (2014). Do phishing alerts impact global corporations? A firm value analysis. *Decision Support Systems*, *64*(Supplement C), 67–78. doi:10.1016/j.dss.2014.04.006

Bouzzine, Y. D. (2021). Stock price reactions to environmental pollution events: A systematic literature review of direct and indirect effects and a research agenda. *Journal of Cleaner Production*, *316*, 128305. doi:10.1016/j.jclepro.2021.128305

Brandon-Jones, E., Dutordoir, M., Frota Neto, J. Q., & Squire, B. (2017). The impact of reshoring decisions on shareholder wealth. *Journal of Operations Management*, *49*(1, Supplement C), 31–36. doi:10.1016/j.jom.2016.12.002

Burdina, M., Wright, M., & Zhu, Z. (2014). Is the stock market sticker shocked? A study of market response to recent CAFE regulations in the US. *Applied Economics*, *46*(34), 4178–4189. doi:10.1080/00036846.2014.952891

Chatjuthamard, P., Jiraporn, P., Jiraporn, N., & Tong, S. (2017). Estimating the market value of Steve Jobs using an event study. *Applied Economics Letters*, *24*(1), 30–34. doi:10.1080/13504851.2016.1158911

Cheng, J. M.-S., Tsao, S.-M., Tsai, W.-H., & Tu, H. H.-J. (2007). Will eChannel additions increase the financial performance of the firm?—The evidence from Taiwan. *Industrial Marketing Management*, *36*(1), 50–57. doi:10.1016/j.indmarman.2006.06.011

Chowdhury, J., & Sarkar, S. (2017). The financial impact of retail store closure announcements. *International Journal of Physical Distribution & Logistics Management*, *47*(6), 536–556. Advance online publication. doi:10.1108/IJPDLM-04-2016-0117

Corrado, C. J., & Zivney, T. L. (1992). The specification and power of the sign test in event study hypothesis tests using daily stock returns. *Journal of Financial and Quantitative Analysis*, *27*(3), 465–478. doi:10.2307/2331331

Dai, Y., Kong, D., & Wang, M. (2013). Investor reactions to food safety incidents: Evidence from the Chinese milk industry. *Food Policy*, *43*, 23–31. doi:10.1016/j.foodpol.2013.08.004

Sorescu, A., Warren, N. L., & Ertekin, L. (2017). Event study methodology in the marketing literature: An overview. *Journal of the Academy of Marketing Science*, *45*(2), 186–207. doi:10.100711747-017-0516-y

Sorokina, N., Booth, D. E., & Thornton, J. H. (2013). Robust methods in event studies: Empirical evidence and theoretical implications. *Journal of Data Science: JDS*, *11*(3), 575–606. doi:10.6339/JDS.2013.11(3).1166

KEY TERMS AND DEFINITIONS

Abnormal Return: The difference between an observed movement in stock returns that is clearly different from the normal or expected return.

Cross-Sectional Regression: The analysis of how multiple variables, drawn from the theoretical model, influence the outcome of the dependent variable usually modeled as abnormal returns in event study projects.

Database: An organized collection of information and data. In event studies, the databases will usually contain accurate data on stock returns and other information pertaining to companies, such as financial data like sales figures.

Event Study: The study of how an event, situation, circumstance influences the performance of a firm, usually evaluated with short-term changes in the stock returns, long-term changes, or changes in operating performance.

News Announcement: A release of information to the market participants that might cause them to re-evaluate the long-term performance of the company. For instance, a news announcement may outline that the company is undertaking a recall of an item they sell, leading to a drop in reputation and lower future sales and costs to undertake the recall, resulting in a negative stock market reaction.

Product Recall: A corrective action taken by companies when they realize there is a product safety issue. Remedies may include a return, replacement, or repair.

Variable: Used in the statistical analysis, where an observation has a value for the variable that may exist in a range of values. For instance, the firm size may be a variable used in the study, with the firm size represented by the annual sales.

Chapter 4
Selecting and Developing a Suitable Topic

ABSTRACT

The selection and match of topic/issue and method are crucial components of the research design process. The event study method requires a particular type of event that is studied, so selecting the appropriate topic is important. Not all topics are immediately amenable to inclusion use in an event study. The author looks at the types of topics that are a 'natural fit' and also how other topics can broadly be investigated with a slight change of the topic to make them amendable to the method. At the end of the chapter, readers are guided step-by-step in selecting an appropriate topic and development of the issue so that, most times, they can use an event study project as part of the investigation.

INTRODUCTION

The event study method relies on a sudden release of news to the market that the investors react to, pricing in the future outcomes from the study and pricing these into the current price. Generally positive events, those improving the company's long-term prospects, result in a positive bump or change in the stock returns. Those that are negative, with overall negative influences on the firm's success, result in a negative change in stock returns.

The need or a sudden and surprising news release that might influence the stock returns suggests two key issues.

1. There must be news and a surprise. (We include more details are below about how to take an otherwise unsurprising project and use it as the basis for an event study.)
2. The issue must be 'large' enough to make a discernible impact on the overall company value. There are many interesting phenomena that may not be large enough to dent corporate costs or revenues and are, therefore, less likely to be suitable for study with this method.

DOI: 10.4018/978-1-7998-8969-4.ch004

Many operations and supply chain studies use primary data collections (Töyli et al., 2008) based on surveys or interviews (Fawcett et al., 2014). But, the range of different topics where the use of secondary data can be quite valuable and beneficial for the study. For operations and supply chain subjects, we are often interested in sustainability outcomes. However, when speaking with a manager or sending them a survey, is a high probability that the managerial perception of outcomes or performance may not actually correlate with the genuine reality. Often with a survey, for example, we use a Likert-type scale where we ask participants to report on the firm's ability to meet various performance metrics, a form of 'soft measure' (Töyli et al., 2008). One good reason for using a survey approach to evaluate this type of measure is that participants and their employers will probably be prepared to report on outcomes and performance using Likert -type scales, as no confidential data needs to be revealed. However, the use of a 'hard measure' such as actual data from the company would be vastly more accurate and would provide more insight. However, the drawback is that many companies would be reluctant and unwilling to share these types of data. Secondary data often allows us to evaluate financial performance in terms of this reliable, secondary data, and it is becoming increasingly relevant in supply chain research in the 2000-2010 decades (Ellinger et al., 2011; Hendricks & Singhal, 2003, 2009).

There have also been calls for more use of secondary data in supply chain management research (Roth, 2007; Töyli et al., 2008). The research often proves easier to collect them primary data, and it often has a more objective nature, which helps improve the reliability of findings. Overall, a body of research (note, not necessarily from a single researcher or research team, but overall) needs to cover a range of methods and data for long-term success (Boyer & Swink, 2008).

Another important factor is the issue of social desirability bias (Walker et al., 2012). This refers to a manager's propensity to enhance their performance by making a self-evaluation. It is particularly an issue when using perceptual data and interviews and survey research to self-report soft measures (Bertrand & Mullainathan, 2001; Dam & Petkova, 2014). Most times, the researchers have not addressed the issue itself, and perception and soft measures are still commonly used for performance measures (Carter & Easton, 2011). The issue is important when considering environmental and sustainability performance, where there is a strong emphasis on improving outcomes and is often used in marketing materials.

Background

As the name implies, the method focuses on an 'event' of interest. In this way, the method is quite limited, as it will not be useful in answering a host of interesting and engaging research questions from a supply chain perspective. It is, therefore, useful for addressing a limited subset of supply chain or management research questions and objectives. Despite the limited direct applicability, it may still be a useful complement to other research approaches as part of a study that triangulates several sources of data and methods to address a particular research problem.

A researcher needs to consider the first consideration that, even though the term 'event' is used, many events will be unsuitable for analysis. The event must be sufficiently 'newsworthy' so that they would report it on in a public news release or in the Wall Street Journal (for instance). The event must be 'sudden'. There should not be a prior warning about it. As we measure the 'stock market reaction' or 'investor' reaction to the event, it must be a sudden news release with no prior warning. If there were prior warnings or rumblings about the event, some investors will have already reacted to it, making it difficult to detect a single 'reaction' to the news.

The event should not be 'confounded' with other events or announced or correlated with other events. As this is analysis based on archival data, there is not the flexibility to run an experiment and separate out the effect of different events.

It is possible to examine the impact of the single event on multiple companies. This is a more complex form of event study analysis and requires a more careful analysis to address cross-sectional correlation, an issue we address in following chapters. (The creation of the sample may be easier, but the analysis may be more complex.)

How, then, would you start an event study project? How do you find the 'right' project idea or topic?

THE NEWS METHOD

As the event must be 'newsworthy', then reading the news is a straight-forward and obvious way to identify events worth of study! What type of events are mentioned in widely distributed and noted publications, such as the Wall Street Journal (WSJ)? Serious supply chain issues of interest to C-suite managers and investors will be reported, as will a host of other important managerial issues of interest to senior manages. Therefore, if WSJ report something on, then the topic may interest us. We often identify instances or specific examples of a wider category of topics or phenomenon of interest when taking this approach. For example, an article about a product failure resulting in a lawsuit (Raymond, 2022) may become one observation in a wider study on product failures, but there will be many other terms to search for to seek other specific examples of the wider topic.

When a suitable announcement of supply chain or management interest is found, the next task is to 'abstract' from this. It is a specific example/case of 'what' general concept/issue that is of interest? This may be the more challenging element as you as: what is the supply chain or management concept of interest here? Beyond this, when the abstract concept is identified, you will be able to develop a keyword search strategy based on a range of terms or phrases associated with several 'concrete' or 'specific' examples of the supply chain and management issues. The approaches to do this are addressed in Chapters 5 and 6.

NEGATIVE EVENTS IN THE NEWS

Using an example can be instructional. We will work through some real-world examples related to a published article (without discussing with the authors!). In essence, the approach can take a real-world negative event and estimate the costs associated with it. The approach is not useful for disentangling complex phenomena such as changing behaviours studied by Sankaran and Wood (2007) in the context of worsening traffic congestion. But it can help to identify costs of failures, such as when auto firms fail to meet environmental requirements (Wood et al., 2018).

Demand and Supply Mismatch

Take, for instance, we next discuss the article by Hendricks and Singhal (2009) that examines the impact of holding more inventory to meet demand than is warranted, creating an expensive mismatch. The title talks about 'demand and supply mis-matches'. This is a very general supply chain and operations issue; the very discipline of operations focuses on balancing demand and supply. (The text by Cachon and

Terwiesch (2018) is titled *Matching demand with supply.*) But what are 'concrete' or specific cases of this that mismatch that may be reported on?

As you read the article, you see the authors' keywords. For example, Hendricks and Singhal (2009, p. 513) note "[t]he final set of key words include inventory or inventories close to words such as obsolete, excess, glut, buildup, reduce, bloated, charge, write-off, write-down, liquidate, accumulate, or revalue."

In addition, we can use these keywords and find some particular announcements that may be relevant. For example, Hendricks and Singhal (2009, p. 513) provide the examples of "Champion International Corp plans to curtail production at two of its paper mills to reduce its office-paper Inventory," and, "Eastman Kodak is cutting 15% to 20% of the prices of older formulations photographic film in a fourth-quarter promotion to liquidate inventory."

New Product Introduction Delays

Another example is the delay in introducing new product developments. New product development and innovation is clearly an important operations and business topic (with cross-overs with engineering and marketing), as evidenced by the wealth of research in this area appearing in many business and engineering journals.

In studying delays in new product introductions, we can see that Hendricks and Singhal use several key terms from major news outlets:

The Wall Street Journal (WSJ) and Dow Jones News Service (DJNS) are our primary sources for the sample of firms that announce product introduction delays. As in Hendricks and Singhal (1997), we use key words, such as "product and introduction," in conjunction with words such as "delay, reschedule, and postpone," along with other relevant phrases, to search the WSJ and DJNS from 1987 to 2003. (Hendricks & Singhal, 2008, p. 881)

Product Crises and Recalls

There are a range of crisis-focused articles that are negative that focus on recalls. A significant category is reserved for 'recall' papers (Gokhale et al., 2014; Rupp, 2001; Rupp & Taylor, 2002; Thomsen & McKenzie, 2001; Wood, Wang, et al., 2017; Zeng & Mu, 2016; Zhao et al., 2013). While they are commonplace, they tend to show relatively comparable outcomes in different regions in the first hypothesis – the recall announcement leads to a negative stock market reaction. However, each study should add some additional alternate factors that may mitigate or worsen the impact.

For example, Chen et al. (2009) examine product recall but examine the strategy used by the firm. Are they proactive and make a recall ahead of when it is required? Or are they passive and only make the recall when required? Selection of the response can lessen the negative stock market reaction.

POSITIVE EVENTS IN THE NEWS

While the other examples have been 'negative' events, the same process is true of 'positive' events as well. Investors welcomed positive events, resulting in a positive abnormal return for the firms involved. As such, it can be used to estimate the benefits to the firm of, for instance, implementing a new technology in Big Data or analytics, which are understood to be operationally valuabe (Bag et al., 2020; Wood, Reiners, et al., 2017) but for which the financial returns are not understood or are difficult to estimate. It can help a firm to understand how to value positive investments (Duong et al., 2021; Wood et al., 2022).

Product Introductions and Innovations

As an example of a positive event, many automakers have been switching and developing non-internal-combustion engines (ICE) vehicles for a long time. Notably, Toyota has experimented with hydrogen powered vehicles and was a leader in hybrid ICE-Electric vehicles with the Prius. However, the shift to electric has become increasingly compelling for auto manufacturers that target both retail/consumers and industrial users. We have seen the shift as a necessary move for ICE manufacturers, even before recent requirements and commitments to shift to electric vehicles (Jessop et al., 2021).

Consequentially, the study by Ba et al. (2013) has focused on the positive news releases of the introduction and development of BEV vehicles. They do not summarize the keywords that they used during the search, but they used the Dow Jones Factiva database for announcements of green vehicle innovations over the 1996-2009 period. As a result, they identified 351 announcements, with 90 being dropped on further examination, providing a sample of 261 announcements for the analysis.

They found a three-day CAR of 0.45%, which was positive at the 5% level. They note the direction and magnitude is comparable to other research on product introductions. For instance, Chaney et al. (1991) demonstrate 0.75% CAR, and Kelm et al. (1995) find an average CAR of 0.96% for announcements about product-focused R&D.

More recent research on R&D spend and product development shows an influence on the firm size and resources (Lee & Chen, 2009). Kaur and Kaur (2019) investigated different strategic investments in India with a range of positive abnormal returns.

Reducing Retail Stores in Uncertain Trading Conditions

The ability for a retailer to maintain a large network of stores is often threatened during difficult trading periods. For instance, during a period of economic uncertainty, many firms may shutter, shut, or reduce their capacity to serve customers to reduce their costs in the current time and remove future commitments (e.g., to paying rent). Consequentially, this can be seen to reduce expenses. Further, by targeting low-performing stores (e.g., those without increasing year-on-year increases), investors may be persuaded that the changes are positive and will be of a net financial benefit to the firm. Consequently, we may see a company that employs this strategy see a positive stock market reaction.

Chowdhury and Sarkar (2017) investigate the closure of stores. A search was made of the WSJ Eastern Edition for the keywords "store/outlet" appearing with "close/closure/shut" in the headlines, for 1995-2016. After investigation, 173 announcements were in the sample. They find a positive overall stock market reaction to store closure announcement. However, they note that future research may look at the long-term impact using a long-term event study. In addition, future research should also account for existing omni-channel distribution strategies, which may influence the stock market reactions. Indeed, as Xia and Zhang (2010) show, online channels improve ROI, inventory, cost, and sales, so controlling for the distribution strategy may be important for future research.

EXOGENOUS ISSUES METHOD

In contrast to the news method, where multiple different events occur over time, with the exogenous method, we are looking for a couple of very large and significant events that shift and shake numerous firms simultaneously. Even as we discuss the exogenous method this way, we can see that it will have some implications for the research design.

Most times, you will get the sense of an exogenous change from a disaster, such as an earthquake (Hendricks et al., 2020) or substantial regulatory changes like the Maritime Transportation Safety Act (MTSA) (Homan, 2007, 2009). Based on the identification of such an issue, you then need to identify the firms that might be affected. In some situations, such as the Rana Plaza disaster, certain firms were affected by sourcing in Bangladesh, where the "sample is based on retailers that signed either the AFBSB or the ABWS" (Jacobs & Singhal, 2017, p. 56). In other cases, it may be more challenging to get a set of firms that will be heavily affected. For instance, Homan (2009) studies Maritime firms that will be affected by the MTSA. Homan reports how the study uses a:

dataset for the analysis consists of daily stock market returns for the 19 marine operators found in the August 2005 WorkBoat Composite Index who are listed on NASDAQ or the NYSE [7]. These operators primary business, or a significant portion of their business, relates to marine transportation services. At the same time, they are diversified businesses. There is not a sample of publicly traded US businesses whose sole line of business is marine transportation services during the sample period. As such, there is not an exact 'pure play' for studying the impact of 9/11 or security policies as there is with airlines. However, these firms represent the closest proxy to a 'pure play' for studying the effects of terrorism on marine operators trading on US markets. (Homan, 2009, p. 107)

The exogenous method does not mean you can simply use a rapidly acquired set of companies. A thorough consideration is still required. For instance, despite the possibility of assessing the impact of the earthquake only on manufacturers, Hendricks et al. (2020) draw on a sample based on the news method of searching publications, press releases, and news wire services.

DEVELOPING THE TOPIC AND ISSUE

In this section, we have explored a range of methods and approaches to ensure an appropriate study design, drawing on news items and abstracting from this to the type of event of interest and also identifying an exogenous event that affects many firms. Several examples are used to illustrate key points. While the event study method relies on that sudden burst of new information to the market participants, this does not mean that all event studies must rely on a sudden or instant change. We provide some notable examples explaining why these approaches still work and how they can be a valuable addition to your study on a particular topic.

A Gradual Change as an Event: Creating an Event Study From an On-Going Process

There are several methods that can study change and gradual events. The event study can sometimes evaluate how these gradual changes impact the firm. Take, for instance, quality improvement programs. On the face of it, an event study is not methodologically suited to study the gradual program of change as the company undertakes the initiative. However, there will still be points in time where information is released or made known/public. At these points, you can isolate the news announcement and use this as the basis for your sample.

Take, for instance, a quality improvement program or initiative. A quality improvement initiative involves significant work and investment of time by teams over a company. There is not necessarily an end-point or any clear 'surprise' to the market. There are, however, ways of perceiving the project as a sequence of events. For instance, many projects may include an announcement, the appointment of a new lead, or an investment or partnership to develop the project. These public news releases show that something will happen (it is a prospective announcement). By itself, this suggests that the project will be implemented and assumed to be successful and bring benefit to the company, suggesting a positive abnormal return that may be evident in the stock market reaction today as this is 'priced into' the current values for the firm.

On the other hand, the conclusion of a project or wrap-up may be announced. This will often be less common, but we can find it sometimes. Again, a successful conclusion (e.g., an announcement of cost savings or defect reductions because of a quality program) shows future benefit to the firm that may cause an abnormal stock return.

Finally, another category can be where an outside body reports on the project. This may take the form of a 'reward' or an 'award'. For example, an award for outstanding quality innovations gives the wider world the perspective that the quality improvement initiative was outstanding and, therefore, the firm is likely to be able to deliver improved and tangible results. Consequently, a positive stock return can reflect this Zhang et al. (2021) use a short-term event study and show a positive stock market reaction to award winners in China. The stock market reaction is found to be particularly strong for those winning their first award. The award may be used to signal investors and the market that the impact of quality improvement programs have been successful.

While TQM involves a process of application and change, Hendricks and Singhal (2001) use the award win as a proxy for an effective implementation of TQM. They use operating income before depreciation as a measure of performance, rather than the stock market reaction. Similarly, Six Sigma is a process. Shafer and Moeller (2012, p. 521) investigate the impact of six sigma on performance based on "Operating Income/Total Assets (OI/A), Operating Income/Sales (OI/S), Operating Income/Number of Employees (OI/E), Sales/Assets (S/A), and Sales/Number of Employees (S/E)."

As a result, when there is an announcement that can crystalize or show an outcome of a commencement of a process, we can find the announcement used in short-term event studies. Note, however, that these represent only an estimation of the event's impact, so the results should be used judiciously. Long-term improvements may need to be evaluated at a later date.

This also begs the question whether a study of firms announcing something is meaningful. Well, it allows us to analyze the stock market reaction, an unbiased investor reaction, to the announcement as an event. In this way, it captures the positive and negative outcomes that are estimated. However, many managers may require or find more convincing a study that provides long-term financial outcomes, such as a buy-and-hold abnormal returns (BHAR) analysis. (This approach is addressed in a later chapter.)

TOPICS LESS AMENABLE TO EVENT STUDY PROJECTS

Ultimately, however, there are going to be several interesting investigations that simply cannot be conducted using event studies. That is perfectly OK, but it means that if you are interested in these other types of studies, and you cannot think of some way to make them 'work' (e.g., see the quality awards above), then you will need a different method.

For example, while I note that studying recalls is common for event studies, the method provides little additional value to guiding managers beyond what we already know about the nuances of how they may engage in a recall process. There is a growing body of literature that shows recalls are not positive. But the method does little to help us address additional questions that arise in terms of how to manage recall situations. For instance, Wowak and Boone (2015) review literature on recalls and generate research opportunities. I review these here to show some limitations of the event study process.

Research Opportunity 1: Top Management Teams (TMT)

Event studies can address past experiences and TMT experiences. This data can be collected and built into a model. Indeed, Hendricks et al. (2014) study the appointment of supply chain executives and show how TMT experience can be incorporated into the analysis. However, the use of upper echelon theory (Hambrick & Mason, 1984) cannot really be used in many wider event studies of recalls, as there is little easy way to incorporate individual biases and understanding of bounded rationality with secondary data collection.

Research Opportunity 2. Recall Processes

The internal management of recalls is difficult to study, as little secondary data is available and readily incorporated into the model. Wowak and Boone talk about strategy formulation (the 'how' of strategy decisions), which we cannot capture in an event study. They also talk about the implementation; some elements of implementation may be captured with blunt variables used to capture the differences, perhaps, of two different implementation of recall process decisions and built into the cross-sectional regression. They also cited orgnizational culture as of interest. It is difficult to evaluate these measures using secondary data.

They cite supply chain complexity as of interest. It is possible to develop a series of measures for the supply chain complexity, such as the diversification of the supply base or using geographic diversification of the business, using secondary data sources (Hendricks et al., 2009). However, it is limited to retrospectively making sense of how this supply chain complexity is correlated to the stock market reaction to recalls. Many would cite this of little value.

It becomes very difficult to understand firm capabilities and actions at detailed news and secondary data. For example, Wowak et al. (2016) use a grounded theory investigation to understand traceability in the face of recall. They used the grounded theory approach because of the complexity and multifaceted nature of the phenomenon of interest. Perhaps most importantly, they note how this type of recall event in the reaction is one that unfolds over time with many complex organizational, team, and individual changes that need to be incorporated. Consequently, they needed to dive into the organization in much more depth and detail to study the changes and understand the processes used by the organizations. Their findings highlight some challenges and limitations of the event study method. While an event study may show an investment strategies can mitigate or lessen the impact of product recalls, it does not show us how to build, implement, or execute the strategies. Event studies also fail to explore the complex interactions between the different components of the organization that is required to successfully undertake the recall, because of the retrospective nature and reliance on secondary data.

Research Opportunity 3: Learning from Failure and Near-Misses

There is little opportunity to study a 'near miss' as firms are unlikely to publicize a near-miss opportunity. Indeed, these may be 'hidden' most times and never talked about. Then, it would be difficult to use secondary data to examine this. Part of the difficulty in understanding a near-miss comes from where the information would come from. A company is unlikely to announce or report on a near-miss voluntarily. In some ways, it has little relevance to investors in the broader market. Further, there would be few outsiders with the insight into the internal activities to know that a near-miss happened. Consequently, a near-miss might be reported by a whistleblower and made public to draw attention and scrutiny to the firm, but this is unlikely. Therefore, an event study is more likely to focus on a failure than on a near miss.

Near misses, therefore, cannot be understood with an event study, but they may be studied using other research approaches that enable the researcher to get close to the process and understand what happened and why it happened. From a comprehensive investigation of this nature using primary data, a researcher might understand factors that influence the near-miss and then devise and advise on approaches and strategies that firms engage in reducing future near-misses and building their resilience.

Research Opportunity 4: Organizational Countermeasures

The event study method can certainly examine the direct effect on guilty firms as they note and the impact on bystander firms the collateral damage to others. Here, the event study process can determine the stock market reaction because of the event being studied. However, they note that there is a range of theories that might be applicable that had not been well-utilized. For example, justice theory (Rawls, 1999) with a focus on procedural justice and distributed justice, as well as interpersonal justice and informational justice. Using these theories and approaches may be difficult in an event study design.

SELECTING DIFFERENT FORMS OF EVENT STUDY

While some projects are less amenable to the short horizon event study, there is another category of circumstances where the research questions can be addressed through other forms of an event study. This type of circumstance can often come about through discussions with supervisors, between supervisors of a doctoral project, between faculty and research members, perhaps departmental seminars, and through discussions and feedback from editors and reviewers or examiners of doctoral dissertations. Although, in those circumstances, file the research questions may be interesting, they are not directly relevant to the short horizon event study focused on stock returns or stock market reactions. Sometimes, there is a need to show enduring long-term change in stock returns or the issues in question might relate more to operational performance. If this is the case, the interested reader can get an insight into these issues in Chapter 14, where we look at other types of event studies. We do not provide sufficient detail to complete such a project, but certainly provide enough insight into what that project might look like and how it might address the related but different research questions.

It can also be interesting to examine a topic where the study is developed using a mixed method. This may include both a short-term abnormal returns, the long-term abnormal return, or other approaches.

For example, in Hendricks et al. (2014), they proposed six hypotheses relating to supply chain and operations management executive (SCOME) positions. The first is that the stock market will react positively to newly created positions; second, the stock market reaction will be different when the appointee is an outsider to the firm. However, hypotheses three, four, five, and six address an issue of likelihood that cannot be addressed with an event study. Underlying the development of their hypotheses, they also argue for how the new appointees may influence the company's operating performance. Here, the study extends beyond merely stock market reaction and includes other variables of interest.

Arora et al. (2020) took a similar approach and find that the appointment of a chief sustainability officer results in a more positive stock market reaction following a prior adverse incident and that an improvement follows the appointment in operating performance. In this way, there is an analysis of operating performance and the financial performance as reflected by the abnormal returns. In a slightly different approach, Modi et al. (2015, p. 35) evaluated long-horizon abnormal returns and include the details of a small experiment (with 84 participants), all providing additional support for their developments.

A more extensive introduction to these types of event studies is provided in Chapter 14.

A Topic With a Sufficient Sample Size for your Event List

One of the key factors in selecting an appropriate topic will be to develop a sample size that will be sufficient for the analysis. The event list should contain hundreds of publicly listed firms that have experienced that event is an ideal. It can accommodate smaller sample sizes; this is perhaps best left to further studies. Some types of events are not well-publicized, even though they may be of interest. An example of this might be the collapse of a strategic alliance which is not well publicized but occurs gradually over time, with few key announcements marking out the decline. It is usually not in the interests of the firms to promote such failures. As a result, there may be a relatively small sample size if this was your selected topic. It may require you to think more broadly about the abstract type of event that is represented by this type of instance, and then broader the event type to include a wider range of specific events.

SUMMARY

There is no right or wrong way to select a suitable subject for the event study method analysis. However, is important to note that not every topical phenomenon and will be amenable to studying with the event study method. This is because of the strong limitations and assumptions made by the method.

If you are mainly focused on a particular phenomenon that is not amenable to the event study method, you will certainly need to find another method. However, most times, it is possible to take a surprise announcement of news about the phenomenon of interest and then start an investigation using an event study method based on this announcement. However, the analysis will remain limited by the use of secondary data and the secondary data sources. You will not gain insight into the complexities and interactions required by firms to navigate and manage concerning that phenomenon.

If you are looking for a new project to start, and you use the event study method as a starting point before looking for a particular topic, this chapter should guide you in selecting an appropriate topic for your study.

Finally, is important to note that your access to resources and data may influence whether an event study method is appropriate for your study. For example, a doctorate of business administration student would usually work full time and have deep and ready access to a wide range of institutional and organizational data. If so, it makes little sense for them to employ an event study method when they could readily access a range of company data. However, they might consider an event study method where they look at how the event influences or changes a particular operational outcome over time for the company to determine whether not there was a substantial change in reaction to the event. It is more likely that they will have access to rich data and company databases or key decision-makers to extract much more insight and interesting data through interviews or other qualitative research methods, and so an event study would be less promising for them.

While the event study is a valuable method, it is important to note that it is certainly not the only method I use. However, I know that other researchers solely devote themselves to the use of one method and develop their careers using and enhancing that methodological approach. Increasingly, we see the method combined with other approaches where, for example, short-horizon studies are combined with long-horizon studies to provide further evidence (Hendricks et al., 2014) or even with other methods, such as an experimental design (Modi et al., 2015).

REFERENCES

Arora, P., Hora, M., Singhal, V., & Subramanian, R. (2020). When do appointments of corporate sustainability executives affect shareholder value? *Journal of Operations Management*, 66(4), 464–487. doi:10.1002/joom.1074

Ba, S., Lisic, L. L., Liu, Q., & Stallaert, J. (2013). Stock market reaction to green vehicle innovation. *Production and Operations Management*, 22(4), 976–990. doi:10.1111/j.1937-5956.2012.01387.x

Bag, S., Gupta, S., & Wood, L. (2020). Big data analytics in sustainable humanitarian supply chain: Barriers and their interactions. *Annals of Operations Research*. Advance online publication. doi:10.100710479-020-03790-7

Bertrand, M., & Mullainathan, S. (2001). Do people mean what they say? Implications for subjective survey data. *The American Economic Review*, 91(2), 67–72. doi:10.1257/aer.91.2.67

Boyer, K. K., & Swink, M. L. (2008). Empirical elephants—Why multiple methods are essential to quality research in operations and supply chain management. *Journal of Operations Management*, 26(3), 338–344. doi:10.1016/j.jom.2008.03.002

Cachon, G., & Terwiesch, C. (2018). *Matching supply with demand: An introduction to operations management* (4th ed.). McGraw-Hill Education.

Carter, C. R., & Easton, P. L. (2011). Sustainable supply chain management: Evolution and future directions. *International Journal of Physical Distribution & Logistics Management, 41*(1), 46–62. doi:10.1108/09600031111101420

Chaney, P. K., Devinney, T. M., & Winer, R. S. (1991). The impact of new product introductions on the market value of firms. *The Journal of Business, 64*(4), 573–610. doi:10.1086/296552

Chen, Y., Ganesan, S., & Liu, Y. (2009). Does a firm's product-recall strategy affect its financial value? An examination of strategic alternatives during product-harm crises. *Journal of Marketing, 73*(6), 214–226. doi:10.1509/jmkg.73.6.214

Chowdhury, J., & Sarkar, S. (2017). The financial impact of retail store closure announcements. *International Journal of Physical Distribution & Logistics Management, 47*(6), 536–556. Advance online publication. doi:10.1108/IJPDLM-04-2016-0117

Dam, L., & Petkova, B. N. (2014). The impact of environmental supply chain sustainability programs on shareholder wealth. *International Journal of Operations & Production Management, 34*(5), 586–609. doi:10.1108/IJOPM-10-2012-0482

Duong, L. N. K., Wang, J. X., Wood, L. C., Reiners, T., & Koushan, M. (2021). The value of incremental environmental sustainability innovation in the construction industry: An event study. *Construction Management and Economics, 39*(5), 398–418. doi:10.1080/01446193.2021.1901950

Ellinger, A. E., Natarajarathinam, M., Adams, F. G., Gray, J. B., Hofman, D., & O'Marah, K. (2011). Supply chain management competency and firm financial success. *Journal of Business Logistics, 32*(3), 214–226. doi:10.1111/j.2158-1592.2011.01018.x

Fawcett, S. E., Waller, M. A., Miller, J. W., Schwieterman, M. A., Hazen, B. T., & Overstreet, R. E. (2014). A trail guide to publishing success: Tips on writing influential conceptual, qualitative, and survey research. *Journal of Business Logistics, 35*(1), 1–16. doi:10.1111/jbl.12039

Gokhale, J., Brooks, R. M., & Tremblay, V. J. (2014). The effect on stockholder wealth of product recalls and government action: The case of Toyota's accelerator pedal recall. *The Quarterly Review of Economics and Finance, 54*(4), 521–528. doi:10.1016/j.qref.2014.06.004

Hambrick, D. C., & Mason, P. A. (1984). Upper echelons: The organization as a reflection of its top managers. *Academy of Management Review, 9*(2), 193–206. doi:10.2307/258434

Hendricks, K. B., Hora, M., & Singhal, V. R. (2014). An empirical investigation on the appointments of supply chain and operations management executives. *Management Science, 61*(7), 1562–1583. doi:10.1287/mnsc.2014.1987

Hendricks, K. B., Jacobs, B. W., & Singhal, V. R. (2020). Stock market reaction to supply chain disruptions from the 2011 great east Japan earthquake. *Manufacturing & Service Operations Management, 22*(4), 645–867. doi:10.1287/msom.2019.0777

Hendricks, K. B., & Singhal, V. R. (2001). The long-run stock price performance of firms with effective TQM programs. *Management Science, 47*(3), 359–368. doi:10.1287/mnsc.47.3.359.9773

Hendricks, K. B., & Singhal, V. R. (2003). The effect of supply chain glitches on shareholder wealth. *Journal of Operations Management, 21*(5), 501–522. doi:10.1016/j.jom.2003.02.003

Hendricks, K. B., & Singhal, V. R. (2008). The effect of product introduction delays on operating performance. *Management Science, 54*(5), 878–892. doi:10.1287/mnsc.1070.0805

Hendricks, K. B., & Singhal, V. R. (2009). Demand-supply mismatches and stock market reaction: Evidence from excess inventory announcements. *Manufacturing & Service Operations Management, 11*(3), 509–524. doi:10.1287/msom.1080.0237

Hendricks, K. B., Singhal, V. R., & Zhang, R. (2009). The effect of operational slack, diversification, and vertical relatedness on the stock market reaction to supply chain disruptions. *Journal of Operations Management, 27*(3), 233–246. doi:10.1016/j.jom.2008.09.001

Homan, A. C. (2007). The impact of MTSA on financial risk and volatility of marine firms. *Maritime Policy & Management, 34*(1), 69–79. doi:10.1080/03088830601103459

Homan, A. C. (2009). The impact of MTSA on investment uncertainty and the persistence of financial return volatility of marine firms. *Maritime Policy & Management, 36*(2), 105–115. doi:10.1080/03088830902868008

Jacobs, B. W., & Singhal, V. R. (2017). The effect of the Rana Plaza disaster on shareholder wealth of retailers: Implications for sourcing strategies and supply chain governance. *Journal of Operations Management, 49–51*(1), 52–66. doi:10.1016/j.jom.2017.01.002

Jessop, S., James, W., & Carey, N. (2021, November 11). *Countries, cities, carmakers commit to end fossil-fuel vehicles by 2040.* https://www.reuters.com/business/cop/six-major-carmakers-agree-phase-out-fossil-fuel-vehicles-by-2040-uk-says-2021-11-10/

Kaur, P., & Kaur, R. (2019). Effects of strategic investment decisions on value of firm: Evidence from India. *Paradigm, 23*(1), 1–19. doi:10.1177/0971890719835442

Kelm, K. M., Narayanan, V. K., & Pinches, G. E. (1995). Shareholder value creation during R&D innovation and commercialization stages. *Academy of Management Journal, 38*(3), 770–786. doi:10.5465/256745

Lee, R. P., & Chen, Q. (2009). The immediate impact of new product introductions on stock price: The role of firm resources and size. *Journal of Product Innovation Management, 26*(1), 97–107. doi:10.1111/j.1540-5885.2009.00337.x

Modi, S. B., Wiles, M. A., & Mishra, S. (2015). Shareholder value implications of service failures in triads: The case of customer information security breaches. *Journal of Operations Management, 35*(1), 21–39. doi:10.1016/j.jom.2014.10.003

Rawls, J. (1999). *A theory of justice* (Revised edition). Belknap Press. doi:10.4159/9780674042582

Raymond, N. (2022, January 28). 3M hit with $110 million verdict in latest U.S. military earplug trial. *Reuters.* https://www.reuters.com/business/aerospace-defense/3m-hit-with-110-million-verdict-latest-us-military-earplug-trial-2022-01-27/

Roth, A. V. (2007). Applications of empirical science in manufacturing and service operations. *Manufacturing & Service Operations Management, 9*(4), 353–367. doi:10.1287/msom.1070.0197

Rupp, N. G. (2001). Are government initiated recalls more damaging for shareholders? Evidence from automotive recalls, 1973–1998. *Economics Letters, 71*(2), 265–270. doi:10.1016/S0165-1765(01)00379-2

Rupp, N. G., & Taylor, C. R. (2002). Who initiates recalls and who cares? Evidence from the automobile industry. *The Journal of Industrial Economics, 50*(2), 123–149. doi:10.1111/1467-6451.00171

Sankaran, J. K., & Wood, L. (2007). The relative impact of consignee behaviour and road traffic congestion on distribution costs. *Transportation Research Part B: Methodological, 41*(9), 1033–1049. doi:10.1016/j.trb.2007.04.005

Shafer, S. M., & Moeller, S. B. (2012). The effects of Six Sigma on corporate performance: An empirical investigation. *Journal of Operations Management, 30*(7–8), 521–532. doi:10.1016/j.jom.2012.10.002

Thomsen, M. R., & McKenzie, A. M. (2001). Market incentives for safe foods: An examination of shareholder losses from meat and poultry recalls. *American Journal of Agricultural Economics, 83*(3), 526–538. doi:10.1111/0002-9092.00175

Töyli, J., Häkkinen, L., Ojala, L., & Naula, T. (2008). Logistics and financial performance: An analysis of 424 Finnish small and medium-sized enterprises. *International Journal of Physical Distribution & Logistics Management, 38*(1), 57–80. doi:10.1108/09600030810857210

Walker, H., Miemczyk, J., Johnsen, T., & Spencer, R. (2012). Sustainable procurement: Past, present and future. *Journal of Purchasing and Supply Management, 18*(4), 201–206. doi:10.1016/j.pursup.2012.11.003

Wood, L. C., Duong, L. N. K., & Wang, J. X. (2022). Business Process Improvement for Sustainable Technologies Investments in Construction: A Configurational Approach. *Sustainability, 14*(9), 5697. doi:10.3390u14095697

Wood, L. C., Reiners, T., & Srivastava, H. S. (2017). Think exogenous to excel: Alternative supply chain data to improve transparency and decisions. *International Journal of Logistics Research and Applications, 20*(5), 426–443. doi:10.1080/13675567.2016.1267126

Wood, L. C., Wang, J. X., Duong, L. N. K., Reiners, T., & Smith, R. (2018). Stock market reactions to auto manufacturers' environmental failures. *Journal of Macromarketing, 38*(4), 364–382. doi:10.1177/0276146718781915

Wood, L. C., Wang, J. X., Olesen, K., & Reiners, T. (2017). The effect of slack, diversification, and time to recall on stock market reaction to toy recalls. *International Journal of Production Economics, 193*, 244–258. doi:10.1016/j.ijpe.2017.07.021

Wowak, K. D., & Boone, C. A. (2015). So many recalls, so little research: A review of the literature and road map for future research. *The Journal of Supply Chain Management, 51*(4), 54–72. doi:10.1111/jscm.12079

Wowak, K. D., Craighead, C. W., & Ketchen, D. J. Jr. (2016). Tracing bad products in supply chains: The roles of temporality, supply chain permeation, and product information ambiguity. *Journal of Business Logistics, 37*(2), 132–151. doi:10.1111/jbl.12125

Xia, Y., & Zhang, G. P. (2010). The impact of the online channel on retailers' performances: An empirical evaluation. *Decision Sciences, 41*(3), 517–546. doi:10.1111/j.1540-5915.2010.00279.x

Zeng, Z., & Mu, Y. (2016). The impact of the product safety crisis on shareholder wealth: Evidence from infant and child products industry. *2016 13th International Conference on Service Systems and Service Management (ICSSSM)*, 1–5. 10.1109/ICSSSM.2016.7538665

Zhang, M., Long, R., Wei, K., Tan, Q., & Zhang, W. (2021). China quality award and the market value of the firm. *Total Quality Management & Business Excellence, 0*(0), 1–16. doi:10.1080/14783363.20 21.1960157

Zhao, X., Li, Y., & Flynn, B. B. (2013). The financial impact of product recall announcements in China. *International Journal of Production Economics, 142*(1), 115–123. doi:10.1016/j.ijpe.2012.10.018

ADDITIONAL READING

Brown, S. J., & Warner, J. B. (1980). Measuring security price performance. *Journal of Financial Economics, 8*(3), 205–258. doi:10.1016/0304-405X(80)90002-1

Brown, S. J., & Warner, J. B. (1985). Using daily stock returns: The case of event studies. *Journal of Financial Economics, 14*(1), 3–31. doi:10.1016/0304-405X(85)90042-X

Dnes, A. W., Kodwani, D. G., Seaton, J. S., & Wood, D. (1998). The regulation of the United Kingdom electricity industry: An event study of price-capping measures. *Journal of Regulatory Economics, 13*(3), 207–226. doi:10.1023/A:1008027419553

Dnes, A. W., & Seaton, J. S. (1999). The regulation of electricity: Results from an event study. *Applied Economics, 31*(5), 609–618. doi:10.1080/000368499324057

Erickson, S. L., Stone, M., Hanson, T. A., Tolifson, A., Ngongoni, N., & Kalthoff, J. (2017). Shareholder value and crisis communication patterns: An analysis of the Ford and Firestone tire recall. *Academy of Strategic Management Journal, 16*(1), 32–53.

Fama, E. F. (1970). Efficient capital markets: A review of theory and empirical work. *The Journal of Finance, 25*(2), 383–417. doi:10.2307/2325486

Fama, E. F. (1991). Efficient capital markets: II. *The Journal of Finance, 46*(5), 1575–1617. doi:10.1111/j.1540-6261.1991.tb04636.x

Fama, E. F. (1998). Market efficiency, long-term returns, and behavioral finance. *Journal of Financial Economics, 49*(3), 283–306. doi:10.1016/S0304-405X(98)00026-9

Fama, E. F., & French, K. R. (1993). Common risk factors in the returns on stocks and bonds. *Journal of Financial Economics, 33*(1), 3–56. doi:10.1016/0304-405X(93)90023-5

Gong, S. X. H., Firth, M., & Cullinane, K. (2008). International oligopoly and stock market linkages: The case of global airlines. *Transportation Research Part E, Logistics and Transportation Review, 44*(4), 621–636. doi:10.1016/j.tre.2007.05.008

Jayanti, R. K., & Jayanti, S. V. (2011). Effects of airline bankruptcies: An event study. *The Journal of Services Marketing, 25*(6), 399–409. http://dx.doi.org.ezproxy.otago.ac.nz/10.1108/08876041111160998

Kothari, S. P., & Warner, J. B. (2007). Econometrics of event studies. In B. E. Eckbo (Ed.), *Handbook of Corporate Finance: Empirical Corporate Finance* (Vol. 1, pp. 3–36). North-Holland/Elsevier. doi:10.1016/B978-0-444-53265-7.50015-9

Sawkins, J. W. (1995). Measuring the effects of regulation: An event study of the English and Welsh water industry. *Applied Economics Letters, 2*(10), 359–362. doi:10.1080/758518989

Xia, Y., Singhal, V. R., & Peter Zhang, G. (2016). Product design awards and the market value of the firm. *Production and Operations Management, 25*(6), 1038–1055. doi:10.1111/poms.12525

Zhan, X., Mu, Y., Hora, M., & Singhal, V. R. (2021). Service excellence and market value of a firm: An empirical investigation of winning service awards and stock market reaction. *International Journal of Production Research, 59*(14), 4188–4204. doi:10.1080/00207543.2020.1759837

Zhan, X., Mu, Y., Nishant, R., & Singhal, V. R. (2020). When do appointments of Chief Digital or Data Officers (CDOs) affect stock prices? *IEEE Transactions on Engineering Management*, 1–14. doi:10.1109/TEM.2020.2984619

KEY TERMS AND DEFINITIONS

Delay: A difference in the expected date and the updated dates. The difference is often new information to market participants, so announcements about delays can be a suitable topic.

Event: The particular type of topic and specific examples of the topic.

Event List: the list of events that occur, capturing both the date of first occurrence and the identity of the company affected.

Exogenous Method: The use of critical exogenous changes in the external marketplace that simultaneously influence multiple firms. Examples may be a regulatory change or a disaster. This causes clustering.

Gradual Change: Many management and operations processes require gradual changes and improvements. These changes are more difficult to study with the event study method, as there is no single point of information where new information is released to market participants. However, often a study can be created around these gradual change processes.

New Information: The release of a surprise piece of news to the market that the market participants then respond to, creating a change in the stock returns that we aim to detect in an event study.

News Method: The approach of identifying cases through examining the news and reading key headlines for inspiration. The cases will be one event affecting one (or few) firms simultaneously, so there is little clustering.

Phenomenon of Interest: The main situation that you are observing and interesting in studying. It will often be quite an abstract understanding that will encompass a range of practical, specific examples of news announcements.

Topic: The major issue and theme being studied in the event study. This may be a gradual change over time where there is an announcement that can be new information to market participants or a sudden change that is new information.

Chapter 5
Developing a Sample:
Strategies and Considerations

ABSTRACT

When considering an event, we need a sample of events to study. We will often start with a few example events that are 'sort of what we want to study' and, from there, develop a deeper and more comprehensive focused category of events. Then, the overall sample consists of examples of this abstract category of events. When a good sample has been collected, the progress and analysis steps are relatively straightforward. However, failure to collect a good sample or skipping key considerations may doom a sample to become unusable and non-viable, risking the overall project. Although there are similarities, the process and considerations may be quite different from those of survey sampling that many readers may be familiar with.

INTRODUCTION

The purpose of this chapter is to discuss the sample. Developing the sample is one of the most important tasks that is often overlooked in this research method. The overall project will be broken or made in the development of the sample. However, this is not always apparent, but many 'failed projects' can often trace the root of their demise to the sample construction, although it is not always directly causal. It is important to understand that "[s]electing a sample is a fundamental element of a positivistic study" (Collis & Hussey, 2003, p. 155).

The sample is a key element of any research project, and when you use the event study method, there is no exception.

This chapter addresses several different methods that are often used in event study projects. First, we discuss the standard search method and an iterative search through the news. This is where the event affects a couple of businesses simultaneously, and the sample consists of a smaller number of events affecting quite a diverse number of companies throughout the project. We also look at the use of specialized databases that contain a set of these events already within them so that you can quickly and rapidly assemble a sample that still may need to be supplemented with new searches. Examples might be a list

DOI: 10.4018/978-1-7998-8969-4.ch005

of award winners or recalls in a database like U.S. Consumer Product Safety Commission (CPSC, 2022). A final step is a recognized event method where a single event simultaneously affects multiple firms, such as changes in regulations and legislation or an exogenous shock to the companies such as a disaster.

We talk about some of the primary considerations and setting up the sample in each case.

We talk about having a sufficient sample size and setting up the sample to create the event list as the output. The final step is the confounding event search, where we eliminate observations from the sample if another event occurs within the same duration of time, as it becomes challenging to ensure that the event of interest in is causing the abnormal stock returns or stock market reaction.

At the end of the chapter, you should have a strategy for developing a sample, understand some of the key steps involved in the sampling, and understand the essentials of conducting a confounding event search. The ultimate objective is to have an event list that can be used as input into the following analytic steps.

As stressed, establishing the sample is crucial as the sample must represent the broader type of event and constituent observations. Each must be influenced by instantiations or concrete, specific examples of the wider, more abstract category of events being studied.

Background

One of the most challenging, time-consuming, and ambiguous parts of the research process is developing the sample for the event list. Done well, and you have a defensible sample of the type of event of interest. Done poorly, and you will spend time collecting worthless data and completing an analysis that generates few valuable insights. Therefore, developing the sample is at the heart of 'good event study practice'.

We introduce three fundamental approaches to develop the sample:

a) The 'standard search' method to identify news releases and press releases of interest within a general news database.

b) The 'specialized database search' uses a specialized dataset held (often by a government agency) that partially addresses the supply chain or management subject of interest.

c) The 'recognised event list' where pre-identified cases have already been identified and compiled.

The Standard Search Method

The standard search method uses a database of news announcements that are searched similarly to an academic (scholarly) article database. Commonly used databases include the Dow Jones Factiva and Lexis Nexis. The search format is similar to that used in a structured literature review and may be dissimilar to the type of search you usually do when looking for research articles.

A two-part search is generally used, with a series of synonyms for:

1. Activities or the type of managerial situation that are associated with the event of interest. This requires clarity about the topic and when it is or is not of interest. Different terms may be used depending on the circumstances. For example, 'expansion' in a study of capacity expansion (Hendricks et al., 1995); when signing agreements for business process outsourcing, this includes words such as 'agreement', 'contract', and 'outsource' (Duan et al., 2009, p. 449)

2. The set of circumstances or the context when the event is of interest to your study. This delimiter begins to narrow down the search results considerably. For example, 'capacity' in a study of capac-

ity expansion (Hendricks et al., 1995); or signing a new agreement in a study of business process outsourcing where they used terms like 'announce', 'purchase', 'sign', and 'award' (Duan et al., 2009, p. 449)

For example, consider what we might do to investigate the stock market reaction to manufacturing/factory expansion, given the intense global environment and competition since the GFC. The issue naturally suggests two groups of keywords – those relating to 'factories' and those relating to 'expansion.'
When we consider synonyms, four activities can be undertaken (in no particular order):

1. Referring to a thesaurus, to understand the range of synonyms and different ways of describing the situation. This is fast and free and is a good starting point.
2. Having conversations with colleagues. This option is readily available for those working in a research lab or a university department. However, be warned that you may get a slightly skewed sample; our research parlance is often quite different to the terms used to describe a situation in mainstream media.
3. Examining articles that are relevant to the sample. However, this is one of the most fruitful ways, and we will touch on this further below.
4. Discussing (over coffee) with a professional in the area. Assuming you have good industry connections, a few emails out to friends or chats over coffee can provide substantial insight.

Given our proposed topic, what are several synonyms?
For factories or manufacturing plants:

- 'plant or factory' are commonly used terms, depending on the region of the world you operate in.
- Other terms may include 'manufacturing facilities.'
- Capacity could also include 'production lines' or 'assembly lines' as a sub-set of an entire plant undergoing expansion.

For expansion in other sectors, such as service firms, we might expand this to include terms such as adding, hiring, or recruitment. Again, working with a colleague in human resource management might support a rapid and easy expansion of the list.
We can create a lengthy list, but it is impossible to use every possible relevant term. This is because some will simply not appear to be practical or may not be relevant to the circumstances you are studying, even if they appear to be relevant (this is particularly true with suggestions you make based on reading the thesaurus!).
When using a database like Factiva, it is convenient to think of a search as consisting of two blocks. The first is a set of synonyms of the issue, topic, or event of general interest. The second is a list explaining when and where this is of interest. For example, Jacobs et al. (2010, p. 433; Table 1) use two blocks consisting of terms that first reflect environmental or green synonyms and the second reflect accomplishments in recognition of success. Similarly, Hendricks and Singhal (2008, p. 881) used a search consisting of terms "such as 'product and introduction,' in conjunction with words such as 'delay, reschedule, and postpone'."
Factiva also has several essential search functions that are worth noting. It is possible to force the results to include only items where the first search string appears within a certain number of words of the

second search string. This means that these two words must be closely related such that a word relating to the environment and a word relating to achievements must be positioned closely together. While it is not a certain outcome, words positioned closely together often have more relevance and meaning in a relationship than words positioned at opposite ends of the article. Factiva enables us to do this with the "NearX" operator we can replace X with a number that determines how stringent this requirement will be. A lower number such as three or four would force these words to be closely positioned; a much higher number such as ten would loosen this restriction enable results to be displayed where the words are positioned further apart. There is no right or wrong way of selecting this number, but as it becomes more stringent or smaller, there are fewer results to read through manually, but it becomes increasingly likely that events and observations have been missed. On the other hand, a relaxed and large number means the search results will be extensive and contain many less relevant outputs. It may be useful to quickly change the number several times and make notes with pen and paper to determine the total number of results. No one would want to be in a position of using Near10 and, for instance, having 500,000 results to manually search through.

My general approach is to use a set of search terms that I am satisfied with (generated iteratively in consultation with other researchers and colleagues with management experience) and then select the news sources of interest. I then vary the NearX term from approximately three to ten to see more stringent and relaxed search results. Often, a Near5 or Near7 will generate a manageable number of articles to search through while assuring that a very high proportion of articles of interest will be captured in the search. As you increase the X in NearX, you will gradually identify an increasing number of articles that you must search through. If you have X set too small, you will undoubtedly miss many items in the search. In practice, there is no clear guideline here, so the search should be conducted reasonably to assure yourself and your readers that you have captured an identifiable and comprehensive sample.

The Iterative News Search

The best way to understand the terms used in news articles of interest is to read and use news articles of interest. Perform a 'quick and dirty' search of Factiva (or google) and identify five to ten articles of interest. (Example, search abstract, and title for the keywords of interest, generating a shortlist of relevant items). These articles should be geared towards the topic of interest, even if not perfectly aligned. Next, read the terminology used; often, the writers use several terms in the article or include two descriptions or words that explain what is happening. Use these additional explanations, capture them, and provide a springboard for identifying a more comprehensive range of articles.

An example may be the news about a verdict against 3M (Raymond, 2022) relating to the failure of the earplugs to prevent damage to the hearing of users in the U.S. military. Reading the announcement suggests terms such as verdict, lawsuit, test results, design flaws, defective, irreparable, compensatory damages, and damage. These are all terms that may be used in a study of product failure to identify announcements relevant to the issue.

By taking the initial search string, identifying further articles, expanding the search terms after reading these articles, then expanding the search term again, it is possible to rapidly and iteratively build up a comprehensive set of search terms. This is demonstrated by Duan et al. (Duan et al., 2009, p. 449), who notes how "[a] list of keywords used to identify a BPO announcement was then created by analyzing the content of 15 highly publicized outsourcing announcements."

We must also consider under what circumstances this event will be of interest. For example, we want to identify what will happen if capacity is increased. We already have several terms that are relevant, such as abstract terms: increase or expand. Articles that mention capacity expansions would be relevant. A thesaurus might provide additional synonyms for 'increase.' Discussions with colleagues, and other researchers will also provide several industry-specific synonyms.

When writing the manuscript, including all possible combinations and permutations is not common. For example, Hendricks et al. (1995, p. 261) note how "[a] variety of keywords were used in the search including "capacity expansion", "plant expansion", "new plant" and other pertinent phrases."

Duan et al. (2014, p. 4678) noted that "[t]he main keywords include 'outsource*', 'agreement', 'arrangement' and 'contract'. Other auxiliary keywords in BPO announcements identified are 'announce', 'purchase', 'sign' and 'award'."

In other cases, a complete list of keywords may be provided. For example, Jacobs et al. (2010, p. 433; Table 1) provides the following keywords:

(accomplishment or accomplishments or admire or admiration or admirable or advantage or advantages or analysis or announcement or approve or approves or approval or approvals or award or awards or awarded or best or breakthrough or breakthroughs or celebrate or celebrates or celebration or celebrations or certification certified or consult or consultant or contribute or contributes or contribution or discovery or distinction or donate or donates or donation or donations or effort or efforts or endeavor or endeavors or endowment or example or excellent or excellence or exceptional or exemplary or gift or gifts or grant or grants or granted or great or greatest or honor or honors or honored or idea or ideas or initiative or innovate or innovates or innovation or innovations or innovative or invent or invents or invention or inventions or inventive or involvement or key or lead or leads or leader or leadership or master or mastery or message or messages or model or outstanding or patent or patents or patented or preeminent or preeminence or principle or principles or principled or prize or prizes or program or proactive or proclamation or proclamations or quality or qualities or qualify or qualified or qualification or recognize or recognizes or recognition or recognitions or reputation or research or researcher or respect or respected or reward or rewards rewarded or solution or standard or standards or star or strategy or strategies or strategic or study or success or successes or successful or super or superb or technology or technologies or top or tribute or tributes or tremendous or trust or venture or win or wins or won). (Jacobs et al., 2010, p. 433; Table 1)

This example also demonstrates the importance of multiple spellings of a word and multiple endings for similar words, such as ' accomplishment' or 'accomplishments.' Alternatively, wildcards might have been used, depending on the database capability.

As we read Hendricks et al. (2009), you see the authors' keywords. For example, they note (page 236): delay, shortfall, shortage, manufacturing, production, shipment, delivery, parts, components" as a brief list. In addition, a complete search statement is provided in the online supplement for the article:

(inventory or inventories) near5 (obsolete or obsolescence or excess or excessive or glut or buildup or builds or build or building or reduce or reducing or reduced or reduces or reduction or reductions or bloated or bloating or charge or charges or charging or write$ or adjust or adjustment or adjustments or adjusts or adjusting or adjusted or liquidate or liquidates or liquidating or liquidated or loss$ or

accumulate or accumulates or accumulated or accumulating or revaluate or revaluates or revaluated or revaluating or revaluation). (Hendricks & Singhal, 2009, p. S1)

There are often some headlines or excerpts from announcements, providing insight into keywords. For example, Hendricks and Singhal (2003, p. 506) cite:

- "Sony Sees Shortage of PlayStation 2s for Holiday Season," The Wall Street Journal, September 28, 2000.
- "Apple Computer Inc. Cuts 4th-period Forecast Citing Parts Shortages, Product Delays," The Wall Street Journal, September 15, 1995.

At this point, there is a list of synonyms that will be useful. However, it is unlikely that this list will capture all possible news announcements the relevant. Regularly reading news articles and publications such as from the Wall Street Journal and other financial news sources will enable an academic researcher to be familiar with business and professional terminology; regular reading provides insight into the language used in news announcements to discuss the issue of interest. When discussing the topics, these announcements will often use different phrases and terminology than academic researchers. For example, industry professionals often use industry jargon or terminology that is very industry-specific, whereas an academic researcher might use a much more abstract term that is valid for many industries. An example of reading articles for guidance about the words to use is provided by Duan et al. (2014, p. 4678; emphasis added) where they note they "created a list of keywords used to identify a BPO announcement by **analysing the content of 15 highly publicised outsourcing announcements**." Similarly, Hendricks and Singhal (2005) explain how they:

determined key search words by carefully analyzing a small number of disruptions announcements to identify words that are typically associated with disruption announcements and how the announcements are structured in terms of the closeness of key words, as well as the location of the key words in the full text. This enabled a more focused search and increased the chances of identifying announcements that are related to supply chain disruptions. (Hendricks & Singhal, 2005, p. 39)

At this point, you should have a string of synonyms. You can iteratively develop this string into a comprehensive search string that will identify many thousands of announcements using a database like Factiva. An initial search, perhaps with a small date range, will enable the identification of several additional articles and news announcements. From there, it is possible to read through and identify other terminology that may be relevant and add this to the search string. Moreover, going through the process several times will enable you to expand the search string considerably.

If you plan to complete a cross-sectional regression (as covered in chapter 11), it may be necessary to read further articles and news announcements to identify any other variables that may be of interest in your study. These might be extracted and coded in your study. For example, using the announcements Duan et al. (2014) was able to determine whether or not the business process outsourcing that they were studied was managed either using relational governance, the value chain position of the processes that were being outsourced, as well as getting a sense of the level of process that experience of the firms involved. These could then be coded using ordinal codes (such as their experience level).

When writing the article, it is often helpful to provide the reader with a sense of the type of announcements you have identified. It is unnecessary to include entire announcements (this would be a terrible waste of space in a journal article, but it might be viable in a thesis or dissertation). In a journal article, that is useful to provide an extract that gives a sense of the company and the type of issues being discussed. It allows the reader to understand the type of announcement and the type of event with several specific examples provided. Emphasis can also be added if there is a longer string of text That might be used in subsequent coding.

In general, news announcements in major news outlets such as Wall Street Journal will cover events significant enough to shift the stock returns for that company. However, sometimes it is necessary to drop into smaller or regional publications. An example of this is provided by Jacobs et al. (2010). Alternatively, if you are working on a topic pertinent to a particular industry, you may be able to use the news database to only return results for that industry (Duong et al., 2021; Wood et al., 2022).

A good example of this type of news search work is Eroglu et al. (2016). Using a list of award-winning firms in safety, quality, and sustainability in logistics, they compiled a list of 525 firms that had received 866 awards throughout their study period.

When searching in the news, it is important that you can attribute the release of news to a particular day. If it is unclear when the news was released or only suggests a month or a week, it has become possible to use this effectively for a short window (for several days). Sadly, such observations could not be included in the sample. An example is given by Xia et al. (2016, p. 1043), who notes that they "exclude announcements that appear in nondaily news sources as it is not clear when the market first gets the information about the winning of the award."

An example of the iterative nature of the searches is provided by Shafer and Moeller (2012, p. 525), who note that "[i]n searching the web for organizations that adopted Six Sigma [a list was compiled and] [t]his list became the starting point for identifying the sample Six Sigma organizations."

The Specialized Database Method

One often convenient approach is to use a pre-determined sample from a specialized database. For instance, the category of events may be widely acknowledged as essential and may already be captured in a database.

Alternatively, there may be an award or public list of awardees. This, by itself, generates a list. Naturally, not all award-winning firms will be eligible for inclusion as it may include privately help companies (e.g., those without stock returns for analysis).

Not all circumstances will be amenable to this approach. It may also not provide a robust approach to securing a list of firms and the event of interest. For example, Eroglu et al. (2016) might have been able to identify several lists of award-winning firms. However, there are likely few listed, and these lists may have been difficult to source after several years. Completing a comprehensive search of databases makes it possible to secure a larger sample, but there may be a trade-off, and some of the awards may not be as recognized or 'excellent.'

Tai and Hwang (2020) use a list of enterprises ranked based on a corporate governance exercise in Taiwan. Therefore, they could use a single list, released on 30th April 2015 (for the first exercise and part of the analysis) that consisted of firms for the sample. A bonus is that these were listed companies, so it was not necessary to determine whether they were listed on the stock exchange.

Similarly, Zou et al. (2020) examine the impact of 'doing good' in emerging markets and use a list of firms included on various socially responsible investment (SRI) indices released in emerging markets. Again, this enables a list of relevant firms to be rapidly established.

There are a range of other databases. Modi et al. (2015) report on developing their sample based on the data held on the Identity Theft Resource Center (ITRC) database. ITRC tracks the affected firms in the U.S. and the date of the breach announcement. Note that Modi et al. undertook an additional news search to identify any earlier press reports. The use of the database provides comprehensive coverage of U.S. organizations, and as the ITRC is a

[r]ecognized non-profit organization that receives funding from the U.S. Department of Justice to track and report information security breaches. In 2005, it began recording incidents of U.S. information security breaches on its website (www.idtheftcenter.org). The ITRC reports incidents where an individual's name plus confidential information (e.g., Social Security number, credit/debit card records) are put at risk. It builds its list of such breach incidents from company statements, press reports, and government sources (CMP TechWeb, 2011). (Modi et al., 2015, p. 26)

Combined Searches

Finally, the specialized database and the news search methods can be combined into a single sample. For example, although their study reflects changes in operating income rather than stock returns, Hendricks and Singhal (2001, p. 274) detail their approach that includes (emphasis added):

First, *from* **announcements** *of quality awards in the Wall Street Journal, PR Newswires, Business Wires, and Dow Jones News Service.* **Second**, *from* **lists of quality award winners published in monthly publications** *such as Automotive Engineering, Business Electronics, Distribution, and Ward's Auto World. Third, by contacting a number of award givers for a list of their award winners. (Hendricks & Singhal, 2001, p. 274)*

That is, first, from news announcements. Second, they use lists published and available. They combine these and also contact award givers to get additional lists.

Another example is provided by Shafer and Moeller (2012, p. 525), who note that how:

In searching the web for organizations that adopted Six Sigma, a list of approximately 400 organizations that were reported adopters of Six Sigma was discovered. This list became the starting point for identifying the sample Six Sigma organizations for this study. Systematically, follow-up Google queries, searches of each organization's website and annual reports, and queries of publication databases were executed for each public organization on the list in an effort to identify the date when the organization adopted Six Sigma. (Shafer & Moeller, 2012, p. 525),

The Recognized Event Method

A final approach to compiling the event list is identifying firms affected simultaneously by a significant, recognized, and extraneous event. For instance, a government policy change or an industry issue. We provide several examples below. It is important to note that the recognized event method, affecting many firms simultaneously, creates a cluster of events simultaneously, creating additional analytic steps later on in the study.

Jacobs and Singhal (2017) focus on a single event – the Rana Plaza disaster, and the impact on retailers. It was widely reported, with much speculation about changes in the global supply chains and outrage at the causes and issues underlying this. Firms can be easily and rapidly identified that were involved in the initiatives taken to overcome the issues, insofar that it is simple to identify the firms that sign either the Accord on Fire and Building Safety in Bangladesh (AFBSB) or the Alliance for Bangladesh Worker Safety (ABWS) following the disaster.

Hendricks et al. (2020) investigated the impact of the large earthquake in Japan over supply chains – using a 'related firms' event study. The nature of the event means that a search of news can be rapidly undertaken, over a short time frame, to identify firms affected by the event.

Homan presented a series of articles focused on the 9/11 disaster and its impact on several related industries, showing the impact not just on the stock returns but also other measures highlighting the impact.

Homan (2007) examines the implementation of the Maritime Transportation Security Act (MTSA) and how it influences the marine operator stocks listed on the NASDAQ and the NYSE. This study involves only those operators listed at the time of the act's implementation. It uses a well-defined list of companies on a specific date; all the companies are influenced the one event simultaneously. The study shows the implementation of the legislation is positive for the industry overall; there is a positive stock market reaction and a reduction in risk for the industry. Therefore, the MTSA reduces the increased financial risk following 9/11 for marine operators.

Homan (2006) focuses on the impact of the 9/11 attacks. The sample consists of the marine operators on the New York Stock exchange. While this is a well-specified list, although to do this retrospectively, one needs to ensure that the list of firms they use is included on the New York Stock exchange during the date of the event.

Homan (2009) examined the volatility or the financial returns. once again this shows the impact of a single event over a spread of companies.

NEXT STEPS – WHEN YOU HAVE YOUR SEARCH STRING

When you have your search string and you are happy with the synonyms, it will be time to search. This must be done systematically for several reasons. First, it is important that another researcher could replicate the study if necessary. You should understand the steps that you are taking and keep a careful record of what you did and how you did it. Second, you should have a systematic approach for your well-being and workflow. What this means is, you should not simply search for your synonyms over all periods. You should instead, as an example, search over smaller time periods step by step. This appears to be the approach used by Duan et al. (2014, p. 4678), who note that each monthly search produced 80 to 300 items. If conducted monthly, the researchers can complete the search in small chunks, for example, perhaps only taking 30 minutes per chunk. That means that any interruptions would not be a problem. Many databases might also remove the user if the system is inactive for some time. Again, breaking this into small chunks and then systematically keeping track of when the searchers were completed over what period provides the researcher with a great deal of flexibility.

As you go through, not every observation will be relevant. There be many irrelevant items also. It's necessary also as you go through to quickly eliminate fairly non relevant items. There will be several that are clearly relevant. And there will be several that are of questionable relevance. I found it helpful to process these quickly in the initial stage and if I'm not sure I'm spending a little bit of time thinking about it I Simply put the announcement into the questionable relevancy bucket with the intention of coming back and analyzing thinking about these more detail later. This also enables the entire set of questionable announcements to be analyzed at once which often provides additional insight. It also means that I can get the help of a colleague or a friend to bounce ideas around with them about how or why these may or may not be relevant. It's also useful at this point to be able to remove any items observations that have popped up and two different searches of different databases as you only want one to be included.

At the end of the process, you should have two key items:

a)   The name of the firm impacted by the event. The firm may be the one that is taking action or the firm directly affected by it

b)   The date of the event. Additional research may be required to determine whether this was the first known announcement about this event. For instance, a company may have announced on a particular day well a news or media outlet may have discussed or promoted this announcement the following day. However, it is usual that when a company makes its announcement, this will be the first release of news to the market about this issue.

A Sufficient Sample Size

The event study method presents an interesting paradox; the event must be somewhat unusual and noteworthy to be meaningful to investors. However, it must also be somewhat common so a sufficiently large size can be collected for the subsequent statistical analysis.

It is important to note that these studies do not use a statistical sampling method so that the sample provides an estimate of the population and the same way that we might expect with the traditional survey approach (Collis & Hussey, 2003; Hair et al., 2014). Rather, the intent is to capture the entire population in the sample for the study. And essence, this means that the sample size need not necessarily be large in the same way in survey sampling to capture and generate a sufficient effect size. Rather, the sample simply must be large enough so that subsequent statistical analysis work effectively. Note that "size of your study and the size of the population under consideration, you may find that you can use the entire population" (Collis & Hussey, 2003, p. 155)

How large a sample size is needed? There are many studies with large sample sizes in the finance literature where the event study method originated. This is because of the nature of the events the finance scholars focus on – they are financially focused events that occur to most/all listed companies. Because of this widespread application to many firms, the event occurs regularly, and sample sizes are larger.

When we look at management actions or techniques, occurrences will be less common, and sample sizes smaller. The phenomenon of interest will not usually apply to 'all firms'; it may be restricted to a subset of sectors. This presents the issue of small sample sizes and the issue of affecting a few firms simultaneously, introducing violations of independence and a time-clustering of events and firms. These can be addressed, and we examine methods for this type of data later in the book. An example may be a quality initiative (Hendricks & Singhal, 2001), such as six sigma or total quality management (TQM), which are more likely to be found in a firm that manufactures products but might also be found in a smaller subset of service-oriented firms.

Most event study projects first estimate abnormal returns and then conduct a cross-sectional analysis using a range of variables to predict the abnormal returns. In all cases, reasonably large sample sizes are required to meet the tests' assumptions. In practice, this may not be easy to achieve. For example, in a review paper, Wood and Wang (2018, p. 71) note in Table 1 that of a small sample of logistics focused event studies, there is a handful with under 100 observations; Table 1 shows the two smallest study sizes were 26 (Chi, 2012) and 56 (Deitz et al., 2009) with the largest being 408 (Filbeck et al., 2016) and 553 (Gong et al., 2008). If a smaller sample is used and independence and normality (required for subsequent analytical steps) requirements are not met, then bootstrapping techniques may be valuable, as they do not require the assumptions to hold true (Barclay & Litzenberger, 1988).

Research in the finance literature often includes event study projects with large sample sizes relative to those in the management literature. The financial actions are often relevant to all publicly listed companies. However, many management or supply chain management projects examine events relevant to their particular industries. Consequentially, supply chain management projects will often have a slightly smaller sample size than those published in finance journals. While the sample size might be concerning during management research, mainly because of assumptions such as normality in many test statistics. If a smaller sample size is available, many bootstrapping methods do not require assumptions of normality to be true (Barclay & Litzenberger, 1988). However, it can be a problem if a larger sample needs to be split into subgroups to learn more about the subject. Researchers should always carefully examine the assumptions for the tests they are using. It is always necessary to determine whether or not these assumptions are true in the particular case being studied.

What To Do With Your Sample

At the end of the sample generation, you will likely have a collection of PDFs that is several hundred large. How do we go from articles to something we can use further in our research? First, we need to extract the company name and the date from each announcement. These will form the basis of the 'event list' for analysis in your software.

Set up a spreadsheet, with the first two columns labeled "Firm Name" and the second "Date." Extract the data appropriately; each announcement becomes one row or observation in your dataset. It may be helpful to include a third column, "Ticker," as many announcements include a ticker code that you can use to locate further details about the stock rapidly. Note that most financial databases (such as WRDS and Datastream) use different unique identifiers for a firm at a given time. You cannot use a ticker later in the analysis as we are using historical data, and you might be looking at data from several decades earlier. Since that time, there may have been several mergers, buy-outs, and re-listings, so the identifier will often change. We discuss this in more detail in Chapter 8. Eventually, we need to provide identifiers for each firm that are appropriate for extracting the firm information.

Which Companies Should be Included in the Sample?

While compiling the sample, it is important to recall that we will only be able to calculate the stock market reaction for publicly listed companies. Consequently, you might include all companies at an early stage before eliminating privately held companies are later. This can be advantageous, as any of the companies fully owned subsidiaries of a publicly listed conglomerate, you can attribute the event to the conglomerate, although this might dilute or weaken the attribution.

You may wish to include all the firms and observations that you find, and then record how many are eliminated from the sample because they refer to privately held companies, where we cannot attribute the event to a publicly listed company. Again, this can be reported on in the manuscript.

If you're not sure whether the company is publicly listed was city area a publicly listed company, many databases will automatically include a ticket number for a publicly listed company. A quick Google search will often also reveal whether it is a subsidiary of a major publicly held conglomerate.

Confounding Event Search

To determine whether or not the event studied impacts stock returns as necessary to ensure that any change in the stock returns can only be attributed to the event of interest. If other factors might influence the stock returns, then these other factors would be confounding factors. As we are studying events, other events become confounding events. If there are two significant events on one day, it becomes impossible to determine which of these caused the change in stock returns. Consequently, the critical approach here is to identify other events that might influence stock returns and remove them from the sample.

For example, Meznar et al. (1994) reported that when using a three-day window, a confounding event check led to 37 percent of observations in the original sample being impacted by confounding events and, then, these needed to be eliminated. Short event windows make it less likely there are confounding events and ensure a larger sample.

In practice, this is completed by taking the event window and then searching for other announcements during this window. If other important announcements are found, it becomes impossible to determine which influences the stock returns. However, other options exist for managing and dealing with confounding events (Foster, 1980), but contemporary research merely illuminates these observations in practice.

With increasing access to accurate information, it may be increasingly possible to shift from end-of-day data to intraday trading data. This would enable the isolation of event St a very rapid changes in stock returns or abnormal trading volumes. For instance, Muntermann and Guettler (2007) show how the stock returns can be altered within 30 minutes of the news announcement. Such a rapid response suggests that if two events occurred on the same day at different times, it might be possible to separate the two separate changes in stock returns at the intraday level. And practice, this would mean event windows of perhaps 30 to 90 minutes each. However, when the daily returns data is being used, it is not possible to separate confounding events in this way.

When writing the report, it is essential to detail the total number of observations initially identified, the steps taken to identify confounding events, which observations were affected by confounding events, and how many were removed from the sample.

Each entry in the provisional event list should be assessed during the confounding event search to eliminate possible candidates. A fundamental assessment is whether there are any entries in the EDGAR securities filing website database that are several days on either side. These tend to be announcements that move the market and, if they are in the period, they will confound the event of interest.

A very robust search would include using a database such as Factiva and then searching for a date range around the event date AND the company name. Of course, this means any announcements about that company or concerning that company should have been picked up. A straightforward way of completing this task would be to use equations in the spreadsheet to take the event day and, for instance, count two days earlier and two days later, then present the dates (e.g., using concatenation) as a final date range.

An example of what this may look like is provided by Eroglu et al. (2016); they detail how they looked for events within five days of the award announcements (presumably, two days before, the day of the announcement, and two days after). They identified 14 potentially confounding events, so the items were removed, leaving them with 244 events in their event list.

OUTCOMES AND OUTPUT FOR THE NEXT STEPS

At the end of the chapter, the reader should have a list of events in the sample. It should be clear why these have been included and why others have been excluded. Ideally, those excluded would also be recorded with a brief note. For example, if they were the wrong focus for one of 3 reasons, a simple drop-down box or a numeric code is sufficient for making this record. It allows you to report on the number of items identified, screened, and how many were removed for which reason.

The event list will be one of the critical components in the event study, enabling the calculation of the abnormal returns as a partial step in a larger project.

Very good practice would include a spreadsheet with observations of those initially identified in the news, including those eliminated in the confounding event check but are still included in the spreadsheet for further analysis. A complete record-keeping process like this will also enable the researcher to accurately and quickly collect the data required to report the number of observations removed due to confounding events. Then, that can be easily added with a simple column such as confounding event check with the note that the observation was removed, allowing a speedy and easy sorting or calculation later on.

Several spreadsheets or several tabs may be generated during the process. At the end of the process, it is essential to have a single clear spreadsheet or tab where the final sample that will be used in the subsequent analysis can be found. It is detrimental to have multiple spreadsheets with a muddled file named system and muddled tabs inside. Although, while you are doing the research, it may seem possible to understand which you should be using, in many cases, you may need to come back to these in later years or months to check something. For doctoral students, this might come during revisions following the oral examination. For research as, it may come from another researcher asking for specific details that were not provided.

(For instance, a researcher recently contacted me for statistical details for the study that had not been reported in the published article, Wood et al. (2018). Due to good record keeping, we could very quickly pull up the file, calculate the statistics, and send them to them. They intended to publish a meta-analysis of this type of research. The meta-analysis combines comparable similar research to understand more about the overall effect size.)

CONCLUSIONS

At this point, you should understand not only the type of event that you might want to study but also how you might go about collecting a list of observations to include in your event list. We have addressed several different strategies for compiling the list; the most appropriate strategy will depend on the nature of the phenomena you are studying.

The issues around the confounding event search are introduced here and expounded in further detail in the following chapters. It is vital to ensure that the event sample contains only those events that can be causally connected to the stock market reaction; if there are two events at almost the same time, it might be challenging to ascertain which drives the stock market reaction. Therefore, managing the confounding event search is important and is often cited as critical in the event study method.

At the end of this chapter, you should know how to create an event list. It contains the observations, each consisting of the date of the event and the firm affected. As an initial step, you might also include a ticker symbol for the firm, although this will not be necessarily a sufficient identifier moving forward but is often an excellent and easy first step at this point.

REFERENCES

Barclay, M. J., & Litzenberger, R. H. (1988). Announcement effects of new equity issues and the use of intraday price data. *Journal of Financial Economics, 21*(1), 71–99. doi:10.1016/0304-405X(88)90032-3

Chi, L.-C. (2012). Price reactions to the announcement of the cross-strait Economic Cooperation Framework Agreement. *Applied Economics Quarterly, 58*(3), 213–221. http://dx.doi.org.ezproxy.otago.ac.nz/10.3790/aeq.58.3.213

Collis, J., & Hussey, R. (2003). *Business Research: A Practical Guide for Undergraduate and Postgraduate Students*. Palgrave Macmillan.

CPSC. (2022). *CPSC Data*. U.S. Consumer Product Safety Commission. https://www.cpsc.gov/Data

Deitz, G., Hansen, J., & Richey, R. G. (2009). Coerced integration: The effects of retailer supply chain technology mandates on supplier stock returns. *International Journal of Physical Distribution & Logistics Management, 39*(10), 814–825. doi:10.1108/09600030911011423

Duan, C., Grover, V., & Balakrishnan, N. (2009). Business process outsourcing: An event study on the nature of processes and firm valuation. *European Journal of Information Systems, 18*(5), 442–457. doi:10.1057/ejis.2009.38

Duan, C., Grover, V., Roberts, N., & Balakrishnan, N. (2014). Firm valuation effects of the decision to adopt relationally governed business process outsourcing arrangements. *International Journal of Production Research, 52*(15), 4673–4694. doi:10.1080/00207543.2014.884289

Duong, L. N. K., Wang, J. X., Wood, L. C., Reiners, T., & Koushan, M. (2021). The value of incremental environmental sustainability innovation in the construction industry: An event study. *Construction Management and Economics, 39*(5), 398–418. doi:10.1080/01446193.2021.1901950

Eroglu, C., Kurt, A. C., & Elwakil, O. S. (2016). Stock market reaction to quality, safety, and sustainability awards in logistics. *Journal of Business Logistics, 37*(4), 329–345. doi:10.1111/jbl.12145

Filbeck, G., Kumar, S., Liu, J., & Zhao, X. (2016). Supply chain finance and financial contagion from disruptions: Evidence from the automobile industry. *International Journal of Physical Distribution & Logistics Management, 46*(4), 414–438. doi:10.1108/IJPDLM-04-2014-0082

Gong, S. X. H., Firth, M., & Cullinane, K. (2008). International oligopoly and stock market linkages: The case of global airlines. *Transportation Research Part E, Logistics and Transportation Review, 44*(4), 621–636. doi:10.1016/j.tre.2007.05.008

Hair, J. F., Black, W. C., Babin, B. J., & Anderson, R. E. (2014). *Multivariate data analysis* (7th ed.). Pearson Education.

Hendricks, K. B., Jacobs, B. W., & Singhal, V. R. (2020). Stock market reaction to supply chain disruptions from the 2011 great east Japan earthquake. *Manufacturing & Service Operations Management, 22*(4), 645–867. doi:10.1287/msom.2019.0777

Hendricks, K. B., & Singhal, V. R. (2001). Firm characteristics, total quality management, and financial performance. *Journal of Operations Management, 19*(3), 269–285. doi:10.1016/S0272-6963(00)00049-8

Hendricks, K. B., & Singhal, V. R. (2003). The effect of supply chain glitches on shareholder wealth. *Journal of Operations Management, 21*(5), 501–522. doi:10.1016/j.jom.2003.02.003

Hendricks, K. B., & Singhal, V. R. (2005). Association between supply chain glitches and operating performance. *Management Science, 51*(5), 695–711. doi:10.1287/mnsc.1040.0353

Hendricks, K. B., & Singhal, V. R. (2008). The effect of product introduction delays on operating performance. *Management Science, 54*(5), 878–892. doi:10.1287/mnsc.1070.0805

Hendricks, K. B., & Singhal, V. R. (2009). Online supplement: Details about constructing the sample of excess inventory announcements. *Manufacturing & Service Operations Management, 11*(3, Suppl.), S1–S3.

Hendricks, K. B., Singhal, V. R., & Wiedman, C. I. (1995). The impact of capacity expansion on the market value of the firm. *Journal of Operations Management, 12*(3–4), 259–272. doi:10.1016/0272-6963(94)00016-8

Hendricks, K. B., Singhal, V. R., & Zhang, R. (2009). The effect of operational slack, diversification, and vertical relatedness on the stock market reaction to supply chain disruptions. *Journal of Operations Management, 27*(3), 233–246. doi:10.1016/j.jom.2008.09.001

Homan, A. C. (2006). The impact of 9/11 on financial risk, volatility and returns of marine firms. *Maritime Economics & Logistics, 8*(4), 387–401. doi:10.1057/palgrave.mel.9100165

Homan, A. C. (2007). The impact of MTSA on financial risk and volatility of marine firms. *Maritime Policy & Management, 34*(1), 69–79. doi:10.1080/03088830601103459

Homan, A. C. (2009). The impact of MTSA on investment uncertainty and the persistence of financial return volatility of marine firms. *Maritime Policy & Management, 36*(2), 105–115. doi:10.1080/03088830902868008

Jacobs, B. W., & Singhal, V. R. (2017). The effect of the Rana Plaza disaster on shareholder wealth of retailers: Implications for sourcing strategies and supply chain governance. *Journal of Operations Management, 49–51*(1), 52–66. doi:10.1016/j.jom.2017.01.002

Jacobs, B. W., Singhal, V. R., & Subramanian, R. (2010). An empirical investigation of environmental performance and the market value of the firm. *Journal of Operations Management, 28*(5), 430–441. doi:10.1016/j.jom.2010.01.001

Meznar, M. B., Nigh, D., & Kwok, C. C. Y. (1994). Effect of Announcements of Withdrawal from South Africa on Stockholder Wealth. *Academy of Management Journal*, *37*(6), 1633–1648. doi:10.2307/256803

Modi, S. B., Wiles, M. A., & Mishra, S. (2015). Shareholder value implications of service failures in triads: The case of customer information security breaches. *Journal of Operations Management*, *35*(1), 21–39. doi:10.1016/j.jom.2014.10.003

Muntermann, J., & Guettler, A. (2007). Intraday stock price effects of ad hoc disclosures: The German case. *Journal of International Financial Markets, Institutions and Money*, *17*(1), 1–24. doi:10.1016/j.intfin.2005.08.003

Raymond, N. (2022, January 28). 3M hit with $110 million verdict in latest U.S. military earplug trial. *Reuters*. https://www.reuters.com/business/aerospace-defense/3m-hit-with-110-million-verdict-latest-us-military-earplug-trial-2022-01-27/

Shafer, S. M., & Moeller, S. B. (2012). The effects of Six Sigma on corporate performance: An empirical investigation. *Journal of Operations Management*, *30*(7–8), 521–532. doi:10.1016/j.jom.2012.10.002

Tai, Y.-H., & Hwang, N.-C. R. (2020). Market reactions to corporate governance ranking announcements: Evidence from Taiwan. *Abacus*, *56*(4), 627–648. doi:10.1111/abac.12209

Wood, L. C., Duong, L. N. K., & Wang, J. X. (2022). Business Process Improvement for Sustainable Technologies Investments in Construction: A Configurational Approach. *Sustainability*, *14*(9), 5697. doi:10.3390u14095697

Wood, L. C., & Wang, J. X. (2018). The event study method in logistics research: Overview and a critical analysis. *International Journal of Applied Logistics*, *8*(1), 57–79. doi:10.4018/IJAL.2018010104

Wood, L. C., Wang, J. X., Duong, L. N. K., Reiners, T., & Smith, R. (2018). Stock market reactions to auto manufacturers' environmental failures. *Journal of Macromarketing*, *38*(4), 364–382. doi:10.1177/0276146718781915

Xia, Y., Singhal, V. R., & Peter Zhang, G. (2016). Product design awards and the market value of the firm. *Production and Operations Management*, *25*(6), 1038–1055. doi:10.1111/poms.12525

Zou, P., Wang, Q., Xie, J., & Zhou, C. (2020). Does doing good lead to doing better in emerging markets? Stock market responses to the SRI index announcements in Brazil, China, and South Africa. *Journal of the Academy of Marketing Science*, *48*(5), 966–986. doi:10.100711747-019-00651-z

ADDITIONAL READING

Ahern, K. R. (2009). Sample selection and event study estimation. *Journal of Empirical Finance*, *16*(3), 466–482. doi:10.1016/j.jempfin.2009.01.003

Arora, P., Hora, M., Singhal, V., & Subramanian, R. (2020). When do appointments of corporate sustainability executives affect shareholder value? *Journal of Operations Management*, *66*(4), 464–487. doi:10.1002/joom.1074

Binder, J. (1998). The event study methodology since 1969. *Review of Quantitative Finance and Accounting, 11*(2), 111–137. doi:10.1023/A:1008295500105

Chen, Y., Singhal, V., & Zhu, Q. (2021). Environmental policies and financial performance: Stock market reaction to firms for their proactive environmental practices recognized by governmental programs. *Business Strategy and the Environment, 30*(4), 1548–1562. doi:10.1002/bse.2693

Corrado, C. J., & Zivney, T. L. (1992). The specification and power of the sign test in event study hypothesis tests using daily stock returns. *Journal of Financial and Quantitative Analysis, 27*(3), 465–478. doi:10.2307/2331331

Duan, C., Grover, V., & Balakrishnan, N. (2009). Business process outsourcing: An event study on the nature of processes and firm valuation. *European Journal of Information Systems, 18*(5), 442–457. doi:10.1057/ejis.2009.38

Duong, L. N. K., Wang, J. X., Wood, L. C., Reiners, T., & Koushan, M. (2021). The value of incremental environmental sustainability innovation in the construction industry: An event study. *Construction Management and Economics, 39*(5), 398–418. doi:10.1080/01446193.2021.1901950

Goldstein, J., Chernobai, A., & Benaroch, M. (2011). An event study analysis of the economic impact of IT operational risk and its subcategories. *Journal of the Association for Information Systems, 12*(9), 606–631. doi:10.17705/1jais.00275

Jayanti, R. K., & Jayanti, S. V. (2011). Effects of airline bankruptcies: An event study. *The Journal of Services Marketing, 25*(6), 399–409. http://dx.doi.org.ezproxy.otago.ac.nz/10.1108/08876041111160998

Park, N. K. (2004). A guide to using event study methods in multi-country settings. *Strategic Management Journal, 25*(7), 655–668. doi:10.1002mj.399

Pérez-Rodríguez, J. V., & González López-Valcárcel, B. (2012). Does innovation in obesity drugs affect stock markets? An event study analysis. *Gaceta Sanitaria, 26*(4), 352–359. doi:10.1016/j.gaceta.2011.07.028 PMID:22244267

Roztocki, N., & Weistroffer, H. R. (2015). Investments in enterprise integration technology: An event study. *Information Systems Frontiers, 17*(3), 659–672. http://dx.doi.org.ezproxy.otago.ac.nz/10.1007/s10796-013-9451-8

Xin, J. Y., Yeung, A. C. L., & Cheng, T. C. E. (2008). Radical innovations in new product development and their financial performance implications: An event study of US manufacturing firms. *Operations Management Research, 1*(2), 119–128. doi:10.100712063-009-0017-3

Zhan, X., Mu, Y., Hora, M., & Singhal, V. R. (2021). Service excellence and market value of a firm: An empirical investigation of winning service awards and stock market reaction. *International Journal of Production Research, 59*(14), 4188–4204. doi:10.1080/00207543.2020.1759837

Zhan, X., Mu, Y., Nishant, R., & Singhal, V. R. (2020). When do appointments of Chief Digital or Data Officers (CDOs) affect stock prices? *IEEE Transactions on Engineering Management*, 1–14. doi:10.1109/TEM.2020.2984619

KEY TERMS AND DEFINITIONS

Confounding Event: An event that occurs at the same time as the event of interest, making it difficult or impossible to assess if a stock market reaction is due to the event of interest.

Event List: The list of observations, each with a date and firm name and identifier.

Recognized Event: A single event that simultaneously affects many firms in related industries. This can often be conducted with reference to specialized databases or datasets.

Sample Size: The number of observations in the sample.

Search String: The combination of keywords, truncations, and Boolean operators used in the database search.

Standard Search: Searching for announcements with a search of news, with a manual screening of relevant news announcements.

Chapter 6
Literature and Archival Data:
Searching, Reading, and Writing

ABSTRACT

The purpose of this chapter is to discuss searching archival databases both for a literature review and searching through secondary data sources or archival data sources. Moreover, while some readers may turn to a Google search, the idea of a systematic, well-structured search is valuable, and this chapter outlines some of the benefits. The use of academic databases may seem quaint or antiquated. However, such academic research databases provide many powerful features to support both fast and thorough searches. The author also addresses notetaking because the reading you do can be limited if you are not taking effective notes that you can use in your writing and in the analysis of whether you have more literature you still must find. The value of notes and how to use them to develop your literature review is also addressed. This chapter discusses some of the challenges of searches and different methods and outlines an array of tips and strategies to both do fast, quick, and dirty searches and more comprehensive and in-depth searches.

INTRODUCTION

Many people are used to searching for information on the Internet using common search engines such as Google. Consequently, many people believe that an academic search is merely an extension of what they do in their everyday lives. However, the truth is vastly different. Many academic research studies will live or die on the foundation built on the search either of the background literature or other archival searches. If you miss something vital when doing a literature review for your doctoral dissertation or thesis, you will probably run into substantial problems and face strong challenges from supervisors or, the worst case, serious challenges from your examiners. The problems will be exacerbated if you have missed key literature that you should have been aware of and drawn on.

Consequently, the use of a more systematic approach and use of academic research databases for search pays big dividends to the scholar or student as they undertake their search. It enables them to create a repeatable or replicable search, which is valuable when working in a postgraduate research

DOI: 10.4018/978-1-7998-8969-4.ch006

environment. It will support you to respond to either reviewers, supervisors, or examiners about how the search was conducted and why.

The chapter first starts with a critique of a general searching and then progresses through to outlining several important tips and considerations when conducting a more systematic search of academic research databases. Next, we talk about the use of search engines, particularly academic research databases, and the strengths and drawbacks of all search engines. Examples will be given of both academic search engines and other archival data sources and how search patterns can be used to effectively and rapidly and cover what you need to know. We turn our attention to notetaking as this enables you to bridge the gap between reading and writing. We introduce, briefly, some ideas to take your notes and begin to write as this can help you to determine gaps where further ligature may be required. While doing this we look at the importance of intellectual honesty, quotations, and paraphrasing.

Background

We often hear of the echo chamber the way in which people's thoughts and beliefs are repeated back to them and reinforces their own beliefs (Flaxman et al., 2016). Some of this comes as a consequence of how social media platforms operate and cluster like-minded groups; then, underlying algorithms can push more of the same or similar content at the users as this is clearly what is most relevant to them (Hosanagar, 2016). Consequently, reading more articles about health and well-being will probably mean that you get targeted with more advertisements and be exposed to more other posts from your network about health and well-being. In a more negative outcome, it can also be used to support the spread of disinformation or misinformation; such as the spread of information about vaccinations in the COVID-19 pandemic (Jennings et al., 2021). People who read conspiracy theories and digest this information will tend to be presented with more conspiracy theory based content digest further reinforcing their beliefs (Puri et al., 2020).

Underlining all of this is a search engine and the capabilities for the search engine to adapt to what is presented to the user so that it gives more of what they want. By itself, this is not so consequential. It is however a problem when people do not realize what is happening or expect others to see the same type of output from their search that they are seeing. For example, when a search is conducted in Google, that attempts to present the most relevant information to the user (Hariri, 2011). Yes, it does weigh up connections and links between pages, but it also will draw on user information to try and generate a better ranking system that will better match what the users are looking for. Again, if I am thinking about general health and wellbeing, this may not have such severe consequences. However, if we are thinking about somebody who searches for dis-information about COVID vaccines and anti-vaccine matches, then it could be a quite dangerous and significant problem.

When we are thinking about research, the problem is fundamental as many students and early career researchers might just jump on Google and assume that what they search and find would be the same for them and everyone else. Unfortunately, the truth is very different. This also has dire consequences when we begin to think about the applicability of your search to your study. If the study draws on archival data sources and everyone runs the same search and gets different results, it becomes impossible for people to replicate those results and it makes it harder to justify whether you have identified all of the relevant sources to your study.

In an academic research database setting, this is not such a problem because when two users have used identical search strings and options, we are sure they will be presented with same data/output. Therefore, a research study design with an academic research database should be replicable by other people with access to their database and the underlying data. Using these academic research databases also allows you to undertake rapid quick and dirty searches that identify a small number of highly relevant articles, or a more thorough and comprehensive search.

The main purpose of this chapter is to introduce the reader to the idea of a well-structured search both when searching for literature and also in developing your sample of news items a search of news archive databases for the event study. The same habits and behaviors can be carried through to other projects and studies where relevant and so I hope that this chapter contains generalizable insight and is useful for many readers. The focus will be to get the most out of a search rapidly and as quickly as possible to reduce ambiguity and uncertainty throughout the process.

LITERATURE REVIEW SPECIFICS

In many ways conducting a literature review is very similar to an archival search and an event study. Many doctoral programs and publishers now require systematic literature review as part of the submission. As a consequence, there is a greater focus on replication and clear and well-defined steps within that review of the literature.

It is very important to be thorough and rigorous and securing, compiling, and interpreting the data used for your study. This is true with any research project, and it can often be addressed using a research journal. You should be able to understand what decisions you are making and why these decisions were made, and these should all be noted (at least in your own research journal and key points made in your dissertation or manuscript). It should be possible to generate a decision support flow chart to help your advisors or other greatest understand the decisions made, the sequence, and any outcomes. Being able to capture this information also assures that there was a rigorous and consistent process applied during the entire data collection process.

When conducting a literature review and preparing the background or literature sections on your dissertation paper, it is not important to be proud of how many articles you have read but rather to develop an understanding and to read with purpose. It is better to have read the small number of highly relevant articles with great thoroughness and we have read dozens of less relevant articles be familiar with intimate details which are not of any importance a distinction to your study.

Searches of Announcements

One of the most important elements in an event study is establishing the sample of relevant announcements to the research project. Out of 100 announcements, you may only find two or three relevant to your project. And a very simple search and skim of the title and lead paragraph will enable you to include or exclude the announcement from your sample quickly. Beyond that, a fast read of the article is usually sufficient to include within the sample. However, there will still be articles for which it is difficult to determine whether they are included. And in these circumstances, it is best to work with an advisor or a colleague to understand what may or may not be worth including this announcement, and the sample and a patch of these ambiguous announcements should be evaluated simultaneously. Through this process and the related discussions, it will usually be possible to generate some ideas about how or why they are included or not. These ideas can then be codified, written up, and included in a decision chart. In general, these decisions will only be made for a very small number of announcements that we look at.

THE LITERATURE REVIEW

There will certainly be some background literature review within an event study project published as an article. Depending on the type of journal and editorial preferences, this could be included in an introduction section that leads directly into a methodology section, or it might be included as a separate section between an introduction and method section. In any case, the literature review should demonstrate an understanding of the core antecedents to the current research. Usually, we see a more narrative review of the literature being used in an event study, with the authors selecting key articles from which they develop their ideas and theories.

While there are several forms of literature reviews, such as more traditional narrative reviews and far more systematic meta-analysis or integrative literature reviews, for the event studies, they are usually used to capture a core understanding of the background in systematic literature reviews are less common. However, as Tranfield et al. (2003, p. 207) asserts, " 'narrative' reviews frequently lack thoroughness, and in many cases are not undertaken as genuine pieces of investigatory science. Consequently they can lack a means for making sense of what the collection of studies is saying. These reviews can he biased by the researcher and often lack rigour." Furthermore, there is often "legitimate criticism of narrative reviews is that they may 'cherry pick' evidence to bolster a particular perspective" (Greenhalgh et al., 2018, p. 4). As such, systematic reviews are sometimes seen by "leading academic journals view as a state-of-the-art (that is, expert-led narrative) review" (Greenhalgh et al., 2018, p. 1) and a superior review.

No one form of a literature review is superior to another and Greenhalgh et al. (2018, p. 4) have argued there are reasons for some preferences, stating that "[t]he under-acknowledged limitations of systematic reviews, along with missed opportunities for undertaking and using narrative reviews to extend understanding within a field, risks legitimising and perpetuating a narrow and unexciting research agenda and contributing to research waste." However, it is also possible to capture the essence of a systematic review without being burdened by an overly constrained procedure. Simsek et al. (2021) present a framework that might guide more systematic approaches to literature reviews.

FINDING LITERATURE

Planning and executing a systematic literature review is far beyond the scope of this volume and chapter. However, discussing some methods and tricks to get the most out of academic research databases is perfectly positioned in this chapter. Being able to rapidly identify some key literature and identify a comprehensive set of literature for the review is important, and we turn our attention to each of these issues next.

A Quick and Dirty Search

When we open up an academic research database to search, several options are usually available. Most commonly, the databases will open up with a simple or user-friendly search page available for us to use.

We can often simply plug in search terms here and rapidly get results. However, there is usually also an option for an advanced search, where we can structure a more complex and comprehensive query that might be useful in narrowing down for looking for a particular type of article. My advice is always to read through the documentation for each academic research database or discuss it with the subject librarian to better understand how it will work and how to get the most out of the search.

Many databases like Scopus use a relatively simple interface that we can expand to generate a reasonably comprehensive search without sacrificing usability. In essence, we can combine several search terms to narrow down on key pieces of literature.

I usually want to find articles and evidence to support something I am working on for a quick and dirty search. I do not necessarily want to engage in a comprehensive review of the literature but just want a very fast take on a particular idea, relationship, or operational management initiative.

As such, a quick and dirty search will be executed with a sequence of key terms. The database itself would usually have the option for identifying key terms in particular segments of the document. That is, does the search term appear in the title, the body, or the keywords? If the keyword is a central part of the article's message and findings, the keyword will almost certainly appear in the keywords list or perhaps in the title abstract. In contrast, if the keyword I am interested in was only cited parenthetically in passing within the article, the article is not likely to be useful for me.

The quick and dirty search then consists of several keywords or phrases, often using quote marks to ensure that multiple words appear in that sequence exactly as I intend them to within the source documents. I usually have one or several key terms or words that appear in the title or abstract. Sometimes, if I am looking for a particular type of study, a key term might be a method or a variable of interest or a type of initiative taken.

Another search term might be if I am looking for studies in a particular context or a particular technology, in which case the term might be one that I want to appear in the title of the source publication. An example is from looking for something in the operations management literature, I may include 'operations management' as a term in the source (journal) title. This can be challenging to achieve because not all operations management journals use that term precisely in the title; an example is the *International Journal of Operations and Production Management*. Each search term can often be related to Boolean operators such as 'and,' to ensure they occur in the abstract.

If we are still left with many potential articles to look through a read, we may have the option of further isolating articles published in recent years or isolating those published by a particular journal in the area. This might enable us to narrow down on a particular area or field only lock the articles that have been recently published. In many cases, we can rapidly and easily assess whether or not an article will be of interest, using the article title, abstract, and a quick read.

In terms of an event study, the quick and dirty method is often useful for finding past studies that shed light on some of the key relationships for the hypothesis development. For example, you can use key variables is one of the search terms and perhaps an industrial context as another. Alternatively, you might use the variable name as one search term and a method such as use of surveys as another search term.

Databases often have different functions for searching for two words in proximity. Scopus, for instance, allows you to search for one term that is 'within' a number of words of another term; the "w/X" operator checks for proximity so there must be within X words of each other (Scopus, n.d.). For instance, looking for an article about innovation in construction, you may search for "(construction OR building) w/5 (innovation OR innovative OR novel)" so that innovation is closely related to construction. It is often useful to become familiar with these less-used functions as they can enable you to complete quick and dirty searches to find key literature rapidly.

When you identify key literature this way, these will often be your "A" ranked articles (more on this below). You might expect such highly relevant articles to be positioned as the key articles you are 'competing' against or extending; as such, you may expect to cite them multiple times at the start (e.g., in the literature review) and near the end of the manuscript (e.g., in the discussion section).

A More Comprehensive Search for the Literature Review

As noted, comprehensive systematic literature reviews are beyond our scope. In this section, a more carefully to targeted and more systematic approach to literature reviews can be developed to help you to dig deeply into a particular body of research and find key articles.

We start with the same foundation of ideas that we just discussed. Academic research databases should be used. Ideally, you should get to know one of your databases and discuss it with your subject librarian to understand some of the nuances are differences between databases. Many databases have sophisticated and complex possibilities for conducting searches using even the frequently used operators. This section only presents an introduction to some of these operators and methods that may be useful but will give you some insight into how you can go about designing a more comprehensive search strategy.

First, the sources that might be searched may need to be widened. For example, we might need to search from scholarly journals and conferences, and some databases may enable us to look through doctoral dissertations.

Second, we need to start thinking about synonyms, different spellings, and related words to search for a range of words that may be relevant. Synonyms can be crucial whether we are searching for academic literature for events. Therefore, we should consider a range of synonyms that might be used and create a part of the search string in parentheses where the search can use any of these synonyms using the OR operator; the search results should contain, for instance, "operations OR production."

The spelling of words is important when considering the differences between U.K. and U.S. English; organization with an S or a Z. Where some commonly used databases would probably be able to address this issue automatically, you may need to check with your database and you may need to replace with a wildcard. In the Scopus database, for example, the use of a Question Mark (?) can be used so that a single character can be substituted (Scopus, n.d.); "organi?ation" would pick up both organization and organisation.

Understanding the common roots for related words is also quite a useful way of searching a wide body of literature. we might be interested in management, managers, managing all as related words. Many databases will have a function that will enable us to enter the root word then truncate so that any other ending would also be appropriate within the search. In Scopus, the Asterisk (*) character can replace multiple characters. Therefore, "behav* finds behave, behavior, behaviour, behavioural, behaviourism, etc." (Scopus, n.d.).

Systematic Literature Reviews

While beyond the scope of this volume, the basic principle is to create a reproducible sequence of activities and document and communicate them. In some areas, such as healthcare, certain standards should be understood and adhered to from the commencement of the project (Page et al., 2021). For instance, the PRISMA guidelines can be followed to enhance success in publishing in journals with this as a requirement. It is much easier to plan and execute the project after reading the PRISMA requirements than to undertake a project and then go back to the PRISMA guidelines and need to re-do substantial work to comply.

In general, I do not think these types of systematic reviews are particularly valuable for an event study, but they can build a strong body of knowledge about factors or variables that may be of interest in the study or any study with a different method. An example includes evaluating surgical cancellations and the location and screening of the studies as part of the systematic review provided by Koushan et al. (2021).

DEVELOPING HYPOTHESES

Many hypotheses are empirically or logically derived in the operations and supply chain management literature. In other bodies of literature, there is a wider emphasis on developing a more theoretically grounded set of hypotheses. We are seeing this emerge more powerful force in the operations management literature. As such, there are several ways of identifying literature related to a hypothesis. In some cases, we may find, for example, what Hendricks et al. (2014) identified and stated, that there is little theoretical background on the appointment of supply chain and operations management executives, and they state eloquently:

To the best of our knowledge, there does not exist any literature that provides theory and evidence directly related to SCOMEs that we could use to develop this hypothesis. However, there is literature on executive appointments, successions, and turnover that we can use to build our hypothesis.(Hendricks et al., 2014, p. 1564)

How, then, do we build a foundation of relevant literature to help develop the hypotheses?

First, we can run a search identifying research that uses those variables within our research. Adding a methodological element to the search string is often useful, such as studies using 'structural equation modeling' as a search term. This can enable us to find articles that provide some research support to key relationships we may be interested in studying. We might want to use a method like structural equation modelling because these will be based on surveys with relatively large sample sizes, providing some degree of generalizability from the study results. We might also use a search that matches up variables of interest with a theoretical framework to see how other researchers have used the same type of variable and theory that we are using.

Second, we can take the variables of interest and brainstorm several other synonyms for these. We can then run a search where any synonyms can be identified in an article using the OR operator. We can then also begin to use another block of terms in the search, much like in the event search outlined in the previous chapter. An article should be identified when it has a synonym of interest within another block which may be the context of interest. This might enable us to identify research within a particular industry or affecting a particular type of company. For example, we might be looking at innovation within the construction industry. Research might involve a range of synonyms for innovation, and all articles that are returned should also include synonyms for 'construction' and 'built environment.'

As we read through the articles, rapidly identify articles that talk about those key variables within the title and the abstract. Skimming these articles will give some insight into whether they include the variables within the study in a meaningful way and how their findings might be relevant to the study.

Just because we are using an event study as the methodology does not mean that all articles cited within the literature review or the hypothesis development need to use the same event study method. As already suggested, we may draw on other sources and cite studies that use surveys or even qualitative case study-based projects.

Keep in mind that if we have some other event studies that use comparable variables and relationships, we may compare the results very directly to their results at a later stage in the study. Each of the studies may be quite comparable, to make an 'apples to apples' comparison.

If, on the other hand, we are drawing from a range of different sources to provide support for these relationships, then when we write the results section, we may be able to argue an 'apples to oranges' comparison with any differences that you may need to discuss as being due to methodological or sampling issues.

A case study is a qualitative research approach that can also be of interest. In many cases, this research uses a very small sample of sites or cases and may draw data from a single company. In this type of situation, we can add to their findings with a wider study that more comprehensively examines this relationship over hundreds of companies in the event study sample.

In the event study, we work with secondary data. Not all hypotheses and variables of interest will have meaningful measures that can be constructed with secondary data for analysis in the cross-sectional regression. This is one of the limitations that we must be comfortable with. However, there are often a range of different variables that can be constructed, even if they are not the ideal proxy for the variable and relationships we are interested in studying.

Theoretically Driven Hypotheses

We can derive the core hypotheses from a single body of work with theoretically-driven hypotheses. However, there are many examples of event studies taking this approach to more theoretically driven hypotheses, and so this is just a very limited subset.

Duan et al. (2014) draw on the transaction cost economics (TCE) approach developed by Williamson (Williamson, 1975, 1981, 2008) to study outsourcing and relational governance. There are three hypotheses. First, a business process outsourcing arrangement with more relational governance adoption is present will lead to a stronger valuation (a stronger stock market reaction). Second, the effect will be stronger for primary (value-creating) processes than secondary (supportive) processes. Third, with greater process experience, the effect will be stronger.

Bilgili et al. (2017) use sensemaking and resource dependence as key theoretical foundations for their hypotheses. The first hypothesis treats the CEO as a resource; a CEO departure leads to a negative stock market reaction. The second hypothesis uses sensemaking and focuses on whether a credible narrative reduces uncertainty; if so, the reaction will be more positive. The third hypothesis follows the theme of the content and style of messaging.

Lo et al. (2014) examine safety in a longitudinal event study. They draw on institutional theory along with normal accident theory (NAT) (Wolf, 2001) and high-reliability theory (HRT) (Colquitt et al., 2011).

READING, NOTES, AND DATA FOR THE LITERATURE REVIEW

It is not reading that creates a manuscript or a thesis, but rather it has the writing as this incorporates the notes and the ideas built and developed into the manuscript. Thinking this way suggests that while reading is important, it is also crucial that we develop our ability to take and condense these ideas, relate them to other ideas, develop relationships between ideas, and then build and construct our own arguments.

Reading carefully is important, but it is also necessary to engage in careful notetaking. A useful way of approaching this is to use a single piece of software that will capture both bibliographic details and core notes for that work. We can assemble direct quotations using cut and paste functions always recording the page number. In this way, we can also use this to paraphrase and capture our ideas. I will often reword key phrases and summarize key concepts from the work. In this way, throughout your reading you might read many hundreds or thousands of pages and summarize this down to a collection of critical notes for your work. The overall volume that you have read is then condensed from thousands of pages to perhaps dozens of pages of notes. This interaction between the reading and the notetaking should help you to become familiar with and understand the core ideas in this area. The more heavily you engage with concepts and ideas and the more you take notes about them the more you will understand, comprehend, and clearly remember these concepts. You will be more able to think through, consider carefully, and re imagine the relationship between core ideas even while you are not at a computer with those notes handy.

When teaching classes, we often implore students to engage in scholarly reading. However, such scholarly reading is only the first part of the puzzle as I noted earlier. It is also necessary to take the scholarly reading and then extend this by creating critical notes, judiciously reading, and then summarizing those core ideas in the notes. In this way, scholarly reading is a key part of your overall purpose and understanding and writing about ideas. It is tightly coupled with the ability to make notes and use notes. Indeed, as you begin to take notes and use the notes about other people's work, you begin to explore that topic and understand and relate it to others' understandings of the topic. As a result, we become more critical of their work and the stance that they are taking without being worried about providing a coherent argument in discussion and finished or polished writing. Notetaking also enables us to think critically about the works read as they will help us really understand the key points being made and the research design they use.

Careful note-taking gives us the building blocks and the raw material to construct our research articles and research work. It provides a connection to core readings and the summary of those key ideas, the analysis, results, and outcomes of those research articles. As a student, notes can also be communication with supervisors; rather than listing what you have been reading, the notes can concisely summarize what was read and understood. Using notes in this way often triggers a very productive conversation about different perspectives on research work if, for example, the supervisor sees your notes present a single perspective on the issue that needs to be further balanced.

Using Bibliographic Management Software

This category of software may also be called reference management software or citation management software. They enable users to (EBSCO Connect, n.d.):

- Create a database of bibliographic details to help with the work of citations
- Generate bibliographies or reference lists at the end of works

- Manage the in-text citations and reference lists.

As an undergraduate student, I would have seen little need of such software. However, as a postgraduate student, I quickly realized that I would be in big trouble without such software. One of the first conversations I now have with any new research student is about adopting a package. I do not have any strong preferences; I would probably make a different choice if I set out today to select software. At the moment, the simple fact that I have been using a particular package for so long has meant that I can use it rapidly and quickly to generate the results that I want, and there is little incentive to change to another package.

One of the main reasons that I advise on the use is that it enables the writing process to rapidly generate in-text citations and reference lists that are perfectly synchronized the entire time. This means that if we deleted a paragraph that is no longer necessary, any references cited only in the paragraph would then be removed from the reference list. It also enables the user to change to a different citation style very rapidly if required to submit an article to a journal. In addition, using the software also enables you to capture notes and analyze the articles stored in the database.

Yes, it is possible to write a manuscript without this type of software, but I personally find myself far more productive while using this type of software.

A note of caution – the software must be actively and carefully used. I have had students protest that they are using the correct referencing style and doing everything correctly. In their defense, they just said that they are using the software just like I told them to. However, when we sit down at their laptop, the problem becomes clear. There is often incomplete, incorrect, or missing data inside of their software. Consequently, the output in terms of in-text citations or references is incorrect. In many cases, the software pulls information from sources where the source has incomplete information; consequently, the database becomes incomplete. In particular, care should be taken to ensure that the volume and issue number (for journals) are complete and the final page number is included (I've seen some databases only note the starting page number for an article). This is simply a principle of "garbage in; garbage out." Some data sources may also have journal titles fully capitalized, which may need to be edited. The exact requirements depend on the software package, but we should become familiar with it at the outset.

Being Proud of Notes Rather than Reading

As a postgraduate student, I fondly recall many discussions about how many articles people had read, how many they had collected in the bibliographic management software, and how many works were being cited in their thesis. I now understand that that was the wrong way of looking at the issue of reading and writing. As you can see from this discussion, the notes about the reading are crucial, not the reading itself. So much time can be taken and reading article after article, particularly when there are so many journals and so much more research being produced, yet this overwhelms many students and postgraduate researchers. Instead, it is much more important to closely read the major articles and then extract from them the key ideas and your notes.

There is also a very important and virtuous cycle. the more we read and the more we practice summarizing key ideas into notes, the more quickly we will find that we can scan a big article, identify pertinent information, and then mentally make sense of this so that you can take a note of it. Like anything else, this is a skill that can be learned and will develop with further practice.

If we are working with pen and paper, we might have a highlighter or a marker to identify key sections of text. With software, we might electronically highlight key sections. Either is appropriate if we are engaged in the reading process, and highlighting or identifying information is a key component of the notetaking process.

When reading a book, it is useful to scan through the table of contents to understand the structure and argumentation that they will be using. For example, when reading an article, quickly reviewing the introduction will often provide a very good understanding of the background, core data and arguments, and contribution of the article. We can also look through the headings and subheadings of the article for inside, being aware that if the article follows a standardized format, in many cases, the headings will be fairly standard and not particularly informative. Getting to grips with the content and value of the work in this way is important because it can help determine whether it is worth reading the rest of the work.

While I have asserted the importance of taking notes, this is still connected to the reading you do. My advice is if you think the article is worth reading, first quickly read through from start to finish to get a feel and a sense of the article's overall content. This skim enables you to more clearly identify the elements that will be important to take notes about. In contrast, if we start reading in detail from the start to the finish while taking notes along the way, we often identify later that much time was spent taking detailed notes about less relevant points, but we can only come to this realization after reading the article.

The content of notes will vary widely depending on the exact nature of the research. However, I tend to use the following key categories for many of my notes:

- What is the core theoretical or conceptual framework for the analysis?
- What method was used and was this a standard approach or did it include any interesting variations. Is this something that is relevant to my own research?
- How does this research compare with my own interests either in this project or other projects?
- What are the major findings?
- Which findings confirmed past research; which are more interesting or novel?
- Does the analysis support the stated conclusions as advertised in the abstract?

Everyone will develop their own style for capturing some way of annotating a text to reflect many of these core ideas. I use sequences of symbols to help me later understand the importance of relative importance of some of the ideas and approaches being used. For example, in many cases, I use a star for a key point with multiple stars indicating my assessment of the importance of this particular segment, coupled with a "TH" for points on theory.

Coming from an operations management background (where we talk about inventory management), I draw on the established ABC classification for inventory to help me to also categorize my own reading by framing how I think about the articles I am reading (Figure 1). This supports in both reading effectively as well as in writing effectively.

A. These will be the core readings that are crucial to my study. That will be the most closely related, most closely competitive, almost closely methodologically linked articles. These are going to be articles that I expect to cite many times. By the time I finish the research, these will be the articles that I will be very intimately familiar with. In principle, this might be one out of every ten or twenty articles that I read.

Figure 1. ABC classification of articles to support reading and writing

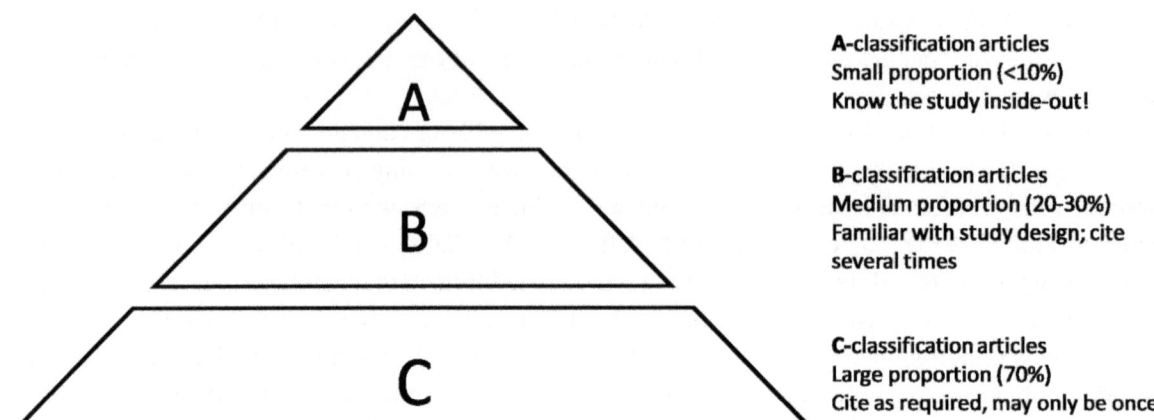

A-classification articles
Small proportion (<10%)
Know the study inside-out!

B-classification articles
Medium proportion (20-30%)
Familiar with study design; cite
several times

C-classification articles
Large proportion (70%)
Cite as required, may only be once.

B. then this category of articles that I will probably cite several times and may even extract a useful quotation or two from. They will often be from the same type of research well. They may be addressing the topic parenthetically to the major focus. While I might cite them in the literature review or introduction several times, it is unlikely that they will take on a leading role in the discussion section where I compare my work to their work to explain the contribution of my study. In principle, I would expect this to be true for two or three out of 10 articles that I read.

C. this is the 'great unwashed' mass of articles and books that we read. In many ways, this is almost like a bibliography. I expect these articles to be cited perhaps once in the literature review, often in passing, providing some evidence and support for a more parenthetical comment that I am making. I would normally expect this to be perhaps seven out of 10 articles that I read.

The best way to manage the notes taken while reading is to make extensive use of the bibliographic management software. As we already use the software to take care of references and citations, it makes sense to double up and begin using it to take notes. Almost all software packages have a page/space for notes. Many now also have a separate section for tags. The tags simply take the place of your current use of keywords. In some cases, the keywords from the article can provide useful tax. However, there is also the opportunity to add specific tags to a project in many cases, particularly if we are taking a particular approach to the subject or the subject and interest is parenthetical to the article's main focus. For example, the article may be focused on a particular issue or context, while your interest in the article may be methodological. Using tags and keywords can enable a search through the database quickly and rapidly for particular citations. For example, if we are not sure whether or not we have read any material on an issue such as product recalls, we would be able to search quickly through the database.

Within the notes section, it is useful to take notes about the main point or the article's main premise to clarify the main stance taken. While we can easily read this within the introduction and conclusion, it is often useful to outline this succinctly. This will be their major contribution and progression on a particular topic in many cases.

It may also be useful to focus on the major or primary point that the article makes. Again, this may appear in an abstract for the introduction, or we may need to paraphrase based on reading the introduction section. Essentially, you are trying to capture a note about why this is important research. The introduction could be clearly outlined with the author saying that "this research is important because [...]" But different disciplines in various subject areas have different conventions, and such points may not always be clearly outlined.

It is useful to clearly capture the article's main premise or primary hypothesis. Again, succinctly paraphrasing this is quite useful and it can also perform a useful note that can be included directly into your own writing when you paraphrased it. It is useful to note the type of data they have used or databases they have drawn from. Many empirical works might also include notes on the unit of analysis, cases, and the types of organizations they have worked with.

Increasingly, is useful to have some insight into the theory framework, model, or approach that has been used within the research. It is also useful to have some insight into the methodology used, emphasizing any novelty or new extensions in the methodology.

Finally, it is useful to have a section for our own free-form notes that summarize some of the key elements and help synthesize our understanding of the research and the connections and relevance of the research. This free-form area provides an area to provide our thoughts about the research. It is important to capture these ideas and insights while reading and note-taking. After a week, we will likely have forgotten many of the main elements of an article we were reading.

CREATING YOUR FREE-FORM NOTES

One of the major benefits of taking free-form notes is that you get engaged with the writing and manage the concepts in the research that you read without engaging any critical faculties that might get in the way of your intended writing process. That is, taking the notes in this way short-circuits any internal critic that might get in the way of writing. There is no need for the writing to be beautiful; there is no need for it to be prose. This will be a private set of notes for your on work. You do not have to worry about introductions and conclusions or structures but merely capturing some of those core ideas and beginning to relate them makes sense to the premise of the articles that you are reading.

These free-form notes form the building blocks for your own writing work in many ways. I believe that this is an important element of preparing to write as:

- they can be quickly captured
- they provide you with a new source of material that summarizes more extensive articles you can make more sense of the short summaries
- you can begin to play with and restructure these notes to cluster your ideas and thoughts about research
- you can begin to analyze trends within these notes rather than dealing with the more unwieldy set of articles that you have been reading

When you have your free form notes, summarizing much of what you have written as a primary note is often very useful. I use these to try and capture the core essence of the research that I have been reading in a way that I believe it is going to be most relevant to my current research work. I give myself several sentences where I paraphrase while also relating those key ideas to the primary purpose of my current writing. Quickly make a note of the author and year as an in-text citation that enables you to take this primary note and use it within the main article that you are writing while still quickly connecting it back to a citation.

While reading an article, I like to capture both free-form and primary notes while reading the article and doing this in one go. The reason is that everything is going to be fresh in my mind. However, I do sometimes come back to these notes, but after reading additional or further material, which gives me new insight or a more deeply reflect on my current work, enabling me to make more use of notes that I have made in the recent past.

One of the next steps is to extract the primary notes into a separate Word file. I then use my bibliographic management tool to provide an in-text citation enabling me to connect the notes through to a particular reference which I can then also cut-and-paste into the main document when I am working on the main body of writing. Working within the management discipline, I often use APA as my primary referencing style; it is a style that I am very familiar with now also because the editing work that I have done for several journals using APA-based styles. In some areas and other disciplines, that may be a different style but is immaterial if we can connect the primary note back to the source material.

In my primary notes file, I usually list a sequence of the primary notes under a citation. This enables me to rapidly take and sequence articles on a particular subject, extract key data, generate primary notes, and then have all these primary notes in one location. I can then go through at the end and cut and paste this list of primary notes and reorganize these under particular themes, topics, or methods. Each primary note must be kept with a citation, enabling me to connect the data I am working with back to the source material

these thematic organizations are entirely free-form and, in many cases, will depend on the purpose of the current reading. If we provide a backdrop or a background to a particular research project, then the organization could be chronologically as we outline the major steps in the development in this area. Alternatively, we might focus on geographical analysis outlining some of the challenges and differences between geographies or regions; alternatively, it might be a sectorial grouping providing insight into differences between sectors. It is also common to outline and categorize our thoughts using the theory or framework we are using in the underlying research. Ultimately, there is no right or wrong way, and much of it will depend on the purpose of the writing.

Of course, nothing stops us from creating several files with several different organizational structures. That is, we might generate one that is intended to provide an overview of the development of the literature in the field. Another might provide an overview of some of the key theoretical frameworks used for research in this field.

This is an important point in the writing and critical thinking process. Using succinct summaries of quite a large amount of reading that we have done enables us to make sense of these. We can then begin to piece them together to fit into the study that we are writing up. Doing it this way should enable us to focus on providing a categorization that will make sense and contribute to the development of the study.

Working in a Group to Support Searching and Note-Taking

It may be useful to form a study group if you are a student, particularly as we take useful notes and run searches as used in this chapter. Taking an article or two articles and having everyone in the group read the articles and then create some notes based on this following this process can be useful. Most importantly, come together and then discuss the notes created. Focus on the thinking process that each person verbalizes as they discuss their notes. How are the outcome notes similar or different? How was the thinking process similar or different? While this may sound tedious or without value, the process will quickly give us more insight into how others approach reading and notetaking, and then, with reflection, we can enhance our approach and process by understanding what others are looking for and how others frame or think about the topic.

Have others also provide insight by asking questions about why we took notes. These types of queries can also lead us to reflect on the process. Such constructive commentary can help us to develop our notetaking and reading approach. Using a group format like this can enable us also to uncover other themes as people question query about the notes taken. As we begin to share our notes about a broader range of research that other people in our group have not read, the questions can also uncover new themes or organizational structures that may have otherwise eluded us. They might also be able to provide some insight into other literature outside of the main area that may be relevant to a theme that is emerging as a prominent and important piece of our work. Therefore, sharing notes and ideas with others in our research group will be encouraging and probably quite a fruitful way of developing our research capability.

PURPOSE STATEMENTS

Many students and writers will be familiar with the concept of a thesis statement. The thesis statement is particularly useful for beginning writers as they learn to develop their first persuasive writing pieces. However, a thesis statement sometimes only emerges later in the writing process. As such, I find it useful to have something early on that provides constraints and boundaries for both thinking and writing. For this purpose, I like to use a purpose statement.

For me, a purpose statement is a short (several sentences long) statement that really provides oversight for the research that will be written about. It captures the essence of the research. It should not be vague or talk in general terms but should instead provide insight into the specifics of the writing's purpose.

It needs to be concise. While I often advocate writing an introduction early on to provide a framework and insight into the reading and writing process, a purpose statement can do the same thing, but it should be much shorter than an introduction. I will often have a purpose statement printed and sitting next to me while I write an article, as it helps to keep me on track. It provides an opportunity to discuss our research with others at a conference or others in your department. Keeping a purpose in mind helps keep the rest of the reading focused as we can always ask if this article will help with the purpose.

Your search string and search strategy can also be compared with the purpose statement. The comparison can help you to ensure that you are 'on track' and the search should deliver literature related to the purpose.

The purpose statement should be a living statement. It is necessary for it to become tighter or wander in focus slightly over time. It should not be static and unchanged in a way that creates enduring and firm constraints. Rather, it should be flexible to extend or shift as reading and research continue. This is particularly needed as an early-stage purpose statement might be slightly longer and slightly vague. Over time, as we write and read more, we should begin to tighten it, so the purpose statements become short, succinct, and increasingly compelling and meaningful to readers.

I do not think there is any need for strict guidelines on what should be contained within the purpose statement. However, it is certainly useful to consider including elements of:

- the particular research question or core issue that we are examining and investigating. This can also help us understand whether it is too narrow or more general, allowing us to communicate the research in the wider field.
- The theory world theoretical framework being used. In some areas theory is very important; in other areas, the theory is less important. Methods might be included particularly where there is an interesting or novel methodological use within the research.
- In some cases, there may be a very strong motivation to guide and frame the research when readers finish reading the research dissertation article – they should be left with a primary message. Do we have a couple of main points that we really want to leave the reader thinking about?
- Do you have a strong sense of the main contribution implication for your work? This could raise a point of dispute between the dominant paradigms or show the value of a new type of analysis or data or application of a theoretical framework in the area.

When writing a purpose statement, I enjoy thinking about it in the first person – "I intend to" or "I will show." It makes it much more personally connected to the research and the research process.

When we think about the list of possible issues to include in the purpose statement, it is useful to think about these and write out answers. While doing this, we will generate quite a long overview of the purpose. Indeed, many of these elements might find their way into the introduction. But when the intent is to create a purpose statement, we will need to boil these down into a more concise summary. For this purpose, it is often useful to chat with a friend or small group of colleagues. Outline the research, give a verbal overview, and then provide them with your purpose outline. They can help to discern the most interesting and key elements that should be retained and made more succinct.

It is often useful to conduct this review of purpose statements in a small group setting. Reading and analyzing purpose statements and hearing others discuss their research can often inspire us to uncover the more pertinent elements of our work that others will find interesting. In addition, it is helpful to receive the thoughts and commentary on our writing in our ideas. The purpose is not to be overly critical but instead to provide a space where people can contribute and provide insight and ideas. We should not be trying to rip apart someone else's idea or have them rip apart our idea. Rather, we should focus on collaboratively querying or questioning and helping to guide each other to create the best possible purpose statements.

If we are at an early stage of research, creating several purpose statements might be an interesting way of getting insight and what other people think is interesting or novel about the ideas we are engaging with. For instance, we can quickly iterate multiple purpose statements relating to a particular topic or theory. From these, we can get quick feedback from the advisers and supervisors about which they believe hold the most potential for the research. They can also help to quickly tighten the approach and discover which type of project we will be most comfortable engaging with for the longer term.

Generating multiple purpose statements in this way enables you to quickly develop project ideas which can then be enhanced and improved on. It is similar to the 'fail fast' approach in entrepreneurship, rapidly throwing not fully developed products to the market and seeing which will be more successful and which are forced to fail so that the best possible ideas are quickly identified so they can be further developed and enhanced.

PLAGIARISM AND INTELLECTUAL HONESTY

When undertaking the literature review and making notes, and writing these notes into the manuscript, it is important to be aware of our intellectual contribution relative to the source material that we use. It is also vital that this distinction is made clear to the reader.

Careful work when making notes enables us to provide correct quotations and paraphrasing and provide the reader with full attribution to where the ideas and quotes are coming from. In this way, the author can give credit where credit is due to others. There are many guidelines on plagiarism and avoiding plagiarism. I always strive to explicitly and thoroughly acknowledge where ideas or data are coming from so that I can always provide insight into what I have used and what debt I owe to other scholars and from this, where my contribution lies.

It is also important to note that many journals, publishers, and universities now require evidence that there is no overlap in content. This takes the form of a very blunt assessment using a similarity checking tool that assesses whether not there is a similarity in the words and text used in the submitted manuscript against those elsewhere on the web or in publishers' databases. Therefore, it becomes increasingly necessary to ensure that manuscripts have been carefully written with correct attributions being made direct quotations properly noted.

Working in the way described in this chapter and elsewhere in this volume should enable us to avoid issues. The key element is taking research articles, paraphrasing, summarizing in your notes, and always capturing quotations and the source to be correctly used when writing up and transforming our notes into finished writing. If some reason, we have forgotten where a particular quote came from because we failed (or were too rushed) to record the source information, we should not use this quote if we cannot identify the source.

Quotations and Paraphrasing

Many students make far too much use of quotations in their work. Quotations should be used judiciously following the suggestions I provide to my students. It is very important always to cut and paste the quotation into the software when collecting quotations. Always ensure that we have the page number noted for the quotation. Using the APA style, which I commonly use, the quotation requires the page number. It is easier to collect this and have it available once rather than flip back through a book later to identify where the quote came from.

New students will often use many quotations in their writing. However, this is disruptive to the reader as it interrupts the flow of the work. The writer should paraphrase the source material and simply provide an in-text citation in most cases. Paraphrasing makes for shorter documents and a more consistent and less disruptive style while acknowledging the contribution of the source.

When determining if a quotation should be included in the manuscript, it is useful to assess whether or not including it will add value beyond what we gain by paraphrasing the source. For example, I tend to use quotations where:

- the quote is a core definition
- the wording is interesting, catches attention, or eloquent
- the author is more authoritative and speaks with this authority

- when providing the source and direct quotation lends gravitas because of the quote source being internationally recognized as an expert or a leading organization

It is also useful to remember that providing a large quote of an entire section is not necessary. You can provide a larger quote and then remove part of the less interesting quote relevant to the current topic. Working in this way, key ideas can be captured with a simple citation of the quote.

When paraphrasing, it is important we summarize with a clear head. The words we capture and provide as our own must not reflect the style and the terminology used in the source material. If we have the original source material open next to us while trying to paraphrase, it is very difficult even for experienced writers not to glance at their source, and for this glance to then flavor would change their interpretation. In a very extreme case, an attempt at paraphrasing with the source material immediately available may lead to an outcome where the sentence structures and arguments are very similar to the source material, with some words simply swapped out for synonyms.

SHIFTING FROM READING AND NOTES TO WRITING

While the chapter is about searching, this is a brief section on writing. The notes are important when searching and compiling literature, and our notes and writing make sense of the reading we are doing. Therefore, writing while reading and searching helps sharpen the ideas and tighten the analysis of the study phenomenon. However, we present a more comprehensive overview of writing the entire manuscript, whether it is a dissertation, thesis, or journal article, within chapter 13, with complete coverage of the structure.

The Skeleton Document

When we consider that we have already taken many notes and we have gained a clear idea of the main purpose and statement of what we want to achieve, we still need several steps to complete a written project or literature review. When we are creating the literature review, we could still consider that we need a framework or structure that we can add to so we can complete a finished piece of writing. In this way, I still like to have an intermediary step for a 'skeleton document.' The approach can be used in the literature review or much larger documents.

Working with a group of peers is often useful for reviewing the purpose statement and asking questions about the topic or project. If they can ask useful questions about the background reading, the background of the methodology, or the background of the theory, this can provide insight and material that we will need to cover within the literature review. The approach can capture the key ideas as statements about what we will need to convince some of or communicate with them. Next, we can use these ideas from the statements and list some quick bullet points underneath. We can then turn back to primary notes and begin including some primary notes under each section where the notes are connected to what has been suggested is needed. As we do this, we get a list that looks a little bit jumbled and perhaps disjointed. However, each of the statements we want to convince the reader about is connected to and contains notes. We can then reorganize and recompile this list to make more sense; it is often useful to have a friend or colleague look at this as we go through this process.

At the end of the process, we should have a list of what we want to convince the reader of and the supporting primary notes. This creates a concise overview of the material that must be covered in the literature review along with some of those key sources.

Building out from the Skeleton

We can begin to move from the skeleton to a more complete draft. Every section of the writing should happen with intent and purpose. Capturing these key questions is important during this process.

Working with a group is useful if your peers can provide you with some insight into what they need to be convinced of as you make an argument in your literature review. For instance, what are some of the core questions they might ask and what do you need to convince them about or what evidence do you need to provide to them? What are the other issues that they must be convinced about?

As we begin to gather these issues, we can begin to frame them as questions that need to be answered. Then, as we consider the answers to these questions, it can guide the writing so that the writing will immediately and more naturally become more persuasive to the reader. When we write to address what our audience wants to know, it helps capture the key ideas in our writing and reading.

Each question that needs to be answered will probably form a paragraph (at least initially). We should write freely and not worry too much about evidence, primary notes, or citations at this point, as we can always come back later and add primary notes to provide evidence later.

Using Primary Notes

Is at this point that the primary notes once more become valuable. As we have the free-form writing about answering and addressing each of these colleagues' questions, we can now return to the primary notes file. I like to print these off and then go through them with my skeleton in front of me. It allows me to highlight the primary notes quickly I think will be valuable and need to be inserted into the skeleton. There should be some overlap in the structure or the theme of the primary notes and the skeleton.

As we go through this process, we should be able to see:

- Sections of your skeleton which are going to be well supported with primary notes
- Lonely sections, with few primary notes, indicate topics we will need to return to while reading sources, read more, and write more primary notes. Alternatively, we may need to create a new theme in the primary notes.

Next, I begin to use primary notes in writing.

I can now open the skeleton file and insert some of the primary notes under the sections of interest. At this time, I find it useful to simply cut-and-paste them into the relevant sections without worrying about the integration so much. This is important as it reduces the level of critical self-reflection required. But it does have the benefit of bringing citations into the literature review. At this point, it will be citations and your own thoughts and argumentation in the skeleton document.

The next step should be relatively simple at this point. I review each question and see my own thoughts on how to address it and relevant citations included in the skeleton. I begin to write out the paragraph integrating relevant material from the primary notes my thoughts on addressing the question with citations already included. Every question will have several paragraphs under it, perhaps as an answer statement that directly addresses it. The question can then be replaced with a subheading relevant to that particular issue. For example, the question might involve a question about the background, such as "what are the theoretical frameworks used to address the topic?" The answer could be several paragraphs underneath explaining the early stages of research, shifting to the more recent work, and expanding the theoretical frameworks used. I include supporting citations using my primary notes; my thinking is derived from and extends the primary notes.

Reviewing your Literature Review with a Critical Friend

At this point, it is useful to get some rapid feedback from a friend and a colleague about the literature review. We will have some core questions that need to be answered in the writing. It is useful to provide a friend and colleague with the actual writing sproduced with paragraphs structured under headings indicating the issue addressed. Make sure that you select a friend who is comfortable being critical and providing meaningful feedback, even if it is not always comfortable to hear. We need someone who we can trust to say something more meaningful than "gosh, that was good!"

Get them to use post-it notes on printed copies of the document to capture their core ideas. Have them post their thoughts on the main purpose for each section using Post-it notes, have them add any questions on the Post-it notes that they have about the content or what is not clear or what needs further elaboration.

When we come together to discuss the writing, it is useful to have the Post-it notes to discuss the purpose and outline what we were trying to convey in that section. This enables us to quickly converge on areas of misunderstanding where we may have assumed prior knowledge that the reader does not have, for example.

Using this feedback from the colleagues enables us to go back to the literature review and craft the paragraph we are trying to write to address the issues or gaps that the friend suggests are important. As we do this, we are writing to serve the readers' needs.

SUMMARY

This chapter covers quite a bit aground and has included making rapid and fast searches of the literature and making sense of what we have read using notes. That then helps to provide a framework for taking these notes and writing a literature review.

When researching the literature, I am a big believer in doing a small series of rapid and frequent searches to ensure that I capture the most relevant material. This does not take the place of a full systematic literature review in all cases, but it certainly enables me to get to grips with some of the primary research that I know I will be reading.

Using primary notes lets us capture the essence and value of each article. Creating primary notes while reading is helpful in the scholarship process; primary notes help us engage more deeply with what we are reading with intent and purpose. They support our writing and scholarship. The primary notes bridge the gap between reading and writing by capturing our thoughts in written format. They can also help identify where we are missing reading, notes, or ideas about key issues in writing.

Using the primary notes to create and add to the skeleton of the work helps to take us from easily written notes to more substantive paragraphs and create a flow and logic to support our readers. I like to use primary notes in this way because it enables me to very quickly use my core database based on my reading to begin addressing key issues and challenges that my readers have about my arguments. I find it easier to take notes first and then cluster them and form them into a coherent piece of writing. For me, this is quite a fast and effective method of going from reading through to writing. I find it easier than other approaches, such as writing a paragraph slowly with a dozen articles next to me and carefully hunting for and then typing in citations as they become relevant.

REFERENCES

Bilgili, H., Tochman Campbell, J., Ellstrand, A. E., & Johnson, J. L. (2017). Riding off into the sunset: Organizational sensegiving, shareholder sensemaking, and reactions to CEO retirement. *Journal of Management Studies, 54*(7), 1019–1049. doi:10.1111/joms.12264

Colquitt, J. A., LePine, J. A., Zapata, C. P., & Wild, R. E. (2011). Trust in Typical and High-Reliability Contexts: Building and Reacting to Trust among Firefighters. *Academy of Management Journal, 54*(5), 999–1015. doi:10.5465/amj.2006.0241

Duan, C., Grover, V., Roberts, N., & Balakrishnan, N. (2014). Firm valuation effects of the decision to adopt relationally governed business process outsourcing arrangements. *International Journal of Production Research, 52*(15), 4673–4694. doi:10.1080/00207543.2014.884289

EBSCO Connect. (n.d.). *What is bibliographic management software?* Retrieved February 2, 2022, from https://connect.ebsco.com/s/article/What-is-Bibliographic-Management-Software?language=en_US

Flaxman, S., Goel, S., & Rao, J. M. (2016). Filter bubbles, echo chambers, and online news consumption. *Public Opinion Quarterly, 80*(S1), 298–320. doi:10.1093/poq/nfw006

Greenhalgh, T., Thorne, S., & Malterud, K. (2018). Time to challenge the spurious hierarchy of systematic over narrative reviews? *European Journal of Clinical Investigation, 48*(6), e12931. doi:10.1111/eci.12931 PMID:29578574

Hariri, N. (2011). Relevance ranking on Google: Are top ranked results really considered more relevant by the users? *Online Information Review, 35*(4), 598–610. doi:10.1108/14684521111161954

Hendricks, K. B., Hora, M., & Singhal, V. R. (2014). An empirical investigation on the appointments of supply chain and operations management executives. *Management Science, 61*(7), 1562–1583. doi:10.1287/mnsc.2014.1987

Hosanagar, K. (2016, November 25). Blame the echo chamber on Facebook. But blame yourself, too. *Wired.* https://www.wired.com/2016/11/facebook-echo-chamber/

Jennings, W., Stoker, G., Bunting, H., Valgarðsson, V. O., Gaskell, J., Devine, D., McKay, L., & Mills, M. C. (2021). Lack of trust, conspiracy beliefs, and social media use predict COVID-19 vaccine hesitancy. *Vaccines, 9*(6), 593. doi:10.3390/vaccines9060593 PMID:34204971

Koushan, M., Wood, L. C., & Greatbanks, R. (2021). Evaluating factors associated with the cancellation and delay of elective surgical procedures: A systematic review. *International Journal for Quality in Health Care, 33*(2), mzab092. doi:10.1093/intqhc/mzab092

Lo, C. K. Y., Pagell, M., Fan, D., Wiengarten, F., & Yeung, A. C. L. (2014). OHSAS 18001 certification and operating performance: The role of complexity and coupling. *Journal of Operations Management*, *32*(5), 268–280. doi:10.1016/j.jom.2014.04.004

Page, M. J., McKenzie, J. E., Bossuyt, P. M., Boutron, I., Hoffmann, T. C., Mulrow, C. D., Shamseer, L., Tetzlaff, J. M., Akl, E. A., Brennan, S. E., Chou, R., Glanville, J., Grimshaw, J. M., Hróbjartsson, A., Lalu, M. M., Li, T., Loder, E. W., Mayo-Wilson, E., McDonald, S., ... Moher, D. (2021). The PRISMA 2020 statement: An updated guideline for reporting systematic reviews. *Systematic Reviews*, *10*(1), 89. doi:10.118613643-021-01626-4 PMID:33781348

Puri, N., Coomes, E. A., Haghbayan, H., & Gunaratne, K. (2020). Social media and vaccine hesitancy: New updates for the era of COVID-19 and globalized infectious diseases. *Human Vaccines & Immunotherapeutics*, *16*(11), 2586–2593. doi:10.1080/21645515.2020.1780846 PMID:32693678

Scopus. (n.d.). *Scopus search guide*. http://schema.elsevier.com/dtds/document/bkapi/search/SCOPUSSearchTips.htm

Simsek, Z., Fox, B., & Heavey, C. (2021). Systematicity in organizational research literature reviews: A framework and assessment. *Organizational Research Methods*. Advance online publication. doi:10.1177/10944281211008652

Tranfield, D., Denyer, D., & Smart, P. (2003). Towards a methodology for developing evidence-informed management knowledge by means of systematic review. *British Journal of Management*, *14*(3), 207–222. doi:10.1111/1467-8551.00375

Williamson, O. E. (1975). *Markets and hierarchies, analysis and antitrust implications: A study in the economics of internal organization*. Free Press.

Williamson, O. E. (1981). The modern corporation: Origins, evolution, attributes. *Journal of Economic Literature*, *19*(4), 1537–1568.

Williamson, O. E. (2008). Outsourcing: Transaction cost economics and supply chain management. *The Journal of Supply Chain Management*, *44*(2), 5–16. doi:10.1111/j.1745-493X.2008.00051.x

Wolf, F. G. (2001). Operationalizing and Testing Normal Accident Theory in Petrochemical Plants and Refineries. *Production and Operations Management*, *10*(3), 292–305. doi:10.1111/j.1937-5956.2001.tb00376.x

ADDITIONAL READING

Aguinis, H., Ramani, R. S., & Alabduljader, N. (2020). Best-practice recommendations for producers, evaluators, and users of methodological literature reviews. *Organizational Research Methods*. Advance online publication. doi:10.1177/1094428120943281

Akter, S., & Wamba, S. F. (2019). Big data and disaster management: A systematic review and agenda for future research. *Annals of Operations Research*, *283*(1), 939–959. doi:10.100710479-017-2584-2

Anderson, M. H., & Lemken, R. K. (2020). Citation context analysis as a method for conducting rigorous and impactful literature reviews. *Organizational Research Methods*. Advance online publication. doi:10.1177/1094428120969905

Antons, D., Breidbach, C. F., Joshi, A. M., & Salge, T. O. (2021). Computational literature reviews: Method, algorithms, and roadmap. *Organizational Research Methods*. Advance online publication. doi:10.1177/1094428121991230

Araújo, A. G., Pereira Carneiro, A. M., & Palha, R. P. (2020). Sustainable construction management: A systematic review of the literature with meta-analysis. *Journal of Cleaner Production, 256*, 120350. doi:10.1016/j.jclepro.2020.120350

Breslin, D., & Gatrell, C. (2020). Theorizing through literature reviews: The miner-prospector continuum. *Organizational Research Methods*. Advance online publication. doi:10.1177/1094428120943288

Carter, C. R., & Easton, P. L. (2011). Sustainable supply chain management: Evolution and future directions. *International Journal of Physical Distribution & Logistics Management, 41*(1), 46–62. doi:10.1108/09600031111101420

Cronin, M. A., & George, E. (2020). The why and how of the integrative review. *Organizational Research Methods*. Advance online publication. doi:10.1177/1094428120935507

Gond, J.-P., Mena, S., & Mosonyi, S. (2020). The performativity of literature reviewing: Constituting the corporate social responsibility literature through re-presentation and intervention. *Organizational Research Methods*. Advance online publication. doi:10.1177/1094428120935494

Hiebl, M. R. W. (2021). Sample selection in systematic literature reviews of management research. *Organizational Research Methods*. Advance online publication. doi:10.1177/1094428120986851

Nill, A., & Schibrowsky, J. A. (2007). Research on marketing ethics: A systematic review of the literature. *Journal of Macromarketing, 27*(3), 256–273. doi:10.1177/0276146707304733

Sharma, G., & Bansal, P. (2020). Partnering up: Including managers as research partners in systematic reviews. *Organizational Research Methods*. Advance online publication. doi:10.1177/1094428120965706

Soheilirad, S., Govindan, K., Mardani, A., Zavadskas, E. K., Nilashi, M., & Zakuan, N. (2018). Application of data envelopment analysis models in supply chain management: A systematic review and meta-analysis. *Annals of Operations Research, 271*(2), 915–969. doi: http://dx.doi.org.ezproxy.otago.ac.nz/10.1007/s10479-017-2605-1

Thomas, J., & Harden, A. (2008). Methods for the thematic synthesis of qualitative research in systematic reviews. *BMC Medical Research Methodology, 8*(1), 45. doi:10.1186/1471-2288-8-45 PMID:18616818

KEY TERMS AND DEFINITIONS

Academic Research Database: A curated and organized collection of scholarly works. They often enable structured searches and may enable you to select only articles that have been peer reviewed.

Hypothesis: A key idea that will be stated that the research will prove. It may start at the point of the literature, which provides some evidence for the relationship that your research will add more evidence to.

Primary Notes: A means of capturing the core ideas about what you read. They create a key piece of information and a bridge between your reading and the writing you do.

Purpose Statement: A statement of the purpose of the piece of writing. This can help you to connect your reading and writing to ensure they match your purpose.

Quick and Dirty Search: A rapid search that involves seeking articles with key words in the title and abstract. It likely generates a shorter list of articles, most of which will be relevant. It runs the risk of excluding important articles or those from other research streams (where, for instance, they may use different terminology for the same topic).

Skeleton Document: A basic collection of core ideas and questions about the writing that the document should answer. This gives you the starting point to bring together a collection of primary notes. A skeleton document should address your purpose statement.

Wild Card: A symbol in a search that takes the place of one or more characters, enabling you to search for a range of related search terms quickly and easily.

Chapter 7
Research Design Considerations

ABSTRACT

The focus of this chapter is the research design and considerations in design that may become apparent part-way through the project. The chapter is positioned at this point in the book as most projects are not perfectly devised at the commencement and then executed with no required changes throughout the project. Instead, there is some messiness early in a project, as research designs are refined and shifted a little as the reality becomes apparent during the project duration. Therefore, this chapter is positioned near the middle of the volume to consider the earlier chapters and discussions and consequences of design decisions. It supports the reader in making decisions that may need to be adjusted or flexed during the project. These considerations include creating the sample, managing outliers, working with a short event window, and managing confounding events.

INTRODUCTION

No research design survives contact with reality. While we might make a few critical design decisions early in the project, they may also come later. After the project has been going for a while, it is often helpful to reflect on the early design decisions made for the project and those made for later stages and then decide whether these are still appropriate design decisions. Consequently, it is helpful to reflect on what had previously been decided and reconsider what still needs to be done in the context of the reality given how the is project shaping up.

This chapter aims to provide a reflection point and encourage you to forgive yourself if you experience a non-linear project where there is some messiness and some readjustment of the design to accommodate and incorporate the reality. While we may consider registered reports as a counterpoint, these are usually prepared at the end of an initial project design phase that establishes substantial groundwork. In most cases, some early engagement with the field or the data often requires change. In many cases, preliminary pilot studies can reveal insight that changes us or forces us to reconsider our key ideas or beliefs upon making the design decisions. Therefore, an early pilot or early search can often provide insight that helps us shape the final form of the study design before we launch into the main data collection and analysis process. Ultimately, we do not know what we do not know until we have had some exposure. Therefore,

DOI: 10.4018/978-1-7998-8969-4.ch007

it is often hard for us to conceptualize and understand the reality of the circumstances we are studying in management and supply chain research until we have engaged meaningfully with the data and project.

BACKGROUND

It is necessary to contemplate the decisions that are made during the project design phase. Every time we make a decision in response to changing circumstances, it is necessary to document what occurred and why. Every design decision will have consequences, and these consequences often create limitations on our research and provide opportunities for further research.

While many assumptions will need to be met when using a range of analytical tools, there are other general design decisions that researchers must carefully consider. These design issues would significantly influence the overall reliability and quality of the outcomes. We consider some of these factors in separate chapters, but below, I summarize some of the key considerations, such as sampling, sample sizes, how outliers are treated, and the impact of the event window and confounding events.

In this way, this chapter can serve as a valuable foundation for reading prior to the study design and execution. The other chapters, in particular chapter 10, are helpful during the study execution when problems have been identified. While there is some overlap, chapter 10 discusses potential solutions or mechanisms that might be useful in overcoming some problems after we identified them.

In principle, a project will always be smoother if we do not need to go back, do rework, and address errors or mistakes. One of the critical intentions of this chapter is to raise awareness of some of the core issues you need to be thinking about early in the project planning stage and the project execution. Even if you have read this chapter early in the project planning phase, and then you realize later that you have a problem, you can come back and check what you are doing and why and assess whether there are any alternatives or options.

GENERATING THE SAMPLE

We must work carefully to generate the sample, as the sample must capture the announcements of interest. Ensuring we have the announcements of interest is particularly important when searching for news sources and press releases. There are a couple of essential elements here.

First, the set of keywords used must be carefully enhanced and expanded so that it is going to capture all the different permutations and examples of the abstract phenomenon of interest. That is, we should take care to work with colleagues, friends, and managers to ensure that there is a range of different descriptions of the phenomenon so that we can capture all the examples and different forms in the announcements we find. Getting multiple perspectives is essential, and relying on managers as part of the team is vital because of the different terminology used concerning different parts of the business or different management areas. For example, an initiative to reduce capacity could relate to plant closures or the retrenchment of staffing levels.

Second, it is vital to ensure that you access the correct range of publications and news sources. The ideal would be a comprehensive database, such as Factiva. However, even if we have access to the right database, selecting appropriate news sources that will capture articles about your phenomena of interest and address issues big enough to lead to a stock market reaction.

Third, it is necessary to manually go through a list of (perhaps!) thousands of announcements and weed out relevant announcements. This requires an element of judgment, and it may be suitable to have multiple people look at announcements that are not immediately clear whether we should include them in the sample. As such, two or more people discussing a specific announcement should agree on whether we will include it within the sample. The process also limits the use of two people examining the announcement, as these are most likely to be borderline. It is possible to use industry-specific searches in some databases, which may provide a more manageable list of possible announcements for inclusion (Wood et al., 2022).

Given that the search can turn up many thousands of articles, the sample creation step can take a considerable amount of time. However, it is crucial to get this right. If we have missed important announcements from the sample, that can influence the overall project outcomes. On the other hand, if we include many less relevant announcements that did not belong in the sample, we may reduce or water down the stock market reaction to the event of interest, and the study finding may be of a weak reaction or no evidence of a reaction to the event.

It is helpful to spend some time reporting on the process to generate the sample, emphasizing the type of keywords and the type of search strategy employed. In addition, most articles provide some insight into the number of articles initially found versus those eliminated during different screening levels to generate the event sample.

An example is provided by Wood et al. (2018) that provides insight into the difficulties and time spent on the event sample. They note that over 17,000 articles were identified while compiling the sample, with a total of 53 distinct events recorded. Many subsequent events were interesting, but these "subsequent developments relating to the main event were recorded as subevents, as often the ramifications and coverage" (Wood et al., 2018, p. 371) of these news items extended the main event, and so they were not included in the final analysis.

Useful specifics are provided by Jacobs et al. (2010) for the keywords they use and the sources. These are listed comprehensively in Table 1 (Jacobs et al., 2010, p. 433), and comprise 15 terms for environmental outcomes (e.g., conservation, ecosystem, environment, and recycle) and 134 words for success or positive outcomes (e.g., breakthroughs, certified, innovate, and reputation). The "Near7" operator ensures that words from each of these sets are within seven words of each other, making the identified items likely to discuss a breakthrough in environmental performance.

EVALUATING AND MANAGING OUTLIERS

Many tests statistics used in invent studies will be very sensitive to statistical outliers, particularly influential ones. The issue is particularly problematic when estimating abnormal returns based on OLS regressions (particularly common in event studies) as the regression is extremely sensitive to outliers (McWilliams & Siegel, 1997). In addition, many events studies in specific disciplines, such as management or supply chain management, may include a relatively small sample size. Smaller sample sizes mean that the sample will be even more sensitive to the presence of single observations that might be rather significant. Therefore, when an event study uses a small sample size, additional care must be taken to interpret the test statistics of abnormal returns. The research team must carefully judge and evaluate whether a positive finding is driven by a few influential observations or actual underlying effect sizes. Researchers should show that they have addressed this issue and provide insight into how they have addressed it and the manuscript. Reporting on the issue is becoming increasingly important in leading journals.

A very pragmatic approach is to use a nonparametric test statistic, as this is a straightforward approach. Nonparametric test statistics will be less sensitive to the presence of outlines. Most commonly used will be the Corrado Rank Test (Ataullah et al., 2011; Corrado, 1989; Corrado & Zivney, 1992) or the Sign Test (Cowan, 1992). Many studies will often report both parametric and nonparametric test statistics for this reason. A reader might generally consider the nonparametric test statistics more valuable given the smaller sample sizes and the often non-normal distributions.

I have also found it helpful to go through the abnormal returns against each observation by ranking them from highest to lowest. It is helpful to assess and get a feel for the overall magnitude. Any observations that seem substantially out of alignment with the others indicate that it is worth going back and ensuring no confounding events, as these might sway the calculated abnormal returns. Please note that I am not suggesting that the sample be adjusted to present a better outcome, but rather pragmatically double-checking to ensure no influential observations may have been created by not accounting for confounding events.

ESTABLISHING A SHORT EVENT WINDOW

The size of the event window used in the study is a key research design consideration that often receives minimal discussion in published manuscripts. However, it is often the case that there is little consistency in the length of the windows reported in different publications, even within a single discipline or a journal. Historically, management research used fairly long windows (McWilliams & Siegel, 1997). Nevertheless, the trend has shifted towards using shorter event windows in recent years, with most research now using one-, two-, or three-day windows to be consistent with the market efficiency hypothesis (Fama, 1970, 1991; Malkiel, 2003; Stiglitz & Grossman, 1980).

When we consider the importance of market efficiency, it implies that there will be an almost constant adjustment and the stock returns in reaction to the news. This constant change is because investors and institutions react and respond to the news; they make rapid assessments and evaluations of the implications for the business. Conceptually, this suggests that a single-day event window would be ideal, and in many cases, it may be practical. However, using short windows is generally justified and practical given the significant research demonstrating how stock returns rapidly adjust to the impact of the news. For instance, early research showed an impact within 15 minutes of a news release (Dann et al., 1977). Furthermore, stock prices have been shown to react within 90 minutes of a news story relating to an industry or market, even if the news item does not name a specific firm (Mitchell & Netter, 1989). This fast reaction is not just true for the U.S. markets, as stock returns also adjust within 30 minutes to ad hoc news announcements in Germany (Muntermann & Guettler, 2007).

Long windows create many problems. For example, an essential issue that a long window will create is more opportunity for other confounding events to occur. Furthermore, from a practical perspective, a long window would mean that the search for confounding events substantially reduces the sample size, as potential confounding events will influence and affect many more observations.

There are also situations where a longer event window might be necessary, such as when information leakage is possible. Such a situation was cited by Kumar et al. (2015) hand was used as a justification for using a longer event window in the study. However, even under these circumstances, the window should not be extended beyond several days in total. It should only be a couple of days before the announcement so that the study captures returns influenced by the information leakage.

Another situation exists when it is difficult to assess a news release's time to connect the news to how it will influence stock prices. For example, it may be difficult to tell whether it was released at 10:00 or 21:00 in New York. If the news was released after the close of the trading day, then the reaction would occur during the next trading day; consequently, it may be pragmatic to extend the event window to one day after the event day to capture these effects. As much as possible, we should minimize these issues.

Another option is to shift towards intraday event windows that are minutes long rather than days long. Using an intraday event window may be possible for studies that focus on stock returns but may be less useful for other events studies, such as those using volumes as they are less well-specified (Marshall et al., 2017). The results from Marshall et al. suggest that both mean and market-adjusted models cannot be used with intraday data and provide well-specified results.

Given these circumstances, there is almost no case where a longer event window of four or more days should be used. If we cannot find an effect size and determine an abnormal return within the short event window, then there may be other problems or no discernible stock market reaction to the event. One option may be to go back to the event list and identify whether the earliest possible release of the news has been identified and included. That is, was there an earlier date when the relevant news was released to market participants that provoked a response from an earlier point in time?

EFFECTIVELY MANAGING CONFOUNDING EVENTS

One of the most crucial design considerations is managing the compounding events. If we recall, we want to attribute the abnormal returns in the study to the event and the phenomenon we are studying. To do this, we need to ensure that no other event coincides with our observed event, which might influence those abnormal returns. What are confounding events? There is a range, but:

Confounding events might include capital events (stock splits and structural changes), damage suits, dividends, executive changes (Cannella and Hambrick, 1993), joint venture announcements (McConnell and Nantell, 1985), merger and acquisition activities (Morck and Yeung, 1992), and earnings announcements (Brown and Warner, 1985). Such types of events may influence the market price in conjunction with particular information systems announcement of concern. (Konchitchki & O'Leary, 2011, p. 107)

A range of studies, syntheses, and reviews have shown that many event studies do not report this very important topic (Bouzzine, 2021; McWilliams et al., 1999; McWilliams & Siegel, 1997; Wood & Wang, 2018).

Using a small event window makes identifying confounding events much more straightforward. This short event window of only one or two days is less likely to contain any other event that might influence stock returns. Longer event windows, as had been commonly used in past studies, inherently mean that there is much more opportunity for a confounding event to be present during that window. A consequence of a multi-day window is that if we rigorously identified compounding events over this wider window, we would end up eliminating and removing many of the observations from the sample. Removing many observations would leave a substantially smaller sample in the study.

There is some disagreement about what constitutes a confounding event and which should be removed. Fundamentally, the analysis would include announcements from the EDGAR database over the same event window that was used for the event study. The EDGAR database is vital as "[a]ll companies, foreign and domestic, are required to file registration statements, periodic reports, and other forms electronically through EDGAR" (U.S. Securities and Exchange Commission, 2022). If we find any confounding events reported in the EDGAR database, it should be noted against the sample so that the observation question can be removed and dropped from the following study. I find it helpful not to delete the observation, but simply to mark on the spreadsheet that the confounding event has affected it. By keeping it on the spreadsheet, I can more easily and rapidly report data on the total number of observations in the sample before the compounding event check versus those after.

When writing up the study, it is helpful to state the window over which the compounding events were checked, against which category of events (such as the EDGAR database), and how many observations we eliminated during the step. In a thesis or dissertation, we may provide extensive details for all the checks and the outcomes; given space constraints in journals, we can report this in a sentence or two. For instance, we could report: "[t]o identify any confounding events, we screened for regulatory or financial announcements during the event window using the EDGAR database; X observations were identified as having confounding events and were removed from the sample." The methods and importance of screening for events are presented in Konchitchki and O'Leary (2011). In an analysis of press releases (official communications) from the company, Sorescu et al. (2017) identified that in a 3-day window (the day of the announcement and one day on either side), approximately 11% of cases had confounding events identified. However, in their analysis, they note that:

This analysis indicates that eliminating confounded observations may be unnecessary for short-term event studies. Particularly in light of the relatively low power of the significance tests for abnormal returns, further reducing a small sample may fail to detect abnormal performance in the case of events that do, in fact, significantly contribute to firm value. Moreover, removing confounded observations becomes increasingly taxing if researchers were to expand the set of what they consider to be contaminating information to any other public mentions of the firm made during the event window. Doing so would essentially eliminate all large firms from the sample; alternatively, biases are also introduced if researchers pick and choose the type of information deemed to be significant enough to qualify as confounding the context of each particular event. (Sorescu et al., 2017, p. pp. 192–193)

A simple option is to use only the EDGAR database as major announcements will affect stock returns. There is, therefore, no ambiguity about whether this may be a confounding event. However, if we search Factiva, there will be a range of different announcements that we may consider as relevant. It then becomes a judgment call whether a particular announcement might be a confounding event, but this is a valuable second step in identifying confounding events, bearing in mind that there is evidence that it is not particularly valuable, may introduce biases, and is taxing (Sorescu et al., 2017, p. pp. 192–193). In Wood et al. (2017, p. 249), we followed the two-step approach (EDGAR database and Factiva search) outlined by Konchitchki and O'Leary (2011); we ended up removing 18 cases and continued the analysis with a sample of 135 observations.

META-EVENTS AS OTHER IMPORTANT EVENTS IN THE MARKET

Many event study projects will collect data over an extended time that could span several years through to several decades. Over a more extended period, there will be many more instances of more significant, exogenous events that are a category of meta-events. These will be independent of the particular companies being studied, but the occurrence of a meta-event would substantially affect the stock market reactions at any given time. For example, in Information Systems studies, the Y2K issue might have affected companies in the late 1990s and therefore generated substantially different stock return results for this period than in 2015 to 2020. The Kyoto protocols could also result in substantially different sustainability initiative outcomes before and after signing the accords in sustainability research. The longer the time, the more likely there are to be meta-events that we should consider. As such, there may be discernible differences in stock market reactions over different periods.

If you can collect data over a shorter period, for example, a decade, this is one way of addressing some of these issues. However, if you need to collect data over an extended time, you may not escape from the presence of meta-events. If you need to accommodate them, we can build them into the analysis with tests to show that the results are robust or comparable over different periods or under different conditions. For example, Filbeck et al. (2016, p. 414) discovered that "[t]he stock market impact from disruptions in automobile companies is affected by market cycle [and there is a] negative stock effect of disruptions occurs in bear markets but not in bull markets."

Another example of a meta-event is one relating to downsizing and layoffs, studied by Scott et al. (2011), where regulatory changes would potentially have made a substantial impact if they had not been considered. They note that:

Events from the years 1990 to 1992, inclusive, were used to develop a sample. This period is clearly past the enactment of the Worker Adjustment and Retraining Notification (WARN) Act of 1988, which was part of the time period studied by Iqbal and Shetty (1995). The WARN Act of 1988 requires companies to provide a 60-day advance notice of plant closings and layoffs. (Scott et al., 2011, p. 2)

There is no magic to identifying these meta-events, and your scholarship and research in the discipline you are working within should make you aware and sensitive to some of these meta-events. Regulatory changes may also influence the particular topic of interest, as noted by Scott et al. (2011), and we may identify this through discussions with business professionals or faculty. From this, we can say that it is good practice to discuss the study with some other colleagues and get their perspective on whether there are any other categories of meta-events that we should know about to build this into an analysis.

SUMMARY

I do not mean this chapter to present a formal checklist or an exhaustive list of all the required issues and considerations. However, it should present an overview of some of the major drawbacks and nuances that you should know when you wish to undertake an event study that can be published in a good journal and generate reliable results.

Working through the chapter, we should understand the design issue and the ramifications of what happens when a critical design issue is ignored. Consequently, we may also become more discerning reviewers of journal articles in the future or users of articles, as we will be better able to assess the articles' design.

While none of these design issues is technically complex, addressing them in an article, dissertation, or thesis is necessary. There may be a short section that notes how these have been addressed with a note as short as one or two sentences regarding a key or seminal article about the issue. Alternatively, there may be a more comprehensive section in the body of a dissertation or thesis or including an appropriate appendix.

REFERENCES

Ataullah, A., Song, X., & Tippett, M. (2011). A modified Corrado test for assessing abnormal security returns. *European Journal of Finance*, *17*(7), 589–601. doi:10.1080/1351847X.2011.554294

Bouzzine, Y. D. (2021). Stock price reactions to environmental pollution events: A systematic literature review of direct and indirect effects and a research agenda. *Journal of Cleaner Production*, *316*, 128305. doi:10.1016/j.jclepro.2021.128305

Corrado, C. J. (1989). A nonparametric test for abnormal security-price performance in event studies. *Journal of Financial Economics*, *23*(2), 385–395. doi:10.1016/0304-405X(89)90064-0

Corrado, C. J., & Zivney, T. L. (1992). The specification and power of the sign test in event study hypothesis tests using daily stock returns. *Journal of Financial and Quantitative Analysis*, *27*(3), 465–478. doi:10.2307/2331331

Cowan, A. R. (1992). Nonparametric event study tests. *Review of Quantitative Finance and Accounting*, *2*(4), 343–358. doi:10.1007/BF00939016

Dann, L. Y., Mayers, D., & Raab, R. J. Jr. (1977). Trading rules, large blocks and the speed of price adjustment. *Journal of Financial Economics*, *4*(1), 3–22. doi:10.1016/0304-405X(77)90034-4

Fama, E. F. (1970). Efficient capital markets: A review of theory and empirical work. *The Journal of Finance*, *25*(2), 383–417. doi:10.2307/2325486

Fama, E. F. (1991). Efficient capital markets: II. *The Journal of Finance*, *46*(5), 1575–1617. doi:10.1111/j.1540-6261.1991.tb04636.x

Filbeck, G., Kumar, S., Liu, J., & Zhao, X. (2016). Supply chain finance and financial contagion from disruptions: Evidence from the automobile industry. *International Journal of Physical Distribution & Logistics Management*, *46*(4), 414–438. doi:10.1108/IJPDLM-04-2014-0082

Jacobs, B. W., Singhal, V. R., & Subramanian, R. (2010). An empirical investigation of environmental performance and the market value of the firm. *Journal of Operations Management*, *28*(5), 430–441. doi:10.1016/j.jom.2010.01.001

Konchitchki, Y., & O'Leary, D. E. (2011). Event study methodologies in information systems research. *International Journal of Accounting Information Systems*, *12*(2), 99–115. doi:10.1016/j.accinf.2011.01.002

Kumar, S., Liu, J., & Scutella, J. (2015). The impact of supply chain disruptions on stockholder wealth in India. *International Journal of Physical Distribution & Logistics Management, 45*(9/10), 938–958. doi:10.1108/IJPDLM-09-2013-0247

Malkiel, B. G. (2003). The efficient market hypothesis and its critics. *The Journal of Economic Perspectives, 17*(1), 59–82. doi:10.1257/089533003321164958

Marshall, B. R., Nguyen, N. H., & Visaltanachoti, N. (2017). *A note on intraday event studies* (SSRN Scholarly Paper ID 3015618). Social Science Research Network. https://papers.ssrn.com/abstract=3015618

McWilliams, A., & Siegel, D. (1997). Event studies in management research: Theoretical and empirical issues. *Academy of Management Journal, 40*(3), 626–657. doi:10.2307/257056

McWilliams, A., Siegel, D., & Teoh, S. H. (1999). Issues in the use of the event study methodology: A critical analysis of corporate social responsibility studies. *Organizational Research Methods, 2*(4), 340–365. doi:10.1177/109442819924002

Mitchell, M. L., & Netter, J. M. (1989). Triggering the 1987 stock market crash. *Journal of Financial Economics, 24*(1), 37–68. doi:10.1016/0304-405X(89)90071-8

Muntermann, J., & Guettler, A. (2007). Intraday stock price effects of ad hoc disclosures: The German case. *Journal of International Financial Markets, Institutions and Money, 17*(1), 1–24. doi:10.1016/j.intfin.2005.08.003

Scott, B. G., Ueng, J., Ramaswamy, V., & Chang, C. L. (2011). Layoff and firm long-term performance. *Academy of Strategic Management Journal, 10*(2), 1–10.

Sorescu, A., Warren, N. L., & Ertekin, L. (2017). Event study methodology in the marketing literature: An overview. *Journal of the Academy of Marketing Science, 45*(2), 186–207. doi:10.100711747-017-0516-y

Stiglitz, J. E., & Grossman, S. J. (1980). *On the impossibility of informationally efficient markets. 70*(3), 393–408. doi:10.7916/D8765R99

U.S. Securities and Exchange Commission. (2022). *SEC - Filings & Forms.* https://www.sec.gov/edgar.shtml

Wood, L. C., Duong, L. N. K., & Wang, J. X. (2022). Business Process Improvement for Sustainable Technologies Investments in Construction: A Configurational Approach. *Sustainability, 14*(9), 5697. doi:10.3390u14095697

Wood, L. C., & Wang, J. X. (2018). The event study method in logistics research: Overview and a critical analysis. *International Journal of Applied Logistics, 8*(1), 57–79. doi:10.4018/IJAL.2018010104

Wood, L. C., Wang, J. X., Duong, L. N. K., Reiners, T., & Smith, R. (2018). Stock market reactions to auto manufacturers' environmental failures. *Journal of Macromarketing, 38*(4), 364–382. doi:10.1177/0276146718781915

Wood, L. C., Wang, J. X., Olesen, K., & Reiners, T. (2017). The effect of slack, diversification, and time to recall on stock market reaction to toy recalls. *International Journal of Production Economics, 193*, 244–258. doi:10.1016/j.ijpe.2017.07.021

ADDITIONAL READING

Arora, P., Hora, M., Singhal, V., & Subramanian, R. (2020). When do appointments of corporate sustainability executives affect shareholder value? *Journal of Operations Management, 66*(4), 464–487. doi:10.1002/joom.1074

Duan, C., Grover, V., & Balakrishnan, N. (2009). Business process outsourcing: An event study on the nature of processes and firm valuation. *European Journal of Information Systems, 18*(5), 442–457. doi:10.1057/ejis.2009.38

Duan, C., Grover, V., Roberts, N., & Balakrishnan, N. (2014). Firm valuation effects of the decision to adopt relationally governed business process outsourcing arrangements. *International Journal of Production Research, 52*(15), 4673–4694. doi:10.1080/00207543.2014.884289

Duong, L. N. K., Wang, J. X., Wood, L. C., Reiners, T., & Koushan, M. (2021). The value of incremental environmental sustainability innovation in the construction industry: An event study. *Construction Management and Economics, 39*(5), 398–418. doi:10.1080/01446193.2021.1901950

Hendricks, K. B., Jacobs, B. W., & Singhal, V. R. (2020). Stock market reaction to supply chain disruptions from the 2011 great east Japan earthquake. *Manufacturing & Service Operations Management, 22*(4), 645–867. doi:10.1287/msom.2019.0777

Hendricks, K. B., & Singhal, V. R. (1996). Quality awards and the market value of the firm: An empirical investigation. *Management Science, 42*(3), 415–436. doi:10.1287/mnsc.42.3.415

Hendricks, K. B., & Singhal, V. R. (2001). Firm characteristics, total quality management, and financial performance. *Journal of Operations Management, 19*(3), 269–285. doi:10.1016/S0272-6963(00)00049-8

Hendricks, K. B., Singhal, V. R., & Stratman, J. K. (2007). The impact of enterprise systems on corporate performance: A study of ERP, SCM, and CRM system implementations. *Journal of Operations Management, 25*(1), 65–82. doi:10.1016/j.jom.2006.02.002

Jong, T., Couwenberg, O., & Woerdman, E. (2014). Does EU emissions trading bite? An event study. *Energy Policy, 69*(Supplement C), 510–519. doi:10.1016/j.enpol.2014.03.007

Papadakis, I. S. (2006). Financial performance of supply chains after disruptions: An event study. *Supply Chain Management, 11*(1), 25–33. doi:10.1108/13598540610642448

Pérez-Rodríguez, J. V., & González López-Valcárcel, B. (2012). Does innovation in obesity drugs affect stock markets? An event study analysis. *Gaceta Sanitaria, 26*(4), 352–359. doi:10.1016/j.gaceta.2011.07.028 PMID:22244267

Roztocki, N., & Weistroffer, H. R. (2015). Investments in enterprise integration technology: An event study. *Information Systems Frontiers, 17*(3), 659–672. http://dx.doi.org.ezproxy.otago.ac.nz/10.1007/s10796-013-9451-8

Whinston, M. D., & Collins, S. C. (1992). Entry and competitive structure in deregulated airline markets: An event study analysis of People Express. *The RAND Journal of Economics, 23*(4), 445–462. doi:10.2307/2555899

Zhan, X., Mu, Y., Hora, M., & Singhal, V. R. (2021). Service excellence and market value of a firm: An empirical investigation of winning service awards and stock market reaction. *International Journal of Production Research*, *59*(14), 4188–4204. doi:10.1080/00207543.2020.1759837

Zhan, X., Mu, Y., Nishant, R., & Singhal, V. R. (2020). When do appointments of Chief Digital or Data Officers (CDOs) affect stock prices? *IEEE Transactions on Engineering Management*, 1–14. doi:10.1109/TEM.2020.2984619

KEY TERMS AND DEFINITIONS

Confounding Event: Another event that occurs in the event window alongside the event we are interested in. As they coincide, we cannot determine which one, or whether they both, influence stock market reactions.

Influential Observation: An observation within the event study dataset that would substantially change the estimated coefficients in the model if it was removed.

Meta-Event: A wider event that affects the events we are interested in within our event study. Examples include business cycles or industry-specific issues such as the Y2K issue for information systems research studies.

Non-Normal Distribution: A distribution where the observations are not normally distributed. This is commonly observed as the abnormal return distributions are frequently non-normally distributed.

Nonparametric Tests: Those tests that do not have assumptions about the form of the distribution of the parameters. Therefore, they can be used with non-normal samples.

Outlier: An observation that is an unusual distance or separate from the other values in the sample. Just because it is an outlier, however, does not make it an influential observation. Conversely, an influential observation is not necessarily an outlier.

Short Window: The window used to estimate the abnormal returns, usually a period of one- to three-days in length.

Chapter 8
Data and Data Management

ABSTRACT

This chapter introduces some challenges and opportunities of working with data in the event study method. There are some similarities and differences in collecting, managing, and analyzing the data. The author also looks at some of the best practices in some issues that researchers may need to be aware of if they are not used to working with the types of data used in the event study method. First, he briefly looks at issues relating to identifying the company at a point in time as required to access the historical financial data. Next, the management of data from several sources is addressed. Finally, the chapter examines the data management lifecycle issues, focusing on the archiving processes at the end of a study. This chapter is not intended to be a comprehensive examination of data management issues, but to provide researchers with enough insight to understand when to get additional help and what sort of support they may need.

INTRODUCTION

Many readers of this book may come from operations other management areas and be used to a broad classification of research methods is either qualitative or quantitative. In general, many foundational research methods classes emphasize collecting quantitative data using surveys and interviews to collect qualitative data. In contrast, the event study method is decidedly quantitative, but it draws on a range of databases and different data types that many management researchers and students may not be familiar with. One of the first things that we address in this chapter is the management of quantitative data and ensuring that we understand some of the fundamental principles that should be followed. Next, we discuss some of the financial and accounting data specifics underlying the event study method.

Together, this chapter should enable researchers to manage their event study data, understand how we can get event study data, and understand how to assess the data for use in the study and manage the data over the data management lifecycle.

The issues relating to data management are important in all studies. The issues may depend on the integrity and management of data and the quality. Failures in these aspects can lead to questions about the reliability and validity of the study results. Further, the effective management of data provides substantial benefits to researchers mainly as they make adjustments to the design during the process of the study

DOI: 10.4018/978-1-7998-8969-4.ch008

but also if they need to adjust, extend, or alter their models during the thesis dissertation examination or the review process. Good data management also helps researchers answer queries or questions about the study, such as when a researcher working on a meta-analysis (Cooper, 2010; Hedges & Olkin, 1985) contacts you to ask about statistics not reported in the published study. If the data has been carefully managed and stored, it will be possible to respond to this request easily and rapidly.

MAIN FOCUS OF THE CHAPTER

It is not the intent or the purpose of this book to advocate for particular databases or software packages. For example, it is possible to undertake an event study with yahoo finance and a spreadsheet (e.g., open spreadsheet) and could, therefore, be conducted for free. However, such approaches have several limitations. First, the quality of data is low, and there is a high likelihood of errors. Second, is the inability to adapt calculations quickly (e.g., running a different estimation model) and tests to determine whether a calculated CAR is statistically significant. A gold standard may be using well-cleansed sets of data, such as provided by the CRSP for U.S. stocks, and software such as Eventus (which has been used for years with the calculations carefully examined and checked). In between, there is a continuum of options. If your institution does not have access to these packages, several options are available. It may be possible to collaborate with a colleague who has an institutional subscription to the services/software required. Alternatively, affordable options can be explored.

Many researchers may be more familiar with spreadsheets for managing data. We cover some fundamentals of spreadsheets to use the type of data we will use in event studies. In terms of calculations, I have found it easiest to run most of my analysis and models in "R" (R Core Team, 2012) because:

1. It is designed for statistical analysis and has a heavy academic/scholarly following. This ensures that researchers constantly update packages and incorporate the latest techniques and tools into packages for wide use.
2. It is free, so I am not locked in and do not need to worry about leaving my employer and finding funding for a new license.
3. It is command-line driven. I admit this is a double-edged sword; there is a steep learning curve, but the model's history and tests are clear, and adjustments can be rapidly made.
    a. A key drawback is the steep learning curve, and it is often challenging to understand what is wrong with a model or a command if it is not working.
    b. On the other hand, you can rapidly develop and change models when you know what you are doing. The model includes the list of inputs, and you can cut-paste these as a record of the model development and analysis. This speed of model development and adjustment can be valuable later as you record the analysis decisions for writing up a manuscript or dissertation.
4. R can generate useful images and figures that may be helpful during the analysis or communication of the study results.

We next turn to the different sources of data, considering both announcements as well as stock returns and financial data. We then begin to consider how we might manipulate the data.

SOURCES OF DATA

Before getting started with any project, it is helpful to assess whether you have access to the required data sources. In many management research projects, access to primary data sources might require additional work in distributing surveys or contacting people for interviews. With such a strong reliance on secondary data, access to appropriate databases is a fundamental project requirement for an event study. If you can identify the university does not have access particular types of data (perhaps due to the cost of maintaining active subscriptions to these services and databases is often incredibly expensive, particularly when considering tight budgets for many public universities), you can look at other options such as forming a partnership with another researcher with access to the data. Therefore, it would be best not to assume that your institution will have access to subscriptions to services noted in this chapter.

Announcements

As noted in earlier chapters, there are many possible sources for announcement data. Sometimes, a specialized database may be used in the data can often be extracted and stored on your computer for subsequent analysis. An example of this is the U.S. Consumer Product Safety Commission (CPSC) database which enables you to search using various parameters. In addition, they have a range of data available that can feed into a research project, as they note on their webpage, the CPSC:

believes in the power of open data and being accessible to the public. This is why we make our data, deliberations, and decisions, accessible to consumers, developers and stakeholders, in accordance with the Open Government Initiative. We use our website to broadcast live webcasts of meetings, hearings, and interactive workshops and trainings. Staff memos, technical analyses, Federal Register notices, Commissioner's statements and public comments are posted online during the course of CPSC's decisional processes. Recalls, safety alerts, safety awareness programs, interpretive rules, final rules and enforcement policies are all available on this site. (CPSC, 2022)

They have, for instance, a "[p]ublic database export of all recalls and unsafe product reports on SaferProducts.gov" (CPSC, 2022) as well as other information such as import and marketplace violations and civil and criminal penalties data. Potentially, a wide range of data in the single database could be used in a recall-based project, whether it is an event study or using other methods. In all cases, it is helpful to create an archive of the data when it is retrieved, as well as sufficient details about where it came from and how it was extracted from the database (e.g., including search terms used) so that you could replicate the extraction process if required.

Alternatively, a search through a full-text database of news and press release announcements may also be valuable. One of the most commonly used powerful, complete, and valuable resources is the Dow Jones Factiva database. This database enables sophisticated advanced searching and enables us to download copies of the announcements for the project records. Note that Factiva limits the number of items that can be downloaded in one batch; consequently, it can be slow to get some data from the system. However, the extensive reach and usability of the database make it a valuable source. Although other web-based searches (for example, using Google) may be conducted to identify an announcement, it would still be good to use Factiva to ensure that this is the first announcement about this event to have the best possible release of information to the market participants.

Information contained within an announcement can, by itself, also be extracted to form a dataset that is useful in the cross-sectional analysis. For example, in a study of executive appointments, the announcement often contains additional information about the appointee's background (Hendricks et al., 2014; Zhan et al., 2020). However, this also illustrates another important point, e are likely to find that not all announcements in the sample will contain sufficient data. While many announcements may include insight into the appointee's background, many may not do so. As researchers, we need to understand what to do and address the problem. Most times, additional work and analysis may be required to uncover the required information to undertake subsequent analysis. Resolving the issue can involve considerable work. For example:

An estimated 78% of [chief digital or data officer, CDO] in our sample are part of the [top management team, TMT] or report to a TMT member in a firm. For the remaining 22% of the sample, no information was available on whether the CDO was part of the TMT or reported to a TMT member. A TMT consists of executives whose names appear under the leadership team, corporate officers, or executive officers on the website of a firm, its annual report, or form 10-K. Some announcements clearly indicate that an appointee is part of a TMT or reports to a TMT member. In cases where such information is unavailable in an announcement, we examine 10-K filings, annual report, and other filings with the US Securities and Exchange Commission to determine whether appointees are part of the TMT or report to a member of the TMT. (Zhan et al., 2020, p. 5)

From this, we can see that while the announcements sometimes contained information, the analysis variable was constructed based on data drawn from several sources.

STOCK RETURNS

Data accuracy is an absolutely element in our event studies. Unfortunately, many freely accessible data sources will contain errors or omissions, and given the volume of data you will work with, it will not be possible to check and evaluate this. Therefore, it is necessary to rely on a trustworthy data source for your stock returns that enables you to calculate abnormal returns. It is helpful to recognize what you need to download to ensure you have the appropriate data to feed into your software for analysis.

CRSP (https://crsp.org) is the most commonly used and reliable data source for event studies. CRSP is the Center for Research in Security Prices, an affiliate of the University of Chicago Booth School of Business. They maintain the quality of the data "with a staff of nearly 80 professionals, CRSP continues its commitment to providing research data for the most rigorous tests in academic research, and in backtesting applications by practitioners" (Center for Research in Security Prices, 2022). Therefore, we are certain of the data quality for our event studies when we draw from CRSP.

The availability of subscriptions to these services will vary between universities. It is important to note that these subscriptions are costly, and sometimes, only leading universities will maintain a current subscription. Other options are available, and more common databases such as Datastream may enable us to continue the process with access to CRSP data through the platform. Datastream has a wide range of methods to access data, such as through Microsoft Office add-ins, a data feed, an API, or integrated within Eikon (Refinitiv, 2022).

Company Identifiers

One of the critical issues when dealing with stock returns data is identifying a particular company so you can extract the appropriate data. When we consider our investments, we often consider a particular stock ticker, the one- to four-letter identifier for the stock (such as T for AT&T, or AMZN for Amazon Inc). However, such tickers can change over time. Another commonly used identifier is the CUSIP (Committee on Uniform Securities Identification Procedures). However, again, these change over time as well. For example, if a company closes, the ticker will cease to be used regarding that company. However, the ticker may later be resurrected for a new company in the future. In addition, there is a range of corporate structural changes which might also result in the CUSIP adjusting to the single company over time. Consequently, when we extract historical data, using these identifiers like a ticker is not particularly appropriate, although they might be helpful when establishing the event and getting to grips with the firms in the sample. We should also ensure the identifier is correct for the company we are interested in, at the time of the event.

Manipulating Data in Spreadsheets

Throughout the process, you may draw data from a range of different sources. As such, you may need to learn simple tricks and techniques if you use a spreadsheet package such as Microsoft Excel (which I assume many readers will be using). The section summarizes some of the critical elements to consider. There be times when a simple cut-and-paste or a formula presents peculiar results. This is not intended as a comprehensive set of suggestions, but rather as a quick review of some elements that you may need or may need to investigate further to clean and manage the data in a spreadsheet. Spreadsheets give you ways to take data from two different cells and combine them or to split apart the data from one cell into several. A quick google search can often help identify solutions to challenges in working with data in spreadsheets. Two particular issues relate to cut-and-paste of 'special' options and ensuring you use the correct data type in the spreadsheet.

Cut-and-Paste: We rarely worry about formatting when we cut-and-paste text and one page to our document. However, sometimes we may want to copy the formula itself in Excel. Also, in some cases, we may wish to take the results of a formula from one source and then paste just the values (the output of the formula in the source cell) only into another cell. Both of these are possible. Therefore, becoming familiar with the 'paste special' options is useful. In addition, many other special paste options are valuable, such as transposing an array of cells.

Cell Format and Data Type: when cutting and pasting from different files, some cells may 'bring with them' the wrong formatting or data type for that cell. For example, I may intend a number such as "10" to be treated as a number in a calculation, but it may be shown and treated as a string of characters (like text in a book). It is often helpful to force the spreadsheet to treat an entire column of data in the same way as the same data type. Sometimes, the problem becomes apparent if some numbers are justified to the right and others to the left.

Preparing for the Cross-Sectional Regression and Subsequent Analysis

There are many possible sources of data and the subsequent cross-sectional regression analysis. First, it is possible to code some announcements and extract additional insight and information from them to generate variables, classifications, or coding analysis. Second, it is possible to use company data for the variables, such as company revenue, to indicate company size.

When looking to extract this data, access to a platform like Datastream may be helpful. Datastream enables us to quickly and rapidly input the companies and data types we want and then extract the data for the required periods.

Downloading stock return data is one thing, but it is also crucial that we incorporate the other data in the file in preparation for the cross-sectional regression analysis. That is, you might download a lot of sales data for a company over particular years, and you may need to convert this (and other downloaded data) by taking the relevant items for the preceding quarter and placing it into your analysis file against each company.

Before starting the cross-sectional regression, my analysis file would have observations on each row with a column that includes the abnormal return as the dependent variable in the regression model in the following columns containing other variables of interest, such as company size represented by revenue.

DATA MANAGEMENT

This section looks at some principles for managing quantitative data for an event study. Effective data management enables us to complete the study, backtrack if required, and understand what happened during the various analytic steps to report on the steps taken. In principle, the data management lifecycle is when:

you start with the idea or the concept for your research journey, then move on to collecting a dataset and analysing it, then cleaning and tidying it up to prepare it for sharing, before finally preserving or archiving it for perpetuity. (Clare et al., 2019, p. 134)

We do need to weigh these elements when managing our projects. Therefore, I pay special attention to archiving and ensuring we have the data fully captured and available to the research team members, as:

most of the time the final archiving step never happens. Instead, data remains with the original researchers and moves around with them. 'What if the researcher retires or dies?' you might ask. Well, often the dataset is lost, unless a colleague can find it and bring it to their institution for preservation, which is rarely the case. (Clare et al., 2019, p. 134)

Initial Downloads

I suspect the many management researchers will be most familiar with software packages such as spreadsheet software like Excel and commonly used statistical analysis packages such as SPSS. It is possible to complete the data management with Excel files, although some software packages may require us to export data into the CSV format before we import it for further analysis.

When we have downloaded a dataset from a source, such as CRSP, it is helpful to use a range of different approaches to check the data. One of the first things to do is to freeze the top line to understand and rapidly evaluate the variable names. Even when we are scrolling down to, for example, row 500, we can still rapidly see what the data is because we can have insight into the variable names. Exploring the initial download of data in this way allows us to evaluate if the data 'looks right.' Is it in the correct type of magnitude and does it match what we expect to see? For example, if we are looking at 'revenue' and most of the figures were between 0 and 1, we have likely made an error. It is helpful to catch these errors quickly with an initial data check.

Excel also benefits us as we can rapidly add new columns and use calculations to construct a particular equation to calculate the value of variables in the model. For example, this enabled us to construct variables, such as geographic diversification, in Wood et al. (2017). We can also rapidly replicate the formula over the column, enabling us to construct variables for further analysis.

It is often helpful to copy the initial dataset downloaded from a database, such as CRSP. I like to back up the initial data before making any changes to the file. I give this a filename such as "Initial_data_date_Project_Name" to simplify file management.

Backing up the initial data is valuable, as we can quickly find a file when searching for filenames. Having a short project code proves beneficial when quickly finding a file. Having the download date is also helpful in case multiple files get used. If we draw data from several databases, we may need to append a note like 'CRSP' to remind us of the data source. After I have an archived copy of the original data, I would usually create a copy that I manipulate for the study.

I have several files throughout the project. For example, there will usually be files containing stock returns for the companies over time, files containing other data such as broom financials or sales figures, and a final analysis file or bring together most of the required data for the cross-sectional regression. We name each type of file accordingly to facilitate the searches for any required file.

Managing Data during Analysis

I am not sure if there is an easy way of managing the data and changes in data files during the analysis. I tend to archive data files during the analysis, mainly as I construct variables or remove events from the sample due to confounding events. However, it is useful to have a record and archive of these files so that I can go back and find the appropriate files if there is a disaster.

BACKUPS, STORAGE, AND ARCHIVING

It almost feels as though I should not need to say this, but it is of absolute importance that we back up and archive our materials during the project. There will always be issues and problems outside of your control that might cause damage to your files. For example, in a worst-case scenario, if the laptop was stolen and contains the only copy of the files, we might lose the data and the work undertaken to construct variables and any further analysis.

Once, I used to backup data and my analysis on multiple floppy disks (for fear that a floppy disk failure would destroy my data!). Now, I use university resources and my own archiving processes. Besides working on a university-provided computer, most universities will also provide network services. Therefore, a regular backup or copy or replication should regularly be made of the data and analysis files to the University network. One of the significant advantages of doing this is that the university network will be professionally managed and backed up. In addition, this ensures an extremely high probability (although not certainty) that if something catastrophic happens to your computer or data file, you can recover a copy from the University network drives that is, at least somewhat, current. While we may not recover all the data (e.g., the backup might miss a week of work if it was old), it is better than losing absolutely everything.

It also seems prudent to at least several times create a backup on external media, whether this is an external USB stick or another approach. We can then place the storage media in a locked file at the university in a safe environment. Because of the manual nature of this type of backup, it is less likely to occur at a regular interval, but it is still a wise idea to create an archive of the project.

Following some of the earlier ideas around managing data files and effective file naming will enable us to rapidly and quickly identify the key required files and any backup.

Managing the Data at the End of the Project

During the project, managing files is also crucial because of the multiple team members using the files of different parts of the process. As a result, there will often be quite a large dataset. For example, in the toy recall project (Wood et al., 2017), we created an archive of all the PDF announcements used in the project. Taken together, a project database could be many hundreds of megabytes particularly if you have replicated some of these files (such as including a subset of announcement PDFs in a separate folder while maintaining the original set in the main folder) and created multiple backups of data files. In addition, when publishing in a leading journal, there may be a rejection from one journal that contains copies of all the relevant files and then other folders for the version accepted in another journal. Even after the paper has been accepted, several folders may have been used to manage the revisions. Within each of these folders, there will often be a separate data file showing the analysis undertaken to address the reviewer and editor comments and often quite extensive 'response to reviewer' letters and updated manuscripts.

After completing a project, I find it very useful to spend even a couple of hours working through the file structure and simplifying this while the project is still fresh in my mind. Therefore, I like to break down the backup and archiving process into several overlapping categories:

1. A simplified but complete backup of all project files. We should back this up on the computer network of at least one of the project team members.
2. A streamlined set of files that contain the critical data, analysis files, and manuscript preparation files for the final accepted article.
3. An archive that contains simply the final data files, analytic notes, and final accepted article. This is most likely to be relevant to all project team members.

Not all co-authors will want or need access to all of these files, but at least one project team member should have access to the complete set of data files. Again, it is wise to back this up on a University network drive to maintain a permanent record.

Depending on the needs, project members may receive a simplified set of files for their own records. In addition, it provides them with some oversight and access to key files if required (for example, distribution to department administrators or other faculty members).

Is it necessary to maintain a record of all the data files? Perhaps not, but I have found it helpful, and sometimes it is interesting to revisit some of the earlier studies. For example, when preparing for faculty research seminars at other institutions, I could return to the toy recall project (Wood et al., 2017) and jump into the archive of toy recall announcements to present some helpful insight into the type of recall and also point out some of the absurdity of product design decisions that are made. (Most times, the seminar attendees will agree that the recall was destined to happen based on the product design!) It is also helpful to have these data to support teaching activities.

In addition, I find the carefully archived files make it easy to discuss the publication process with research students. It enables me simple access to a comprehensive archive so I can retrieve reviewer comments, how we addressed these comments, and the analytic processes required. It gives emerging researchers more insight into the challenges I experienced and how other researchers can similarly address some issues. Alone, these archives enabled me to prepare several voluntary seminars for research students to support their ongoing education, based on my research, the initial analysis, and subsequent revisions.

CONCLUSION

This chapter aims to raise awareness of the different data sources, the types of data needed, and give some insight into how we might handle this data. The considerations of the different data sources are essential going into the project to ensure that we have access to the data required to complete the project before we start. If we have, for example, identified that we will not have access to the full range of data, we may wish to identify a co-author and partner at an institution who will have access to the required data. Further, it is beneficial to have some insight into how to handle the data and manage start over the process both during the analysis involving the combinations of types of data but also during the final archiving processes so that you can assure your co-authors also have a copy of the project and the underlying data sources that will be suitable for their needs.

Given the diversity of software packages, products, and platforms that could be used throughout the project, the chapter has deliberately not gone into specifics. This process means we may find value and get insight from collaborating with an accounting or finance department researcher. If we collaborate, we can undoubtedly pick up many valuable tips and tricks that they can teach us that will speed up the search and acquisition of data. However, my experience is that most researchers in a management department will not have the expertise or experience with the databases that colleagues in an accounting or finance department will have.

Ultimately, partnering with another researcher who has done an event study before, particularly someone from an accounting and finance background, will be handy for many management researchers. They can provide additional insight into and interpret existing studies and explain some of the commonly used variables that might be constructed to support the analysis. In addition, they can translate between what we want to study and a more abstract sense and help us identify what data to extract from which database and then how to manipulate the data to construct a variable of interest for the study.

REFERENCES

Center for Research in Security Prices. (2022). *Why CRSP?* https://crsp.org/main-menu/why-crsp

Clare, C., Cruz, M., Papadopoulou, E., Savage, J., Teperek, M., Wang, Y., Witkowska, I., & Yeomans, J. (2019). *Engaging researchers with data management: The cookbook.* Open Book Publishers. doi:10.11647/OBP.0185

Cooper, H. M. (2010). *Research synthesis and meta-analysis: A step-by-step approach* (4th ed.). Sage.

CPSC. (2022). *CPSC Data*. U.S. Consumer Product Safety Commission. https://www.cpsc.gov/Data

Hedges, L. V., & Olkin, I. (1985). *Statistical methods for meta-analysis*. Academic Press.

Hendricks, K. B., Hora, M., & Singhal, V. R. (2014). An empirical investigation on the appointments of supply chain and operations management executives. *Management Science*, *61*(7), 1562–1583. doi:10.1287/mnsc.2014.1987

R Core Team. (2012). *R: A language and environment for statistical computing*. http://www.R-project.org/

Refinitiv. (2022). *Datastream Macroeconomic Analysis*. https://www.refinitiv.com/en/products/datastream-macroeconomic-analysis

Wood, L. C., Wang, J. X., Olesen, K., & Reiners, T. (2017). The effect of slack, diversification, and time to recall on stock market reaction to toy recalls. *International Journal of Production Economics*, *193*, 244–258. doi:10.1016/j.ijpe.2017.07.021

Zhan, X., Mu, Y., Nishant, R., & Singhal, V. R. (2020). When do appointments of Chief Digital or Data Officers (CDOs) affect stock prices? *IEEE Transactions on Engineering Management*, 1–14. doi:10.1109/TEM.2020.2984619

ADDITIONAL READING

Arora, P., Hora, M., Singhal, V., & Subramanian, R. (2020). When do appointments of corporate sustainability executives affect shareholder value? *Journal of Operations Management*, *66*(4), 464–487. doi:10.1002/joom.1074

Briney, K. (2015). *Data management for researchers: Organize, maintain and share your data for research success*. Pelagic Publishing.

Brown, K. C., Harlow, W. V., & Tinic, S. M. (1988). Risk aversion, uncertain information, and market efficiency. *Journal of Financial Economics*, *22*(2), 355–385. doi:10.1016/0304-405X(88)90075-X

Brown, S. J., & Warner, J. B. (1980). Measuring security price performance. *Journal of Financial Economics*, *8*(3), 205–258. doi:10.1016/0304-405X(80)90002-1

Brown, S. J., & Warner, J. B. (1985). Using daily stock returns: The case of event studies. *Journal of Financial Economics*, *14*(1), 3–31. doi:10.1016/0304-405X(85)90042-X

Chen, Y., Singhal, V., & Zhu, Q. (2021). Environmental policies and financial performance: Stock market reaction to firms for their proactive environmental practices recognized by governmental programs. *Business Strategy and the Environment*, *30*(4), 1548–1562. doi:10.1002/bse.2693

Cox, A. (2018). *Exploring research data management*. Facet Publishing. doi:10.29085/9781783302802

Duong, L. N. K., Wang, J. X., Wood, L. C., Reiners, T., & Koushan, M. (2021). The value of incremental environmental sustainability innovation in the construction industry: An event study. *Construction Management and Economics*, *39*(5), 398–418. doi:10.1080/01446193.2021.1901950

Fama, E. F. (1998). Market efficiency, long-term returns, and behavioral finance. *Journal of Financial Economics*, *49*(3), 283–306. doi:10.1016/S0304-405X(98)00026-9

Fama, E. F., & French, K. R. (1993). Common risk factors in the returns on stocks and bonds. *Journal of Financial Economics*, *33*(1), 3–56. doi:10.1016/0304-405X(93)90023-5

Gong, S. X. H., Firth, M., & Cullinane, K. (2008). International oligopoly and stock market linkages: The case of global airlines. *Transportation Research Part E, Logistics and Transportation Review*, *44*(4), 621–636. doi:10.1016/j.tre.2007.05.008

Kothari, S. P., & Warner, J. B. (2007). Econometrics of event studies. In B. E. Eckbo (Ed.), *Handbook of Corporate Finance: Empirical Corporate Finance* (Vol. 1, pp. 3–36). North-Holland/Elsevier. doi:10.1016/B978-0-444-53265-7.50015-9

McWilliams, A., Siegel, D., & Teoh, S. H. (1999). Issues in the use of the event study methodology: A critical analysis of corporate social responsibility studies. *Organizational Research Methods*, *2*(4), 340–365. doi:10.1177/109442819924002

Tibor, K. (2021). *Research data management and data literacies*. Elsevier Science & Technology.

Wood, L. C., Wang, J. X., Duong, L. N. K., Reiners, T., & Smith, R. (2018). Stock market reactions to auto manufacturers' environmental failures. *Journal of Macromarketing*, *38*(4), 364–382. doi:10.1177/0276146718781915

Xia, Y., Singhal, V. R., & Peter Zhang, G. (2016). Product design awards and the market value of the firm. *Production and Operations Management*, *25*(6), 1038–1055. doi:10.1111/poms.12525

Zhan, X., Mu, Y., Hora, M., & Singhal, V. R. (2021). Service excellence and market value of a firm: An empirical investigation of winning service awards and stock market reaction. *International Journal of Production Research*, *59*(14), 4188–4204. doi:10.1080/00207543.2020.1759837

Zhan, X., Mu, Y., Nishant, R., & Singhal, V. R. (2020). When do appointments of Chief Digital or Data Officers (CDOs) affect stock prices? *IEEE Transactions on Engineering Management*, ●●●, 1–14. doi:10.1109/TEM.2020.2984619

KEY TERMS AND DEFINITIONS

Archive: The process of taking the data used in the study, cleansing it, and creating a copy in another destination. The process should create files that other researchers will quickly understand if they need to access the archived files.

Backup: The process of creating a copy regularly that can be used if the working file is damaged or the data is lost.

CRSP: CRSP is the Center for Research in Security Prices, an affiliate of the University of Chicago Booth School of Business. The team at CRSP curates the data and ensures data accuracy.

Data Accuracy: Ensuring that the data is accurate and is free from errors. Given the large amount of data we may use in an event study, data accuracy is best assured by using reliable sources, like CRSP.

Data Management: The set of approaches used to process, store, and organize the data used in the study.

Data Manipulation: The process of modifying the data structure and data types to make sure we can use it effectively in the event study analysis.

Firm Identifiers: An identifier for a firm. This identifier should be unique (i.e., not shared with another firm) and can be used to extract appropriate information from databases or data providers such as CRSP. Examples include the ticker symbols and the CUSIPs.

Chapter 9
Running the Event
Study Analysis

ABSTRACT

This chapter introduces the running of the event study analysis and calculating the abnormal returns causally connected to the event being studied. The author does not examine the cross-sectional regression, but instead focuses on the key elements, design decisions, and analytical steps required to calculate the abnormal returns. This includes evaluating estimation windows, event windows, and the estimation model of the normal and abnormal returns. Following this, he examines a range of different test statistics that can be used to determine whether the estimated abnormal returns are statistically significantly different from zero, allowing you to make a conclusion. The focus is on using software tools and interpretation rather than the mathematical treatment and calculations behind estimating abnormal returns and statistics.

INTRODUCTION

Within the book, this is one of the most fundamentally important chapters as this is where we calculate the abnormal returns and use these to estimate whether the event that any discernible impact through the stock price reaction. Having said that, keeping in mind that the audience for the chapter includes researchers and students in the management and supply chain areas, the treatment in this chapter is not heavily mathematical and does not emphasize calculations and formulae behind the estimation procedures and test statistics. Interested readers can reference additional reading lists that they so desire. Instead, bearing in mind that in the era of SPSS, many postgraduate students are used to the point-and-click approach, our focus is on preparations and design decisions. We develop a fundamental understanding of some of the key parameters and interpretation of outcomes that will enable us to use a range of different software packages depending on which are available.

Many software packages can calculate the cumulative average abnormal returns (CAARs). However, you will need to become quite familiar with the tricks for the particular software package that you are using. Eventus is probably the gold standard. In more recent years, they have also integrated with the WRDS database to enable many researchers and subscribing universities to collect the financial data

DOI: 10.4018/978-1-7998-8969-4.ch009

from WRDS and conduct some reasonably sophisticated analyzes online at the same time. So, if your institution has a subscription, this could be a very simple and effective way of conducting an event study where the firms in your sample are U.S. businesses.

There is a range of packages on STATA and on R, online, or in specialized software packages like Eventus, where you can upload data in correctly formatted CSV files and conduct the analysis. The packages range in terms of the capability and sophistication of the type of analyzes that they can manage. Depending on the type of project you might want to do, you may need to carefully select the software to analyze the data. For example, running a multi-country study (with firms based outside the U.S.) can be tricky in some packages and easier in others.

This chapter provides an overview of calculating abnormal returns for the study. It first examines the concept of the windows for estimation and then examines the different abnormal return estimation models that can be used.

What we need to run the analysis, and what we will get out of it

As expected from previous chapters, the key items will be an event list (a list of dates and company identifiers) and stock returns or stock price data. In previous chapters, we have addressed how to retrieve these files. Each package may require different formats and presentations of the input files, so we have not addressed the specifics of any particular package in this chapter. However, in the preceding chapter on data management, we give some insight into what may be required as well as some tax on trips to how we might be able to manage some datasets so that we can prepare, transform, and ascertain that our data files are in a format suitable the software package that we are using. In addition, some approaches do not even require data on the stock prices/returns to be provided, such as Event Study for WRDS, which requires a list of firm identifiers and dates to be provided, and then it draws on its dataset to complete the analysis.

There are two things that we need as output. First is the output from the abnormal return tests and the test statistics to know whether the event appears to have caused a significant stock market reaction over the event window. Second, the list of individualized abnormal returns as output against each of the observations in a sample so that we can use these and pair them up with the other data for subsequent cross-sectional regression.

An Overview of Software Packages

It is impossible to have no opinion on the packages that may be used for the analysis. This section is not a full review of the packages and reflects only my own (often limited) experience and insight from trialling, using, or investigating the options. These are options available at the time of writing that could be adopted. It does not guarantee that they are still available or that better options have not been introduced. This is by no means a comprehensive listing.

Event Study for WRDS. This package, as noted, is embedded within the WRDS features. If your institution has a subscription, check to see whether you have access to this feature. If you can use it then you can simply and quickly run a series of event studies on U.S. listed firms or even in other markets. Note that it does not appear to support a multi-country study (a single study with a sample of firms listed in different markets), but only a sequence of studies one country at a time. It is remarkably easy to use and has some powerful features, such as the ability to draw on the internal database for simple access to quality data.

Eventus. This package remains the 'gold standard' and probably most comprehensive and powerful package available. It runs under SAS and is, therefore, possibly less user-friendly than 'Event study for WRDS' when it is used by itself. However, Eventus provided an option for 'Eventus WRDS' that reads data directly from WRDS and, therefore, makes it more user-friendly. It can be set up to draw from Datastream or CRSP databases or downloads. When users understand how to manage the software for their particular setup, it can be fast and simple to use and it presents very reliable and trustworthy estimations and test statistics.

STATA. There is a package and methodology for running an event study in STATA software (Ullah et al., 2021) and this may be appropriate if the user is already familiar with the STATA package.

R. There have been several packages in R available over the years. These have the benefit of being freely available but they do require the user to be familiar with R. It is, therefore, an option that has a steeper learning curve and requires the user to have access to a rich source of trustworthy data (e.g., from CRSP).

Eventstudytools.com. This is a relatively low-cost option, where users can pay for analyses required. For a postgraduate project, therefore, it can prove to be a relatively low-cost option where only a single analysis is required or a small number of analyzes are required. Data will need to be source (e.g., from CRSP) but there are plenty of examples of how the different options can be used on the website for a fairly wide range of event study analysis project types. There are also good resources to help readers with less background understand the method and how to set up their data for the options. It does have a data files compilation service that allows new users to relatively cheaply have the service pull together the required data for analysis.

For STATA, Eventus, and WRDS databases, the subscriptions can be expensive and if the institution does not already have a subscription then it may not be financially feasible for a postgraduate project.

WORKING WITH YOUR ESTIMATION WINDOWS

It is necessary to convert our calendar time into a standardized format around the event. As noted in previous chapters, there is little consensus on how wide the estimation window should be, but there is consensus that the event window should be as short as practically possible.

Event Window

The event window is simply the period that is used to capture the abnormal return. The intention is that there should be higher stock price variability within that event window than at other periods. The changes in the event window occur because the marketplace absorbs new information that is material meaningful to the stock returns (Hillmer & Yu, 1979). The selection of the event window length as a primary design issue that needs to be carefully considered. Historically, many management studies used longer event windows (McWilliams & Siegel, 1997). However, the use of a long event window is concerning as it reduces the power of the test statistic commonly used, leading to false inferences about the events' significance (Brown & Warner, 1980, 1985).

The event window should be as small as is practical (McWilliams et al., 1999; McWilliams & Siegel, 1997). There are two primary reasons why an event window should be kept very short. First, McWilliams and Siegel (1997) warn that along event window violates the assumptions of the efficient market hypothesis. It would be peculiar to accept one of the foundational assumptions of the method of then violating it and setting up the study.

The second is a pragmatic reason for a short window. As noted in the other chapter, a longer event window is more likely to encompass other confounding events. When the confounding events have been identified over a long window, and the observations affected have been eliminated, there is often a substantial drop in the number of observations included in the sample, as you will be few remaining observations with no confounding events. A wider event window suggests more opportunities for each observation to be confounded by other events.

Most studies will incorporate an event window now of two or perhaps three days, with some even electing to use a single-day window representing the day of the event. It is, however, sometimes tricky to find out on which date we may observe a stock market reaction to a given announcement. For example, if we know that a news announcement was made on 26 January, we may be tempted to say that the stock market reaction occurs on that date. However, if the announcement and the information were released or made public at 11:55 at the end of 26 January, there will be no stock market reaction until the following day. Consequently, even though the information was released on the 26th of January, a stock market reaction would probably occur on 27 January. While this is an extreme case of a very late release of information, the same basic principle applies to after-hours release of information to the market.

One way of addressing the ambiguity where it is not always known whether the event is after hours or during hours is to use both the day of the event and the following day, that is, a window of day zero and day +1.

International studies can also suffer from time zone challenges where the news may be released in one time zone at one time, then absorbed into a different day in the market and another time zone. Therefore, it may even be prudent to include the day before the identified event day for multi-country studies.

However, in practice, many different event windows have been used. I suspect that many studies make errors in identifying the first occurrence or the first release of the relevant information to the market. For instance, consider Figure 1; if we identify a news release on 26 January unbeknownst to us, an earlier press release was made on 25 January, then we may not observe a stock market reaction to that news within the window as our assumed event date of 26 January is incorrect, and the window does not include the event date of 25 January. Wider windows can be used to overcome errors or mistakes that have been made in identifying the earliest release of information.

The window can be described in the manuscript as day 0, representing the day of the event with days counted either before (using, for example, -1 to represent the day immediately prior to the event day) or after (using, for example, 2 to represent two days immediately after the event day). Using this notation, an event window of (-1, 1) would represent the day before the event day, the event day, and the day after the event day, giving a three-day event window.

Increasingly, however, reviewers, editors, and authors are reporting multiple event windows. The use of multiple event windows also demonstrates that they have accounted for investor anticipation (Bhattacharya et al., 2000), information leakage (McWilliams & Siegel, 1997), or learning effects (Bebchuk et al., 2013). Examples of multiple windows being presented in a single paper can be found in many papers, such as the extensive analysis in Hawn et al. (2018).

Figure 1. The event window with three markers for time using the event date as the central marker. Here, for example, an event occurred on January 26, 2022.

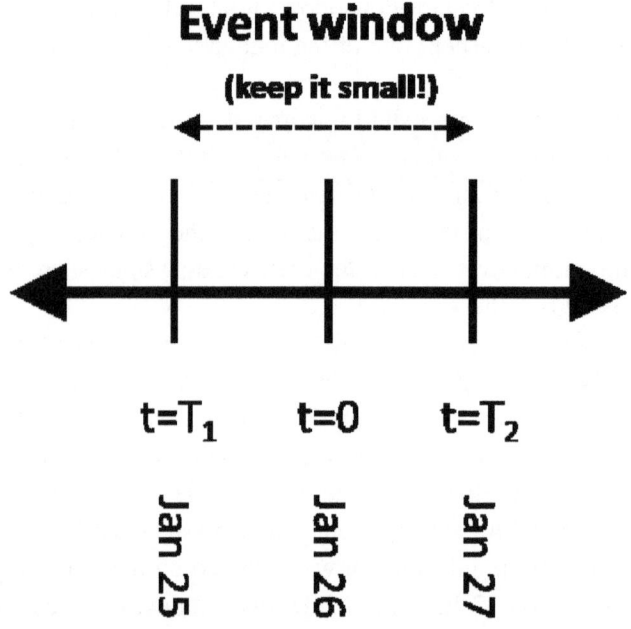

Estimation Window for the Normal Returns Estimation

Surprisingly, there is little guidance on the estimation period required when calculating the normal returns. McWilliams and Siegel (1999) note that it tends to be 250 days to 50 days. In a review of environmental pollution studies, Bouzzine (2021) noted a wide range from approximately 100 days through to nearly 350 days. Most commonly was a number that was approximately 100 to 250 days. There is certainly very little consistency. One key point is that the longer the estimation window, the greater the likelihood that we are in a situation where we cannot get the full set of data required to estimate the normal returns during this period. For example, assume we wanted to estimate the normal returns with ten years of proceeding data in an extreme situation. While this might seem reasonable for a firm that has been around for many decades, our sample might also include relatively new firms with much less history as publicly traded companies even though they may have existed a long time. Consequently, not all firms in the sample will have the entire ten years of historical stock price data to draw on. The longer the estimation window for the normal returns, the greater the likelihood of having a higher proportion of firms with incomplete data. Some software packages have robust procedures to manage this and can accommodate a small amount of missing data, while other packages are incredibly sensitive to missing data and may force us to drop a relatively large proportion of the sample because of even a small amount of missing data. McWilliams and Seigel (1999) provide an example of how this can substantially reduce the sample size:

Posnikoff (1997) identified 52 companies that made "distinct public and published announcements of divestment" between 1977 and 1992 (p. 78). Of these, she found that 40 had complete data on financial

Figure 2. Normal return estimation window and isolation window placed before the event window

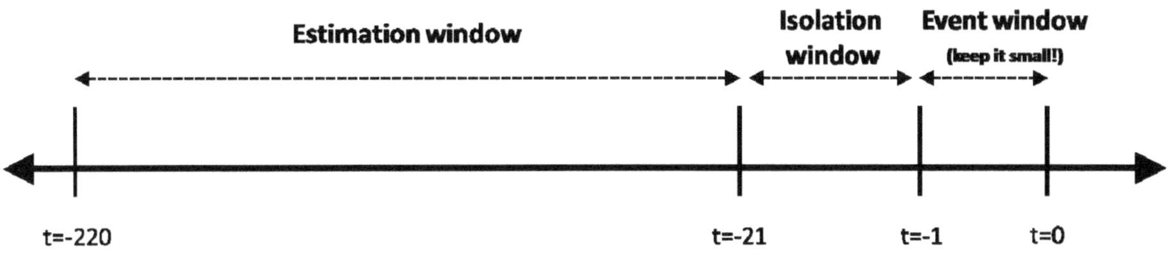

returns for the estimation period from 1980 to 1991. That is, she defined the event as the announcement of divestment by all firms but located returns data for only 40 of these firms. (p. 351)

So, in an extreme case, the estimation window normal returns would exclude a large proportion of our sample simply because we do not have the top stock data available. How short, then, are we able to make this window? For example, many studies use a value between 120 to 200 trading days, where 200 trading days represent approximately one year prior to the event.

A further conceptual issue is if the sample comprises a few firms that experience repeated events. If this happens, we may have a situation where the estimation window for a given observation also encompasses an earlier event of interest. On the other hand, a large sample that consists primarily of one event per firm does not have this difficulty. A shorter estimation window for normal returns may be pragmatic in this particular case. However, it is also important to note that in that estimation. For the normal returns, each of the firms of interest will have experienced several abnormal stock returns in reaction to different types of events, such as poor earnings announcements. This is all part and parcel of that calculation of normal returns.

In addition, there will usually be an isolation window between the window used to estimate the normal returns and the event window. Including the isolation period is crucial "in order to shield the estimates from effects of the announcement and to ensure that any non-stationarities in the estimates are not an issue" (Jacobs et al., 2010, p. 434). In their study, Jacobs et al. (2010) used a 10-day isolation period and an estimation window of (-210, -11). The isolation period might be longer at 20 days, as used in Xia et al. (2016, p. 1047) with a 200-day estimation window, represented as an estimation period of -220 to -21. They also note that their approach required only 40 stock returns during the 200 days of trading, allowing for a few observations to be dropped due to unavailable stock returns data. In Figure 2, we can see an estimation window of 200 days, an isolation window of 20 days, and the event window of two days (-1, 0), reflecting what we observe in Xia et al. (2016).

ESTIMATION MODELS

The key outcome of the event study is to calculate the abnormal returns. A primary corollary of this is that we need to understand the normal returns to evaluate what is abnormal and the magnitude of the abnormal returns. When we think about this, several different research design decisions become of crucial importance.

Given how well-meaning researchers do their best to remove bias in the research, we expect to see a range of different estimation models being used in most contemporary research. However, over the last ten years, I think we have gone some way towards seeing an improvement in studies being published in leading journals that show the results of a range of different estimation models. The use of different estimation models demonstrates that the researchers have not selectively picked results from a particular model which provides the best possible outcome. Instead, it shows an effect from the event that has a discernible impact on stock market reactions regardless of the estimation model that we have used.

At the most basic level, the estimation model requires few parameters to be estimated. The more comprehensive the model used, the greater the range of parameters that need to be estimated. Most researchers in practice find that the three- or four-factor models present a sufficient balance and tend to be used in most management research projects for U.S.-based samples.

We consider that our goal is to identify the stock return on the event day (or during the event window) that is unusual relative to other normal days. Normal returns are estimated before the event to evaluate the impact of the returns in reaction to the event. In this way, the abnormal return is the primary indicator of the stock market reaction to the news in the marketplace. As noted, this feeds into further calculations and analyses. On the other hand, the normal returns are what we expect to occur and encompass the expected volatility and variation in stock returns. Therefore, it is a benchmark that we can use to assess whether or not the identified fluctuations in stock returns in response to the event are meaningful.

As noted, the standard now is to use several measures to estimate the normal returns that help to demonstrate that the stock market reaction to the event in question is robust to our model specification. However, when several models have been used, and they all generate rather different results, we would begin to doubt whether the stock market reaction in response to the event was meaningful. Instead, we might believe that any results identified in this study are simply due to selecting the most favorable model.

Most contemporary event study research uses models for normal returns that are based on equity indices or stock market indices. They include a range of variables that have been identified and verified to explain stock returns better. Using the stock market indices is important as these represent a collection of stocks that enable us to observe the performance of particular sectors or gauge the economy's performance as a whole (such as the S&P500). (Similarly, many investors and mutual funds also use an appropriate equity index as a benchmark to demonstrate their investing outperformance.) There are a range of market indices that might be used in the U.S., for instance:

- One of the oldest equity indices as the Dow Jones industrial average which represents a small number of leading U.S.-based industrial companies.
- One of the most commonly referenced indices today is the S&P 500. It represents the 500 largest companies on NYSE or NASDAQ. The index is weighted by market capitalization; large firms (such as Microsoft and Apple, in 2021) represent a considerable proportion of the index.
- The NASDAQ 100 index represents 100 of the largest non-financial real estate companies that are technology-related.
- In contrast, the Russell 2000 Index represents the 2000 small-capitalization U.S. firms. They are a sub-set of the broader Russell 3000 Index representing most investable companies across the U.S.

Other global indices might be used in event studies. For example, the FTSE 100 represents the top 100 firms on the London stock exchange by capitalization (U.K.). The Nikkei 225 represents the top-rated companies listed on the Tokyo Stock Exchange (Japan).

The Mean Return or Naïve Benchmark

The first model that we consider is the most simple model of stock returns. However, this ignores many of the characteristics of stocks that have been identified and studied. It excludes elements of the riskiness of stocks and different factors that influence stock returns. Instead, the mean model estimates a normal return based on the market return as given by the broader stock market index. The broad market index essentially presents the expectation of normal returns over all the traded stocks. This allows a calculation of abnormal returns for the securities under examination with reference to the market.

The mean model assumes a constant expected stock return that will be the same for each of the stocks (regardless of their characteristics), that is equal to their market return, so that:

$$R_{it} = R_{mt} + \varepsilon_{it},$$ (1)

where R_{it} is the stock i's return on the share price at time t; R_{mt} is the return on a value-weighted market portfolio of stocks at period t; and, ε_{it} is the error term in the model (where $E(\varepsilon_{it})=0$). For example, R_{it} may be the rate of return of AT&T stock (ticker T) over the estimation window.

We can then estimate the normal returns (NR) using this mean return by stating that:

$$\widehat{NR}_{it} = R_{mt},$$ (2)

where $\widehat{NR}_{it}$ is the estimated normal returns for stock i during time t. From this, we can derive that:

$$\widehat{AR}_{it} = R_{it} - \widehat{NR}_{it} = R_{it} - R_{mt},$$ (3)

where $\widehat{AR}_{it}$ is the estimated abnormal return (AR) for stock i at time t.

When we consider what this means, this benchmark suggests that anything that diverges from the average market behavior is, therefore, an abnormal return. The constant mean return is a basic and fundamental model that is naïve as it ignores common economic understandings. For example, the model ignores the fundamental concept that riskier stocks should have higher expected returns to compensate investors for the greater risks they take on during the investment.

One benefit of this benchmark is that no parameter estimation is required for the calculations. Therefore, we rarely consider it the main estimation model appropriate for event study applications. However, it could be valuable as part of a general test of the robustness of the calculations for the abnormal returns. My personal experience with the abnormal return estimations from the model suggests that they can differ from those produced using the other, more sophisticated estimation procedures detailed below.

The Market Model as a Single-Factor Benchmark

The next benchmark that can be used for assessing whether we have abnormal returns is based on the single factor estimation model. This is based on Sharpe (1963, 1964) building on the working on the theory of portfolio selection of Markowitz (1952). The estimation is slightly more sophisticated as it assumes a linear relationship between the stock in the market returns, modeled with the following equation:

$$R_{it} = \alpha i + \beta i R_m t_+ \varepsilon it_, \qquad (4)$$

where Ri_t is the stock i's return at time t; αi and βi are the estimated parameters, Rm_t is the market return at time t; and, εi_t is the model's error term. In general, the parameters are estimated using a linear regression model. We model the stock returns as the dependent variable, with the market return as an independent, or explanatory, variable. Clearly, the estimates need to be separated from the impact of the event being studied, and therefore, the data range used during the regression needs to be selected to reduce any influence of the event. Therefore, the estimation should be separate from the event window (using an isolation period). In this way, the estimation of the normal stock returns will not be contaminated by including the intended detection of abnormal returns.

The parameters are specific to each stock are calculated relative to their specific (observed) behaviors in relation to the broader market to which they belong. The beta measures the stock's systematic risk based on how it moves with a broader stock market. We can consider that a 1% increase in market returns would correspond to a change of the β_i percent in stock i's return. The beta values for stocks can differ depending on the companies' nature. For example, utility firms have much lower betas than high-technology stocks. In contrast, the alpha value can be interpreted as a return expected if the market return had been zero.

From the estimation in equation (4), we can then derive an estimated daily abnormal return for firm i using:

$$\widehat{AR}_{it} = R_{it} - \left(\hat{\alpha}_i + \hat{\beta}_i R_{mt} \right), \qquad (5)$$

where:

$\widehat{AR}_{it}$ is the estimated AR at time t for stock i;
R_{it} is the stock i's return at time t;
R_{mt} is the market return at time t; and,
α_i and β_i are the estimated model's parameters.

As such, the single factor benchmark represents an improvement over the mean model because it incorporates the reality that there are specific differences between stocks. It captures some differences using the stocks betas. Further, these parameters can be used to estimate the expected normal returns with reference to the market return so that the model can capture a more accurate assessment of the normal behaviors of the stock, allowing us to capture a better perspective on what would be considered an abnormal return in reaction to the event under study. Again, the parameters must be estimated based on data outside the event window of interest. This is why an isolation gap is used between the estimation window and event window to buffers the parameter estimates (in the event window) from the calculations of normal returns (in the estimation window).

While many contemporary studies use three- or four-factor models, Bouzzine (2021, p. 10) notes that many environmental studies use the market model. A possible reason for this may be the estimation difficulty executing a multi-country study, as the estimation of additional factors (in the three- or four-factor models) is more challenging for samples with non-U.S. firms. In contrast, using this single-factor model, the market returns can be derived from the major stock market indices used in the countries being studied.

Three-Factor Model

The work of Fama and French (1993) forms the basis of the multifactor family of benchmark models. The emphasis is on providing a better model for stock returns than the previously introduced models by comprehensively modeling a wider range of systematic stock return sources. In addition, the emphasis is on the model accounting for a greater proportion of possible return variability. However, as more factors are added and the more advanced benchmarks, more complex structures are likely prone to greater estimation errors. This suggests that the simple return models still have some benefits.

Regardless, multifactor benchmarks are commonly used in most contemporaneous event studies.

Over the last several decades, various factors have been suggested as mechanisms to enhance the explanatory power of this type of return model. The three- and four-factor return models have been widely recognized as providing substantial explanatory power.

There has been an enduring sequence of research to develop models that use risk factors to help estimate stock returns (Fama, 1991, 1998). The first is the same market factor that the single-factor model uses. The second relates to the company size, that is, the firm's overall market capitalisation or market value. The third is a ratio of the book and market equity values. Therefore, the return for a single stock i can be represented by the three-factor model as follows:

$$R_{it} - R_{ft} = \alpha_i + \beta_{i1}\left(R_{mt} - R_{ft}\right) + \beta_{i2}SMB_t + \beta_{i3}HML_t + \varepsilon_{it}, \tag{6}$$

where R_{it} is the stock i's return at time t; R_{ft} is the risk-free return at time t; R_{mt} is the market return at time t; $\alpha_i, \beta_{i1}, \beta_{i2}$, and β_{i3} are firms-specific parameters in the model; SMB_t is the size factor; HML_t is the book-to-market factor; and ε_{it} is the model's error term.

Given this, then, the abnormal returns AR_{it} for stock i on day t can be estimated as:

$$\widehat{AR}_{it} = R_{it} - (\hat{\alpha}_i + R_{ft} + \hat{\beta}_{i1}\left(R_{mt} - R_{ft}\right) + \hat{\beta}_{i2}SMB_t + \hat{\beta}_{i3}HML_t, \tag{7}$$

where:

$\widehat{AR}_{it}$ is the estimated abnormal return for stock i at time t;
R_{it} is the stock i's return at time t;
R_{ft} is the risk-free return at time t;
R_{mt} is the market return at time t;
SMB_t is the size factor;
HML_t is the book-to-market factor; and,
$\hat{\alpha}_i, \hat{\beta}_{i1}, \hat{\beta}_{i2}, \hat{\beta}_{i3}$ are the estimated model's parameters.

Researchers do not need to construct these factors in many cases, as a wide range of available sources have complete factors, particularly for key markets such as the U.S.

Four-Factor Model

While there have been a range of different portfolio suggestions and different factors that can be included, the most commonly added fourth factor is that of momentum as noted by Carhart (1997). This is identified as a variable of importance as it takes into consideration the observation that stocks of the rising stock prices continue to rise. That is, when in motion the stock tends to stay in motion. As a consequence, stock i has a return that can be represented by the four factor model as follows:

$$R_{it} - R_{ft} = \alpha_i + \beta_{i1}\left(R_{mt} - R_{ft}\right) + \beta_{i2}SMB_t + \beta_{i3}HML_t + \beta_{i4}UMB_t + \varepsilon_{it}, \tag{8}$$

where, R_{it} is the stock i's return at time t; R_{ft} is the risk-free return at time t; R_{mt} is the market return at time t; $\alpha_i, \beta_{i1}, \beta_{i2}, \beta_{i3}$, and β_{i4} are firm-specific parameters in the model; SMB_t is the size factor; HML_t is the book-to-market factor; UMB is the momentum factor (i.e., the difference in returns between firms with high and low past stock performance), and ε_{it} is the model's error term.

From this, we can then estimate the abnormal returns AR_{it} for stock i on day t as:

$$\widehat{AR_{it}} = R_{it} - (\hat{\alpha}_i + R_{ft} + \hat{\beta}_{i1}\left(R_{mt} - R_{ft}\right) + \hat{\beta}_{i2}SMB_t + \hat{\beta}_{i3}HML_t + \hat{\beta}_{i4}UMB_t, \tag{9}$$

where

$\widehat{AR_{it}}$ is the estimated abnormal return for stock i at time t;
R_{it} is the stock i's return at time t;
R_{ft} is the risk-free return at time t;
R_{mt} is the market return at time t;
SMB_t is the size factor;
HML_t is the book-to-market factor;
UMB_t is the momentum factor; and,
$\hat{\alpha}_i, \hat{\beta}_{i1}, \hat{\beta}_{i2}, \hat{\beta}_{i3}$, and $\hat{\beta}_{i4}$ are the estimated model's parameters.

Therefore, the four-factor model includes a one-year momentum factor, which Carhart (1997) shows to improve the model's fit. Consequently, the inclusion of the factor should allow for a more accurate measurement of the normal returns, and therefore, a better estimation of how the market reacts to the event that we are studying.

Multi-Country Models

An effective and comprehensive guide to conducting a multi-country study is provided by Park (2004). One of the key challenges is to extend the stock return model to accommodate different countries and markets. The simple solution is to develop a model of normal returns that reflects the stock return in the home country, relative to the appropriate market index. While there are many U.S. indices, most multi-country studies use the dominant index as a wider reflection of the local market. For example, in our study of the stock market reaction to auto manufacturers' environmental failure, we used data from the

U.S., Germany, France, Japan, Korea, and the U.K., with the local index used for each country reported in Table 1 (Wood et al., 2018, p. 372).

TEST STATISTICS TO DETERMINE THE SIGNIFICANCE

Over several decades, a great deal of work has been put into identifying the best way to evaluate the abnormal returns and determine whether not they are statistically significant. As different test statistics have been proposed, subsequent research has been conducted using simulation practice to determine whether each test statistic is beneficial or has weaknesses.

This section summarizes some of the commonly used test statistics and some weaknesses and drawbacks of each. We look at under what circumstances we might rely on or find a particular test statistic more credible than others. Given the nature of this volume, we have not included the calculations of the test statistics. Interested readers can go to the source material to learn the calculations required. In most cases, using a software package will enable these test statistics to be rapidly and easily brought up, reducing the need to understand the calculations behind the scenes. Many event study papers do not include the calculations for the test statistics in the paper, while in other cases, such as Jacobs et al. (2010, p. 435), these details are included.

One of the fundamental assumptions of many test statistics is a normal distribution. For example, assuming the stock price returns will be normally distributed would open up a range of test statistics. However, in practice, not all returns will be normally distributed, and those in multicountry event studies are certainly unlikely to be normally distributed (Campbell et al., 2010).

Another important issue is the additional volatility because of the events we study. In most cases, there will be an event-induced increase in stock returns volatility, which has been well-discussed in several papers. For example, an important early analysis of the problem by Brown and Warner (1985) identified how volatility and the increasing variance of the stock returns could cause mis-specification of commonly used test statistics. More recently, others have also noted that adjustments would need to be made in the calculations used to calculate statistical significance (Aktas et al., 2007; Harrington & Shrider, 2007; Higgins & Peterson, 1998).

Boehmer et al. (1991) suggested that the standard deviation from the estimation period can standardize the returns. The BMP parametric test assumes that all firms in the sample experience the same event-induced variance. In contrast, Corrado (1989) suggests that a nonparametric test better addresses the variation caused by events.

Another core problem is how event-date clustering can create the potential for cross-correlation of the stock returns (Kolari & Pynnönen, 2010). This is true when a common event date affects several firms in the sample. For instance, a study of an external event that affects several firms in the industry would cause this problem. Even if the cross-correlation is relatively low, event-date clustering will mean that there is no rejection of the null hypothesis, even if this hypothesis is true (Kolari & Pynnönen, 2010).

A good overview of nonparametric tests for event studies, along with discussions on some of the strengths and weaknesses of particular studies, is provided by Kolari and Pynnonen (2011). We next provide a short overview of some of the prime tests that may be useful, depending on their availability on the platform used to estimate abnormal returns.

Time Series T-Test

The time series t-test is a classic parametric test based on the assumption of normality of the abnormal returns and that the abnormal returns are cross-sectionally uncorrelated (MacKinlay, 1997; McWilliams & Siegel, 1997). The calculation examines the difference between the expected and actual returns, with no hypothesis that the abnormal returns are not statistically significant. The alternative hypothesis is that there is a difference, as what we are generally looking for if we believe our event will cause a stock market reaction.

Cross-Sectional T-Test

The cross-sectional t-test is another commonly used parametric test. The approach assumes that the abnormal returns are independent and identically distributed. Therefore, it cannot account for the variance in the estimation window. If there is event-induced volatility or the abnormal returns are correlated between firms, then the test statistics may be mis-specified (Brown & Warner, 1985).

Patell test of Standardized Residuals

This test may be referred to as a standardized residual test and is a third parametric test that is robust to heteroscedastic abnormal returns (the distribution) within the (cumulated) event window (Patell, 1976). However, it is sensitive to event-induced volatility and cross-sectional correlation of abnormal returns.

The Adjusted Patell Test

Introduced by Kolari and Pynnönen (2010), this accounts for the cross-sectional correlations that the original Patell test was sensitive to.

Standardized Cross-Sectional Test or BMP Test

This parametric test was developed by Boehmer, Musumeci, and Poulson (1991), and it largely is robust against the issues in the Patell test. In addition, it is robust against event-induced volatility; it accounts for serial correlation; and it is robust to variance in the distribution of abnormal returns. However, it remains sensitive to cross-sectional correlation.

Corrado Rank Test

The Corrado rank test is a nonparametric test that is commonly available (Corrado, 1989; Corrado & Zivney, 1992). While useful as a nonparametric test, it has a weakness where it will lose power with studies employing a wide event window (-10, 10). It has been shown to be more robust and powerful than parametric tests if there is no increase in return variability (Cowan & Sergeant, 1996).

Sign Test

The sign test (sometimes called the generalized sign test) is a nonparametric test that is robust against the skewness of the returns distribution (Cowan, 1992). Similar to the Corrado rank test, however, it performs poorly when a wider event window is used.

Wilcoxon Signed-Rank Test

This nonparametric test accounts for both the magnitude and the sign or direction of the abnormal returns (Wilcoxon, 1945)

CONCLUSION

This chapter has provided an overview of what abnormal returns are, how to consider the estimation window and event window, and then how to calculate the estimated abnormal returns with a range of models. These are the commonly used models, with the three- and four-factor models now becoming more prominent in studies, often with other model results provided to show that the selection of model is not driving the significant abnormal returns being reported. A range of test statistics are also discussed, showing the range of parametric and nonparametric options. Some of the benefits and drawbacks of each are presented. While the full range are not available in all packages, the options provided here should provide insight into which will be more reliable, based on the characteristics of the study you are conducting.

REFERENCES

Aktas, N., de Bodt, E., & Cousin, J.-G. (2007). Event studies with a contaminated estimation period. *Journal of Corporate Finance*, *13*(1), 129–145. doi:10.1016/j.jcorpfin.2006.09.001

Bebchuk, L. A., Cohen, A., & Wang, C. C. Y. (2013). Learning and the disappearing association between governance and returns. *Journal of Financial Economics*, *108*(2), 323–348. doi:10.1016/j.jfineco.2012.10.004

Bhattacharya, U., Daouk, H., Jorgenson, B., & Kehr, C.-H. (2000). When an event is not an event: The curious case of an emerging market. *Journal of Financial Economics*, *55*(1), 69–101. doi:10.1016/S0304-405X(99)00045-8

Boehmer, E., Masumeci, J., & Poulsen, A. B. (1991). Event-study methodology under conditions of event-induced variance. *Journal of Financial Economics*, *30*(2), 253–272. doi:10.1016/0304-405X(91)90032-F

Bouzzine, Y. D. (2021). Stock price reactions to environmental pollution events: A systematic literature review of direct and indirect effects and a research agenda. *Journal of Cleaner Production*, *316*, 128305. doi:10.1016/j.jclepro.2021.128305

Brown, S. J., & Warner, J. B. (1980). Measuring security price performance. *Journal of Financial Economics, 8*(3), 205–258. doi:10.1016/0304-405X(80)90002-1

Brown, S. J., & Warner, J. B. (1985). Using daily stock returns: The case of event studies. *Journal of Financial Economics, 14*(1), 3–31. doi:10.1016/0304-405X(85)90042-X

Campbell, C. J., Cowan, A. R., & Salotti, V. (2010). Multi-country event-study methods. *Journal of Banking & Finance, 34*(12), 3078–3090. doi:10.1016/j.jbankfin.2010.07.016

Carhart, M. M. (1997). On persistence in mutual fund performance. *The Journal of Finance, 52*(1), 57–82. doi:10.1111/j.1540-6261.1997.tb03808.x

Corrado, C. J. (1989). A nonparametric test for abnormal security-price performance in event studies. *Journal of Financial Economics, 23*(2), 385–395. doi:10.1016/0304-405X(89)90064-0

Corrado, C. J., & Zivney, T. L. (1992). The specification and power of the sign test in event study hypothesis tests using daily stock returns. *Journal of Financial and Quantitative Analysis, 27*(3), 465–478. doi:10.2307/2331331

Cowan, A. R. (1992). Nonparametric event study tests. *Review of Quantitative Finance and Accounting, 2*(4), 343–358. doi:10.1007/BF00939016

Cowan, A. R., & Sergeant, A. M. A. (1996). Trading frequency and event study test specification. *Journal of Banking & Finance, 20*(10), 1731–1757. doi:10.1016/S0378-4266(96)00021-0

Fama, E. F. (1991). Efficient capital markets: II. *The Journal of Finance, 46*(5), 1575–1617. doi:10.1111/j.1540-6261.1991.tb04636.x

Fama, E. F. (1998). Market efficiency, long-term returns, and behavioral finance. *Journal of Financial Economics, 49*(3), 283–306. doi:10.1016/S0304-405X(98)00026-9

Fama, E. F., & French, K. R. (1993). Common risk factors in the returns on stocks and bonds. *Journal of Financial Economics, 33*(1), 3–56. doi:10.1016/0304-405X(93)90023-5

Harrington, S. E., & Shrider, D. G. (2007). All events induce variance: Analyzing abnormal returns when effects vary across firms. *Journal of Financial and Quantitative Analysis, 42*(1), 229–256. doi:10.1017/S002210900000226X

Hawn, O., Chatterji, A. K., & Mitchell, W. (2018). Do investors actually value sustainability? New evidence from investor reactions to the Dow Jones Sustainability Index (DJSI). *Strategic Management Journal, 39*(4), 949–976. doi:10.1002mj.2752

Higgins, E. J., & Peterson, D. R. (1998). The power of one and two sample t-statistics given event-induced variance increases and nonnormal stock returns: A comparative study. *Quarterly Journal of Business and Economics, 37*(1), 27–49.

Hillmer, S. C., & Yu, P. L. (1979). The market speed of adjustment to new information. *Journal of Financial Economics, 7*(4), 321–345. doi:10.1016/0304-405X(79)90002-3

Jacobs, B. W., Singhal, V. R., & Subramanian, R. (2010). An empirical investigation of environmental performance and the market value of the firm. *Journal of Operations Management, 28*(5), 430–441. doi:10.1016/j.jom.2010.01.001

Kolari, J. W., & Pynnönen, S. (2010). Event study testing with cross-sectional correlation of abnormal returns. *Review of Financial Studies, 23*(11), 3996–4025. doi:10.1093/rfs/hhq072

Kolari, J. W., & Pynnonen, S. (2011). Nonparametric rank tests for event studies. *Journal of Empirical Finance, 18*(5), 953–971. doi:10.1016/j.jempfin.2011.08.003

MacKinlay, A. C. (1997). Event studies in economics and finance. *Journal of Economic Literature, 35*(1), 13–39.

Markowitz, H. (1952). Portfolio selection. *The Journal of Finance, 7*(1), 77–91. doi:10.1111/j.1540-6261.1952.tb01525.x

McWilliams, A., & Siegel, D. (1997). Event studies in management research: Theoretical and empirical issues. *Academy of Management Journal, 40*(3), 626–657. doi:10.2307/257056

McWilliams, A., Siegel, D., & Teoh, S. H. (1999). Issues in the use of the event study methodology: A critical analysis of corporate social responsibility studies. *Organizational Research Methods, 2*(4), 340–365. doi:10.1177/109442819924002

Park, N. K. (2004). A guide to using event study methods in multi-country settings. *Strategic Management Journal, 25*(7), 655–668. doi:10.1002mj.399

Patell, J. M. (1976). Corporate forecasts of earnings per share and stock price behavior: Empirical test. *Journal of Accounting Research, 14*(2), 246–276. doi:10.2307/2490543

Sharpe, W. F. (1963). A simplified model for portfolio analysis. *Management Science, 9*(2), 277–293. doi:10.1287/mnsc.9.2.277

Sharpe, W. F. (1964). Capital asset prices: A theory of market equilibrium under conditions of risk. *The Journal of Finance, 19*(3), 425–442. doi:10.1111/j.1540-6261.1964.tb02865.x

Ullah, S., Zaefarian, G., Ahmed, R., & Kimani, D. (2021). How to apply the event study methodology in STATA: An overview and a step-by-step guide for authors. *Industrial Marketing Management, 99*, A1–A12. doi:10.1016/j.indmarman.2021.02.004

Wilcoxon, F. (1945). Individual comparisons by ranking methods. *Biometrics Bulletin, 1*(6), 80–83. doi:10.2307/3001968

Wood, L. C., Wang, J. X., Duong, L. N. K., Reiners, T., & Smith, R. (2018). Stock market reactions to auto manufacturers' environmental failures. *Journal of Macromarketing, 38*(4), 364–382. doi:10.1177/0276146718781915

Xia, Y., Singhal, V. R., & Peter Zhang, G. (2016). Product design awards and the market value of the firm. *Production and Operations Management, 25*(6), 1038–1055. doi:10.1111/poms.12525

ADDITIONAL READING

Arora, P., Hora, M., Singhal, V., & Subramanian, R. (2020). When do appointments of corporate sustainability executives affect shareholder value? *Journal of Operations Management*, *66*(4), 464–487. doi:10.1002/joom.1074

Chen, Y., Singhal, V., & Zhu, Q. (2021). Environmental policies and financial performance: Stock market reaction to firms for their proactive environmental practices recognized by governmental programs. *Business Strategy and the Environment*, *30*(4), 1548–1562. doi:10.1002/bse.2693

Duong, L. N. K., Wang, J. X., Wood, L. C., Reiners, T., & Koushan, M. (2021). The value of incremental environmental sustainability innovation in the construction industry: An event study. *Construction Management and Economics*, *39*(5), 398–418. doi:10.1080/01446193.2021.1901950

Eilert, M., Jayachandran, S., Kalaignanam, K., & Swartz, T. A. (2017). Does it pay to recall your product early? An empirical investigation in the automobile industry. *Journal of Marketing*, *81*(3), 111–129. doi:10.1509/jm.15.0074

Gokhale, J., Brooks, R. M., & Tremblay, V. J. (2014). The effect on stockholder wealth of product recalls and government action: The case of Toyota's accelerator pedal recall. *The Quarterly Review of Economics and Finance*, *54*(4), 521–528. doi:10.1016/j.qref.2014.06.004

Hendricks, K. B., Hora, M., & Singhal, V. R. (2014). An empirical investigation on the appointments of supply chain and operations management executives. *Management Science*, *61*(7), 1562–1583. doi:10.1287/mnsc.2014.1987

Hendricks, K. B., Jacobs, B. W., & Singhal, V. R. (2020). Stock market reaction to supply chain disruptions from the 2011 great east Japan earthquake. *Manufacturing & Service Operations Management*, *22*(4), 645–867. doi:10.1287/msom.2019.0777

Hendricks, K. B., & Singhal, V. R. (2009). Online supplement: Details about constructing the sample of excess inventory announcements. *Manufacturing & Service Operations Management*, *11*(3, Suppl.), S1–S3.

Hu, H., Djebarni, R., Zhao, X., Xiao, L., & Flynn, B. (2017). Effect of different food recall strategies on consumers' reaction to different recall norms: A comparative study. *Industrial Management & Data Systems*, *117*(9), 2045–2063. doi:10.1108/IMDS-10-2016-0464

Jacobs, B. W., & Singhal, V. R. (2020). Shareholder value effects of the Volkswagen emissions scandal on the automotive ecosystem. *Production and Operations Management*, *29*(10), 2230–2251. doi:10.1111/poms.13228

Wood, L. C., Wang, J. X., Olesen, K., & Reiners, T. (2017). The effect of slack, diversification, and time to recall on stock market reaction to toy recalls. *International Journal of Production Economics*, *193*, 244–258. doi:10.1016/j.ijpe.2017.07.021

Zhan, X., Mu, Y., Hora, M., & Singhal, V. R. (2021). Service excellence and market value of a firm: An empirical investigation of winning service awards and stock market reaction. *International Journal of Production Research*, *59*(14), 4188–4204. doi:10.1080/00207543.2020.1759837

Zhan, X., Mu, Y., Nishant, R., & Singhal, V. R. (2020). When do appointments of Chief Digital or Data Officers (CDOs) affect stock prices? *IEEE Transactions on Engineering Management*, 1–14. doi:10.1109/TEM.2020.2984619

KEY TERMS AND DEFINITIONS

Estimated Parameter: While the parameter is a descriptive measure of the population, we are estimating this by providing a point estimate of the most likely value of the population parameter.

Four-Factor Model: Sometimes called the Carhart four-factor model, this extends the factors used in the three-factor model by also including the momentum, representing the speed of price changes, usually over the prior year.

Market Model: Sometimes referred to as a single-factor model, the model is used to estimate normal and then abnormal returns for the stock, drawing on the market returns, and providing estimates of alpha and beta.

Nonparametric Test: In contrast to the parametric tests, the nonparametric statistical tests do not rely on assumptions about the distribution (they are 'distribution free') but may instead rely on ranking or ordinal data.

Parametric Test: A statistical result to evaluate whether there is sufficient evidence to reject the null hypothesis. The statistical test depends on critical distribution assumptions, such as the population having a normal distribution.

Three-Factor Model: Sometimes referred to as the Fama and French model, this model extends earlier work by including abnormal return estimates that include size-risk and value factors, incorporating how small-cap stocks and value stocks tend to out-perform.

Chapter 10
Resolving Issues and Troubleshooting Problems

ABSTRACT

This chapter takes many of the research project design steps and analysis at this point and looks at things that can (and may) go wrong and what can be done about this. The author discusses how the issue may have been mitigated with effective research design decisions ahead of time and how to recover from an issue when it is identified later. As such, this chapter provides an overview of design decisions and why they are essential. It provides a range of remedies and actions that can be taken if issues and problems are identified part-way through a project. Several examples are provided of how different scholars have resolved the issues in their published articles, showing that resolutions are possible and practical.

INTRODUCTION

The purpose of this chapter is partially to provide a point for reflection on the book's content so far, with a particular focus on identifying what may have gone wrong. The root causes may be earlier in the journey through the project, problems may have been identified earlier or later, and there may be elements that you are uncertain about as a researcher. As such, the main focus of this chapter is on troubleshooting and identifying a range of different issues that researchers may experience at this point in the analysis and project. Some of these issues may be rectified with effective research design ahead of time; reading this chapter head of a project can give insight into the rationale and reason for some of the project design decisions being what they are. However, the chapter also provides insight into how problems can be rectified and overcome once they are identified.

The student whose research project progresses as planned with no deviations from what is expected is indeed a lucky student. However, many students find that because of shortcuts or rushing through different steps in the process; they do get results, but they are not quite the results they are looking for or expected; or there are some serious problems that they uncover part-way through the process. This is not, by itself, unusual. However, it can be a significant source of stress, mainly when there are time pressures that students are working under.

DOI: 10.4018/978-1-7998-8969-4.ch010

However, faculty research tends to have more luxury regarding how long the researcher takes to address issues and problems. However, there are often points where something has not worked as expected, and it is useful to identify what can be done to rectify and mitigate these problems.

The rest of this chapter progresses through a range of key issues that can be identified and commentary and ideas on how they can be resolved either proactively or reactively following identification of the problem.

PROBLEMS AND TROUBLESHOOTING

It is often difficult to isolate and separate out specific problems you may have. Consequently, it may be necessary to read through the chapter quickly and identify whether or not any of the issues are apparent with your project. In other cases, the troubleshooting problem has been reported to me in similar language terminology by some of my postgraduate students.

I Do Not have a Significant Result for My Abnormal Return

I recognize that it is often a gutwrenching experience to collect and analyze data and then seeing that the result shows no indication there is an effect of interest. But, unfortunately, this can happen to all of us. In an event study, this would indicate that you have found no significant evidence for an abnormal return based on a sample.

There are several ways of considering what this means the implications for your research. Number one, it could be the fact that there simply is no stock market reaction to the particular type of event that you are studying. It is not considered sufficiently important to the company's future in a way that will materially impact its future prospects. For many projects, this will result in a frustrating end to the study and may mean that further analysis such as a cross-sectional analysis is not considered.

First, I will discuss why no significant result for estimating abnormal returns is not necessarily a big problem stop. Second, I present some pathways that may be used to overcome this problem.

First of all, an absence of any significant evidence for an abnormal return is not, by itself, necessarily a problem. However, if you are expecting an abnormal return and that is none evident, this could be of great interest given the controversial nature of the particular problem being studied.

Two notable studies include the study by of the Rana Plaza disaster, showing no discernible stock market reaction, and a study of medical device recalls by Thirumalai and Sinha (2011).

When considering the Rana Plaza disaster, this falls into the category of an interesting and controversial problem. Based on the expansive and sweeping media commentary on such employee safety and social issues, we might expect a strong stock market reaction to the event. However, the study by Jacobs and Singhal (2017) show that no meaningful reaction transpired.

Also, merely because there is no substantial finding of an abnormal stock market reaction, that does not mean that understanding the determinants of the abnormal returns is unneeded, and thus, we can see that:

it is appropriate to examine the determinants of CARs [with a regression model] even if the average CAR is not significantly different from zero, particularly if the variance of CARs is relatively large. This could help authors determine subgroups of events for which the average CARs are significantly different than zero, even though they are not so for the entire sample. (Sorescu et al., 2017, pp. 199–200; emphasis added)

In other cases, where we might expect reaction and there is no reaction, such as with medical device recalls (Thirumalai & Sinha, 2011), this can be partially overcome by constructing interesting cross-sectional regression results to provide insight and add to our knowledge more broadly. Even though there is no discernible stock market reaction, the abnormal returns can still be the dependent variable in a cross-sectional regression. The cross-sectional regression may show statistically significant results that are also of practical significance to managers and researchers. Of the immediate impact of no significant findings for the primary hypothesis, Thirumalai and Sinha (2011, p. 376) note in the abstract that "[c]ontrary to our expectations, the findings of the study indicate that at an aggregate level, the market penalties for medical device recalls are not significant, i.e., at the aggregate level, the costs of poor quality are not severe."

When reading the article, it is clear they tried a range of approaches to discover a meaningful abnormal return, such as breaking the sample into sub-samples for analysis by using the severity of the recall issue as a classifier. Despite these efforts, they note how the

We wanted to estimate the market reactions to recalls, this time focusing only on the most severe recalls, i.e., class I recalls. We redrew a subset of events from our data, such that events were those of public firms that had class I recalls. At the end of this step, we arrived at a sample of 26 events. (Thirumalai & Sinha, 2011, p. 384)

Ultimately, despite a range of tests, they find the "pattern of results, similar to those for class II and class III recalls, suggests that regardless of the type of recall, on average, the abnormal returns are not significant" (Thirumalai & Sinha, 2011, p. 384). However, using the abnormal returns in the cross-sectional regression, they identify that "The results suggest that the product scope, sales, growth prospects, and the capital structure of a firm affect the magnitude of the financial consequences of recalls" (Thirumalai & Sinha, 2011, p. 385). A key section that, therefore, outlines critical findings notes that:

The findings from the analyses suggest that capital market penalties for medical device recalls are not severe and that market reaction to recall announcements is varied across heterogeneous firms. The results also indicate that as firms broaden their product scope, the likelihood of product failures and recalls increases, owing to a decreased operational focus. Lastly, the results suggest that firms do learn from recalls. (Thirumalai & Sinha, 2011, p. 387)

With the Rana Plaza collapse, we may expect a negative stock market reaction to the disaster, as investors drive an economic impact that would suggest a cost to the businesses of operating this way and may, for instance, suggest that sourcing should shift to countries or regions with better health and safety records. However, they found that:

From a retailer perspective, since negative economic impacts from the Rana Plaza disaster were insignificant, they have limited economic incentive to move sourcing out of Bangladesh to other low-cost countries such as Cambodia and China, both of which have well-developed garment industries, let alone to higher-cost countries in North America or Europe. This evidence is counter to the widely-held as-

sumption that the risks of sourcing in developing, low-cost countries might lead to increased sourcing in developed, high-cost countries. (Jacobs & Singhal, 2017, p. 63)

This outcome is based on an extensive range of tests not just of the collapse but also the development of two pro-worker initiatives that would be seen to be positive for the retailers: the Accord on Fire and Building Safety in Bangladesh (AFBSB), and the Alliance for Bangladesh Worker Safety (ABWS). However, ultimately, the new accords to protect workers also generated no significant stock market reaction. Furthermore, they noted that "[t]he combined sample of AFBSB and ABWS signees experienced no significant reaction to the announcement of the AFBSB" (Jacobs & Singhal, 2017, p. 59). Broadly, the range of tests used and different tests to ensure the robustness of their results, led them to state:

Although stock market reaction to retailers on the day of the Rana Plaza disaster is negative and significant, its magnitude and significance dissipates when considering the following day's stock market reaction. There is no evidence of significant stock market reaction over 11 trading days (approximately two weeks in calendar time) after the Rana Plaza disaster. Further, for the 60 trading days (approximately 3 months in calendar time) after the Rana Plaza disaster, the stock market reaction adjusted for other contemporaneous announcements unrelated to the Rana Plaza disaster is statistically insignificant. (Jacobs & Singhal, 2017, p. 61)

This particular case, given the broad interest in the type of disaster, the social implications of the event, and the meaningfulness of the outcome, the strong societal expectations for a negative stock market reaction that was not found suggests that this is still an important finding which policymakers and managers do need to consider very carefully.

There Seem to be no Statistically Significant Results in the Cross-Sectional Regression Analysis

If the estimation of the abnormal returns showed no evidence of abnormal returns different from zero, then finding no meaningful statistically significant results for the cross-sectional regression would represent a double blow. However, there several ways of addressing the lack of statistically significant returns of the cross-sectional regression analysis. Therefore, several elements need to be checked. It is also worth noting that every hypothesis does not need to find support in the manuscript.

First, given the type of data available for the cross-sectional regression, quarterly data may have be used. The type of data and the calculations should be thoroughly checked for errors. This may include having one of the other researchers on the team coming in to independently checks that the variables are being constructed correctly. The data may also need to be transformed with a log function. This transformation may improve the analysis, particularly where there is a wide range of values, such as may be identified for revenue values as a measure of firm size.

The quarterly data should be that for the quarter before the event of interest. It would not make sense to use cross-sectional data reported the quarter during which the event occurs as a be reported after the event and reduces the predictive value of the regression – the use of future data to estimate something the past is not logical. This is something that I have also seen several times while reviewing leading journals where the regression analysis was not thoroughly and carefully set up. In many cases, this may not make much difference but is certainly something that needs to be carefully investigated.

With reference to the chapter on the regression analysis, it is important to understand that conducting the regression in SPSS with standard OLS estimators is not necessarily can provide a very good outcome. This is because the abnormal returns tend to be nonnormally distributed. However, a speedy examination of the estimated abnormal returns on the project should illuminate the nature of the issue. Consequently, it may be more appropriate to use different standard error calculations such as robust standard errors. Please see the chapter on cross-sectional regression for additional details on this.

Finally, it may be the case that the variables that have been constructed to measure what is of interest and the hypothesis represent a poor measure. Ultimately, this is hard to avoid given the nature of secondary data use and the inability to change or collect different forms of variables, as you might do with primary data collection using a survey. However, there are often different ways of addressing the core relationship of interest with different ways of measuring the variables of interest. Therefore, it is worth checking through the literature to carefully identify whether or not there are any other variables or measures that could be used or constructed. In some cases, reference to the finance literature (where they have used the method extensively for many years) may indicate acceptable and sensible measures that can be used.

When this does not work, it is worth going back to the variables and the hypotheses that have been generated. As noted elsewhere in the book, a theory-based study is more likely to generate statistically significant and meaningful results. On the other hand, if the hypotheses were based on gut reactions or assumptions rather than clear theoretical frameworks, there is less likely an observable abnormal return effect that can be identified and the hypotheses themselves are less likely to be significant. Therefore, it may be worth looking at the hypotheses and understanding whether they can be changed or should be changed to align with a guiding theoretical framework.

It is certainly not good practice to go back and develop a range of new hypotheses and try out a sequence of variables until something works. This approach is simply slinging mud at a wall and hoping some of it sticks. Moreover, when the manuscript is written, it becomes clear that there is a jumble of hypotheses with the unifying thread or theme. As a result, such a manuscript may be rejected from many leading journals because it has an insufficient theoretical grounding.

A related approach may be to go back to the broader sample, where the sample is sufficiently large, and identify a relevant subgroup where the event of interest may be more prominent, significant, or meaningful. The isolated subgroup may be able to provide evidence of a more meaningful abnormal return and a stronger relationship between the variables of interest in the cross-sectional regression. This approach may work in some cases but is certainly not a guaranteed fix to the problem.

Another mechanism that might be useful for refining the hypotheses of interest is going back to the announcements and reading through them carefully. There is no magic to the approach. As you read through and consider the similarities and differences between the different announcements, you may discover that you can categorize the announcements in different ways this might include the severity of the product recall (Chen et al., 2009; Thirumalai & Sinha, 2011), or the type of business process outsourcing that is being used (Duan et al., 2009), or the type of IT system has been implemented (Hendricks et al., 2007). Consequentially, a new hypothesis might be formed based on this where there is reason to suspect that the stock market reaction to each of these categories may be different. For instance, Duan et al. (2014) discuss how they read the announcements carefully to determine whether the business process outsourcing is managed using relational governance, the value chain position of the process, and the process experience of the firms.

Challenges with multicollinearity may drive related issues. A traditional evaluation has been whether the variance inflation factors are below 10 (Cohen et al., 2003), although many researchers will now use a value of below three. Lower values indicate less multicollinearity, usually resulting in a more meaningful regression model. Whether or not there is an influential observation can be determined using Cook's distance or the protocols Fox outlined (2002). The distribution of daily stock returns can be an issue that heteroscedasticity tests can evaluate. It may require the use of robust standard errors (White, 1982) where the heteroscedasticity consistent covariance matrix estimation processes will be robust, even with a slightly smaller sample size as you may have with an event study in management (Kleiber, 2008; MacKinnon & White, 1985). Addressing these issues may positively impact the analysis but requires careful consideration. It may be beneficial to consult with another researcher to ensure you are doing everything correctly and addressing all underlying issues that may be apparent in the data.

My Sample was Ruined When I Removed Confounding Events

If you have searched for confounding events within the event window and discovered that removing most of the observations from your sample was necessary, this is most likely a reflection on having a wider window to estimate the abnormal returns. When looking for confounding events by increasing the width of this window, it is much more likely to increase the chances that a particular firm has something else going on and other pertinent news is released to the market. This is one of the primary reasons that a smaller event window is recommended from a practical perspective (in addition to the fact that the efficient market hypothesis suggests that the small event window should be as small as possible) (McWilliams et al., 1999; McWilliams & Siegel, 1997).

If the removal of confounding events is problematic, it could also suggest there were few events in the sample to begin with. It may be necessary to work out how to increase the sample size.

Some of the mechanisms that you can use to address this include:

- **checking the event window.** In general, this is likely to be between one and three days in length. Even if it is three days, you may wish to examine this and evaluate with another can be fruitfully reduced to 2 days. This would decrease the number of confounding events identified by perhaps 1/3 and may result in a substantial gain in the final number of observations in the sample.
- **You may have been too ruthless in terms of what qualifies as a confounding event.** At the most basic level may be necessary to check on the Edgar database but perhaps no further. A simple search for news about the firm of interest over that event window will likely turn up dozens or even hundreds of news articles, commentaries, even press releases from the company itself over several days. Clearly, not all of this will be sufficient to shake the market. In principle, the EDGAR database information releases will be enough to move the market, and it also has the benefit of being a simple way of reducing the ambiguity in terms of what constitutes an announcement released to the market.

Jacobs and Singhal (2017, p. 59) looked at the removal of confounding events and identified "20 contemporaneous announcements for the 39 sample firms over the 6-day period that are unrelated to the Rana Plaza disaster, and estimate abnormal returns by removing the abnormal returns around these announcements." While this did not reduce the sample size from 39 to 19 (the difference due to 20 events), it reduced the sample size used each day to 29 to 33.

I Cannot Find a Very Large Event Sample and There Does Not Seem to Be Actual Any Events That I can Find That are Related to the Phenomenon I am Studying

When searching for events, we often have a pretty strict concept of what we think we are looking for. It is important to recall that the event study will focus on quite an abstract category of events; managers may be more interested in specific sub-categories of the events, while researchers will often work at quite an abstract level.

As we get interested in doing this study, we often become quite narrowly focused on a particular type of event representing, in reality, only a tiny set of possible instantiations or examples of the wider category of event. I think this is entirely normal and useful to consider in advance of the study.

It is possible that when the sample is being created is just possible to find very few examples of news announcements that are relevant to the event type.

If there are not very many announcements that appear to be relevant, there could be several issues. First, there may simply be very few announcements about this type of event. In some cases, this may be simply because of the nature of the event. For example, whereas many firms exclaim about gaining or signing new contracts, very few firms make public announcements about the change of the critical vendor or the loss of the primary customer, which may reflect poorly on the parties involved.

Second, the search may simply have been created to be far too narrow, which often comes from a very narrow disciplinary perspective on the topic. To address this issue, there are two fundamental approaches. First, expand the search string to include more specific events related to the event's more abstract category. This can be conducted by expanding on the keywords in consultation with equity and other researchers, particularly those from other disciplines who might explain the terminology used in the field that might relate to the broader category. Another source of valuable ideas is managers or employees, who can explain specific terminology employed in the business articles when discussing the phenomenon of interest. For example, when we think about capacity and operations management perspective, we may be inclined to consider capacity only in terms of, for example, capacity at a factory plant. In this case, capacity might initially be considered equipment, an increase in capital expenditure, and a plant, factory, or facility. However, when we think about the expansion of capacity, there is quite a range of other ways of thinking about capacity. For example, if we think about capacity in the service sector, it may be more related to hiring decisions for recruitment or job advertisements. Moreover, expansion of IT capacity may involve other terminologies, such as noting servers or data centers. For instance, from an operations perspective, Hendricks and Singhal (1995, p. 261)use 'capacity expansion,' 'plant expansion,' and new plant among other phrases, betraying a strong production focus for the research that need not necessarily relate to the broader concept of 'capacity' in other sectors. Another operations example is focused on production delays. Here, Hendricks and Singhal (2003, p. 506) use "[k]ey words used in the search include combinations of words such as delay, shortfall, shortage, manufacturing, production, shipment, delivery, parts, components, and other relevant phrases."

Third, it may be that the search is focused on too narrow a set of publications. For example, while articles appearing in the Wall Street Journal will undoubtedly change the market and result in the stock market reaction, very few of these announcements may be made in those key publications. It may become necessary to search for more regional publications for announcements of interest. Additionally, rather than focusing on a single region such as the USA, and it might be advantageous to consider the event in other regions such as Europe, Australia, or China. To do this, the media sources you search in for announcements may need to be expanded to address other geographic regions. However, note that this will create other challenges such as a much larger set of announcements to search. In addition, the analysis steps subsequently may be more challenging, and a wider event window may be required for a multi-country study to accommodate the different time zones.

Fourth, extending the search back in time may be possible. Some issues will be timeless, such as capacity expansions, contractions, or supply chain glitches. However, some announcements and issues may be relevant to particular periods. For instance, cyber attacks and cyber security would not have been considered an issue of such consequence before the development of the Internet. As such, the studies will naturally have a point in time where they cannot go past the data collection.

A small sample, by itself, is not a terminal issue as it is possible to go back and expand the search parameters to try and increase the sample size. However, it may be necessary to get additional help, insight, and eyes considering the terminology used in search parameters. Different publications may need to be used or even searching using publications from different geographic regions. (Note that if you expand the search to accommodate different geographic regions, you may need to run a multi-country study to estimate the abnormal returns.)

There is no wonder set rules for how big sample size should be in there have been event studies with relatively small sample sizes and those with many hundreds and even thousands of observations, particularly in the finance sector. However, in general, larger sample sizes will be preferable for identifying an abnormal return, particularly those that are slightly smaller of this magnitude, and conducting an effective and robust cross-sectional analysis after calculating the abnormal returns.

Examples of a range of sample sizes used over several studies, showing small and large management studies, include:

- 406 firms in Hendricks et al. (2007) studying ERP, CRM, and SCM focused system implementations
- 780 in Jacobs et al. (2010) studying announcements of environmental performance
- 39 publicly traded global apparel retailers in Jacobs and Singhal (2017)
- 261 firms in the Ba et al. (2013) study on green vehicle innovations
- 135 toy recall announcements in Wood et al. (2017)
- 298 announcements of business process outsourcing events in Duan et al. (2009)

Another possible remedy to improve the sample size may come from considering news amount moments that mention the company of interest and those that affect the company of interest. For example, when conducting a project on toy recalls we were able to attribute announcements to the broader holding company about some of these critical brands that they managed and owned, and so Wood et al. (2017, p. 249) explained they "searched for key brands or subsidiaries, e.g., in addition to searching for Mattel we also sought announcements regarding the Mattel-owned Fisher-Price brand." That is, recall associated with a brand held by a subsidiary of the broader listed parent company impacts the broader parent company. Consequently, this requires a bit more careful consideration and work, but it becomes a manageable way to attribute a broader set of events to publicly listed companies, mainly when you are familiar with the industry and the type of companies in the industry.

Finally, it may simply be that there are not many examples of what you want to study. For example, it may be the case that a project needs to be abandoned or the scope or nature of the event needs to be substantially broadened. Then, the final analysis may contain a group-to-group comparison of fairly specific event types against other types of similar or comparable events.

CONCLUSIONS

This chapter presents some common problems or issues that may occur mid-project. In most cases, this underscores the importance of advice and discussions in the earlier chapters and addresses some issues that may occur during the process. In some cases, the issue may have several remedies that can be applied to address the underlying problem.

By working through the chapter, the researcher should take the problem they are experiencing, understand the core problem, work out how to address the problem, and come back to the analysis. In most cases, the underlying issues can be resolved. However, this is not to say that the resolution will be free of pain or work; additional analysis and scrutiny may need to be applied at different steps, and some elements may need to be re-worked to address the problem. In some cases, this simply addresses a step that was, perhaps, not as thoroughly completed as it should have been, with the consequences only apparent part-way through the analysis.

The following chapters look at the final analyses and make sense of the results before progressing through the write-up of the manuscript. Again, it is helpful to identify and remedy issues before writing up, although notes may be taken about the steps and processes used as they can form an essential component of the write-up.

REFERENCES

Ba, S., Lisic, L. L., Liu, Q., & Stallaert, J. (2013). Stock market reaction to green vehicle innovation. *Production and Operations Management, 22*(4), 976–990. doi:10.1111/j.1937-5956.2012.01387.x

Chen, Y., Ganesan, S., & Liu, Y. (2009). Does a firm's product-recall strategy affect its financial value? An examination of strategic alternatives during product-harm crises. *Journal of Marketing, 73*(6), 214–226. doi:10.1509/jmkg.73.6.214

Cohen, J., Cohen, P., West, S. G., & Aiken, L. S. (2003). *Applied multiple regression/correlation analysis for the behavioral sciences* (3rd ed.). L. Erlbaum Associates.

Duan, C., Grover, V., & Balakrishnan, N. (2009). Business process outsourcing: An event study on the nature of processes and firm valuation. *European Journal of Information Systems, 18*(5), 442–457. doi:10.1057/ejis.2009.38

Duan, C., Grover, V., Roberts, N., & Balakrishnan, N. (2014). Firm valuation effects of the decision to adopt relationally governed business process outsourcing arrangements. *International Journal of Production Research, 52*(15), 4673–4694. doi:10.1080/00207543.2014.884289

Fox, J. (2002). *An R and S-Plus companion to applied regression.* Sage Publications.

Hendricks, K. B., & Singhal, V. R. (2003). The effect of supply chain glitches on shareholder wealth. *Journal of Operations Management, 21*(5), 501–522. doi:10.1016/j.jom.2003.02.003

Hendricks, K. B., Singhal, V. R., & Stratman, J. K. (2007). The impact of enterprise systems on corporate performance: A study of ERP, SCM, and CRM system implementations. *Journal of Operations Management, 25*(1), 65–82. doi:10.1016/j.jom.2006.02.002

Hendricks, K. B., Singhal, V. R., & Wiedman, C. I. (1995). The impact of capacity expansion on the market value of the firm. *Journal of Operations Management, 12*(3–4), 259–272. doi:10.1016/0272-6963(94)00016-8

Jacobs, B. W., & Singhal, V. R. (2017). The effect of the Rana Plaza disaster on shareholder wealth of retailers: Implications for sourcing strategies and supply chain governance. *Journal of Operations Management, 49–51*(1), 52–66. doi:10.1016/j.jom.2017.01.002

Jacobs, B. W., Singhal, V. R., & Subramanian, R. (2010). An empirical investigation of environmental performance and the market value of the firm. *Journal of Operations Management, 28*(5), 430–441. doi:10.1016/j.jom.2010.01.001

Kleiber, C. (2008). *Applied econometrics with R*. Springer New York. doi:10.1007/978-0-387-77318-6

MacKinnon, J. G., & White, H. (1985). Some heteroskedasticity-consistent covariance matrix estimators with improved finite sample properties. *Journal of Econometrics, 29*(3), 305–325. doi:10.1016/0304-4076(85)90158-7

McWilliams, A., & Siegel, D. (1997). Event studies in management research: Theoretical and empirical issues. *Academy of Management Journal, 40*(3), 626–657. doi:10.2307/257056

McWilliams, A., Siegel, D., & Teoh, S. H. (1999). Issues in the use of the event study methodology: A critical analysis of corporate social responsibility studies. *Organizational Research Methods, 2*(4), 340–365. doi:10.1177/109442819924002

Sorescu, A., Warren, N. L., & Ertekin, L. (2017). Event study methodology in the marketing literature: An overview. *Journal of the Academy of Marketing Science, 45*(2), 186–207. doi:10.100711747-017-0516-y

Thirumalai, S., & Sinha, K. K. (2011). Product recalls in the medical device industry: An empirical exploration of the sources and financial consequences. *Management Science, 57*(2), 376–392. doi:10.1287/mnsc.1100.1267

White, H. (1982). Maximum likelihood estimation of misspecified models. *Econometrica, 50*(1), 1–25. doi:10.2307/1912526

Wood, L. C., Wang, J. X., Olesen, K., & Reiners, T. (2017). The effect of slack, diversification, and time to recall on stock market reaction to toy recalls. *International Journal of Production Economics, 193*, 244–258. doi:10.1016/j.ijpe.2017.07.021

ADDITIONAL READING

Arora, P., Hora, M., Singhal, V., & Subramanian, R. (2020). When do appointments of corporate sustainability executives affect shareholder value? *Journal of Operations Management, 66*(4), 464–487. doi:10.1002/joom.1074

Binder, J. (1998). The event study methodology since 1969. *Review of Quantitative Finance and Accounting, 11*(2), 111–137. doi:10.1023/A:1008295500105

Binder, J. J. (1985). On the use of the multivariate regression model in event studies. *Journal of Accounting Research*, *23*(1), 370–383. doi:10.2307/2490925

Brown, S. J., & Warner, J. B. (1980). Measuring security price performance. *Journal of Financial Economics*, *8*(3), 205–258. doi:10.1016/0304-405X(80)90002-1

Fama, E. F. (1970). Efficient capital markets: A review of theory and empirical work. *The Journal of Finance*, *25*(2), 383–417. doi:10.2307/2325486

Fama, E. F. (1991). Efficient capital markets: II. *The Journal of Finance*, *46*(5), 1575–1617. doi:10.1111/j.1540-6261.1991.tb04636.x

Fama, E. F. (1998). Market efficiency, long-term returns, and behavioral finance. *Journal of Financial Economics*, *49*(3), 283–306. doi:10.1016/S0304-405X(98)00026-9

Fama, E. F., & French, K. R. (1993). Common risk factors in the returns on stocks and bonds. *Journal of Financial Economics*, *33*(1), 3–56. doi:10.1016/0304-405X(93)90023-5

Kothari, S. P., & Warner, J. B. (2007). Econometrics of event studies. In B. E. Eckbo (Ed.), *Handbook of Corporate Finance: Empirical Corporate Finance* (Vol. 1, pp. 3–36). North-Holland/Elsevier. doi:10.1016/B978-0-444-53265-7.50015-9

Mitchell, M., & Stafford, E. (2000). Managerial decisions and long-term stock price performance. *The Journal of Business*, *73*(3), 287–329. doi:10.1086/209645

Oh, C. H., Shapiro, D., Ho, S. S. H., & Shin, J. (2020). Location matters: Valuing firm-specific nonmarket risk in the global mining industry. *Strategic Management Journal*, *41*(7), 1210–1244. doi:10.1002mj.3153

Riley, S. M., Michael, S. C., & Mahoney, J. T. (2017). Human capital matters: Market valuation of firm investments in training and the role of complementary assets. *Strategic Management Journal*, *38*(9), 1895–1914. doi:10.1002mj.2631

Wassmer, U., & Dussauge, P. (2012). Network resource stocks and flows: How do alliance portfolios affect the value of new alliance formations? *Strategic Management Journal*, *33*(7), 871–883. doi:10.1002mj.973

Zhan, X., Mu, Y., Hora, M., & Singhal, V. R. (2021). Service excellence and market value of a firm: An empirical investigation of winning service awards and stock market reaction. *International Journal of Production Research*, *59*(14), 4188–4204. doi:10.1080/00207543.2020.1759837

Zhan, X., Mu, Y., Nishant, R., & Singhal, V. R. (2020). When do appointments of Chief Digital or Data Officers (CDOs) affect stock prices? *IEEE Transactions on Engineering Management*, •••, 1–14. doi:10.1109/TEM.2020.2984619

KEY TERMS AND DEFINITIONS

Abnormal Return: The divergence from the expected, 'normal' return that we would expect to see, indicating that the event has influenced the stock returns or that there is evidence of a stock market reaction.

Event List: The list of observations of an event, including the date and the firm affected.

Heteroscedasticity: The error variance that is different or varies with some level of dispersion.

Independence: The assumption of independence is at the core of many assumptions for test statistics. It suggests that each event or observation has no connection with the others; it has no influence on another event occurring. Logically, we may see some problems with this where, for instance, a firm with poor quality control measures may experience multiple product failures and consequential recalls.

Multicollinearity: A case where several of the variables in the model are highly correlated. This may include both the control variables as well as the variables of interest and used to test the hypotheses.

Regression Model: The analysis using abnormal returns as the dependent variable, used to test hypotheses and determine the importance of factinrs influencing the abnormal returns.

Sample Size: The number of observations in the sample. In an event study, one firm may have different events impact them over time, and so while there may be many observations in the sample, there may be fewer firms.

Sampling: the process of creating a sample for the analysis. Errors in sampling create consequential problems in the analysis.

Chapter 11
Cross–Sectional Regression

ABSTRACT

This chapter revisits some of the major considerations in undertaking the cross-sectional regression. The author uses the abnormal returns as the dependent variable, with the other hypotheses tested to understand the determinants of the abnormal returns. Examining the principles of setting up the models, he uses several examples and provides commentary to add additional insights. In addition, he looks at some of the common issues and problems and how they might be addressed. Next, he outlined some important diagnostic steps. Again, examples from the literature are used to illustrate important principles. Finally, the reporting of results is examined, with some conclusions drawn about the presentation of results and reporting on the use of multiple models. Together, these steps and cautions should enable researchers to draw on their experience with regression modeling in other areas and produce valuable and useful contributions using a cross-sectional regression model.

INTRODUCTION

As always, this chapter may not be sufficient to resolve all issues and problems, but the included citations and ideas on where to look for further answers should benefit many readers. Regression analysis has been, for a long time, a fundamental technique used in both academic research and decision-making processes. It is commonly understood and presents a very versatile analysis of dependence. It can accommodate a broad range of issues and problems from wider estimations of economic output, for example, 30 much more specific analyses of a particular business problem. It can be used as a supplement in event studies that enable us to evaluate how several different determinants play in affecting abnormal returns. This enables us to see how these independent variables influence the dependent variable and how the managerial choices might influence abnormal returns.

This chapter presents some guidelines for using the cross-sectional regression within the analysis in the event study project. We present some guidelines for the appropriateness of regression and some distinctions from other regression studies that are important to keep in mind. Finally, we provide some suggestions for interpreting the analysis from both the statistical and managerial perspectives. In preparing the chapter, I assume most operations and supply chain and broader management researchers are at

DOI: 10.4018/978-1-7998-8969-4.ch011

least passingly familiar with the multiple regression method. If your background is qualitative research, it may be helpful to refer to a good research methods book with strong coverage of multiple regression, such as Hair et al. (2014).

Drawing on your background of regression in other areas, whether it is multivariate methods or structural equation modeling (Kock, 2017, p. 207; Kock & Hadaya, 2018; Ringle et al., 2012), much of what you know will be applicable here. First, however, we focus on some of the core issues. These issues are both conceptual and in terms of the analysis technicalities that we must consider when working with event study data.

THEORY DRIVEN HYPOTHESES AND MODELS

Publishing in leading journals and management in supply chain management requires an increasingly strong contribution to theory. The need for a theory-basis challenges the use of the event method in this area as it is necessary to connect the event and the underlying model being studied to a theory. By itself, a single event study showing the change in the market value of the companies in reaction to this event is not a substantial contribution to theory in most cases, and inclusion of an appropriate theoretical model will usually come through the cross-sectional regression analysis based on the abnormal returns calculated by the event study.

See, for example, the empirical study of re-shoring of manufacturing, with an analysis of the short-run stock market reaction in Brandon-Jones et al. (2017), where they note that future studies may include analysis of the determinants. The study itself provided evidence of shareholder value implications.

For example, Duan et al. (2014) studied the business process outsourcing and relied on transaction cost economics (TCE) as a theoretical foundation for studying outsourcing. TCE informed the development of the key hypotheses which had tested in the cross-sectional regression. While using theory makes sense and is encouraged, practice of including theory to inform the development of the model in the cross-sectional regression remains challenging as we often do not have access to data appropriate to test hypotheses derived from the theory. For example, during a survey or when conducting qualitative research, we often have the flexibility to ask a different type of question or to adapt our questions to provide a better measurement that allows us to capture and measure the variable of interest. When collecting and compiling the data for an event study, in contrast, we remain limited by the type of data and often the data availability. For example, while it might be of great interest to study the power difference in an outsourcing study, this may be easily accomplished with a survey and established scales of questions. However, it remains difficult to effectively measure power when using archival data for the cross-sectional regression in an event study.

As an example, if we are interested in how the innovativeness of a company will influence the stock market reaction, several measures may be used. For example, we could incorporate research and development (R&D) spend or patents granted to the firm. However, when we search databases to try and secure this type of information, they will often be big gaps or a large proportion of firms for which we cannot get appropriate data. This is true even within the U.S. market, and the data availability decreases when we start to look at firms listed on non-U.S. markets

DETERMINING VARIABLES OF INTEREST FROM THE ANNOUNCEMENTS

It is often very difficult to determine what data in an announcement might be relevant to a project. In many cases, variables or information pertinent to the project will be encoded or hidden within a particular set of announcements. It will often be possible to determine this while looking through the announcements one-by-one. We should share some announcements with a colleague or advisor to help identify any additional variables of interest. Taking a shared approach is helpful because it will not always be apparent which factors are relevant to the project.

In many cases, relevant information may not be directly reported using keywords we may have trained ourselves to recognize. For example, the range of terminology used might be quite broad, so we may not pick up cues. Or we might need to translate the terminology used as the announcement may report on a particular instance of a more general category of events we study. Again, discussing and talking with other experienced researchers often helps with this step.

CONTROL VARIABLES

In developing the model is important to include appropriate control variables. We want to address the control variables indirectly within the study; they will be held constant as they are not a key focus of the study, but we recognize that they could influence the outcome. Reducing the influence of these other variables will help you develop a stronger correlational relationship between the variables of interest. By developing a multiple model approach where you first include control variables that are recognized to influence the dependent variable, you can then present the second model with the variables of interest. When the second model shows that the variables of interest are statistically significant, we confidently assert that we have identified important relationships. This enables us to make a stronger, more compelling theoretical contribution.

The commonly used control variables are the firm's size, which can often be represented by the revenue or sales for the firm. There is a great deal of evidence that large firms, when faced with a crisis, have a greater ability to cover their costs associated with the adverse event (Jones & Rubin, 2001) and may therefore be less affected by a crisis, while smaller firms gain a relatively greater benefit from positive news in large firms.

They may vary depending on the focus and type of issue we are addressing. For instance, in a study of product design awards, Xia et al. (2016) use controls for the research and development (R&D) intensity, number of awards received at the same time, and the overall reputation of the company. In a study of supply chain glitches, Hendricks and Singhal (2003) use the capital intensity, the R&D intensity, the industry competitiveness, and whether there are previous glitches to the one in the study. In their study of investments into human capital, Riley et al. (2017) use the firm size, whether the award was to a division or subsidiary, whether they had received an award in the immediately preceding year, and the industry classification.

There is little consensus on the exact control variables, so a degree of flexibility exists here. However, if we can control for known effects and identify an effect in the analysis, it becomes a more compelling finding. On the other hand, we do not want to be in a situation where an examiner or reviewer requires the list of control variables to be updated and, in doing so, the main effects in the study are diminished or become no longer statistically significant.

CONSTRUCTING THE HYPOTHESES VARIABLES

The hypothesis may be drawn from a theory foundation, but it is or remains fairly abstract. If we were doing survey research, there are often a series of scales and previously validated items that provide a satisfactory measure of the variable. However, any one of these measures is probably insufficient and open to interpretation as to whether this is satisfactory. In an event study, we cannot simply draw any particular type of data, and we are limited to what is available in the databases that we have on offer or the types of variables we can use to construct another variable. Therefore, when we do an event study, we may find there are no direct or simple measures of many managerial issues of interest that may be available.

However, contemporary research often draws on accounting and operational data to construct variables for hypothesis testing. In addition, information can be drawn from announcements themselves, often used to create categories such as the seven corporate environmental initiative categories based on the announcement content in Jacobs et al. (2010), the categories of compensation for customers noted in the announcements (Wood et al., 2018), or from other sources such as geographic information systems (Oh et al., 2020).

RUNNING THE ANALYSIS

In principle, the study can run cross-sectional regression using the same principles that we may remember from elementary statistics lessons at university. However, some nuances require additional thought and care. It is on these factors that we focus our attention.

One element that is often used in event study papers is a two-stage modeling process. In the first stage, we use the control variables in the model. The comprehensive model that includes variables of interest or interaction terms is introduced in the next stage. In this way, we can see the impact of adding the variables of interest on top of the control variables. We can report VIF factor scores as a measure of collinearity for the final model only. The final or most comprehensive model results are usually discussed in subsequent sections.

DIAGNOSTICS AND VALIDATION

Developing the models within R enables us to access a range of different diagnostics and modeling tools and techniques that can be used. One of the first elements to consider is whether there is any evidence of multicollinearity within the model. We also need to consider whether there are any outlier observations or influential observations of concern.

Stock returns are unlikely to be normally distributed, which can impact the results and study (Brown & Warner, 1985). Consequently, the studentized Breusch-Pagan test can be used to evaluate the level of heteroscedasticity (Breusch & Pagan, 1979). If there is a level of heteroscedasticity, we should use robust standard errors in the analysis (White, 1982). The issues of distribution represent a common problem, as:

data typically exhibit some form of autocorrelation and/or heteroskedasticity. If the covariance structure were known, it could be taken into account in a (parametric) model, but more often than not, the form of the autocorrelation or heteroskedasticity is unknown [...] for valid inference a consistent covariance matrix estimate is essential. Over the last 20 years, several procedures for heteroskedasticity consistent (HC)[...] covariance matrix estimation have been suggested (Kleiber, 2008, p. 106)

An example of this in practice is reported by Xia et al. (2016, p. 1050) who note how "[t]he Breusch-Pagan test for all models in Table 7 has p-values higher than 0.15, indicating that the null of homoscedasticity cannot be rejected. The t-statistics reported in parenthesis are computed using robust standard errors."

A range of HC estimators have been proposed to work with robust standard errors: HC0, HC1, HC2, HC3, HC4. The selection is important for several reasons:

The first version is the standard estimator for homoskedastic errors. All others produce different kinds of HC estimators. The estimator HC0 was introduced by Eicker (1963) and popularized in econometrics by White (1980). The estimators HC1, HC2, and HC3 were suggested by MacKinnon and White (1985) to improve the performance in small samples. A more extensive study of small-sample behavior was conducted by Long and Ervin (2000), who arrive at the conclusion that HC3 provides the best performance in small samples, as it gives less weight to influential observations. HC3 is the default choice in vcovHC(). More recently, Cribari-Neto (2004) suggested the estimator HC4 to further improve small-sample performance, especially in the presence of influential observations. (Kleiber, 2008, p. 107)

Another issue can be collinearity and multicollinearity, where several variables are closely correlated. For instance, if we include multiple measures of firm size (e.g., sales market value of the equity and total assets), the separate measures may be closely related and highly correlated. Multicollinearity can be evaluated with variance inflation factors (VIF) which should be below a threshold value which may usually be 10 (Cohen et al., 2003), 5 (Hair et al., 2017), or even as low as 3.3 to be conservative (Kock & Lynn, 2012). My experience is that there is often a level of collinearity, and a VIF value of below five is usually satisfactory, although I have seen many studies aim for less than three.

SETTING UP THE MODELS

Because of the lack of data in the databases that we may draw from, we are often in a situation where we have missing data for many observations. As a result, for instance, Riley et al. (Riley et al., 2017, p. 1905) note that because of "gaps in the reporting of data for the independent variables, testing Hypotheses 2–5 with one comprehensive model was not feasible," and so separate regressions were used with a consistent set of control variables. A common approach is to use a first model that has the main variables, then a second with interactions, such as how:

The independent variables enter the model in two steps. Model A includes award types, an indicator variable for first-time winners and firm characteristics (return on assets and firm size). In Model B, interactions between award types and firm characteristics are added. (Eroglu et al., 2016, p. 337)

In each case, we can draw conclusions about the study outcomes and the changes in statistical significance.

When we use a package such as R, we can establish a regression model and update the model to include new variables as we extend the model. This enables a rapid assessment of the different models and the ability to quickly compile such output tables as required for an article or a dissertation.

SOFTWARE PACKAGES

As noted earlier, we should calculate robust standard errors when using smaller samples. Unfortunately, SPSS, a commonly used statistical analysis package, struggles to do this meaningfully. It also has other drawbacks, such as the difficulty in setting up or remembering exactly which parameters and options were being used.

In contrast, my preference is to run models in R (R Core Team, 2012). While it has a steep learning curve, it has the benefit of capturing the commands used to develop the model, enabling me to quickly and rapidly go back and change the model development if required. This approach is also useful for the replicability of the research design and for communicating with colleagues and co-authors about what the model accommodates. In addition, it also becomes much easier to calculate a range of different test statistics and standard errors. These can be useful when completing the analysis.

An example of a regression model code in R can be seen in Kleiber (2008, p. 66):

```
R> cps_lm <- lm(log(wage) ~ experience + I(experience^2) + education + ethnicity, data = CPS1988)
```

In this case, it is the estimation of wages, using a dataframe from the U.S. Census Bureau data to examine the impact of education, experience, and ethnicity on wages. From this, the following command generates the output that can be used to generate tables in publications (Kleiber, 2008, p. 66): R> summary(cps_lm)

From this, it is clear that the approach in R is not as user-friendly as other statistical analysis packages used in management research, such as SPSS or SmartPLS. However, the advantage is that we can see how a model was constructed, what components were included, we can update the models rapidly and easily, and use a wide range of test statistics or standard errors while keeping a record or journal of what was done and why.

REPORTING RESULTS

The primary output that needs to be reported on a manuscript will be a table showing the cross-sectional regression analysis results. This will usually include multiple control variables and an independent variable list.

Important to ensure that we have correctly identified which coefficients are significant, and the reader can evaluate what significance level. Different journals and disciplines have slightly different expectations for what level of significance should be reported and how they should be denoted. The table usually includes the coefficient and a robust standard error for each independent variable. We might include VIF factors for the final model.

We might include multiple models where additional terms are added, such as variables of interest on top of the control variables or interaction terms on top of an existing model. For example, a first model may include just the control variables with the other variables, those of theoretical interest in the study, being added in the next model or the subsequent models. We could gather the control variables either at the top of the table or at the bottom. It is best to include these as a block, with an indicator that they are control variables, to simplify the interpretation of the table results.

Some studies estimate the abnormal return over a range of different windows. We should then make it clear for the reader which set of abnormal returns (correlating to which event window) are then used in the cross-sectional regression. Most studies will have models used to estimate abnormal returns and may have different numbers of observations used in the calculations because of data availability. Consequently, the table should report the number of observations used in the regression and which set of abnormal returns are used (e.g., stating that the abnormal returns estimated with the market model in the (0,1) window are used in the table).

These tables can be quite complex at first glance. For example, Hawn et al. (2018, pp. 965–966) in Table 5 present data relating to five different models with different variables of interest and interaction terms over the different models. At the bottom, they include the control variables of size, profitability, analysts following, the age, country ESG, and the constant variable. They report the observations used in each model, which is consistent over the first four models with a larger number for the placebo testing in the final model. They also report R squared values for each model. Finally, they report robust standard errors in the parentheses and *p*-values.

One interesting point to note is that cross-sectional regression following the calculation of abnormal returns tends to have rather low spread of values. For example, Hawn et al. (2018) report a maximum adjusted R^2 value of 4.61% in model 4. Xia et al. (2016) report up to 11.56% in Model 4; 9.6% for the interaction model in Jacobs and Singhal (2014); and 0.52% for Model 2 with the full [-1,1] in Modi et al. (2015). Whether or not the R^2 is adjusted is not always apparent when reading studies. When presenting several models, the R^2 value is usually used to measure the model's predictive accuracy. However, this is important that we include the adjusted R^2 as the primary metric for evaluation. The range of models we usually see when results are presented include an increasing number of independent variables; the increase of variables included in the model inflates the R^2 value and the adjusted R^2 value addresses this important issue, particularly as there may be a substantial number of variables in the model.

FUTURE OPPORTUNITIES USING OTHER ANALYSIS APPROACHES

Traditionally, cross-sectional regression has been employed to extend the core estimation of the abnormal return in response to the event. Although the chapter has addressed regression approaches, that is not to say that these are the only possible analytic approaches. Over time, we will see a range of different approaches and different uses for the abnormal return of subsequent analyzes.

First, there is a possibility that we might use structural equation modeling (SEM) sometimes where a range of different variables and factors are used to predict the abnormal return. In this way, it is similar to the cross-sectional regression approach, although it handles and addresses the issue of latent variables and more complex causal relationships between latent variables (Hair et al., 2011, 2017; Sarstedt et al., 2016). The development of latent variables is not common in event studies, but such combinations are possible, where, for example, Oh et al. (2020) used not only data from a geographic information system (GIS), dummy variables, as well as a more complex variable as for the:

third moderator, institutions supporting collective actions, is measured as the sum of three standardized variables, including WGI's Voice and Accountability, Reporters Without Borders' WPFI [...], and GCI's Judicial Independence. We based these measures on the social movement literature [which] suggests three factors that increase the likelihood of collective action: mobilizing structures; political opportunities; and framing structures. (Oh et al., 2020, p. 1225)

As the range of data and variables extends in our research, there is the possibility of accommodating further latent variables, such as measures of overall slack. This approach might include a formative measurement model, assuming that other measures cause the construct, and it may include, for instance, operational forms of slack like excess capacity, inventory slack, supply chain slack (Hendricks et al., 2009), as well as other measures such as financial slack (Wood et al., 2017). At present, this avenue for analysis has been employed infrequently with few published examples (Saftiana et al., 2018).

Perhaps the most speculative approach to extending the estimation of abnormal returns is using ARs in other types of more qualitative research and other mixed methods. For example, case studies have been commonly conducted using only qualitative analyses, and there is a wider range of data that can be used to build into a case study, including the opportunity to cases built on much greater quantities of numeric and quantitative data (Ketokivi & Choi, 2014). In this way, abnormal returns might present the opportunity for additional analyzes as a data source within a broader case study.

Another potential approach is qualitative comparative analysis (QCA) (Rihoux & Ragin, 2009; Schneider & Eggert, 2014). The QCA approach is similar to regression in that "QCA studies typically involve learning about facts we do not know by using the facts we do know—that is, they establish inference" (Thomann & Maggetti, 2020, p. 358). QCA can accommodate both quantitative data and ordinal data. An important sub-set of QCA is using fuzzy sets or fsQCA, allowing a fine-grained analysis based on the development of ordinal categories (Afonso et al., 2017; Mendel & Korjani, 2012; Meneses et al., 2016; Oyemomi et al., 2016). In addition, QCA can incorporate a larger sample (than a qualitative case study approach) and evaluate patterns, as the:

<u>*Condition-oriented*</u> *applications understand cases primarily in terms of a well-defined set of conditions. The results are mainly interpreted as patterns across cases and are not complemented with an in-depth, qualitative treatment of individual cases [...] This approach typically uses QCA on large samples, which are often implicitly or explicitly deemed representative of an underlying population. This largely precludes intimacy with all cases but facilitates resorting to complementary statistical techniques and parameters to evaluate QCA models. (Thomann & Maggetti, 2020, p. 363)*

In contrast to the linear modeling approach of regression that might establish a relationship between, for example, more inventory slack being associated with a less negative stock market reaction (Wood et al., 2017), QCA analyzes the configuration of multiple factors. For example, maybe more inventory slack in combination with reduced leverage might be associated with a less negative stock market reaction, while an entire lack of inventory slack might be associated with a less negative stock market reaction if several other causal conditions are also present at the same time. This example shows a primary value of QCA as:

it allows researchers to unveil how certain profiles of variables (thought of as independent variables in linear studies and termed causal conditions or attributes in QCA) are related to an outcome of interest (thought of as a dependent variable in linear studies). (Ketchen et al., 2021, p. 4)

We derived the value of QCA from the ability to move beyond the more simple linear relationships and interactions used in regression-based models to present a more complex understanding of how to achieve the outcomes of interest. Therefore:

QCA helps to work out the inner logics behind complex phenomena by moving away from traditional net-effect thinking and encouraging scholars to compare, contrast, and most importantly synthesize different causal mechanisms. Indeed, QCA actively acknowledges that mechanisms coexist and therefore show up in different configurations via the interplay of different causal conditions (e.g., economic and psychological constructs). As a consequence, concepts from previously separate fields can be integrated in order to facilitate a more holistic understanding. Relatedly, because QCA allows for the combination of causal conditions from different levels— both higher levels such as the firm and lower levels such as the team and the individual—it is well suited to explore if and how elements from different levels configure to shape outcomes of interest. (Ketchen et al., 2021, p. 5)

While there have been few examples of this combination of approaches, Wood et al. (2022) shows how the approach of QCA can incorporate the estimation of abnormal returns, instead of taking a cross-sectional approach. The analysis presented by Wood et al. also highlights how prior related research may fail to reach conclusions about the role of factors. By providing two analyses, Wood et al. show how different 'mixes' of factors may be related to either strong performance or weak performance as measured by abnormal returns, such as adopting novel vs incremental innovations. As such, they show how "how investors are cautious and risk-averse about the likelihood of positive returns. The analysis can show multiple combinations of factors relating to a weak or strong performance that cannot be identified using a cross-sectional regression" (Wood et al., 2022, p. 11).

CONCLUSIONS

This chapter presents how we can use the abnormal returns calculated to present a more sophisticated and complete analysis that allows for greater theoretical development using the cross-sectional regression approach. We outline many of the key steps and issues that may arise while using these techniques and provide insight into how some of these factors can be addressed. In addition, we summarize and provide an opportunity to investigate alternative methods of extending and supplementing the analysis, such as structural equation modeling (SEM), qualitative comparative analysis (QCA), and including abnormal returns within case studies.

REFERENCES

Afonso, C., Silva, G. M., Gonçalves, H. M., & Duarte, M. (2017). The role of motivations and involvement in wine tourists' intention to return: SEM and fsQCA findings. *Journal of Business Research.* Advance online publication. doi:10.1016/j.jbusres.2017.11.042

Brandon-Jones, E., Dutordoir, M., Frota Neto, J. Q., & Squire, B. (2017). The impact of reshoring decisions on shareholder wealth. *Journal of Operations Management, 49*(1, Supplement C), 31–36. doi:10.1016/j.jom.2016.12.002

Breusch, T. S., & Pagan, A. R. (1979). A simple test for heteroscedasticity and random coefficient variation. *Econometrica, 47*(5), 1287–1294. doi:10.2307/1911963

Brown, S. J., & Warner, J. B. (1985). Using daily stock returns: The case of event studies. *Journal of Financial Economics, 14*(1), 3–31. doi:10.1016/0304-405X(85)90042-X

Cohen, J., Cohen, P., West, S. G., & Aiken, L. S. (2003). *Applied multiple regression/correlation analysis for the behavioral sciences* (3rd ed.). L. Erlbaum Associates.

Duan, C., Grover, V., Roberts, N., & Balakrishnan, N. (2014). Firm valuation effects of the decision to adopt relationally governed business process outsourcing arrangements. *International Journal of Production Research, 52*(15), 4673–4694. doi:10.1080/00207543.2014.884289

Eroglu, C., Kurt, A. C., & Elwakil, O. S. (2016). Stock market reaction to quality, safety, and sustainability awards in logistics. *Journal of Business Logistics, 37*(4), 329–345. doi:10.1111/jbl.12145

Hair, J. F., Black, W. C., Babin, B. J., & Anderson, R. E. (2014). *Multivariate data analysis* (7th ed.). Pearson Education.

Hair, J. F., Matthews, L. M., Matthews, R. L., & Sarstedt, M. (2017). PLS-SEM or CB-SEM: Updated guidelines on which method to use. *International Journal of Multivariate Data Analysis.* https://www.inderscienceonline.com/doi/abs/10.1504/IJMDA.2017.087624

Hair, J. F., Ringle, C. M., & Sarstedt, M. (2011). PLS-SEM: Indeed a Silver Bullet. *Journal of Marketing Theory and Practice, 19*(2), 139–152. doi:10.2753/MTP1069-6679190202

Hawn, O., Chatterji, A. K., & Mitchell, W. (2018). Do investors actually value sustainability? New evidence from investor reactions to the Dow Jones Sustainability Index (DJSI). *Strategic Management Journal, 39*(4), 949–976. doi:10.1002mj.2752

Hendricks, K. B., & Singhal, V. R. (2003). The effect of supply chain glitches on shareholder wealth. *Journal of Operations Management, 21*(5), 501–522. doi:10.1016/j.jom.2003.02.003

Hendricks, K. B., Singhal, V. R., & Zhang, R. (2009). The effect of operational slack, diversification, and vertical relatedness on the stock market reaction to supply chain disruptions. *Journal of Operations Management, 27*(3), 233–246. doi:10.1016/j.jom.2008.09.001

Jacobs, B. W., & Singhal, V. R. (2014). The effect of product development restructuring on shareholder value. *Production and Operations Management, 23*(5), 728–743. doi:10.1111/poms.12074

Jacobs, B. W., Singhal, V. R., & Subramanian, R. (2010). An empirical investigation of environmental performance and the market value of the firm. *Journal of Operations Management, 28*(5), 430–441. doi:10.1016/j.jom.2010.01.001

Jones, K., & Rubin, P. H. (2001). Effects of harmful environmental events on reputations of firms. In M. Hirschey, K. John, & A. Makhija (Eds.), *Advances in Financial Economics* (Vol. 6, pp. 161–182). Emerald Group Publishing Limited. doi:10.1016/S1569-3732(01)06007-8

Ketchen, D. J.., Kaufmann, L., & Carter, C. R. (2021). Configurational approaches to theory development in supply chain management: Leveraging underexplored opportunities. *Journal of Supply Chain Management*. Advance online publication doi:10.1111/jscm.12275

Ketokivi, M., & Choi, T. (2014). Renaissance of case research as a scientific method. *Journal of Operations Management, 32*(5), 232–240. doi:10.1016/j.jom.2014.03.004

Kleiber, C. (2008). *Applied econometrics with R*. Springer New York. doi:10.1007/978-0-387-77318-6

Kock, N. (2017). Going Beyond Composites: Conducting a Factor-Based PLS-SEM Analysis. In H. Latan & R. Noonan (Eds.), *Partial Least Squares Path Modeling: Basic Concepts, Methodological Issues and Applications* (pp. 41–53). Springer International Publishing. doi:10.1007/978-3-319-64069-3_3

Kock, N., & Hadaya, P. (2018). Minimum sample size estimation in PLS-SEM: The inverse square root and gamma-exponential methods. *Information Systems Journal, 28*(1), 227–261. doi:10.1111/isj.12131

Kock, N., & Lynn, G. (2012). Lateral collinearity and misleading results in variance-based SEM: An illustration and recommendations. *Journal of the Association for Information Systems, 13*(7), 546–580. doi:10.17705/1jais.00302

Mendel, J. M., & Korjani, M. M. (2012). Charles Ragin's Fuzzy Set Qualitative Comparative Analysis (fsQCA) used for linguistic summarizations. *Information Sciences, 202*, 1–23. doi:10.1016/j.ins.2012.02.039

Meneses, R., Quelhas Brito, P., & Coelho Gomes, P. (2016). From offshore-provider to brand creator: FsQCA of footwear industry. *Journal of Business Research, 69*(11), 5540–5546. doi:10.1016/j.jbusres.2016.04.168

Modi, S. B., Wiles, M. A., & Mishra, S. (2015). Shareholder value implications of service failures in triads: The case of customer information security breaches. *Journal of Operations Management, 35*(1), 21–39. doi:10.1016/j.jom.2014.10.003

Oh, C. H., Shapiro, D., Ho, S. S. H., & Shin, J. (2020). Location matters: Valuing firm-specific nonmarket risk in the global mining industry. *Strategic Management Journal, 41*(7), 1210–1244. doi:10.1002mj.3153

Oyemomi, O., Liu, S., Neaga, I., & Alkhuraiji, A. (2016). How knowledge sharing and business process contribute to organizational performance: Using the fsQCA approach. *Journal of Business Research, 69*(11), 5222–5227. doi:10.1016/j.jbusres.2016.04.116

R Core Team. (2012). *R: A language and environment for statistical computing*. http://www.R-project.org/

Rihoux, B., & Ragin, C. C. (2009). Configurational comparative methods: Qualitative comparative analysis (QCA) and related techniques. *Sage (Atlanta, Ga.)*. Advance online publication. doi:10.4135/9781452226569

Riley, S. M., Michael, S. C., & Mahoney, J. T. (2017). Human capital matters: Market valuation of firm investments in training and the role of complementary assets. *Strategic Management Journal, 38*(9), 1895–1914. doi:10.1002mj.2631

Ringle, C. M. S., Sarstedt, & Straub. (2012). A critical look at the use of PLS-SEM in MIS Quarterly. *Management Information Systems Quarterly, 36*(1), iiv–8. doi:10.2307/41410402

Saftiana, Y., Sulastri, S., Isnurhadi, I., Adam, M., & Muthia, F. (2018). Diversification: Complementary assets and super additive synergy. *Journal of Advanced Research in Law and Economics, 9*(2), 664–679. doi:10.14505//jarle.v9

Sarstedt, M., Hair, J. F., Ringle, C. M., Thiele, K. O., & Gudergan, S. P. (2016). Estimation issues with PLS and CBSEM: Where the bias lies! *Journal of Business Research, 69*(10), 3998–4010. doi:10.1016/j.jbusres.2016.06.007

Schneider, M. R., & Eggert, A. (2014). Embracing complex causality with the QCA method: An invitation. *Journal of Business Market Management, 7*(1), 312–328.

Thomann, E., & Maggetti, M. (2020). Designing research with qualitative comparative analysis (QCA): Approaches, challenges, and tools. *Sociological Methods & Research, 49*(2), 356–386. doi:10.1177/0049124117729700

White, H. (1982). Maximum likelihood estimation of misspecified models. *Econometrica, 50*(1), 1–25. doi:10.2307/1912526

Wood, L. C., Duong, L. N. K., & Wang, J. X. (2022). Business Process Improvement for Sustainable Technologies Investments in Construction: A Configurational Approach. *Sustainability, 14*(9), 5697. doi:10.3390u14095697

Wood, L. C., Wang, J. X., Duong, L. N. K., Reiners, T., & Smith, R. (2018). Stock market reactions to auto manufacturers' environmental failures. *Journal of Macromarketing, 38*(4), 364–382. doi:10.1177/0276146718781915

Wood, L. C., Wang, J. X., Olesen, K., & Reiners, T. (2017). The effect of slack, diversification, and time to recall on stock market reaction to toy recalls. *International Journal of Production Economics, 193*, 244–258. doi:10.1016/j.ijpe.2017.07.021

Xia, Y., Singhal, V. R., & Peter Zhang, G. (2016). Product design awards and the market value of the firm. *Production and Operations Management, 25*(6), 1038–1055. doi:10.1111/poms.12525

ADDITIONAL READING

Binder, J. (1998). The event study methodology since 1969. *Review of Quantitative Finance and Accounting, 11*(2), 111–137. doi:10.1023/A:1008295500105

Binder, J. J. (1985). On the use of the multivariate regression model in event studies. *Journal of Accounting Research, 23*(1), 370–383. doi:10.2307/2490925

Blume, M. E. (1975). Betas and their regression tendencies. *The Journal of Finance, 30*(3), 785–795. doi:10.1111/j.1540-6261.1975.tb01850.x

Chen, Y., Singhal, V., & Zhu, Q. (2021). Environmental policies and financial performance: Stock market reaction to firms for their proactive environmental practices recognized by governmental programs. *Business Strategy and the Environment, 30*(4), 1548–1562. doi:10.1002/bse.2693

Cohen, J., Cohen, P., West, S. G., & Aiken, L. S. (2003). *Applied multiple regression/correlation analysis for the behavioral sciences* (3rd ed.). L. Erlbaum Associates.

Cook, R. D., & Weisberg, S. (1982). *Residuals and influence in regression*. Chapman and Hall.

Fox, J. (2002). *An R and S-Plus companion to applied regression*. Sage Publications.

Gelman, A., & Hill, J. (2006). *Data analysis using regression and multilevel/hierarchical models*. Cambridge University Press. doi:10.1017/CBO9780511790942

Hair, J. F. Jr, & Sarstedt, M. (2019). Factors versus composites: Guidelines for choosing the right structural equation modeling method. *Project Management Journal, 50*(6), 619–624. doi:10.1177/8756972819882132

Hair, J. F., Sarstedt, M., Ringle, C. M., & Mena, J. A. (2012). An assessment of the use of partial least squares structural equation modeling in marketing research. *Journal of the Academy of Marketing Science, 40*(3), 414–433. doi:10.100711747-011-0261-6

Long, J. S., & Ervin, L. H. (2000). Using heteroscedasticity consistent standard errors in the linear regression model. *The American Statistician, 54*(3), 217–224. doi:10.1080/00031305.2000.10474549

Olive, D. J. (2017). *Linear regression*. Springer. doi:10.1007/978-3-319-55252-1

Renaud, O., & Victoria-Feser, M.-P. (2010). A robust coefficient of determination for regression. *Journal of Statistical Planning and Inference, 140*(7), 1852–1862. doi:10.1016/j.jspi.2010.01.008

Sarstedt, M., Hair, J. F. Jr, Cheah, J.-H., Becker, J.-M., & Ringle, C. M. (2019). How to Specify, Estimate, and Validate Higher-Order Constructs in PLS-SEM. *Australasian Marketing Journal, 27*(3), 197–211. doi:10.1016/j.ausmj.2019.05.003

Sarstedt, M., Ringle, C. M., & Hair, J. F. (2017). Treating Unobserved Heterogeneity in PLS-SEM: A Multi-method Approach. In H. Latan & R. Noonan (Eds.), *Partial Least Squares Path Modeling: Basic Concepts, Methodological Issues and Applications* (pp. 197–217). Springer International Publishing. doi:10.1007/978-3-319-64069-3_9

Weisberg, S. (2005). *Applied Linear Regression* (3rd ed.). Wiley. doi:10.1002/0471704091

Zhan, X., Mu, Y., Hora, M., & Singhal, V. R. (2021). Service excellence and market value of a firm: An empirical investigation of winning service awards and stock market reaction. *International Journal of Production Research*, *59*(14), 4188–4204. doi:10.1080/00207543.2020.1759837

Zhan, X., Mu, Y., Nishant, R., & Singhal, V. R. (2020). When do appointments of Chief Digital or Data Officers (CDOs) affect stock prices? *IEEE Transactions on Engineering Management*, ●●●, 1–14. doi:10.1109/TEM.2020.2984619

KEY TERMS AND DEFINITIONS

Dependent Variable: The variable being predicted in the model, using a range of independent variables. In the case of the event study, the dependent variable is the abnormal returns calculated in the previous steps.

Heteroscedasticity: A situation when the variance of the error terms is not constant over the range of the independent variables.

Independent Variable: The variables used to predict or explain the abnormal returns (dependent variable) to improve our theoretical understanding of the phenomenon under study.

Influential Observation: An observation that has a significant influence on the final regression estimates. Extreme independent or dependent variables may cause it. It may be an outlier, but not necessarily.

Linear Regression: A general statistical technique to analyze the relationship between a dependent variable and an independent variable. The model predicts values that are in a linear nature with a constant slope or unit change. When there are multiple independent variables, it is a multiple regression model.

Moderator: When one of the independent variables influences the relationship of another independent and dependent variable, depending on the value of the moderator in a particular case.

Multicollinearity: When an independent variable is correlated with a range of other independent variables. This causes problems when, in an extreme case, it causes singularity, where two independent variables are perfectly correlated.

Outlier: An observation that differs significantly and is, therefore, a poor representation of the wider population and may be discounted or removed from the sample for subsequent analysis because of the unrepresentative nature.

Chapter 12
Interpreting the Results:
Making Sense of Study Findings

ABSTRACT

This chapter focuses on the steps following the analysis. First, the main results have been identified, but their meaning, consequence, and implications must be derived and communicated. Second, scholars must analyze their findings to work out 'what does this mean' and establish how to write up the results. Third, the chapter examines past studies' findings and then discusses how they can be interpreted. Several examples are provided throughout to illustrate key points being made. Finally, the chapter examines the writing process, distinguishing between writing a dissertation for examiners and articles to be read by other researchers. The writing process involves discussing the findings and extracting implications for practice and research.

INTRODUCTION

A big part of any study is understanding the outcome, what was found, and the statistics. Next, as a researcher and scholar, you must make sense of the findings to be communicated to others in a dissertation or journal article. In this chapter, we step through several critical elements of this process. Ultimately, one of the primary objectives is to communicate research findings to others through publishing. Therefore, the communication of results is a critical element of this chapter.

In the other chapters, we have seen a range of different events being discussed. In some cases, the stock market reaction is negative; in other cases, the stock market reaction is positive. A range of analyses will be conducted with different results presented in a table of cross-sectional regression results in each case. However, it remains necessary to take these results and create meaning from them so it is meaningful to the reader. When we consider how the results can be interpreted, we might consider that there will be two or three primary audiences of writing the results up:

- your peers and other researchers in the area. What can the reader learn from your results; what are the implications for research and research advancement in this area?

DOI: 10.4018/978-1-7998-8969-4.ch012

- managers and business professionals. While they may not consume the research directly, they may source at the other (perhaps management-focused) journals. In this way, you need to explain the interesting research and theory findings and what this would mean in practice for somebody sitting in an office struggling with these management concepts and events that you have been researching.
- examiners of the thesis or dissertation for postgraduate research students. In terms of the results and findings, they want an obvious contribution to knowledge. You can demonstrate the contribution by discussing the results in the context of past studies to show how this research extends, contributes to, or conflicts with past studies.

We next look at the interpretation of the overall stock market reaction. This search for the stock market reaction is usually the first hypothesis, and the results of the estimation of abnormal returns are the primary input to this section.

RESULTS – THE OVERALL STOCK MARKET REACTION

The expected first result reported on and interpreted is usually the overall market reaction before covering the other results. The first paragraph in the section will probably provide an overview of some of the different periods examined for the event window, giving an understanding of the mean abnormal returns. It is also valuable to report median abnormal returns, the proportion of the sample with positive negative returns, and some level of interpretation about what all of this means.

In general, the primary focus will be the event window that was used to generate the abnormal returns that were subsequently used in the cross-sectional regression. Hence, they should be reported on carefully. An example of a first paragraph outlining the primary results relating to the overall market reaction is given by Chen et al. (2021):

the abnormal returns for the day of the announcement (Day 0), the day following the announcement (Day 1), and the CARs for the two-day event period [Days (0, 1)]. The mean abnormal returns for Day 0, Day 1 and Days (0, 1) are −0.01% 0.03% and 0.03%, respectively, and statistically insignificant. The median abnormal return for Days (0, 1) is marginally negative (−0.08%) but insignificant. About 48% of the sample has positive abnormal returns, which is insignificantly different from 50%. (Chen et al., 2021, p. 1557)

There is a fairly standard reporting on some of the event windows and a little overview of the type of direction and proportion of firms reporting that finding. So, for example, in Duong et al. (2021), we see the results first noting the use of test statistics, including non-parametric tests, to establish significance, before they report that:

[i]n the event window (0, 1), the mean (median) CAR is 0.80% (0.53%), and significant at the 5% level (two tails) across all tests. The result indicates that there is a positive stock market reaction to sustainability innovations announcements in the construction industry. Thus, H1 is supported. The ARs/CARs on other days/event windows in Table 2 provide a robustness test. All other ARs/CARs are not statistically significant by any of the tests, indicating CAR (0, 1) incorporates the stock market reaction to the announcements. (Duong et al., 2021, p. 407)

In this case, only the abnormal returns for the main window are reported on with insight provided in the accompanying table. Reporting in this way keeps the text brief and more easily read.

If the results section also includes some discussion, the following paragraph might explain the meaning and interpretation of what this means. For example, when the primary hypothesis was developed and suggested that the event in question causes an abnormal stock market reaction, five to ten pieces of literature were likely cited to support the case. When the articles are identified, it is possible to return to these specific articles and explain what they studied and what they found versus what was found in the current study and, therefore, what we know now that we do not know before.

In undertaking this comparison, it might be helpful to compare periods, geographic regions, sectors, and regulatory environments as these might influence the stock market reactions of various studies even if they are comparable event studies. For instance, Jacobs and Singhal (2014, p. 739) make a direct comparison with a review article of similar research, where they note differences in outcomes where they find a positive finding that conflicts with the past review: "Compared to the positive results in our sample of PDR layoffs, Capelle-Blancard and Couderc (2007) find that abnormal returns for layoffs are generally negative regardless of time period or geographic region."

Further, the classification or categorizations used in studies can differ, so that the process of making comparisons challenging. Jacobs and Singhal (2014, p. 739) note this by stating: "Given that action categorizations differ across papers, it is difficult to compare our results with previous empirical studies. However, definitions are generally consistent in the case of layoffs."

When interpreting the results, it is important not to make sweeping generalizations and comparisons as much as possible. Instead, comparisons should be contextually sensitive to the context and study parameters differences.

If there is no evidence that the estimated abnormal returns are statistically different from zero, then the first thought may be deflating: there are no study findings to report. However, Thirumalai and Sinha (2011) provide an example of this outcome. Moreover, they have undertaken several subsequent analyses to provide more insight into the problem (e.g., examining whether the different classes of recalls may result in evidence of a stock market reaction). Their study provides novel findings and interesting variables constructed to analyze the determinants of abnormal returns.

CROSS-SECTIONAL ANALYSIS RESULTS

Suppose there is a range of models in the cross-sectional regression that have been generated for various reasons. For example, Xia et al. (2016) note that several models are developed due to missing research and development (R&D) intensity data. However, they show consistency in the model before proceeding with the subsequent discussions for a particular model. Therefore, they used model 3 results in their subsequent discussions, which incorporated all the hypotheses while it was generated with a smaller data set due to missing data problems.

One of the most important things to look for is the existence of particular relationships with the *p*-value below five (in some management disciplines). Such relationships tend to indicate that there is a statistically significant relationship present. The next thing to look for is the beta coefficient for that relationship. Interpretation of these coefficients is often challenging to understand. For example:

The interpretation of the coefficients of the determinants of abnormal or cumulative abnormal returns is straightforward, unless researchers wish to also interpret the effect that the variable has on the stock returns of the firm. In that case, the effect of a significant determinant of CARs is akin to an interaction: the determinant either magnifies or mitigates the effect of the event on stock returns (e.g., Martin et al. 2016). **Finally, we note that it is appropriate to examine the determinants of CARs even if the average CAR is not significantly different from zero,** *particularly if the variance of CARs is relatively large. This could help authors determine subgroups of events for which the average CARs are significantly different than zero, even though they are not so for the entire sample. (Sorescu et al., 2017, pp. 199–200; emphasis added)*

The commentary from Sorescu et al. (2017) supports the approach taken in several studies that report no substantial evidence of an overall stock market reaction, like Thirumalai and Sinha (2011). Nevertheless, some examples may be helpful and instructive.

Turning back to the study that we used in earlier chapters, the Wood et al. (2017) toy recall project identified a negative stock market reaction to the news of the recall. However, the coefficient for business diversification was positive, while the coefficient for capacity slack was negative. Both have evidence of a significant relationship, and the results suggest that companies with a higher business diversification have a less negative stock market reaction to the toy recall. Moreover, the positive coefficient means that while the firm may experience an overall negative stock market reaction, they would have a less negative stock market reaction if this factor were favorable. Similarly, firms with high capacity slack experience a more negative stock market reaction to a record event.

A specific example drawn from Xia et al. shows how they report on and explain the finding that supports their hypothesis:

As predicted, the coefficient of product type is positive and significant at the 5% level, indicating that the market reacts more positively for consumer products than for industrial products. The coefficient of the industry-adjusted market-to-book ratio is negative but insignificantly different from zero. This suggests that the stock market reaction to winning design awards is not influenced by the growth potential of the firm and that good product design is important for both high growth potential and low growth potential firms. As predicted the coefficient of the industry competitiveness is positive but insignificantly different from zero. This suggests that good product design matters irrespective of how intense the competition is in an industry. (Xia et al., 2016, p. 1050)

In contrast, when reporting on a finding where there is no support for the hypothesis, this can be relatively simple, as Xia et al. (2016) show:

We had also argued that winning any award, regardless of whether it is the first-time winning or not, provides information about the success of the products that win the awards. The statistically insignificant coefficient of winning the first design award suggests that the stock market seems to react more to the information about the success of the products that win the award than to the updated expectations about the design capability of the firm. (Xia et al., 2016, p. 1050)

The terminology and the wording are also crucial in constructing the hypotheses earlier in the manuscript. For example, hypotheses three and four in Hendricks and Singhal (2003) contrast in the directionality. First, "H3. Supply chain glitches by **high growth prospects firms** will have a **more negative** stock market reaction than low growth prospects firms" (Hendricks & Singhal, 2003, p. 505; emphasis added). The hypothesis suggests that where the firm is a high growth prospect firm, it will have a more negative outcome; the stock market reaction with be more negative than it would otherwise be. In contrast, the following hypothesis is, "H4. The **higher the debt–equity ratio**, the **less negative** will be stock market's reaction to supply chain glitches" (Hendricks & Singhal, 2003, p. 505; emphasis added). This suggests a less negative stock market reaction. Note that it relates to the overall abnormal return in both cases, which is expected to be negative; that is, a firm that experiences a supply chain glitch or disruption will experience an adverse stock market reaction. Consequentially, when examining the results for H3 and H4, we would expect the coefficients to be negative and positive, respectively.

The terminology and the wording may be a bit confusing at first, but before long, you will get the hang of understanding how to phrase the hypotheses and then how to interpret the coefficients in the results table.

PREPARING YOUR DISCUSSION OF RESULTS

There are no set ways to provide a discussion. Each hypothesis may have several key articles drawn from the literature review and brought into the discussion section for a compare and contrast discussion. You may also add another level of analysis and pose several other explanations and discussion points. For instance, Wood et al. (2017) note how their findings relating to business diversification mean that companies can:

*develop opportunities in additional product segments, providing a greater level of security to the firm if it does face a toy recall. While Hendricks et al. (2009) found no significant relationship between business diversification and the stock market reaction to supply chain disruptions, we identified the significant contribution of business diversification to toy recalls. Traditionally, **toys are low-cost products.** Hence, firms may encounter market competition, reducing their **profit margins**. In addition, the common requirement for extensive assembly processes means that toy production is often outsourced (Wong et al., 2005), which decreases the reserve of operational resources in the traditional toy segment. **Less diversified firms** are unlikely to accumulate sufficient financial and operational resources to cushion against urgent costs associated with a recall, and the negative impact may influence a larger proportion of their total business. In contrast, a **more diversified firm** is less likely to be financially or operationally strained while managing a recall, or when faced with another adverse event. Moreover, the **more diversified firms are likely** to find it easier to raise external capital as there will be less dependence between product lines and, therefore, there is a 'coinsurance' effect between their product segments that reduces overall risk (Hendricks et al., 2009). **More diversified firms may benefit from the reallocation of internal funding and resources** ensuring the steadiness of the overall business. Therefore, our analysis on business diversification is likely to be particularly relevant to firms in other low-cost industries where outsourcing is commonplace as it is in this industry. (Wood et al., 2017, pp. 254–255; emphasis added)*

There is a use of more vs less diversified firms with additional insight into some of the mechanisms that may be relevant. These could form the foundation for additional studies. Finally, there is a reminder on the nature of the event being studied, focusing on the low-cost and tight profit margins related to the product.

The compare-and-contrast effect is also evident in the study of chief data officers by Zhan et al. (2020), who note how:

*the estimated coefficient of Outsider is positive but insignificant, indicating the lack of support for H4 (both H4a and H4b). Our **finding is consistent** with that of Mian [35] and Arora [2], wherein the market reactions are not significantly different between announcements of CFO and CSO hires from outside versus inside the firm. **But our findings depart from** Hendricks et al. [24], who find that the market reacts more positively when the SCOME appointee is an outsider rather than an insider. (Zhan et al., 2020, p. 10; emphasis added)*

they relate their findings to three comparable studies of executive appointments – all different types of executives; Mian (2001) studying the appointment of chief financial officers; Arora et al. (2020) the appointment of corporate sustainability executives; and Hendricks et al. (2014) the appointment of supply chain and operations management executives. The direction of the estimated coefficient is also reported even though it is insignificant.

The finding that the estimated coefficient is not significantly different from zero can also be interesting in the context of past studies. For instance, Arora et al. (2020) note that:

*the estimated coefficient of [sustainability performance] is negative but not significantly different from zero. Although Flammer (2015) finds that the stock market reaction to the passing of **CSR-related proposals in annual board meetings** is more positive for firms with **weaker sustainability performance**, our finding suggests that the stock market reactions are not significantly different for **announcements of CSE appointments** by firms with **weaker versus stronger sustainability performance**. The results continue to hold if instead of using the firm's strengths along the six sustainability-related dimensions in the KLD database, we use the firm's strength on only the environment dimension as an alternative measure for [sustainability performance]. (Arora et al., 2020, p. 476; emphasis added)*

The studies being compared are not identical in nature but closely related enough to compare, as noted in the discussion. The comparison draws out some of the study samples and distinctions that may lead to this different result (in the added emphasis). In addition, they report on the additional robustness check of using different compositions to measure sustainability performance and find no substantial difference in the outcome.

IMPLICATIONS FOR RESEARCH AND PRACTICE

While these are relevant, it is also interesting to make sense of what this means to managers by addressing how these results (from the stock market reaction and the determinants of the reaction from the cross-sectional regression) translate into important managerial implications? In a straightforward sense, the management team should maximize, work towards, or enhance variables with a positive coefficient. Conversely, variables with a negative coefficient are those the management team should avoid or minimize.

For instance, when considering the communications around CEO departures, communications should emphasize authenticity and tone. As the cues relating to activity are associated with a negative return, the team should consider shifting communications to reduce this. Working from the results to extract meaning for practice and management, they interpret the importance of the cues and language by saying:

Specifically, managers are encouraged to reduce information-based disadvantages by not only engaging in substantive management of their relationships with key stakeholders (e.g., succession planning and disclosure of material information), but also paying major attention to 'soft' informational cues (e.g., the one and emotional quality of language used) that are embedded in organizational disclosures. However, we also caution against the use of overly optimistic language, especially when it is not grounded in reality, as this form of pure impression management may be conceived as manipulative and misleading by external resource providers, who appear to value credible, assuring, and transparent communications. (Bilgili et al., 2017, p. 1043)

So the results translate into direct suggestions about what to do and what not to do. They can provide insight into where to place attention and care to enhance outcomes and what elements may be reduced or removed. In addition, we see that it is not just about what the firm does but also how they communicate or encode information in the announcement, where Bilgili et al. caution about "overly optimistic language," Jacobs et al. (2010) discuss the content of the announcements about environmental initiatives as they assert that:

*announcements of voluntary emission reductions efforts should be accompanied by **formal justifications** as to **why** these efforts are being conducted (for example, preparing for future legislation, competitive lobbying, or anticipated carbon trading) and **what the expected value** from these efforts is likely to be.* **(Jacobs et al., 2010, p. 439)**

When considering outsourcing, Duan et al. (2014), their results and the difference over the hypotheses suggest that the outsourcing process should be considered carefully with different governance forms for each outsourced process. Also provided a framework based on their results is a suggestion that the framework can also be applied to other outsourcing arrangements and the firm currently, to ensure that that fit suggestion from the framework is what is being achieved in the company. Ultimately, they know that there are elements that cannot be changed

*In general, **managers cannot change** the physical (VC position) or temporal nature (experience) of the processes to be outsourced. However, **this should not inhibit them from managing each of the outsourced processes attentively**. The maximum group-mean difference in ARs by VC position and process experience alone is only about 1.5%. However, as illustrated in Figure 3, when we factor in the governance issue in the calculations, the maximum group-mean difference triples to about 4.5%. This implies that on the margin considerable valuation enhancements are determined by the managerial mechanisms applied. (Duan et al., 2014, p. pp. 4686–4688; emphasis added)*

The results suggest that while not all elements can be managed, the difference in group-means suggests that managers will unlock substantial value for the firm with appropriate managerial mechanisms and decisions around the business process outsourcing activities.

At this point, it is also worth reflecting on what we mean by 'value'. The managerial implications are essentially based on the concept that the management action can lead to a greater abnormal return (or a less negative abnormal return). These are good for the firm because a positive stock market reaction implies that the company's value has increased. The stock market reaction reflects the overall benefit to the company of the event and the underlying factors studied. The determinants, assessed in the cross-sectional regression, also suggest areas to enhance the stock market reaction.

Based on this analysis, these considerations, the straightforward approach to creating managerial implications suggests positive changes in practice, how to take the results with a statistically significant difference, and from these work out how a manager would enhance those variables to create the most favorable outcome possible. Hypotheses generating a positive coefficient should be enhanced, for those with a negative coefficient should be mitigated or reduced.

WRITING FOR THE EXAMINERS

Writing a thesis or dissertation can be nerve-racking because it is unclear what the examiners are looking for to award a pass. However, we can be confident with certain elements in a doctoral thesis. Primarily, universities have a criterion or requirement for a doctoral dissertation or thesis to contribute to knowledge or have some novel contribution. Therefore, this will be one of the primary elements that an examiner will be hunting for when assessing the thesis or dissertation.

There are some simple tips and techniques that we can use when writing for an examiner. For example, a thesis or a dissertation may not heavily focus on implications for research or practice that we see in many leading journals. (Implications for practice may still play a role, particularly for more applied projects or for Doctore of Business Administration students.) However, the dissertation will require a substantial section on the discussion. While this is covered in more detail in the following chapter, a very simple conceptualization of this problem is that you need to make sense of the results and report and compare the study results against other critical research articles.

Consider the top ten comparable studies that were cited in the literature review earlier in the project. These studies do not need to be event studies; they can use other methodologies but must focus on the type of event or phenomenon you are interested in or are investigating the same type of relationships between variables. Next, create a table where each row compares past study to the current study. In this table, each row should be a point of comparison over multiple columns, focusing on:

1. the critical finding in the past study
2. your finding that is relevant and comparable or similar to this finding
3. how the findings are similar or different
4. an explanation about what this difference means in practice. It is most useful where the findings are different and for the core results that extend our knowledge. If the findings are comparable, this may highlight differences in the study designs that mean the results are generalizable to other settings.

Working this way, it is possible to rapidly generate a starting point that compares the current finding to the past studies. If the current study appears to show comparable findings that confirm results from past studies primarily, you can report this. You should then examine your sample and study design and those used in the previous research to determine similarities or differences. When differences are identified, it may enable the comparison to note that these results are similar in general but that the study demonstrates that these results may hold true even with a different type of company, industry, or sector.

If the results are conflicting, showing the opposite of the previous studies, this could be interesting and represent an essential contribution. Similarly to the treatment of confirming results, it may be necessary to go back and examine the study design for the earlier research to understand whether or not any other factors may influence the different results and find each study. When writing this up, it is important not to say that the earlier study was wrong but to state that there is a difference in outcomes and findings and provide some insight and reflection on what might be driving these differences.

The translation of the table into a written format for the manuscript can proceed, at least in a draft format, in the simple translation of the table rows into paragraphs.

CONCLUSIONS

Interpreting and making sense of results in and of themselves can be challenging in any study. The fact that we are working with stock market data as an extra layer of interpretation as required by the researchers. The results may not be as immediately comprehensible to colleagues conducting other management-focused studies. Therefore, some additional insight is required in the interpretation and write-up of the study results so that others can 'make sense' of the results and what they mean.

In the following chapter, we examine the construction of the entire manuscript, whether this is an article or a thesis/dissertation. We bring together many of the issues discussed elsewhere in the book and understand how these components are connected to make sense of the final manuscript sections.

The chapter covers the interpretation of both the abnormal returns and stock market reaction (usually the first hypothesis in the study) and the subsequent analysis results (usually in the cross-sectional regression). The comparison to past studies is addressed with a table-based format to provide an initial method to frame the comparison for the discussion section. Using a table to prepare the manuscript supports a more detailed write-up by using a more mechanical process to force a clear comparison.

REFERENCES

Arora, P., Hora, M., Singhal, V., & Subramanian, R. (2020). When do appointments of corporate sustainability executives affect shareholder value? *Journal of Operations Management*, *66*(4), 464–487. doi:10.1002/joom.1074

Bilgili, H., Tochman Campbell, J., Ellstrand, A. E., & Johnson, J. L. (2017). Riding off into the sunset: Organizational sensegiving, shareholder sensemaking, and reactions to CEO retirement. *Journal of Management Studies*, *54*(7), 1019–1049. doi:10.1111/joms.12264

Chen, Y., Singhal, V., & Zhu, Q. (2021). Environmental policies and financial performance: Stock market reaction to firms for their proactive environmental practices recognized by governmental programs. *Business Strategy and the Environment*, *30*(4), 1548–1562. doi:10.1002/bse.2693

Duan, C., Grover, V., Roberts, N., & Balakrishnan, N. (2014). Firm valuation effects of the decision to adopt relationally governed business process outsourcing arrangements. *International Journal of Production Research*, *52*(15), 4673–4694. doi:10.1080/00207543.2014.884289

Duong, L. N. K., Wang, J. X., Wood, L. C., Reiners, T., & Koushan, M. (2021). The value of incremental environmental sustainability innovation in the construction industry: An event study. *Construction Management and Economics*, *39*(5), 398–418. doi:10.1080/01446193.2021.1901950

Hendricks, K. B., Hora, M., & Singhal, V. R. (2014). An empirical investigation on the appointments of supply chain and operations management executives. *Management Science*, *61*(7), 1562–1583. doi:10.1287/mnsc.2014.1987

Hendricks, K. B., & Singhal, V. R. (2003). The effect of supply chain glitches on shareholder wealth. *Journal of Operations Management*, *21*(5), 501–522. doi:10.1016/j.jom.2003.02.003

Jacobs, B. W., & Singhal, V. R. (2014). The effect of product development restructuring on shareholder value. *Production and Operations Management*, *23*(5), 728–743. doi:10.1111/poms.12074

Jacobs, B. W., Singhal, V. R., & Subramanian, R. (2010). An empirical investigation of environmental performance and the market value of the firm. *Journal of Operations Management*, *28*(5), 430–441. doi:10.1016/j.jom.2010.01.001

Mian, S. (2001). On the choice and replacement of chief financial officers. *Journal of Financial Economics*, *60*(1), 143–175. doi:10.1016/S0304-405X(01)00042-3

Sorescu, A., Warren, N. L., & Ertekin, L. (2017). Event study methodology in the marketing literature: An overview. *Journal of the Academy of Marketing Science*, *45*(2), 186–207. doi:10.100711747-017-0516-y

Thirumalai, S., & Sinha, K. K. (2011). Product recalls in the medical device industry: An empirical exploration of the sources and financial consequences. *Management Science, 57*(2), 376–392. doi:10.1287/mnsc.1100.1267

Wood, L. C., Wang, J. X., Olesen, K., & Reiners, T. (2017). The effect of slack, diversification, and time to recall on stock market reaction to toy recalls. *International Journal of Production Economics*, *193*, 244–258. doi:10.1016/j.ijpe.2017.07.021

Xia, Y., Singhal, V. R., & Peter Zhang, G. (2016). Product design awards and the market value of the firm. *Production and Operations Management*, *25*(6), 1038–1055. doi:10.1111/poms.12525

Zhan, X., Mu, Y., Nishant, R., & Singhal, V. R. (2020). When do appointments of Chief Digital or Data Officers (CDOs) affect stock prices? *IEEE Transactions on Engineering Management*, 1–14. doi:10.1109/TEM.2020.2984619

ADDITIONAL READING

Binder, J. J. (1985). On the use of the multivariate regression model in event studies. *Journal of Accounting Research*, *23*(1), 370–383. doi:10.2307/2490925

Booth, W. C., Colomb, G. G., & Williams, J. M. (2008). *The craft of research* (3rd ed.). University of Chicago Press.

Chen, Y., Singhal, V., & Zhu, Q. (2021). Environmental policies and financial performance: Stock market reaction to firms for their proactive environmental practices recognized by governmental programs. *Business Strategy and the Environment, 30*(4), 1548–1562. doi:10.1002/bse.2693

Cheung, A. W. K. (2011). Do stock investors value corporate sustainability? Evidence from an event study. *Journal of Business Ethics, 99*(2), 145–165. doi:10.100710551-010-0646-3

Goldstein, J., Chernobai, A., & Benaroch, M. (2011). An event study analysis of the economic impact of IT operational risk and its subcategories. *Journal of the Association for Information Systems, 12*(9), 606–631. doi:10.17705/1jais.00275

Hair, J. F., Black, W. C., Babin, B. J., & Anderson, R. E. (2014). *Multivariate data analysis* (7th ed.). Pearson Education.

Hawn, O., Chatterji, A. K., & Mitchell, W. (2018). Do investors actually value sustainability? New evidence from investor reactions to the Dow Jones Sustainability Index (DJSI). *Strategic Management Journal, 39*(4), 949–976. doi:10.1002mj.2752

Hendricks, K. B., & Singhal, V. R. (1996). Quality awards and the market value of the firm: An empirical investigation. *Management Science, 42*(3), 415–436. doi:10.1287/mnsc.42.3.415

Jayanti, R. K., & Jayanti, S. V. (2011). Effects of airline bankruptcies: An event study. *The Journal of Services Marketing, 25*(6), 399–409. doi: http://dx.doi.org.ezproxy.otago.ac.nz/10.1108/08876041111160998

McGuire, S. J., & Dilts, D. M. (2008). The financial impact of standard stringency: An event study of successive generations of the ISO 9000 standard. *International Journal of Production Economics, 113*(1), 3–22. doi:10.1016/j.ijpe.2007.02.045

Oh, C. H., Shapiro, D., Ho, S. S. H., & Shin, J. (2020). Location matters: Valuing firm-specific nonmarket risk in the global mining industry. *Strategic Management Journal, 41*(7), 1210–1244. doi:10.1002mj.3153

Raithel, S., & Hock, S. J. (2021). The crisis-response match: An empirical investigation. *Strategic Management Journal, 42*(1), 170–184. doi:10.1002mj.3213

Roztocki, N., & Weistroffer, H. R. (2015). Investments in enterprise integration technology: An event study. *Information Systems Frontiers, 17*(3), 659–672. http://dx.doi.org.ezproxy.otago.ac.nz/10.1007/s10796-013-9451-8

Wassmer, U., & Dussauge, P. (2012). Network resource stocks and flows: How do alliance portfolios affect the value of new alliance formations? *Strategic Management Journal, 33*(7), 871–883. doi:10.1002mj.973

Wood, L. C., Wang, J. X., Duong, L. N. K., Reiners, T., & Smith, R. (2018). Stock market reactions to auto manufacturers' environmental failures. *Journal of Macromarketing, 38*(4), 364–382. doi:10.1177/0276146718781915

KEY TERMS AND DEFINITIONS

Abnormal Returns: The divergence from the expected, 'normal' return that we would expect to see, indicating that the event has influenced the stock returns or that there is evidence of a stock market reaction.

Comparison: The process of taking earlier study findings and comparing them to the current study's findings to draw a comparison. The comparison process lets the researcher draw distinctions about where the current study confirms past results, extends them, or conflicts with them. The comparison provides a starting point for the discussion.

Cross-Sectional Regression: A regression model where the abnormal returns are the dependent variable explained by the variables of interest as independent variables, where the variables are associated with one point in time. (This is in contrast to, for example, a time-series regression.)

Interpretation: The process of taking the statistical test results, making sense of them for the readers, and explaining what the test results mean in terms of the hypothesis of interest and past studies.

Managerial Implications: The discussion section where the study's implications are made clear to managers, often focused on decisions and processes that managers or other business professionals may address in their day-to-day work.

Results: The output from the models, reported as statistics. These results require additional interpretation for a robust comparison with past studies and the explanation for managers or business professionals.

Stock Market Reaction: A sudden and short-lived change in the stock prices in reaction to the event. The stock market reaction, measured by the abnormal returns, is usually the focus of the main hypothesis in the event study project.

Chapter 13
Writing the Manuscript

ABSTRACT

This chapter introduces a structured approach to writing the manuscript, focusing particularly on the results and discussion section. Many of the core issues and factors that must be considered in the write-up are addressed. Also covered are presentation pitfalls that are commonly encountered. To help conceptualize how the manuscript can synthesized, the author introduces the "V-Model" structure. The model structure explains the connections and relationships between the various portions of a manuscript, what the readers may look for in each section, and outlines some differences between dissertations and journal articles. Finally, several tips are provided on ensuring that each section of the manuscript contains the necessary components and connects with the appropriate sections.

INTRODUCTION

Completing a research project is one crucial step in the process of research. However, having made sense of the data and getting a research answer is only one part of the problem. The next part, and arguably the more difficult component, is communicating the findings and results to others to use, build on, and improve the study. In this chapter, we turn to writing the manuscript and providing guidance on how each section and its relationships can be framed. By propounding the "V-Model", introduced by Sheffield (2005), this chapter provides a structure that ensures the writing process is repeatable and can produce consistent results. In addition, the framework should remove some of the ambiguity from the task for students writing dissertations and support researchers in writing up their own results persuasively.

It is also important to note that there is no strict right or wrong for many writing decisions. We may design the final manuscript in part in consultation with editors or reviewers or the dissertation or thesis supervisors. This chapter seeks to provide a basic overview that can accommodate a range of different event studies and even other empirical project write-ups. Throughout, several essential guidelines are explained and the intention and purpose of each section of the manuscript. The guidelines and framework should help remove some ambiguity in what editors, reviewers, and examiners are looking for when reading a manuscript.

DOI: 10.4018/978-1-7998-8969-4.ch013

Several design decisions include different ways of structuring or presenting material into sections; we provide a short overview of some of these options with some examples. By doing this, I hope to remove some of the uncertainty that new researchers or postgraduate students may feel as they present the results. Of course, they might not be doing it in the 'right way' that their supervisor may expect, but there is usually precedent for many of these decisions on structure, presentation, and writing up the research results.

Further, this chapter summarizes some guidelines for structuring and writing research. It uses the V-model introduced by Sheffield (2005). This can be a fundamental way of considering an article or dissertation write-up. We do not present the concepts as strict controls of how the material is written and organized. However, regarding the basic structure and formula, the new researcher or a postgraduate student can have more confidence about what they should write in each section and understand a little more about why a particular section may include particular insights, materials, or information. Using the basic framework would enable postgraduate students to write their results rapidly about the project into a manuscript while reducing the uncertainty about whether this would be acceptable to an examiner. The framework also ensures that appropriate information is included in places an examiner may look for it. In this way, the V-Model framework provides a good starting point for writing a manuscript, whether an article, thesis, or dissertation.

I designed this chapter to guide and provide general explanations about writing and structuring the work. I strongly advise postgraduate students to check with the supervisors and advisers about departmental expectations, which should always be heeded over the advice in this chapter. However, I hope that the advice in this chapter aids in reducing ambiguity and uncertainties about what should be in each section, and it provides a general framework for postgraduate students as they work.

USING THE V-MODEL TO STRUCTURE A MANUSCRIPT

We can consider no research project complete until it can be communicated to an audience. The communication will either be through our dissertation or other scientific/scholarly journal articles for most of us. In each case, the writing of results and discussion of these results is important, as is the overall ability to help readers find and digest our study. This chapter focuses on aiding the reader to craft effective sections or chapters that will help the reader understand the core study findings and structure the entire manuscript to support the readers.

We often focus on the linear presentation of work, following a standard design. For instance, the flow of topics and chapters/sections of the manuscript is reflected in **Figure 1**. The model is what is physically/actually presented to us (as we read) and likely reflects how many of us read work (from start to finish). However, there are other ways of perceiving a manuscript, and exploring other approaches can add value. While the manuscript is presented as a consistent and linear flow, the underlying work is usually anything but linear. During the research, there will often be significant twists and turns or re-work on certain project elements. Sometimes, a dead-end is reached, or surprising findings precipitate new approaches.

The linear conception (Figure 1) has drawbacks. It suggests one-to-one relationships between each chapter and only with the two adjoining chapters. However, readers of research articles and theses/dissertations will know different manuscript sections are relatable but not adjacent most times.

Figure 1. A linear conception of the manuscript structure

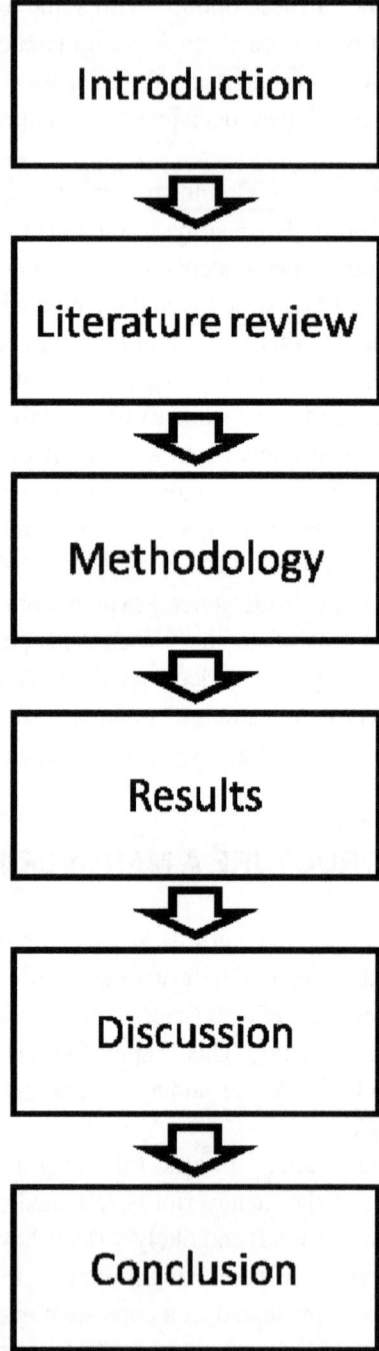

The V-model (Figure 2) allows a different layout and model of the connected components. The V-model enables you to understand better what should be in each section and how the sections are related. It allows us to understand what readers may look for and why these elements should be expected in the

Figure 2. The V-model approach to manuscript structure

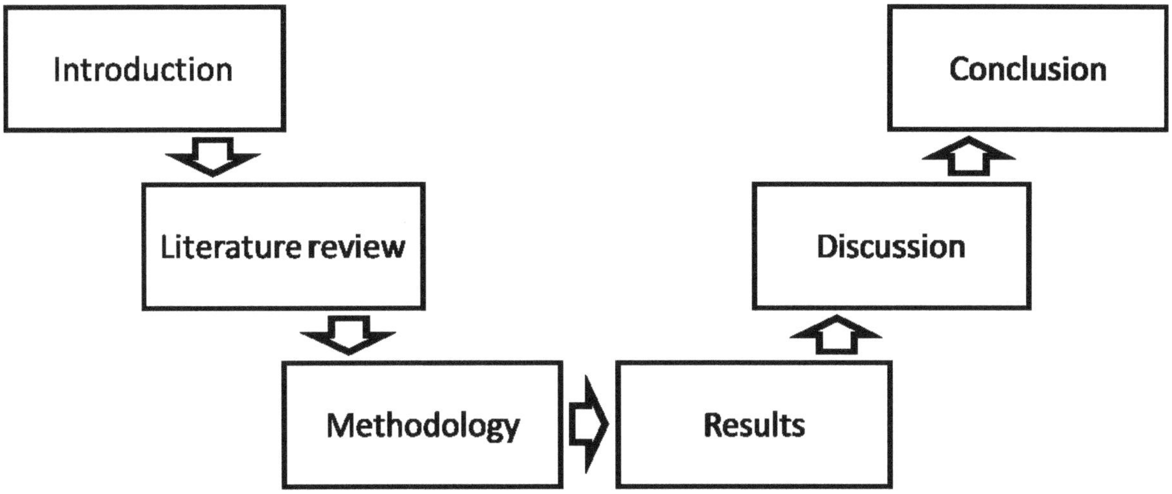

relevant sections. I first learned about the V-Model concept from Sheffield in a research methods class at the University of Auckland. He later published some elements of the discussions in Sheffield (2005).

Not all readers take a linear approach to their reading of a manuscript. Many experienced academic readers will focus on core elements they are most interested in; they will read with a purpose. This will be different for all readers, but may, for instance, include an initial focus on the introduction and conclusion chapter pairings (Figure 3) for evaluating a dissertation, then a look at the methods and results pairing (Figure 5). When looking at a journal article, the results and discussion sections may draw the most attention, with the methods section receiving a cursory look (assuming, of course, they published the article in a leading journal with a strong quality assessment procedure). Dissertations, in particular, are often long and might be read over several sittings. The dissertation style is often ponderous and stylistic, with a surprising amount of repetition. For example, there are often sign-post statements like "this previous section covered this, now we will examine this," and other statements designed to help guide the reader through the lengthy document. Likewise, the linear flow of materials should be sign-posted for the reader. In particular, a dissertation will often have a strongly stylized and large section that sign-posts and guides the reader through the development of the dissertation.

It is valuable to read through several recommended dissertations from your department or your advisors' past students when writing the dissertation. As an exercise, it may be useful to look through three different dissertations and apply the template in this chapter to the dissertations. Then, evaluate how well they fit with the template. To do this, you do not need to read comprehensively, but enough to understand the structuring and organization of the work. For example, a dissertation may have several chapters containing different results or discussions; how would you say the different chapters fit into the categories presented in Figure 2?

When writing, we must understand the need to make a contribution. The ability to assert the contribution will come from your results and your literature review. It relies on the pairing of the literature review and the discussion sections (Figure 4).

Figure 3. V-model demonstrating the relationship between the introduction and conclusion

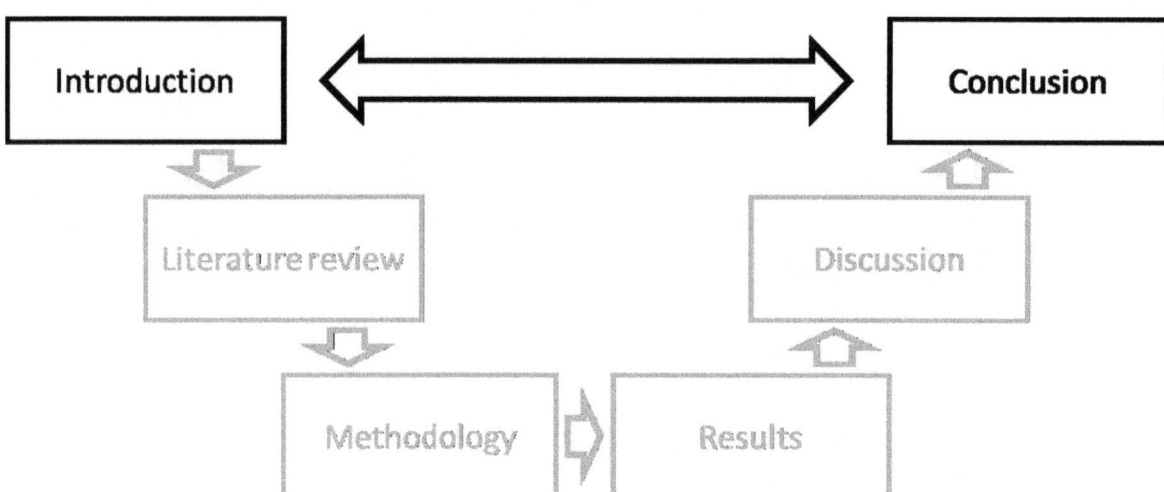

Figure 4. V-model demonstrating literature review and discussion relationships

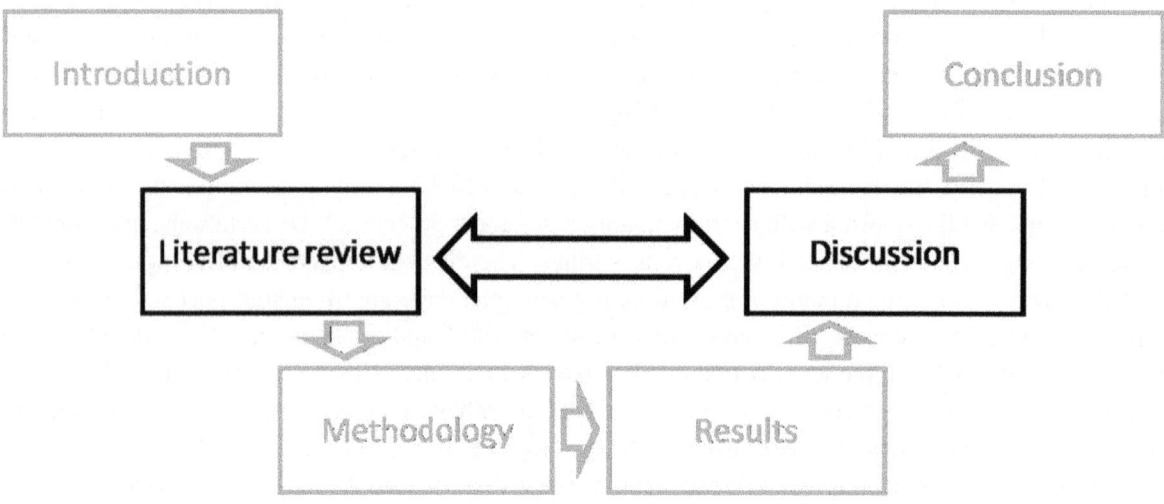

While it may appear fairly rudimentary, I routinely use the model when advising my students and when completing my writing. When writing, the V-Model provides me with a very simple framework and a constant reassurance that I have met the requirements. Using the model, I can check my writing against the V-model's suggestion. It helps to ensure that the internal structure of the writing is sound and it contains all the links and connections that my readers would be looking for. Many students have expressed to me that they are not productive at writing, as they are confused or unclear about what is required in each section. It helps them understand the challenges of writing a thesis that makes it easier by giving them a clear understanding of each section's content and how they are related to the other sections. In this way, the V-Model provides certainty about how the manuscript components should be written about and how these components should be related (Figures 2-5).

Figure 5. V-model demonstrating the methodology and results relationships

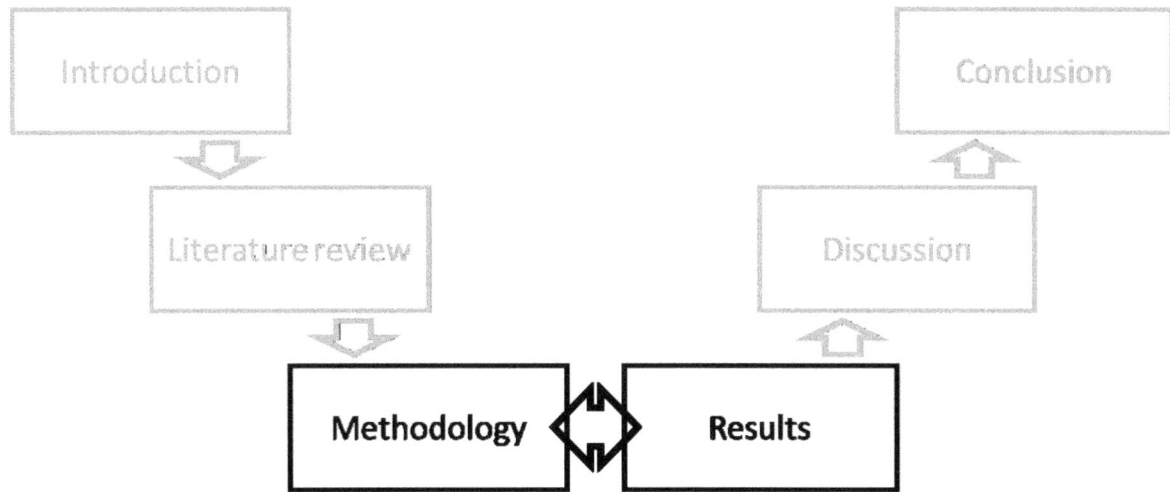

In all cases, if we understand what the reader is expecting to find in a particular section or chapter, we can best present the information there to help them. If we understand what we should present and how, then we can remove unnecessarily repeated materials and include the materials in the appropriate places where the reader may expect to find the materials.

As the section title implies, the abstract is an abstracted and summarized version of the research work. Assume that we will include sufficient information here to help the reader understand if they read it. Journals often have different formats, with some management journals requiring a 'block of text' while others request a structured abstract. Initially, I was uncertain about writing structured abstracts and felt it ruined creativity, but I have grown to appreciate that it includes all the key elements of the abstract. Now, I frequently use the structured abstract to write all my abstracts. Use the headings, fill in the blanks, remove the headings, then combine the sections into a single paragraph. It ensures that I have the core information, there is no repetition, and I include the information in appropriate places.

In all cases, assume that your writing should be persuasive. For example, with a dissertation or journal article, assume that we are trying to persuade the reader that this is good research (carefully conducted) and important. Each paragraph should have a single point that we are trying to communicate. When we read a paragraph, and it seems to tackle two purposes or two issues, we should split the paragraph. (If a paragraph needs to be split, it may also be possible to shuffle some of the constituent sentences to other locations to improve the flow and development of ideas elsewhere.) This is one of the biggest problems I have; the more I write in one sitting, the more frequently the paragraphs become longer and less coherent and need to be edited out or split into two (or more) sections. When reviewing your writing, try to capture the purpose (of what you are trying to persuade the reader) in a single sentence and use a post-it note to summarize this. It is useful to have someone else read through your work and understand if they are taking away the same message and core issue that you wanted to communicate.

You can think about the writing as a sequence of persuasive statements that leads the reader to the conclusion you want them to reach. If we want the reader to agree with the conclusions, they must also agree with the prior arguments. Ultimately, if we can convince them of the sequence of arguments that we make, the reader should agree with the study's conclusions. It may be helpful, for example, to use post-it notes to ensure that each paragraph we write has a clear purpose (as on the post-it note) and that these notes capture a coherent argument. This process can help us as authors to interrogate the argument and ensure that it is persuasive and contains all the required elements.

When in doubt about the thesis or dissertation requirements, it is best to remove the concerns by talking with supervisors, advisors, or faculty members in the department. Ask if they can recommend a comparable dissertation to read through and make sure that they consider this was at least 'well received' or scored highly. It is often difficult to assess which dissertation was well-written (as assessed by the examiners!), and you should not simply read a recent example (written by someone who completed it just before you) or another recent example in your area. Instead, get a good example that gives a sense of what examiners may be looking for and those conventions that are essential to follow.

STRUCTURING THE MANUSCRIPT AND WHAT YOU NEED IN EACH SECTION

There is no right or wrong way to do this, and it may be an editor/reviewer or journal's style or preference. The event study manuscript will generally follow the same sequence of topics/sections as in the V-Model approach. However, in event studies published in journals, the 'data' section is sometimes presented before the models section, and there is no section called 'methods'. This structure may seem strange to many readers, but the sections still match the basic flow and logic to the V-model. In general, my advice for a dissertation or manuscript is to follow the 'standard' approach. The primary reason is that this minimizes risks (particularly important or a dissertation submission); many examiners or reviewers will expect to see things presented under standard headings. You should not be creative; follow the standard models for your field, department, or journal.

WRITING THE INTRODUCTION

The introduction will follow a similar pattern for the dissertation or a journal manuscript with a different emphasis. The dissertation will likely focus heavily on the contribution and the importance of the research. On the other hand, the journal manuscript focuses more on the antecedents and the value of the manuscript. This is restating the same thing; however, the dissertation contribution will be more theoretically focused, at least in the New Zealand system. The introduction also presents some antecedents that are the earlier or prior research in this area; we need to be at least familiar with and understand this work as we use it to establish the contribution of our study. In addition, the introductions will contain a reason or a particular hook to get readers interested in understanding why this type of study is essential. Finally, the manuscript's structure will be presented in both cases, which will usually follow a fairly standard formula.

My thinking about the introduction has been influenced by "the introduction formula" (Head, n.d.). I used to find the introduction very difficult to write. While it remains a challenge, the systematic approach to structuring the introduction has made it more manageable. The structure supports the writing in understanding what they should try to achieve in the introduction. It can be used as a checklist to ensure that we have achieved what we need to achieve and include all the required elements. It also allows us to take a draft and compare it against the checklist to ensure that each paragraph in our draft introduction serves a purpose against the checklist; everything that we want to do is achieve and actually contributes to the objectives.

First, we want to establish a **hook** to capture the readers' interest. In a dissertation, the hook might take the form of a controversial statement or quote from a senior public figure or an important document. It could be a series of quotes from newspaper articles about a recent phenomenon showing the importance and currency of the event. In general terms, the hook will be quite a broad and abstract paragraph, very much at the societal level. It is much broader than the particular focus of the study and positions why it will contribute to our understanding and the bigger picture and help improve business and society.

The antecedents and the prior studies are important because they help the reader contextualize past research in this area. There is no hard and fast rule, and in a dissertation, we might describe the antecedents section as a background section and provide some context. While we can include similar works in the field, this is not the place. Instead, it is possible to present an overview of some of the key research over the last five years, leading us up to this point. The focus should be on developing that narrative and explaining what must be done and why. There should be a realization that there is an issue that still needs to be solved. It is against this problem that you are positioning your work to present a solution or a partial solution to this underlying problem. By clearly showing this issue and problem, we enable the reader to evaluate the study's contribution and value. It must be matched to the hook section because that enables the reader to see the value in the wider context, not just within the discipline or the narrow field of research.

At some point, we will need to be very clear about the problem we are solving or the research question we are addressing. In all cases, I think it is very useful and important to include this statement clearly and explicitly, preferably using words such as objective, aim, or research question. Using these terms is important for the reader; it signposts or signals the intention or purpose of this statement. In a dissertation, it becomes increasingly important to do this so that the examiner can better understand and match up what we are doing with the area and the problem and how we interpret it. Clarity enables examiners to assess the study results and how the results address the problem.

In terms of the contribution or the importance of the research or the value-added section (in the introduction formula), this will often be one of the hardest sections to write. When we think about this logically, it is probably only possible to write this in the end. The reason is that we must know what we have actually achieved in order to report on this and promote or sell this. A journal manuscript may have a strong practical positioning and practical value to professionals in the field, that may have a strong policy focus suggesting changes or alterations and policy development settings nationally, it might have a very strong theoretical development focus enabling us to understand an extension to theory or the development of a new midrange theory. In New Zealand, it is common to see a subsection and the dissertation that explains the theoretical contribution or the contribution of this research. Including these terminologies in the subsection heading provides a clear sign to a thesis/dissertation examiner and enables them to identify and read through the section.

The approach taken, or the method used to address these questions, is sometimes reported in journal manuscripts introductions but is commonly reported in dissertations. Then a dissertation, as often useful to explain the approach taken briefly, shows the philosophically appropriate nature of the approach and the exact method used. In this way, the introduction section is an essence of an extended abstract that presents the reader with everything they need to know. At the end of the introduction, the examiner should be very aware of what the study is about, the purpose, the primary research question and objectives, whether this must be solved, and how the researcher went about solving problem.

It is much less common in journal articles for the method to be so explicitly stated in the introduction. My personal experience has been mixed; while I usually include a little information about the approach, whether reviewers or editors prefer this to be included varies considerably. I like to provide a little paragraph about the method, particularly with an interesting twist or an extension to commonly adapted methods. For example, if I felt it was an extensive data set, or there are some particular challenges that the readers might appreciate and the collecting or analysis of the data, then I will try to insert this, and the introduction section is a way of showing the value or the importance of this work.

Presentation of the manuscript structure, whether a dissertation or journal article, should be relatively standard and should not take long to write in either case. As explained elsewhere, I very much favor a very standard approach. However, I think it is important not just to say this is the literature review section, but also to explain the key elements of the literature review section and provide concise and clear summaries. For example, the literature review section might focus on a theory, combine or juxtapose it against another theory, and position it as an extension of the theories at that intersection point. If so, say that here. This way, we can take this standard section and extend it further.

Another key factor to be included in the introduction is the motivation to complete the research. There can be multiple motivations for the research, and I tend to think of them within the following categories.

1. Further theoretical development is needed. Theory does not appear to explain practice or actual events that we can observe in the industry.
2. Disagreement in the research that is suggesting further theoretical refinement is needed. There seems to be some conflict in the theoretical explanations for particular phenomena, and additional research is needed.
3. There is a business-based motivation or a call for further research to support practice. They commonly used this approach in supply chain literature, where research requires substantial advancements and enhancements. Most times, the business practice may be substantially ahead of research, motivating us to 'catch up' with our research.

While it is instructive to look at different examples, I drew most of my examples from the operations and supply chain management domain. Many researchers provide compelling and clear motivations for their work, and this is not an exhaustive review of how they work, but merely highlights several key examples

Articles including Carter as an author usually have an obvious practice-focused motivation for the research. The introduction usually has a clear articulation about why this research is essential, and they usually ground this within practice-based motivation to complete the work. Most times, the introductions will reference non-academic research or grey literature, providing insight into why this is a critical issue to solve from a professional or practice-based perspective. For instance, the following quote provides insight into early disconnects between professional practice and academic research:

In addition, companies are beginning to rapidly adopt the term sustainability. About 68 percent of the Global 250 firms generated a separate annual sustainability report in 2004 which considered environmental, social, and economic issues, in contrast to the primary emphasis on environmental reporting in 1999; in addition, 80 percent of these reports discuss supply chain-related issues (KPMG, 2005). Unfortunately, a review of the literature will show that the term sustainability has been inconsistently defined and applied in the extant research. (Carter & Rogers, 2008, p. 361)

There is a reference to a report by the consulting group KPMG, providing a good review of business practice. Note how this is contrasted with academic research in the area; while businesses are heavily using sustainability concepts, academic research is less well-defined on this topic. Here, research lags practice. A further example of how research may lag practice is provided by Jacobs et al., where they note that:

Even though Wal-Mart's energy conservation and recycling initiatives, and Unilever's forays into low-cost water purification and eco-friendly detergents are well received by the popular press, the question remains as to whether the market perceives the returns on such initiatives to be as attractive as returns on alternative investment opportunities. In other words, can a firm increase shareholder value through improvements in its environmental performance? The controversy continues to receive attention in the press. (Jacobs et al., 2010, p. 430)

We can also make calls for more research when the outcomes will support managers. For example, when considering social network analysis (SNA), Carter et al. (2007, p. 138) note that "[f]rom a managerial perspective, SNA is a powerful tool that allows managers to map informal networks of communication and workflow," showing the value to professionals from using SNA.

In their event study examination of supply chain disruptions, Hendricks and Singhal note (2005) that:

Our analysis of the long-run stock price effects of disruptions is important for a number of reasons. First, managers and investors are likely to have more faith in estimates of economic impact that are based over long horizons, as it provides them with a more complete picture of the economic implications of disruptions. By examining the long-run stock price effects of disruptions, we are able to shed light on the time pattern of abnormal stock price behavior in terms of when it starts, how long it lasts, and whether firms recover quickly from disruptions. These issues are important for setting realistic expectations of the likely consequences of disruptions. (Hendricks & Singhal, 2005, p. 36)

They clearly state that this is necessary research, and they start with a clear connection to providing managers with a benefit. Further, many business-focused research articles can also show the importance of the phenomenon that they study with examples from practice, as highlighted by Jacobs and Singhal (Jacobs & Singhal, 2014) in their introduction, where they note that:

Consistent with the literature, firms are also concerned with how product development is structured. Firms often undertake firm-level product development restructuring (PDR), a form of organizational restructuring that realigns, refocuses, reorganizes, or streamlines a firm's product development activities and organization. We note that organizational restructuring is a rather broad term that conveys changes in organizational structure that can have different purposes and forms. For example, Toyota restructured its vehicle development group into three geographic regions and streamlined final design decision making in an effort to cut costs and improve product design (Dawson 2012). GlaxoSmithKline realigned its research group into a number of small units to reduce bureaucracy and spur innovation (Whalen 2010). There is limited literature that examines such changes to product development structure at the firm level or its economic consequences. (Jacobs & Singhal, 2014, p. 728)

Event study research can also provide insight into areas of current disagreement between researchers. Jacobs et al. (2010) provide insight into environmental performance. The introduction outlines two different discussions in the research and the lack of consensus. They note:

Second, academics have studied the relationship between environmental performance and financial performance, both theoretically (Walley and Whitehead, 1994; Hart, 1995; Porter and van der Linde, 1995) as well as empirically (Ullman, 1985; Margolis and Walsh, 2003). Friedman (1970) argues that any environmental expenses beyond those required for regulatory compliance are not in the best interest of shareholders and will result in degradation of firm performance and value. However, Barnett and Salomon (2006) suggest that good social performance attracts resources to the firm, including better quality employees and expanded market opportunities. Also, since proactive approaches to environmental performance require greater intangible skills (e.g., cross-disciplinary activity and problem solving) than do reactive approaches, related efforts create more valuable resources and can be a source of competitive advantage (Hart, 1995; Russo and Fouts, 1997). In contrast, Walley and Whitehead (1994) propose that instances where environmental efforts can improve firm performance are rare. In analyzing the market reaction to a broad range of environmental initiatives, we shed light on whether such initiatives affect firm value. (Jacobs et al., 2010, p. 431)

WRITING THE LITERATURE REVIEW

In the dissertation, the primary purpose of the literature review will be a demonstration of scholarship. The author should show they understand the context or the field of research in which they are positioning the research. The literature review structure will vary depending on the background and the type of study. Increasingly, I see the use of systematic literature reviews or systematic reviews, or meta-analyses (Berman & Parker, 2002; Carlson & Ji, 2011; Cooper, 2010). However, when I started, the narrative analysis was the primary mechanism for developing the literature review, which seems to be common in event studies.

While you have probably read a huge amount of literature during the study, perhaps 1000 articles, not all will feature within the literature review. For example, there is more scope for an extensive discussion of research around this topic in a dissertation. On the other hand, a journal article will be much more constrained in the type of research and depth of the literature review.

Your advisor or department may have some suggestions on the length of the doctoral dissertation. However, it is vital to provide an overview of the field, acknowledge seminal works or key thinkers and essential contributions, and explain or trace the evolution of the problem to where we are today. The literature review section will probably end on a note that says something along the lines of: "this is the problem; I have shown you how we have reached this, and this is still an open area for investigation."

Despite the huge amount of research and reading we have done, it is still necessary to coherently piece this and provide a story for the reader. Even in systematic literature reviews, we still have a huge opportunity to provide exciting and innovative ideas and be quite creative in discussing the meaning. In a narrative literature review, we have much more flexibility.

We might include seminal articles and research ideas and a dissertation tracing back the theory's origins to original thinkers. For example, transaction cost economics (TCE) went back to work in the 1930s, which attempted to explain firms' nature (Coase, 1937). Now, we probably do not need to dwell on seminal studies, but rather show an understanding of where key ideas originated and how they evolved. For instance, after discussing the seminal works behind TCE, we might discuss Williamson's development of the concepts further into what we recognize as TCE (Williamson, 1975, 1981, 1985, 1994), before then positioning and contrasting that with the more recent explosion and work in this area (Brewer et al., 2014; Duan et al., 2014; Williamson, 2008).

Assumptions will also be important. For example, in a dissertation, we may include quite a large section discussing the assumptions behind a theory or an idea, as these are often influential in the theoretical developments.

I only want to select the most relevant material that will fit this discussion of the seminal work and more recent contributions in this area when looking through the reading. We can consider the key categories or issues that emerge through the seminal work and the more recent work and the key features of these categories. Search through the background reading completed, and select the A or B category articles (see chapter 6) that have the most relevance to your work. We might use sorting techniques such as post-it notes or a mind map to understand how these relate. Use them to provide the context for the study.

We can be critical, and this is encouraged. However, this is perhaps one of the hardest elements of writing the literature review for a postgraduate student. After all, what place do we have to criticize research and leading journals, the journals in which we aspire to publish? It is important to note that all research designs include a sequence of decisions that are made by the research team. Each of these decisions has implications. Some of these decisions might be good or bad decisions well might lead to large and problematic limitations in the study. Considering the past research's limitations is often a handy place to start with criticism. Alternatively, we can often look at the type of data collected and the type of industry context they collected the data from and reflect on whether some decisions made here influence or bias the outcomes.

Literature and Hypotheses

The literature section may be separate from the hypothesis section in event studies. There is no right or wrong way of doing this. Editor or reviewer preferences may guide the final (published) article structure. There are several approaches we can observe, such as

- Hypotheses in the literature review. For example, Jacobs and Singhal (2017) present the hypotheses in their second section, titled 'Shareholder wealth impacts of Rana Plaza.'
- Hypotheses separate from the literature review. For example, Xia et al. (2016) have a second section on 'literature review' before the third section that presents the development of hypotheses.
- Hypotheses developed with no explicit literature review. For example, Hendricks et al. (2014) do not present a section for the literature review and instead present their second section for the hypothesis development. The section combines a literature review with a thorough analysis of their hypotheses' development and rationale.

WRITING THE METHODS

The methods or methodology section is perhaps the most crucial section in all studies and is usually one of the easiest sections to write. The structure and emphasis of dissertations and journal articles will be similar; however, dissertation writers should explain that they understand the hell and why for selecting this method and that this was an appropriate choice and philosophically congruent with the problem.

When writing and advising my students, I often suggest that the methods chapter is one of the first chapters they write through to completion to create a good draft. The chapter will often be the most straightforward chapter to write. It is, after all, reporting on what was done in the study. If we kept a research journal and detailed the steps we took in the research, including why we have taken these steps and what those outcomes are, we have a huge amount of material that can be adapted to help write this chapter.

In a journal article that uses an event study, there will often be a section on data. It should detail what data was used, where it was collected from, and what analytic process was used. In the journal article, these sections might be fairly brief. Moreover, a dissertation might be more extensive, explaining in great depth and detail the sequence of steps used and what those outcomes were.

In my mind, one of the key attributes that we should aspire to within the methods chapter will be replication. Can a reader replicate our study based on this methods section? Could the reader replicate the analysis they had access to the dataset that we used? Ultimately, we want to provide sufficient details here that somebody else could replicate the study and come up with similar or comparable conclusions or outcomes. If we can achieve this, we can be reasonably confident that we have included everything in the methods section that should be in there.

How to dissertation, you should probably start with an introductory paragraph. This introductory paragraph should explain the main features of the method you used and the chapter's overall organization. An event or quantitative study can use a short statement after this, outlining the procedures adopted, the sampling methods hypothesis, and statistical techniques employed. Qualitative studies will usually be more flexible. If you are a postgraduate student, your advisor can help you with what might be expected based on intended publication outputs.

In positivistic studies, like events studies, the methods chapter will explain precise steps to address the research question. In a journal article, if you are using well-understood or standard processes and tests, you do not necessarily need to describe these in great detail, but you should instead refer to them and include citations to a reference work. However, if you modified or extended any of these tests, you need to describe what you have done in more detail. This methodological extension may be part of your contribution in a doctoral dissertation. If you are using an approach that is not well understood in your field or which is more common in another field but less common in your field, then it is helpful to describe this approach and more detail to help assure the reader about the method and provide them with a little more background.

Event Study Nuances for the Methods and Data

Event study projects often have a slightly different format than other studies in management literature and other areas. While many studies will often follow a traditional introduction, literature, methods, results, discussions, conclusions, an event study will often replace the methods section with 'data and sample' before presenting the results. For instance, Xia et al. (2016) first outline the 'data and methodology' in Section 4, with an overview of the data collection process followed by the method. Similarly, Ba et al. (2013) use their section on 'research methodology' to first discuss data collection, followed by data analysis.

In contrast, Hendricks and Singhal (2003) present a section on 'Sample selection procedure and data description' before a section on 'methodology.' Hendricks et al. (2014) first present a section on the 'sample' before outlining the method used in their next section titled 'stock market reaction to [supply chain and operations management executive] appointments.' There is no right or wrong way to present these sections. Departmental, editorial, or journal guidelines may provide some suggestions. If guidance is absent, presenting the sample and data details in the 'methods' section might be convenient.

WRITING THE RESULTS SECTION

The results chapter will differ depending on whether we are engaged in more phenomenological or qualitative research vs positivist or statistically based research. While a qualitative work will often be replete with quotes and the words of the participants, the positivist and statistical approaches will often have a short section that is more focused on the presentation of data and tables.

Event studies will usually show the results in two key formats. First, there will be a table showing the CAR calculation outcomes. There will be the provision of test statistics to show that these results are, in fact, statistically significant and do not occur because of random chance. Again, model diagnostics will often show that this is a reasonable and appropriate model. It is not, for example, simply a good model because of an influential observation (e.g., an observation that was included and substantially changed the results to look better than they would if we excluded the observation from the sample). The focus is on simply showing the results. We should pair this section against the methods section, showing that what was promised in the methods section was delivered in the results section.

Results for Event Studies

We can include a wide range of possible materials in the results section. Most times, there may be alternative study designs where the results are included here to show the robustness of the analysis. For instance, Xia et al. (2016) provide an extensive results section. They first summarize the actual event study results, providing a written summary of the key results and a table showing day -1, 0, and (-1,0) abnormal returns and other statistics, such as test statistics. This section also provides an explanation and the equations for calculating abnormal returns using a different approach as part of their sensitivity analysis. (Note that they may also include this in earlier sections, as some research articles show.) Next, they summarize the cross-sectional analysis results, with an example of comparable past studies, citations, and the abnormal returns so you can gauge their results against key literature. Next, they present their results section that includes the variable constructions and final regression model used while providing a cross-sectional regression table showing parameter estimates for several models. They discuss the models and outcomes afterward. Finally, they provide descriptive results, as these provide further insights.

In contrast, much of this information may be included in earlier sections. For instance, Wood et al. (2017) use a section on 'methodology' that includes the variable constructions, sample construction, establishment of time windows, an overview of descriptive statistics for the sample, and an overview of the regression modeling used. The results section first provides the abnormal return estimates with a table showing how the results are robust and validates the selection of windows. Next, the regression results and parameter estimates for the model are presented. Finally, sections on model diagnostics and sensitivity analysis assure the reader of the research design decisions. Another approach is taken by

Jacobs et al. (2010), where they first summarize the abnormal returns and then analyze the different categories of the event they studied.

The focus next turns to the discussion section of the manuscript.

WRITING THE DISCUSSIONS

The primary purpose is to show that we understand the results and what they mean in the context of past research. We might consider how this section can show that the results extend, contradict, or confirm other results. For example, in a dissertation, we may partly replicate other results or studies, showing that the results confirm that the general understanding of the phenomenon holds in the context studied. However, we could still find that the results are slightly different, in which case the change of contexts may be significant. For instance, if the past studies were on U.S.-based firms and you did a similar study on Australian firms, with slightly different results, you would note how this shows or adds to our knowledge of the phenomenon, with a comparison of context and culture providing insight into the theory.

Event studies by themselves will not usually create a new theory or result. Instead, it will extend our knowledge of a theory or phenomenon, or it may contradict an established understanding.

If our results differ from what we expect or contradict past studies, we will want to investigate why this is the case. What is different about the sample? Was it a different type of company, a different sector? Is there something distinct about these sectors that may explain this? Is it because of a different country, where its business culture may influence this?

Practical Issues

Take the hypotheses you generated. Did they confirm, contradict, or extend past results? My approach to addressing this practically, that speeds the process and reduces ambiguity is to start with a table, then write the section based on the table. Next, take the "A" rated articles from the literature review and key articles to generate the hypotheses. The table should have four columns:

1. Past study citations
2. What their results were (relevant to your study)
3. What you found (outline your results)
4. How your results confirm, contradict, or extend those results.

Each row should represent one study, allowing us to compare that study to our study. When done, we should have between five to 15 articles listed here and a clearer (mechanical) picture that notes your results, past results, and conclusion.

The next step is to write these comparisons over the table to create paragraphs. Again, use the table format and 'shuffle' the results to match the hypotheses or other key issues. When the rows are clustered together, we have the material to write several paragraphs. At the simplest approach, the discussion section brings together the results, past study results, and explains the contribution or what we know now that we did not before. We can take the primary notes and write these up as paragraphs using this format with a conclusion statement for each paragraph that summarizes the discussion in that paragraph.

The main reason that I prefer this approach is that it enables me to assert a contribution that becomes almost unarguable. Assuming that I interpret the results of the earlier study correctly and my study results, then by carefully placing them together, it shows to the reader that we knew something before; we know something now, and there is an extension or a contribution to our knowledge. Done this way, the discussion section is relatively simple to craft, and it will remove ambiguity and uncertainty while making it easier to write the discussion sections in most masters or doctoral dissertations.

An important element of this approach is that it also provides a very strong connection between the literature review and the discussion section. The V-model provides a clear connection between the background, key articles, and study results. This connection helps us ground our research in past research and enables us to show the contribution of the present research. An example of the comparison of past studies to current study results is provided by Jacobs et al. (2010, p. 439), when they note how:

Finally, the market reaction to environmental awards in our study is different than in Klassen and McLaughlin (1996), who find significant and positive market reaction. Our evidence indicates that LEED certifications and government awards are value-neutral, but non-governmental awards have a negative market reaction. (Jacobs et al., 2010, p. 439)

Note the clear contribution and contrast with past research. The past research concluded that there was a significant and positive market reaction. In contrast, Jacobs et al. (2010, p. 439) find the situation is nuanced, and researchers may need to break the sample into smaller groups to understand the critical differences between them.

Implications for Practice, Research, and Policy

Another section in the discussion or conclusion will be the implications section. We can fruitfully consider this section as having three components:

1. Practice-based contributions (professional). Based on these results, what is the outcome for a professional, a manager, and a CEO? There may also be other categories of implications, such as how Jacobs and Singhal (2017) investigated the Rana Plaza collapse and broke down the 'implications for managers' section into the different components of retailers, factory owners, and non-governmental organizations (NGOs).
2. Academic or theoretical contributions. Given this outcome, how should future research be changed or adjusted? If the theory has been extended or boundary conditions established, how may that influence future study designs and why?
3. Policy contributions. Based on these results, how might a policymaker change policy settings? This is, perhaps, the least common form of contribution, but is likely to see increasing importance in the next decade as more management scholars (particularly in supply chain management research) realize the broader ramification of management issues on the broader society. For instance, if there is an indication that a particular event is more dangerous or disadvantageous to a particular category of a firm (or a firm with a particular characteristic), should a policymaker consider changes to encourage firms to remedy this ahead of time, to mitigate the future damage or outcome from these types of events?

As a simple heuristic, look at the core findings (outcomes of the hypotheses) that were supported in your study. Given this information, how might an operations manager change their approach? For instance, if the event is adverse (i.e., a negative stock market reaction is experienced), and a particular feature (e.g., high inventory levels) makes this worse (i.e., a negative beta-coefficient), what could a manager do with this information? The results may provide ammunition or evidence to support them with a project to reduce inventory levels to reduce the risks associated with this event. Of course, we should not consider this type of outcome without wider consideration, but when balanced against other needs, it suggests that the Operations Manager should judiciously consider the added risks of an elevated inventory level.

The location of the implications sections can vary in each manuscript. For example, it may be in the discussion section or the conclusion, depending on the manuscript's style and the editorial and reviewer preferences.

Jacobs and Singhal (2017) provide an example of policy implications. The article originally suggested that a strong and negative stock market reaction might force managers to attend to health and safety issues. However, as they note,

it is evident that the popular press and many stakeholders placed much of the blame for the Rana Plaza disaster on retailers rather than regulators, expecting market forces to rectify the problem. Our finding of an insignificant stock market reaction to the Rana Plaza disaster lends rigorous, empirical evidence to the claim of Rivoli (2009) that market forces alone are insufficient: The Bangladeshi government must set and consistently enforce clear and comprehensive regulatory guidelines. (Jacobs & Singhal, 2017, p. 64)

The outcome suggests no financial threat to the company owners, so policymakers may need to take a larger role. As a result, they note that "[t]he governments of buying firms in more developed economies can also play a role by altering trade agreements to pressure Bangladesh to improve worker rights and safety" (Jacobs & Singhal, 2017, p. 64).

Another example comes from Homan, who identifies that the 9/11 disaster led to negative stock market reactions for marine firms. This negative reaction suggests policy consequences, and Homan notes that:

The paper also shows that 9/11 resulted in significant and negative abnormal returns for affected firms. Given the ancillary societal costs resulting from the increased financial risks following 9/11, the results suggest that policy actions that reduced these risks would be welfare enhancing. (Homan, 2006, p. 400)

It may be pragmatic to approach the discussion and conclusions as a single section or chapter. In an earlier revision of Wood et al. (2017), we had separated these into separate sections. One reviewer rightly noted (and the editor agreed, and we subsequently agreed, also!) that we had some replications or duplicated material at the end of the manuscript between the two sections and that combining the sections would make for a shorter manuscript that is easier to read. If this is done, I suggest we still focus on the conclusion and discussions section as having distinct components. For example, the first paragraph might contain the summary section of the background, method, and main results; the rest might cover the comparison to past studies as part of the discussions material.

Some journals and editors may have strong feelings or style guides we need to conform to; others may be more relaxed and publish a range of articles with different structures at the end. In all cases, be clear about the purpose of the paragraphs and what they are trying to achieve. For example, ensure that we focus some paragraphs on the discussion section, and others are crafted to emphasize the study conclusions.

WRITING THE CONCLUSIONS SECTION

The conclusion section will be the shortest and perhaps the easiest one to write. It is, however, matched up with or paired with the introduction section. Some examiners may be inclined to read first the introduction section and then the conclusion section immediately after. When we think about it, the introduction section explains the background and antecedents to the study, why it is important to answer it, and exactly what the study aims to achieve. On the other hand, the conclusion section can then present the answer to that research question and some details about these research problems and then present to the reader hell this contributes back to the bigger picture.

The conclusion section should start with a summary of the primary objectives of the research and focus on those particular outcomes. It will then broaden that discussion and assert or explain clearly how this has contributed to and helped solve the wider problems in the area. It is essential that the claims made about the importance and the results are not grandiose and do not exceed or go beyond the claims that can be made with the data being used. This is going to be particularly true with an event study. Event studies will be very well bounded by the type of data collected and analyzed the type of analysis being made. The type of event will also be carefully bounded. It becomes difficult to claim generalization from the events studied to other event categories, even if they are comparable or similar. While it is tempting to make sweeping claims, it is also important not to overreach and be too ambitious. We must remain humble in the interpretation of our study results.

As several chapters or sections may be concurrently read, it is important that the same ideas, concepts, terminology, and keywords are being used throughout. If particular theories or issues are discussed in the introduction, these should be reflected or mirrored within the conclusion section. If we have made promises in the introduction section, such as presenting a research question, it is clear that the reader should look to the conclusion section to see whether we have delivered on this promise. Therefore, while the introduction section might present a clear research question, the conclusion section should explain the answer to that question.

In terms of managing risk, I am also a firm believer that while the presentation of the answer to the research question should be clear and precise, the answer must not overreach and go beyond the claims that could be made with the data and the analysis presented and the manuscript. It is useful to the reader to note that we addressed the research question in a particular section. The cross-reference tool (in word processors) can connect back to a particular subsection number.

Taking this approach enables you to show the reader that: "yes there was a question, and yes, there was an answer; I am summarizing it here in the conclusion, but look if you want further information, it was presented earlier, and here is the exact place where you can get these details." This will present a strong chain of evidence for an examiner and reassure them we are not making any leaps or jumps through the dissertation. Cross-referencing creates an explicit strong chain throughout the dissertation about where elements were presented and where the details can be found.

In my mind, it is perfectly acceptable for the conclusions section to be relatively brief in both manuscripts and theses or dissertations.

When looking to publish in a journal, we should be aware whether the journal can enable us to publish the conclusions and discussions separately or together. There are certain advantages to combining these in the singles section, as it may reduce the compulsion to summarize the core discussion elements twice, once in the discussion section and then again in the conclusion section. For instance, Xia et al.

(2016, p. 1052) use the title "Summary, Implications, and Future Research" for their final section and provide implications for research and practice.

Limitations and Future Research

As already asserted, the research process involves making many decisions. Some of these are of crucial importance to the project, and others will be of lesser importance. However, every decision made has ramifications for yotheur study. In many cases, the decisions made will introduce limitations. Therefore, the limitations section may be relatively simple to write. We take some of the key decisions that were made, perhaps those where we struggled, and it was not easy to decide on the research design. Then, we can write about the decision made, why it was made, and the implications for the study. For example, we may have selected particular respondents to speak with in a qualitative study, or we may not have reached a particular group of respondents. Consequently, the selection of the participants may introduce some bias into the type of data that we could collect or the perspectives that the research may represent. The limitations are simply an outline of the potential weaknesses in the research; all research design decisions create potential weaknesses. It is important not to let the limitations section become overly large; if there is a substantial section and limitations, the reader can correctly question whether or not there is value in the research at all. Consequently, the focus should be on fundamental limitations.

Future research is also of importance. Sometimes, the research design decisions we made present limitations or weaknesses in the research. A simple idea for future research would be a design decision that would overcome this limitation.

There are also going to be new questions that are raised by the research. For instance, if something became apparent that was not expected, that might raise the question about whether this was generalizable to other settings or whether it might be something particular to the research context in the study. Further, if we expect to find or discover a relationship that is not apparent when we analyze the data, future research might be required to uncover why. So, again, design decisions, particularly around sampling and the type of industries we draw participants from, might be useful in determining new research questions.

Future research can also be based on increasing the generalisability of the study findings. In particular, many researchers draw on samples where institutions might restrict data access in empirical work. For example, it might be expensive to travel long distances, so those companies might bound the sample, and the participants are those we can physically reach at a low cost. In other cases, a university may have good access to a group of companies and industry associations that the research can leverage. Consequentially, while we might find a good research result, it is difficult to argue the generalizability of results beyond this group. This provides an ample opportunity for future research that can be expressed as a limitation (i.e., weakness) of the study.

THE PROCESS OF WRITING UP

Like many people reading this chapter, I often have difficulty writing. When I open up a blank manuscript, I find it difficult to get words on the page and organize my thoughts. Like others, I experience writer's block. However, using the V-model provides several simple solutions to writer's block.

First, if we examine **Figure 6**, we can see that the manuscript structure has different levels of specificity and abstraction. One consequence is that the methods and results sections are often the easiest to write; they are the most specific and report on what happened. Therefore, I often advise my students that these are the chapters that they should aim to draft up and completeness various. The reason is that it is easier to capture and record details about the method used.

Ideally, a journal has been kept that details all the design decisions made during the process. If so, this provides very useful source material for the methods section. Consequently, the methods section reports on what was done and provided quite a high level of detail. As the overall manuscript may describe relatively abstract events of interest or phenomenon, what we detailed in the methods section will often be very concrete and specific. For example, while the overall project may be about supply chain disruptions, the methods section may include specific examples of news articles of what these events may look like in practice. The chapter becomes easy to write simply because very little creative thinking is required. Instead, the writer simply adopts a reporting mindset that reports what was done and why.

The results chapter can be framed similarly. It simply reports on the results of the findings with no interpretation or creativity required. Clearly, one must follow and understand the norms and expectations of the readers in the audience for whom we write. For a thesis or dissertation, this means following departmental or advisor guidelines. In addition, this means understanding the journal's expectations for an article, which can be ascertained relatively quickly by examining recently published comparable manuscripts.

Together, these two chapters report the project's specifics and can be written up fairly quickly in a format that will be nearly ready for a final draft. See the earlier sections regarding what material needs to be included in the sections. One very simple heuristic that I use is to report on what I would be interested in reading as a reader. In this way, I often query myself about what I want to know about the manuscript. Being old school, I often use Post-it notes to highlight key questions about the research project that I believe many readers will be interested in. Then, as I complete the section reporting on that element, I discard the Post-it note.

The next section or chapter that I would write is the discussion section. From the results, I have a fair idea of what is interesting, novel, and compelling about this research project. Consequently, considering the previously read literature, I can take the results and make sense of them. It is important to note that my literature review has been drafted but not finished. All of the sections in the literature review must still be re-evaluated with reference to the results, determining which sections are most relevant and if any are now less relevant or completely not relevant.

For this reason, I prefer to draft the discussion section before commencing the finalization of the literature review section. Then, using the study results as an input, I can isolate what the literature review must cover, considering the connections in Figure 4. It is the next section that should be logically written. We would have just used the key articles for the discussion section. These would be the A-ranked articles; those are the most crucial, relevant, and closest 'competitors' to the current study.

There is an element of creativity that must be applied during this chapter, so it becomes more difficult to write. I provided insight into some heuristics that can create a mechanical template that can get you started. However, creative interpretation and synthesis are still required.

Following the write-up of the discussion chapter, then go back to the literature section and evaluate whether all the sections are still required. Most times, the early literature review may have identified several areas of research and interest that, while promising at the start, have become less relevant during the research and the examination of the results. Consequently, the sections might be substantially removed from the literature review, or they may be summarized (as a parenthetical issue) in a sentence or two.

Figure 6. Levels of abstract and details

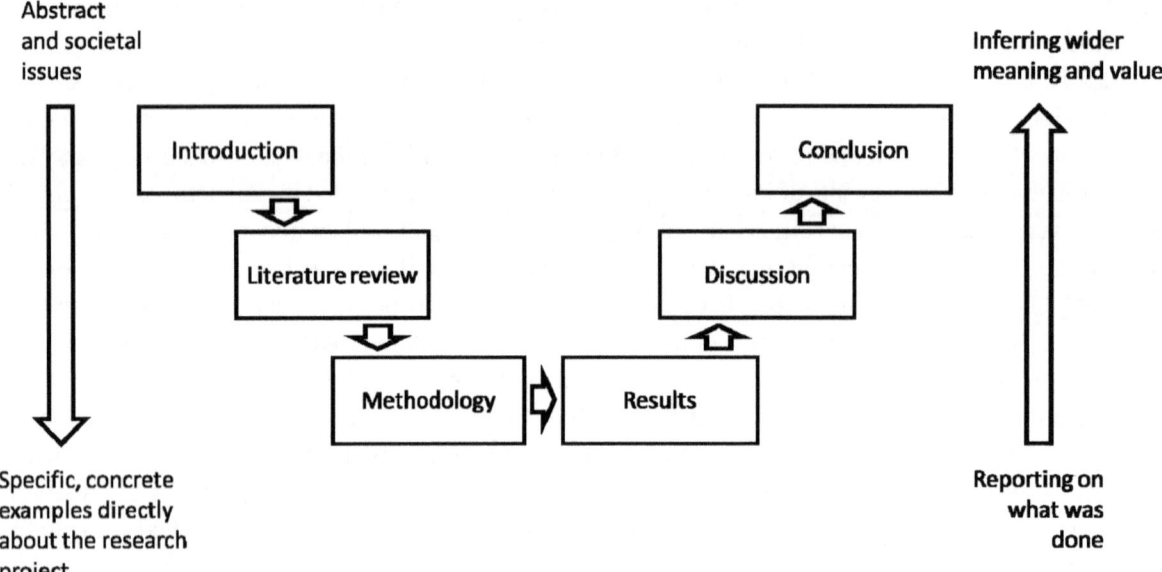

Next, I would tackle the introduction with an emphasis on using the introduction formula approach outlined earlier. At this point, most of what I need to write the introduction I will have at hand. Now, I understand the contribution and the study's importance; I have an overview of key antecedents required to understand the study. I can also explain the method applied and other observations that may interest the reader of the introduction. The introduction will also be one of the big picture sections that provide a sense of the overall meaning and importance of this piece of work so the reader can place it in the context of how this study leads to the betterment of society. What are the meaning and the consequences of solving this particular problem, and how does this improve society?

Finally, I would turn to the conclusions chapter, which is frequently read alongside the introduction. Here, the emphasis will be on the big ideas and providing a key summary of the key elements of the study. We return to the importance of this work and reiterate how it addresses a wider societal problem. We can write some of the limitations earlier identified out in full in the limitations section. This can then inform the future research section. The future research section can also be enhanced by presenting the study findings in a departmental seminar. Many colleagues will then contribute ideas and pose challenging questions that will provoke you to examine new areas and avenues for investigation.

MANAGING WRITERS' BLOCK

I strongly suspect that all writers find themselves faced with writer's block at one point or another. They sit or stand at the desk to write but struggle to string together the words on the page. I am no exception, but I have developed a range of approaches to help me overcome writer's block. I already covered many of these ideas in this chapter and the preceding chapters. This section addresses the issue directly.

First, I like to use dictation software. Windows and Apple devices now come with capable voice dictation software. However, my preference has been the Dragon suite of software for years. Although freely available packages have been closing the gap recently, Dragon always provided exceptionally good results. Second, I enjoy dictation software because I can sit back, relax, and get some ideas on paper. They may not be perfect; the software sometimes dictates words incorrectly, and sentence structures will be conversational. However, there are words on paper; the desolate wasteland of a blank page is gone. Moreover, that is an essential point to get started. Many people think the creative side of writing will be the most difficult. Yet, the second component where we are critical and edit our work comes more naturally than the creative writing process for many of us. It is also easy and legitimate to outsource the evaluation and checking of writing, in terms of the final proofreading steps are preparing a manuscript or thesis.

Second, using the outline approaches and the V-model described earlier, I can provide myself with much structure. In particular, using the purpose statements, I can sit down and directly craft the words that will go into a particular segment that will serve a particular purpose. By breaking the manuscript down to components based on the structural design suggested by the V-Model, it becomes easier and clearer to identify what content needs to appear in each segment. Consequently, the ambiguity and uncertainty related to creating the content drop away, and it becomes easier and faster to fill the manuscript with the words they need to be there and ensure the sections meet the readers' needs.

Third, I am fond of fostering the writing habit. Like all good habits, the writing habit will come through persistence and perseverance. One approach I found useful was to chart my writing successes, particularly given the busyness of academic life and the number of directions and jobs, activities, and tasks faculty must complete. For this purpose, I created a simple chart where I could mark the amount of writing completed in 15-minute increments each day against set targets. Summing the time spent writing, this acts like a bowling chart (Kesterson, 2015). At the end of the week, I could go back and see where the peaks and troughs were and understand the consistency of the week's writing. By posting this on the wall behind the monitor, I was constantly (and, perhaps, punishingly) reminded of my aspirations to write; the chart also showed me when I was failing to meet requirements and targets. We can make this approach more potent by buddying up with a colleague and committing to completing a certain amount of writing every week and being held accountable. Belcher (2009) observes that "[i]n fact, writers who write a little bit every day produce more manuscripts than those who alternate weeks/months without writing with extended writing sessions" (p. 20). Indeed, there is evidence that this approach of developing the habit of writing can be beneficial. For example, it has been noted in a study of writing habits and how this relates to productivity that:

Those who write in regular, unemotional sessions of moderate length completed more pages, enjoyed more editorial acceptance, were less depressed and more creative than those authors who wrote in emotionally charged binges. (Boice, 1997, p. 435)

Fourth, the combination of these approaches embodies the principle of separating the creativity of writing from the critical component of writing. My focus is always to separate creation from critique; most of the time, I can generate the words on paper if I solely focus on writing creativity. Then, later, I come back and synthesize, create, shuffle, and rewrite as required.

CONCLUSIONS

Great writing must support great research. It is all very well to undertake world-class research, but we also need to have this published in order for the research to have value for the broader community. A key issue that makes publication challenging may be writing; clarity in writing, and a concise presentation of important results, makes it easier to convince others of the study's merit. In addition, the importance and value of the work must be immediately apparent to the handling editorial team and the reviewers as they go through the manuscript. Publishing in leading journals requires submitted manuscripts to be in good condition, well-written, and clearly articulating the importance and value of the research.

Working through this chapter, I hope readers can develop some ideas and frameworks that will help them to craft an exceptionally well-written article or thesis, or dissertation. I structured the chapter to provide insight into what readers will look for in different sections and how the writer can ensure that their manuscript meets their expectations. As usual, I provided a range of heuristics and simple rules of thumb, which are not intended to be strict guidelines but show how much may be the minimum required to meet requirements. By systematically working through the chapter, you should have a checklist and an opportunity to ensure that you communicate your research in a way that reaches the intended audience.

REFERENCES

Ba, S., Lisic, L. L., Liu, Q., & Stallaert, J. (2013). Stock market reaction to green vehicle innovation. *Production and Operations Management, 22*(4), 976–990. doi:10.1111/j.1937-5956.2012.01387.x

Belcher, W. L. (2009). *Writing your journal article in 12 weeks: A guide to academic publishing success.* SAGE Publications.

Berman, N., & Parker, R. (2002). Meta-analysis: Neither quick nor easy. *BMC Medical Research Methodology, 2*(1), 10. doi:10.1186/1471-2288-2-10 PMID:12171604

Boice, B. (1997). Which is more productive, writing in binge patterns of creative illness or in moderation? *Written Communication, 14*(4), 435–459. doi:10.1177/0741088397014004001

Brewer, B., Wallin, C., & Ashenbaum, B. (2014). Outsourcing the procurement function: Do actions and results align with theory? *Journal of Purchasing and Supply Management, 20*(3), 186–194. doi:10.1016/j.pursup.2014.02.004

Carlson, K. D., & Ji, F. X. (2011). Citing and building on meta-analytic findings: A review and recommendations. *Organizational Research Methods, 14*(4), 696–717. doi:10.1177/1094428110384272

Carter, C. R., Ellram, L. M., & Tate, W. (2007). The use of social network analysis in logistics research. *Journal of Business Logistics, 28*(1), 137–168. doi:10.1002/j.2158-1592.2007.tb00235.x

Carter, C. R., & Rogers, D. S. (2008). A framework of sustainable supply chain management: Moving toward new theory. *International Journal of Physical Distribution & Logistics Management, 38*(5), 360–387. doi:10.1108/09600030810882816

Coase, R. H. (1937). The nature of the firm. *Economica, 4*(16), 386–405. doi:10.1111/j.1468-0335.1937.tb00002.x

Cooper, H. M. (2010). *Research synthesis and meta-analysis: A step-by-step approach* (4th ed.). Sage.

Duan, C., Grover, V., Roberts, N., & Balakrishnan, N. (2014). Firm valuation effects of the decision to adopt relationally governed business process outsourcing arrangements. *International Journal of Production Research, 52*(15), 4673–4694. doi:10.1080/00207543.2014.884289

Head, K. (n.d.). The introduction formula. *Keith Head*. Retrieved February 11, 2022, from http://blogs.ubc.ca/khead/research/research-advice/formula

Hendricks, K. B., Hora, M., & Singhal, V. R. (2014). An empirical investigation on the appointments of supply chain and operations management executives. *Management Science, 61*(7), 1562–1583. doi:10.1287/mnsc.2014.1987

Hendricks, K. B., & Singhal, V. R. (2003). The effect of supply chain glitches on shareholder wealth. *Journal of Operations Management, 21*(5), 501–522. doi:10.1016/j.jom.2003.02.003

Hendricks, K. B., & Singhal, V. R. (2005). An empirical analysis of the effect of supply chain disruptions on long-run stock price performance and equity risk of the firm. *Production and Operations Management, 14*(1), 35–52. doi:10.1111/j.1937-5956.2005.tb00008.x

Homan, A. C. (2006). The impact of 9/11 on financial risk, volatility and returns of marine firms. *Maritime Economics & Logistics, 8*(4), 387–401. doi:10.1057/palgrave.mel.9100165

Jacobs, B. W., & Singhal, V. R. (2014). The effect of product development restructuring on shareholder value. *Production and Operations Management, 23*(5), 728–743. doi:10.1111/poms.12074

Jacobs, B. W., & Singhal, V. R. (2017). The effect of the Rana Plaza disaster on shareholder wealth of retailers: Implications for sourcing strategies and supply chain governance. *Journal of Operations Management, 49–51*(1), 52–66. doi:10.1016/j.jom.2017.01.002

Jacobs, B. W., Singhal, V. R., & Subramanian, R. (2010). An empirical investigation of environmental performance and the market value of the firm. *Journal of Operations Management, 28*(5), 430–441. doi:10.1016/j.jom.2010.01.001

Kesterson, R. K. (2015). *The Basics of Hoshin Kanri*. CRC Press.

Sheffield, J. (2005). Systemic knowledge and the V-model. *International Journal of Business Information Systems, 1*(1–2), 83–101. doi:10.1504/IJBIS.2005.007401

Williamson, O. E. (1975). *Markets and hierarchies, analysis and antitrust implications: A study in the economics of internal organization*. Free Press.

Williamson, O. E. (1981). The modern corporation: Origins, evolution, attributes. *Journal of Economic Literature, 19*(4), 1537–1568.

Williamson, O. E. (1985). *The economic institutions of capitalism: Firms, markets, relational contracting*. Free Press.

Williamson, O. E. (1994). Transaction cost economics and organization theory. In N. J. Smelser & R. Swedberg (Eds.), *The handbook of economic sociology* (pp. 77–107). Princeton University Press.

Williamson, O. E. (2008). Outsourcing: Transaction cost economics and supply chain management. *The Journal of Supply Chain Management, 44*(2), 5–16. doi:10.1111/j.1745-493X.2008.00051.x

Wood, L. C., Wang, J. X., Olesen, K., & Reiners, T. (2017). The effect of slack, diversification, and time to recall on stock market reaction to toy recalls. *International Journal of Production Economics, 193*, 244–258. doi:10.1016/j.ijpe.2017.07.021

Xia, Y., Singhal, V. R., & Peter Zhang, G. (2016). Product design awards and the market value of the firm. *Production and Operations Management, 25*(6), 1038–1055. doi:10.1111/poms.12525

ADDITIONAL READING

Arora, P., Hora, M., Singhal, V., & Subramanian, R. (2020). When do appointments of corporate sustainability executives affect shareholder value? *Journal of Operations Management, 66*(4), 464–487. doi:10.1002/joom.1074

Binder, J. (1998). The event study methodology since 1969. *Review of Quantitative Finance and Accounting, 11*(2), 111–137. doi:10.1023/A:1008295500105

Booth, W. C., Colomb, G. G., & Williams, J. M. (2008). *The craft of research* (3rd ed.). University of Chicago Press.

Cheung, A., & Roca, E. (2013). The effect on price, liquidity and risk when stocks are added to and deleted from a sustainability index: Evidence from the Asia Pacific context. *Journal of Asian Economics, 24*, 51–65. doi:10.1016/j.asieco.2012.08.002

Hawn, O., Chatterji, A. K., & Mitchell, W. (2018). Do investors actually value sustainability? New evidence from investor reactions to the Dow Jones Sustainability Index (DJSI). *Strategic Management Journal, 39*(4), 949–976. doi:10.1002mj.2752

Oh, C. H., Shapiro, D., Ho, S. S. H., & Shin, J. (2020). Location matters: Valuing firm-specific nonmarket risk in the global mining industry. *Strategic Management Journal, 41*(7), 1210–1244. doi:10.1002mj.3153

Paltridge, B. (2002). Thesis and dissertation writing: An examination of published advice and actual practice. *English for Specific Purposes, 21*(2), 125–143. doi:10.1016/S0889-4906(00)00025-9

Papadakis, I. S. (2006). Financial performance of supply chains after disruptions: An event study. *Supply Chain Management, 11*(1), 25–33. doi:10.1108/13598540610642448

Raithel, S., & Hock, S. J. (2021). The crisis-response match: An empirical investigation. *Strategic Management Journal, 42*(1), 170–184. doi:10.1002mj.3213

Randolph, J. J. (2009). A guide to writing the dissertation literature review. *Practical Assessment, Research & Evaluation, 14*(13), 1–13.

Swanson, K. W., West, J., Carr, S., & Augustine, S. (2015). Supporting dissertation writing using a cognitive apprenticeship model. In V. C. X. Wang (Ed.), *Handbook of Research on Scholarly Publishing and Research Methods* (pp. 84–104). Hershey, PA: Information Science Reference.

Wood, L. C., Wang, J. X., Duong, L. N. K., Reiners, T., & Smith, R. (2018). Stock market reactions to auto manufacturers' environmental failures. *Journal of Macromarketing*, *38*(4), 364–382. doi:10.1177/0276146718781915

Zhan, X., Mu, Y., Hora, M., & Singhal, V. R. (2021). Service excellence and market value of a firm: An empirical investigation of winning service awards and stock market reaction. *International Journal of Production Research*, *59*(14), 4188–4204. doi:10.1080/00207543.2020.1759837

Zhan, X., Mu, Y., Nishant, R., & Singhal, V. R. (2020). When do appointments of Chief Digital or Data Officers (CDOs) affect stock prices? *IEEE Transactions on Engineering Management*, 1–14. doi:10.1109/TEM.2020.2984619

KEY TERMS AND DEFINITIONS

Discussion Section: The section of the manuscript that takes the results and uses thee results to explain the importance of the study, drawing on the key elements of the literature review.

Introduction: The initial section of the manuscript that makes the research interesting explains past studies, the main contribution, and importance of the current study, and how the research is structured.

Section Pairing: The pairing of several sections, showing a conceptual relatedness between the sections that are not necessarily adjacent to each other in a written document.

Structure: The considerations of the constituent blocks of writing and how they are related.

Transaction Cost Economics: The study of the costs of making a trade and not making a product inside the firm. The approach has a rich history and is essential in many supply chain studies.

V-Model: A model that takes six major components of the scholarly manuscript and presents them with clear connections and pairings between sections.

Writer's Block: The feeling of being stuck and unable to progress in writing. Writer's block can be overcome with a series of tricks and writing structure models like the V-Model.

Chapter 14
Alternative Study Designs:
Going Beyond Short–Run Abnormal Returns

ABSTRACT

While the authors has a clear preference for an event study that estimates the short-run calculations of abnormal stock returns over a short multi-day window, there are other forms that readers should be familiar with. Further, you should be aware of the challenges of conducting and interpreting these studies. Therefore, this chapter addresses long-run studies and some difficulties, criticisms, and interpretation issues of using these studies. Finally, it looks at studies that do not use abnormal stock returns but use changes in operational data. Using these alternatives can enable a project to extend its contribution by using several studies (e.g., both short- and long-run studies) in one journal article or dissertation to converge on insights into the phenomenon being studied.

INTRODUCTION

This book focuses on the short-run abnormal returns estimated in an event study, based on the stock market reaction. The results show the stock market reaction and market participants' expectation of how the event affects the companies (Sorokina et al., 2013). Other approaches will often focus on permanent or long-term effects showing or demonstrating an enduring impact. For instance, a short-run effect may be indicated based on the stock market reaction, which provides an immediate estimate of the impact of an event. However, as we know from operations management, forecasts will frequently be wrong. Therefore, a long-term study can often determine whether there is a permanent and enduring impact from the event, often over a one- to five-year time period (Bremer et al., 2011).

This chapter examines these operational and long-term event study approaches. We provide a brief overview so that the reader is aware of some of the key distinctions and differences between the study types. The chapter does not contain sufficient detail and depth for a reader to use to design and execute the studies. In this way, the reader can become familiar with the other types of event studies they might find

DOI: 10.4018/978-1-7998-8969-4.ch014

and will be able to evaluate and assess the quality of the research they read. However, interested readers should continue to advance their knowledge of these other types of studies before conducting the rain.

It can also include a mixture of studies to extend the findings. For instance, Hendricks et al. (2014)use a short-horizon study, a long-horizon study, and an operational performance event study. They provide three reasons why the newly created positions might elicit a positive stock market reaction. They find evidence to support the third reason, that past performance is relatively normal, and the stock market participants expect that this newly created position will enable the company to lift their performance in the future. Through examining the operational data and the changes in the return on assets and sales, they find no evidence of poor performance prior to the new position being created. In the post position operational performance analysis, they find performance results consistent with stock price performance results were a relative improvement in performance. In this way, the mix of event study types provides useful supplements and enables Hendricks et al. to test alternative hypotheses. For instance, they note how they:

We also analyze the abnormal stock price performance in the period after the SCOME appointments to see whether such appointments are associated with subsequent improvement in stock price performance. We estimate CARs over a 250-day postannouncement period that starts on day 21 and ends on day 272, which spans a year that starts one month after the announcement and ends 13 months after the announcement. The reason we start one month after the announcement is to reflect the possibility that the new SCOME may join sometime after the announcement. We use day 282 to day 481 as the estimation period to compute the CAR. The reason for using a forward estimation period is that the appointment of a SCOME may cause a shift in the parameter estimates, and the forward estimation period will better reflect any such shift. The results are based on 582 firms because 99 firms did not have sufficient data during the estimation period and/or the postannouncement period to compute CARs. Panel B of Table 6 presents these results. (Hendricks et al., 2014, p. 1575)

Following the appointment, they were also interested in any change in operating performance, as measured using return on assets (ROA), sales over assets (SOA), as measured by sales/total assets, and cost of goods sold (CGS), and selling, general, and administrative expenses (SGA) summed then the total divided by sales, and CSGA divided by sales. Again, they find interesting operational performance changes, as they note how:

For the full sample as well as for all subsamples, the abnormal ROAs from year 0 to year 2 are insignificantly different from zero. Overall, the evidence suggests that new SCOME appointments are not followed by an immediate improvement in operating performance. However, there is no further decline in operating performance, suggesting that the decline in operating performance observed in the preappointment period under the existing SCOME does not appear to continue under the new SCOME. (Hendricks et al., 2014, p. 1577).

As seen, we can provide additional insights when a research project incorporates multiple event study types. It enables a wider range of research questions to be addressed and added value provided to the reader.

LONG-RUN STUDIES WITH STOCK MARKET DATA

When we consider conceptually whether the event has changed the firms' performance, we need to know the outcome and a benchmark for the comparison to be made. So, in contrast to the short-term event studies outlined in the rest of the book, here we will measure the actual outcomes over time. However, this still leaves open the issue of what we use as a benchmark to make the comparison.

The most commonly used approaches include matching firms affected by the event with other firms that are comparable but not affected. The study then proceeds with an analysis over time, comparing the performance of the two sets of companies to determine if there is a difference in performance that appears to be affected only by the event's occurrence. In this way, we are, in essence, creating both 'control' and 'treatment' samples.

One of the challenges will be the selection of the most appropriate firms with which to compare, that is, selecting the firms in the control group. The most commonly used approach was popularized based on characteristic-based matching, proposed by Barber and Lyon (1997). The abnormal stock returns may occur both before and after an announcement. Using this approach, Hendricks and Singhal (2005) examined the abnormal stock performance before the announcement of a supply chain disruption in their first hypothesis. Then, they coupled this with an examination of the subsequent impact on their equity risk (modeled by an increase in volatility), their financial leverage (the debt relative to the value of equity), and an increase in asset risks.

Buy-and-Hold Abnormal Returns (BHAR)

The most commonly used and popular estimator of long-term abnormal returns is the buy-and-hold abnormal return (BHAR) calculation. In essence, the investors' perspective is used, where the stock is bought and held over a long period. BHAR takes this outcome and the returns for the investor and compares it to the buy-and-hold returns that would have been realized in the control group to deduce the abnormal returns from the treatment group. Despite the popularity, the basic approach suffers from skewness and individual long-horizon abnormal returns and statistical inference challenges in early studies; estimates can also arise from rebalancing issues, skewness, and new listings (Mitchell & Stafford, 2000). The use of large samples can reduce some of these biases. In general, the common perception is that the measurement and evaluation of long-term abnormal performance using event studies is challenging.

The strong case against BHAR methodologies was provided by Fama (1998). The primary contention is that the bad model problem is compounded with long-term return estimates. In addition, many approaches ignore cross-sectional dependence, where several observations are closely together in calendar time. As a result, many test statistics from BHAR are overstated. Fama suggests that the monthly calendar-time portfolio approach is more appropriate.

On the other hand, many scholars still prefer the BHAR approach. It is easy for many readers to understand, and it provides an accurate representation of the investor experience concerning the event. In addition, we can accommodate issues of statistical inference by using bootstrapped procedures (Ikenberry et al., 1995).

More recently, the primary approach for overcoming some of these problems is to run long-term event studies using a more careful creation of benchmarks. However, the care put into these estimations suggests that these may be conservative estimates; where evidence of an effect is found, it may understate the actual impact of the event on firms (Mitchell & Stafford, 2000).

PORTFOLIO CONSTRUCTION

There has been substantial debate, ongoing about the appropriate long-run abnormal returns calculation methods. As noted,

This debate has centered on two issues. The first issue is the appropriate factors that one should control for in computing long-run abnormal returns. Earlier long-run abnormal stock price studies mainly controlled for the systematic risk (or beta) of a firm's stock. Recent research indicates that size and market-to-book ratio (Fama and French 1996) as well as prior performance (Cahart 1997 and Jegadeesh and Titman 1993) are important predictors of stock returns. The current consensus seems to be that abnormal returns should be computed after controlling for size, market-to-book ratio, and prior performance. (Hendricks & Singhal, 2005, p. 40)

The core long-horizon study that is used to calculate the long-run abnormal returns may control mostly for the systematic risk but other predictors also need to be included. This is part of the natural progression of science and investigation, allowing our models to become increasingly sophisticated. Unfortunately, it means that while an in-built solution may easily address the basic matching problem, it may not be able to support a more sophisticated matching over other parameters that are important in the determination of the performance.

Mis-Specification and Cross-Sectional Dependency

There are additional challenges in the long-run abnormal returns for researchers seeking to evaluate if there is a statistically significant difference. First, it is important to realize that most test statistics are mis-specified (Barber & Lyon, 1997; Kothari & Warner, 2007). Consequentially, we can observe that:

A primary source of misspecification is the presence of cross-sectional dependency that arises because of overlapping time period among sample firms that usually exists in long-run stock price studies. Cross-sectional dependency (positive or negative) leads to biased test statistics. Recent simulation results suggest that abnormal returns computed using matching portfolios or one-to-one matching give well-specified tests. (Hendricks & Singhal, 2005, p. 40)

BHARs with One-to-One Match Samples

The approach used by Hendricks and Singhal (2005, p. 40) is to use a "matching portfolio approach [that] computes abnormal returns using as benchmarks portfolios of firms that are similar in size, market-to-book ratio of equity, and prior performance." From this, they detail four steps:

1. Match firms by size and split them into deciles.
2. Match by prior performance.
3. Match by Market-to-book ratio.
4. Industry matching using the SIC code matching.

The following steps are undertaken for each month. These are relatively standard approaches, as outlined in several studies (Hendricks & Singhal, 2005; Lyon et al., 1999). Nevertheless, this overview provides insight into the steps to compile the one-to-one match samples.

First, the U.S. listed firms are sorted into deciles based on the market value of the firms, while the smallest is then sub-divided further into five, giving a total of 14 size-based portfolios. Each portfolio is then split into quintiles based on the market-to-book ratio, giving a total of 70 portfolios. Each is then split by three based on the price performance over the last year, giving 210 total portfolios each month. Through this construction, if we look at any one portfolio that month, the firms inside will be similar in size (first division), market-to-book ratio, and finally, also their prior price performance.

Second, we identify which portfolio matches which firm in the sample. We then can go back 12 months earlier (the start of the measurement period), and the portfolio comprising matched firms to our sample firm will remain the same. This means that, all other things held equal, we would expect the abnormal returns for our sample firm to be comparable to those 'similar firms' in the portfolio.

Third, we complete the BHAR for each of the sample firms. The BHAR for each of the matched firms is also computed. The benchmark, therefore, for each of the sample firms becomes the matched firms in the portfolio; the abnormal return for the sample return is the difference between the return for the sample firm and those returns of the portfolio. (Note that adjustments need to be made if the matching firm or sample firms are delisted during this period. Given that multi-year time-spans are common with long-run calculations, this issue of delisted firms will occur.)

Fourth, a simulation approach supports the statistical inference, providing well-specified test statistics (Ikenberry et al., 1995; Lyon et al., 1999). Pseudo-samples are created, and abnormal performance is calculated. This process is repeated to develop a set of average abnormal return observations. Finally, the mean abnormal returns from the sample portfolio is compared to those from the pseudo-portfolios.

A relatively less complex approach can be used in BHAR, as promoted by Barber and Lyon (1999), who simply note that:

When we match on both size and book-to-market, we first identify all firms with a market value of equity between 70% and 130% of the market value of equity of the sample firm; from this set of firms, we choose the firm with the book-to-market ratio closest to that of the sample firm. Variations on this matching scheme, such as filtering on book-to-market and then matching on size, work well in most sampling situations, but we find that filtering on size and then matching on the book-to-market ratio yields test statistics that are well specified in virtually all sampling situations that we analyze.(Lyon et al., 1999, p. 355)

In each case, however, the performance level of the benchmark, or control, is what we expect to see in the sample firm's performance. Deviations, where the sample firm exhibits a significantly different return, indicate an abnormal return. Similarly, control portfolios can be are generated by first taking U.S. listed firms, ranking by size (e.g., revenue), then dividing them into quintiles. Each group is then sub-divided by five again based on book-to-market values to give 25 portfolios (Fama & French, 1993).

Calendar Time Portfolio

At the most simple approach, the Calendar-time portfolio method (Mitchell & Stafford, 2000) is when the researcher:

Constructs portfolios of firms experiencing the event in the previous T months (e.g., a year), which are rebalanced monthly to add firms experiencing an event and to drop all firms reaching the end of their one-year period. Abnormal performance over the T post-event months is assessed by the significance of the estimated intercept, or alpha, of these monthly portfolio returns in a multifactor regression incorporating the Fama–French three-factor model portfolio regressions and a momentum factor. (Modi et al., 2015, p. 32)

For example, the sample firms will be compared to control portfolios. As such, a method to address the problem is:

An alternative approach to measuring long-term stock price performance is to track the performance of an event portfolio in calendar time relative to either an explicit asset-pricing model or some other benchmark. […] The event portfolio is formed each period to include all companies that have completed the event within the prior n periods. By forming event portfolios, the cross-sectional correlations of the individual event firm returns are automatically accounted for in the portfolio variance at each point in calendar time. (Mitchell & Stafford, 2000, p. 308)

The calendar time portfolio method is superior to BHAR in terms of the bad model problem. Fama (1998) makes a case against BHAR due to the difficulties in calculating the expected returns because of the bad model problem. These problems ignore the issue of cross-sectional dependence when there is an overlap in the calendar-time of the observations in the sample (Mitchell & Stafford, 2000). The calendar-time portfolio approach overcomes many of these problems.

RUNNING THE LONG-HORIZON STOCK RETURN STUDIES

Most software applications that support event study analysis have built-in options for conducting long-term stock price studies. For instance, they might have a buy-and-hold abnormal return (BHAR) calculation even though this may be based on a more rudimentary analysis than the approach outlined by Hendricks and Singhal earlier. However, the basic analysis offered in many packages will be satisfactory to determine at least whether there is an abnormal return that is large enough to be of interest and further investigation. Therefore, it is possible to use these rudimentary analytic approaches to determine whether it is worth investing more time to develop a more comprehensive portfolio for matching.

For instance, the WRDS Event Study module includes the WRDS Long Run Event Study (in Beta) that allows BHAR calculations to be rapidly and easily computed. Similarly, Eventus allows rapid BHAR calculations. The eventstudytools.com website also allows BHAR calculations (https://www.eventstudytools.com/long-run-event-study)

If the long-horizon study is a supplement to a short-horizon study or another study, then a rudimentary analysis with one-to-one matching for a limited number of firms may be sufficient to enhance the credibility of the main study.

ESTIMATING ABNORMAL OPERATING PERFORMANCE

It is also possible to understand how an event affects performance, not regarding the stock price data, but other operational data. In this case, researchers are working with data reported far less frequently; in contrast to stock prices that change by the minute, operational data is reported quarterly.

In essence, the dependent variables are to be measured before the event of interest, and after the event of interest. This enables an investigation of the long-term effect of the event of study. The comparison needs to be made to the control firm. As such, a simple definition provided by Hendricks and Singhal (2008, p. 882) is:

Abnormal operating performance is the actual performance with the event minus the expected performance if the event had not happened

As with a short-horizon event study, we cannot observe the 'normal' performance, so it must still be estimated. Several methods can be used to estimate the expected performance (Hendricks & Singhal, 2008, pp. 882–883):

1.   A naïve approach would use past performance to estimate the expected performance. However, this would not account for meta-events or exogenous circumstances that may mean the wider economic or industrial success changes suddenly during the period of the announcements being studied. Consequentially, it is little used.
2.   Analyst estimates, published ahead of the event can be used to estimate the expected return. However, these are not available for all firms; smaller firms may have few analysts following them. As such, many observations may need to be dropped, and this may cause bias by, for example, dropping a greater proportion of smaller firms.
3.   Develop a benchmark for the expected performance using firms of comparable characteristics. (As we can see, the approach is similar to studies of stock return.)

There remain considerable differences between studies designed to estimate the abnormal operating performance. Selection of control firms should be based on the size, industry, and prior performance (Barber & Lyon, 1996). Each of these is important. For instance, a firm that has previously adopted a successful strategy to dominate their market will probably have superior prior performance that we would expect to continue; controlling for prior performance would continue regardless of the event of interest. There are also important industry-specific operational effects (McGahan & Porter, 1997).

We can generate different control groups. For instance, Hendricks and Singhal (2008, p. 883) generated three comparison groups:

1.   A group matched by performance and industry where firms are identified with a closely matching ROA using the same SIC code.
2.   Matched by performance, industry, and size, which takes the first group, then only includes those that are an effective match on size.
3.   Performance and size matched, taking firms with a comparable level of assets and then those with a tight matching ROA.

From this, an evaluation of, firstly, the normal or expected operating performance can be established, considering that (Hendricks & Singhal, 2008, p. 884):

The sample firm's expected performance if there had been no event is the performance of the sample firm in the base period plus the change in the median performance level of the benchmark firms throughout the study period.

Then,

The sample firm's abnormal performance is its observed performance minus its expected performance.

When the matching and benchmarking process is complete, the esimations and calculations can be relatively straightforward. For example, Lo et al. (2014, p. 272) provide the following formulae for their calculation of abnormal performance:

$$AP_{(t+j)} = PS_{(t+j)} - EP_{(t+j)} \tag{1}$$

$$EP_{(t+j)} = PS_{(t+j)} + \left(PC_{k(t+j)} - PC_{k(i+j)} \right) \tag{2}$$

where PS is the observed performance; AP is the estimation of the abnormal performance. EP is the expected performance of the firms in the sample. The EP is derived with reference to the median (not mean) performance of the control firms; t designates the year of certification; i is the base year of year minus two; finally, j is the year for comparison (raning from -1, 0, 1, or 2).

Lee et al. (2017) provide an interesting example of different dependent variables such as ROA, ROS, COGS/Sales, and Sales Growth. A window is used of two years before and two after the event of interest to study the impact of ISO 14,001 certification. Perhaps the most important finding is that the ISO 14,001 certification improves sales growth rates. There was a noticeable lag between certification and sales growth rate increases, and this is probably a key driver of the certified firms' improvements in profitability. Overall, they "conclude that ISO 14001 certification provides benefits to the firm in terms of profitability and market benefits" (Lee et al., 2017, p. 118).

Operational data is also included in the analysis presented by Hendricks et al. (2014). In their case, poor operational performance may precede the appointment of a supply chain and operations executive. If so, we might expect to see operational improvements following the appointment. As such, they built this expectation into the study, and they found:

*the operating performance results for the postappointment period [...] the evidence suggests that new SCOME appointments are **not followed by an immediate improvement in operating** performance. However, there is no further **decline in operating performance** (Hendricks et al., 2014, p. 1577; empahsis added)*

In this way, they established an immediate impact of the appointee with the estimation of the short-term abnormal returns. They supplemented it with an analysis of the operational data, providing insight into the longer-term impact and consequences of the appointment.

CONCLUSION

There are certainly many options for different types of event studies. However, the short-term focus on stock price changes remains one of the easiest, most assessable approaches. Short-run study methods are well understood, well-specified, and powerful. This compares to other approaches outlined in this chapter. However, it is useful to understand how different approaches can be applied to understand how an event affects performance. These other event study forms demonstrate different outcomes and effects. A combination of different event study methods can provide considerable insight into events.

While the chapter does not include sufficient details to allow readers to run their additional event studies, it should provide some insight into possible management and supply chain topics that can be addressed with these methods.

REFERENCES

Barber, B. M., & Lyon, J. D. (1996). Detecting abnormal operating performance: The empirical power and specification of test statistics. *Journal of Financial Economics*, *41*(3), 359–399. doi:10.1016/0304-405X(96)84701-5

Barber, B. M., & Lyon, J. D. (1997). Detecting long-run abnormal stock returns: The empirical power and specification of test statistics. *Journal of Financial Economics*, *43*(3), 341–372. doi:10.1016/S0304-405X(96)00890-2

Bremer, R., Buchanan, B. G., & English, P. C. II. (2011). The advantages of using quarterly returns for long-term event studies. *Review of Quantitative Finance and Accounting*, *36*(4), 491–516. doi:10.100711156-010-0191-2

Fama, E. F. (1998). Market efficiency, long-term returns, and behavioral finance. *Journal of Financial Economics*, *49*(3), 283–306. doi:10.1016/S0304-405X(98)00026-9

Fama, E. F., & French, K. R. (1993). Common risk factors in the returns on stocks and bonds. *Journal of Financial Economics*, *33*(1), 3–56. doi:10.1016/0304-405X(93)90023-5

Hendricks, K. B., Hora, M., & Singhal, V. R. (2014). An empirical investigation on the appointments of supply chain and operations management executives. *Management Science*, *61*(7), 1562–1583. doi:10.1287/mnsc.2014.1987

Hendricks, K. B., & Singhal, V. R. (2005). An empirical analysis of the effect of supply chain disruptions on long-run stock price performance and equity risk of the firm. *Production and Operations Management*, *14*(1), 35–52. doi:10.1111/j.1937-5956.2005.tb00008.x

Hendricks, K. B., & Singhal, V. R. (2008). The effect of product introduction delays on operating performance. *Management Science*, *54*(5), 878–892. doi:10.1287/mnsc.1070.0805

Ikenberry, D., Lakonishok, J., & Vermaelencqd, T. (1995). Market underreaction to open market share repurchases. *Journal of Financial Economics*, *39*(1), 181–208. doi:10.1016/0304-405X(95)00826-Z

Kothari, S. P., & Warner, J. B. (2007). Econometrics of event studies. In B. E. Eckbo (Ed.), *Handbook of Corporate Finance: Empirical Corporate Finance* (Vol. 1, pp. 3–36). North-Holland/Elsevier. doi:10.1016/B978-0-444-53265-7.50015-9

Lee, S. M., Noh, Y., Choi, D., & Rha, J. S. (2017). Environmental policy performances for sustainable development: From the perspective of ISO 14001 certification. *Corporate Social Responsibility and Environmental Management*, *24*(2), 108–120. doi:10.1002/csr.1395

Lo, C. K. Y., Pagell, M., Fan, D., Wiengarten, F., & Yeung, A. C. L. (2014). OHSAS 18001 certification and operating performance: The role of complexity and coupling. *Journal of Operations Management*, *32*(5), 268–280. doi:10.1016/j.jom.2014.04.004

Lyon, J. D., Barber, B. M., & Tsai, C.-L. (1999). Improved methods for tests of long-run abnormal stock returns. *The Journal of Finance*, *54*(1), 165–201. doi:10.1111/0022-1082.00101

McGahan, A. M., & Porter, M. E. (1997). How much does industry matter, really? *Strategic Management Journal*, *18*(S1), 15–30. doi:10.1002/(SICI)1097-0266(199707)18:1+<15::AID-SMJ916>3.0.CO;2-1

Mitchell, M., & Stafford, E. (2000). Managerial decisions and long-term stock price performance. *The Journal of Business*, *73*(3), 287–329. doi:10.1086/209645

Modi, S. B., Wiles, M. A., & Mishra, S. (2015). Shareholder value implications of service failures in triads: The case of customer information security breaches. *Journal of Operations Management*, *35*(1), 21–39. doi:10.1016/j.jom.2014.10.003

Sorokina, N., Booth, D. E., & Thornton, J. H. (2013). Robust methods in event studies: Empirical evidence and theoretical implications. *Journal of Data Science: JDS*, *11*(3), 575–606. doi:10.6339/JDS.2013.11(3).1166

ADDITIONAL READING

Binder, J. (1998). The event study methodology since 1969. *Review of Quantitative Finance and Accounting*, *11*(2), 111–137. doi:10.1023/A:1008295500105

Hendricks, K. B., & Singhal, V. R. (2001). The long-run stock price performance of firms with effective TQM programs. *Management Science*, *47*(3), 359–368. doi:10.1287/mnsc.47.3.359.9773

Hu, Q., Yayla, A. A., & Lei, Y. (2014). Does inclusion of CIO in top management team impact firm performance? Evidence from a long-term event analysis. *2014 47th Hawaii International Conference on System Sciences*, 4346–4355. 10.1109/HICSS.2014.537

Kim, J. (2010). Assessing the long-term financial performance of ethical companies. *Journal of Targeting. Measurement and Analysis for Marketing, 18*(3–4), 199–208. doi:10.1057/jt.2010.8

Pinar, M., & Ozgur, C. (2007). The long-term impact of ISO 9000 certification on business performance: A longitudinal study using Turkish stock market returns. *The Quality Management Journal, 14*(4), 21–40. doi:10.1080/10686967.2007.11918044

Scott, B. G., Ueng, J., Ramaswamy, V., & Chang, C. L. (2011). Layoff and firm long-term performance. *Academy of Strategic Management Journal, 10*(2), 1–10.

Shafer, S. M., & Moeller, S. B. (2012). The effects of Six Sigma on corporate performance: An empirical investigation. *Journal of Operations Management, 30*(7–8), 521–532. doi:10.1016/j.jom.2012.10.002

Zhan, X., Mu, Y., Hora, M., & Singhal, V. R. (2021). Service excellence and market value of a firm: An empirical investigation of winning service awards and stock market reaction. *International Journal of Production Research, 59*(14), 4188–4204. doi:10.1080/00207543.2020.1759837

Zhan, X., Mu, Y., Nishant, R., & Singhal, V. R. (2022). When do appointments of Chief Digital or Data Officers (CDOs) affect stock prices? *IEEE Transactions on Engineering Management, 69(4), 1308-1321.* doi:10.1109/TEM.2020.2984619

KEY TERMS AND DEFINITIONS

Bad Model Problem: The difficulty in assessing normal returns to determine whether the observed returns are abnormal or not. An accurate estimate of abnormal returns requires the estimation of the underlying normal returns and the abnormal returns.

Buy-and-Hold Abnormal Return (BHAR): Abnormal returns are estimated by comparing the firms affected by the event (the treatment group) with a reference (a control group) that is not affected. The difference in returns, gained by holding over time, indicates abnormal returns attributable to the event.

Calendar-Time Portfolio: The construction of a portfolio each calendar month of firms affected by the event the prior month to assess abnormal returns.

Long-horizon event study: a study that estimates the abnormal return over a long period.

Model Mis-Specification: The situation where a model in the regression violates the underlying assumptions; for instance if the data distribution does not match those assumed in the model.

Operational Data: Data produced by the company's day-to-day operations, relevant to operations and supply chain management executives.

Operational Performance: The measureable aspects of performance relating to outcomes of the operations department, such as the processes, quality, inventory, and reliability.

Short-Horizon Event Study: A study that estimates an abnormal return over a short event window.

Chapter 15
Event Study Examples:
Management and Supply Chain Cases

ABSTRACT

This chapter addresses different uses and styles of event studies, giving a flavor and overview of the styles that might be possible. Inclusion does not imply endorsement, and the chapter will include commentary on research design decisions and issues. The examination of various articles on different topics draws attention to factors such as the complexity of study design, use of interactions or moderators, drawing from a range of diverse data sources to construct variables properly in the study. Consequently, this chapter helps to develop a sense of the richness of the study designs and issues that might be addressed through the event study method.

INTRODUCTION

This chapter comes at the book's conclusion and summarizes the possible types of projects using the event study method. A range of studies has been selected from various leading journals, focusing on supply chain management and logistics methods, with several other general management studies also included. (The concentration is partly pragmatic as I am more familiar with the supply chain management studies and already have several of them I use as teaching examples.) Throughout the chapter, I present various perspectives on the studies and the research design issues. Note that these are not comments or criticisms of the authors but are used to provide some contrasts or point out salient features of the studies that the reader may find interesting. Most times, the published article may not reflect the authors' preferences or design decisions; they may have made changes during the review process, suggested both by reviewers and the editorial team handling the manuscript. As a result, manuscripts may have been submitted and look somewhat different from those finally published; the publication process can span years and include new designs, tests, and data collection to provide enhanced models.

While the rest of the book has focused on building skills and capabilities, have been few examples and commentary on specific articles. While it is necessary to understand some of the background and

DOI: 10.4018/978-1-7998-8969-4.ch015

the techniques, it is also helpful to have a more holistic perspective on the type of research, and actual publications to understand both the process and the opportunities for research using this method.

The first section provides supply chain management examples that should interest managers and researchers in the area. I selected the articles from a range of leading operations and supply chain journals with a more systematic approach. The overview of articles provides insight into what is required to publish these journals.

The second section provides more general management examples. I collected these with a less systematic approach, and they provide a broad perspective on the variety of topics that can be addressed with event studies, other issues and opportunities, and some differences that we need to be aware of when publishing different management areas.

The chapter concludes with a discussion of some of the interesting elements and lessons we can draw from the comparisons and summarization of the studies.

SUPPLY CHAIN MANAGEMENT EXAMPLES AND DISCUSSIONS

Deitz, Hansen, and Richey (2009) presented an early study of changes over the supply chain. They examined how Walmart mandated the use of RFID and influenced major suppliers. This was an interesting case where a dominant buyer and the supply chain required their suppliers to adjust and alter the operational practices by including RFID capability for the supply chain. Because of their size and scale, Walmart would have benefited from the additional value of using RFID within the supply chain. Deitz et al. identified a positive stock market reaction for the suppliers in response to the news. Those suppliers with stronger cash flows, suggesting developed operational capabilities, experienced an even greater stock market reaction. In contrast to many other comparable event studies, the firm's size did not appear to influence the magnitude and stock market reaction. In terms of supply chain power, negotiation capability, and influence over the supply chain, they identified that the supplies most reliant on Walmart (by evaluating the proportion of company sales to Walmart) were even more positively affected. The result suggests that the stock market investors perceived the close-knit relationship as potentially experiencing benefits in the future, as the firms make increasingly specific investments in the relationship. It opens the door to additional research that focuses on using event study methods to use power-based studies.

The topics of distribution channels and capacity will clearly be of interest to operations and supply chain researchers. Given the changing omni-channel distribution, direct to consumer (D2C), and other e-commerce initiatives, particularly in the COVID-19 era, the role of retail stores interests many managers and researchers in the area. While prior research focused on the capacity expansion (Hendricks et al., 1995), we can also study capacity contraction as the closure of retail stores. While we may see the announcement that stores be closed as a negative, reducing the footprint of the retail store and suggesting staff cuts might signal that the firm is in trouble. However, Chowdhury and Sarkar (2017) found that the store closure is perceived as a positive outcome judged by the positive stock market reaction, particularly when the firms are experiencing strong sales growth. However, where there is a particularly competitive industry and environment, stock market reaction to store closures may be reduced. Together, these elements suggest that more work needs to be conducted to understand under what circumstances store closures may be a viable method for managers to enhance performance. A range of event windows was used to detect the abnormal return, suggesting that shorter windows are satisfactory for picking up the stock market reaction. They cite signaling theory (Connelly et al., 2011) as a critical foundation for their work.

As noted in earlier chapters, the role of operational disruptions provides fertile room for investigation using the event study (Hendricks et al., 2009; Hendricks & Singhal, 2005). Disruptions are a significant category of adverse conditions that can influence the firm's success and profitability. In addition, a significant disruption might not only affect a particular firm but may also cause adverse conditions along the supply chain. Filbeck, Kumar, Liu, and Zhao (2016) turn their attention to this broader category of research where an event study was used to determine the impact on related permits. They opted for an unusually wide event window (-5, +5) with the rationale that this would account for the possible leakage of news. They also examine the impact of the business cycle that the firm is currently experiencing. This paper captures the broader business markets that may influence the general stock market reaction to the news. They also suggest that U.S. and Japanese automotive firms react differently to different market conditions. Indeed, they find that U.S. automotive firms experience larger negative shocks during a bear market. Similarly, the reaction to the disruptions is more intense for U.S. automotive firms during a bear market. While it is not necessarily possible to say with authority from these results, it suggests that Japanese firms may be more resilient than their U.S. counterparts and therefore less prone to negative stock market reactions. Local research, there are limitations in the research. In this particular case, the research is conducted within the single automotive sector. It is relatively distinct and has a high degree of concentration in the industry. Consequently, these results may not be generalizable to other industries, particularly where there is substantially less competition.

When we consider the importance of international agreements on trade in relationships and how this influences the flow of goods across supply chains, regulations, and agreements that are made may affect stock market reactions for logistics companies. This is the topic that Chi (2012) investigated as they examined how the Economic Cooperation Framework Agreement (ECFA) impacted Taiwanese shipping and transportation firms, as reflected in the stock market reaction to ECFA-related news. They identified a positive stock market reaction for these transport firms when the agreement was announced, suggesting that investors see this as a positive for these companies in the industry as a whole. The sample consists of all of the listed firms in the country's sector, which suggests a high level of generalisability to other logistics firms within Taiwan that are not publicly listed. The research also uncovers important insight into credit risk rating; firms of the port risk rating have less positive stock market reactions, suggesting that investors see they will be less able to capture the value from this agreement. However, firms that have demonstrated management capability are affected by a higher return on assets experience more favorable stock market reactions. Furthermore, as we often see in other event study research, smaller firms experience larger, more positive reactions to the ECFA news.

Firms that do well experience a better stock market performance; when firms win logistics awards, they are shown by Eroglu et al. (2016) to experience a positive stock market reaction. This follows similar past research on firms with exceptional quality outcomes as evidenced by winning awards, where they experience positive stock market reactions (Hendricks & Singhal, 2001; Shafer & Moeller, 2012). The sample was collected using a range of different approaches using both a list of award winners from different sources, searching the Factiva database, and looking for announcements of awards that logistics firms make that they have gained. They investigated a range of award categories, including quality safety and sustainability successes. As we commonly see, smaller firms experience a more large positive stock market reaction to this news. The result follows a common theme that smaller firms experience more pronounced stock market reactions. In addition, sustainability awards appear to be more beneficial, suggesting that investors in the stock market place more considerable significance on developing the capability to enhance sustainability, suggesting that this may lead to positive market advantages for revenue growth in the future. Firms with strong financial performance in the past also experience more positive reactions. The sample consists only of U.S. firms; whether other firms in other markets experience a similar positive stock market reaction to award-winning news is an open question. Indeed, there are substantial differences between the internal U.S. market and other markets such as cross European Union or throughout Southeast Asia. Furthermore, despite the work completed by the firms to gain the award, the stock market reaction is to the announcement of the award. The finding suggests that investors believe there has been a long-term positive benefit from the award. Consequently, future research might use a long-term study to identify whether additional benefits accrue to the award winners in contrast to those in the control group, suggesting that there are long-term and enduring benefits to logistics capability and success.

Kumar et al. (2015) provide an additional study on the impact of supply chain disruptions. In contrast to many studies that focus only on U.S.-listed firms, this research examines disruptions reported by Indian companies. Given the differences between the India and U.S. stock markets, the researchers opted for a large (-5, +5) window because of information leakage. The results suggest that the stock market reaction to disruptions suggests they are more damaging to Indian firms in this context, and they are the U.S. firms based on past U.S.-focused research. The stock market in India appears to treat internal causes of the disruption as more severe, as evidenced by a more negative stock market reaction. The finding suggests that they held firms to account with punishment for the poor operational management of the situation. In contrast to other studies, there is no sign that smaller firms experience a more extreme stock market reaction.

Gong et al. (2008) restrict their study to a single industry and focus on the impact of one company's success on key rivals. Within the airline industry, they identify firms that make surprise earnings announcements. They then examine the abnormal return at the key rivals for this company, presenting a related firms study. Like many event studies, they explain the background and calculate how they account for and measure the level of rivalry. The calculation focuses on the overlap and exposure of routes served by the airlines in the sample. As with all research, there are important limitations considered. Foremost, the sample consists only of passenger services, suggesting that cargo carriers may experience different outcomes to surprise earnings announcements. However, unlike some of the other cases, the global nature of the airline industry suggests that investors and external parties can follow the international news and earnings announcements of firms around the world; such international news can be used to evaluate local airline firms.

Wassmer and Dussauge (2012) provide an investigation of supply chain alliances and partnerships between logistics firms. They focus on network resources and how one firm can access new resources by creating and leveraging an alliance. This research, therefore, uses the resource-based view (RBV) (Barney, 2012; Bharadwaj, 2000) as the underpinning theoretical perspective. However, they note that further research might need to rely on transaction cost economics (Ellram et al., 2008; Gibbons, 2010; Williamson, 2008). From the announcements and the sample, they extracted further information that gave insight into the resources available to the firms. In particular, this allowed them to assess how the alliance would enable a company to access new city-pair markets. When an alliance is considered a way of integrating resources between the firms involved, a single alliance needs to be considered more than a single strategic exercise. Rather, alliances need to be considered as part of a broader portfolio. The new alliances are assessed as to how they add value to the firm.

MANAGEMENT EXAMPLES AND DISCUSSIONS

As noted earlier, the following examples are hand-picked, and this does not mean to imply that any of these are superior or perfect; but instead, they are selected to provide an interesting insight commentary on different issues and opportunities. They come from a range of good and leading management journals, focusing deliberately on various topics.

Basuil and Datta (2015) investigate cross-border acquisitions by U.S. firms. They examine the acquiring firms' previous experiences in that same industry and region and how this influences the stock market reactions. They use a buy-and-hold abnormal returns (BHAR) methodology. Their organizational framework is based on organizational learning (Argote & Miron-Spektor, 2011) and learning transfer theory (Ellis et al., 2011) argumentation to provide the theoretical foundation for the study. The conceptual framework suggests that industry-specific acquisition experience leads to the acquiring firm experiencing a greater stock market reaction. However, this relationship is moderated by the cultural similarity between the home and host countries, and the region-specific acquisition experience also moderates the moderation. This creates a two-way interaction and multiple moderated relationships in the study. Rather than a search of news articles, Thompson Financial's SDC Platinum database was used. Reference portfolios were constructed for the approach, with each acquiring firm was matched to one of 210 portfolios generated based on the appropriate size, book-to-market ratios, and recent performance. Previous industry-specific position experience was measured using the total number of identified cross-border acquisition within the same three digit SIC industry code over the prior five years. In contrast, the cultural similarity was provided by the GLOBE study (House et al., 2004), addressing some limitations of the early measures by Hofstede.

In their study of the airline industry, Wassmer and Dussauge (2012) focus their investigation on alliances. Considering the resource-based view (RBV) (Barney, 2012), the formation of alliances allows an airline company to access and benefit from resources held by their partners. The research examined several clients' formation circumstances and showed how alliance formation is a step towards developing a portfolio of alliances with complementary value.

Bilgili et al. (2017) used an event study to examine how CEO retirements influence stock market returns. Drawing on the resource dependence theory (RDT), they find the CEO's departure will usually result in an adverse stock market reaction. Further, they find that the narrative spun by the organization and published using the executive retirement announcement can influence the size and magnitude of the stock market reaction. The results show the importance of the CEO from the eyes of shareholders and investors and how crucial corporate communication is to managing stock market reactions. Finally, they acknowledge that while resource dependence theory is usually focused on the external environment; they take perspective where they examine the role of the CEO as an internal resource and how this flow out of the organization of the internal resource influences the stock market reaction.

Continuing the theme of CEOs, Jory et al. (2015) investigate corporate scandals that have been explicitly linked to the company's CEO. This is important, as many scandals occur with larger organizations where managers were granted substantial stock options as a component of an incentive package. They find a substantial and noticeable increase in the stock price volatility following the announcement. Firms with substantial operating cash flows are less severely affected by the CEO scandal. Further, they also conduct buy-and-hold abnormal return calculations, showing little evidence of long-run post-announcement impacts on stock returns.

While not an event study paper, the systematic literature review of stock price reactions to environmental pollution events by Bouzzine (2021) provides insight into the use of the event study method for studying this category of issue and event. It provides a valuable oversight of many events studies focusing on pollution, drawing from a range of journals and different discipline areas. It covers pollution disclosures, violation disclosures, and disaster disclosures. Table 4 (Bouzzine, 2021, p. 10) shows various estimation models, checking for compounding events and nonparametric testing over the publications and samples.

While published in an operations-focused journal, the study by Jacobs and Singhal (2020) provides insight into corporate scandals, and the broader contagion effect over an ecosystem accompanies. They look at the Volkswagen emission scandal and how it influences the broader automotive ecosystem of suppliers and companies. Being a large European company, it is perhaps no surprise that they found that the adverse stock market reaction most affected European supplies. Those supplies that were more dependent on Volkswagen, particularly those that supplied engine components, were emission systems, were more impacted. These results suggest while firms must consider identifying responsible suppliers, we can say the same in the other direction: they must also consider developing responsible customers. They also note the importance of broader legal system changes. The study shows "the evidence from the scandal clearly signals that the market can severely punish wrongdoers, market forces alone were not sufficient to prevent the illegal activity" (Jacobs & Singhal, 2020, p. 2247), suggesting that legal changes may also be required to influence corporate behavior further. Therefore, they note that:

The legal system should bring to justice individuals who knowingly perpetuated and supported this irresponsible behavior. Prosecutors in the United States have convicted a few VW managers with jail terms and have recently indicted the former CEO of VW and other senior executives. A legal system that quickly and fairly enables compensation of victims of such scandals, and convicts and punishes responsible individuals might act as a strong deterrence for future scandals. (Jacobs & Singhal, 2020, p. 2247)

There is a rich history of studies on the impact of corporate social responsibility. Most times, the context of study plays some role. Given recent changes in the Chinese economy, the study by Qiao et al. (2021) provides an interesting insight into corporate efforts at poverty alleviation. Given the substantially different nature of the Chinese economy between state-owned enterprises and non-state-owned enterprises, they divided the group into two. They found that the non-state-owned enterprises experienced substantial positive effects from the poverty alleviation disclosures. This suggests that companies benefit from taking on social responsibilities, particularly poverty alleviation, to benefit from greater abnormal returns in the Chinese economy.

Qiu et al. (2021) provide additional insight into the benefits of corporate social responsibility, emphasizing how this can be used during a crisis (such as the COVID-19 pandemic). They note that "[a]lthough spending on CSR seems painful under financial pressure, stock market returns should justify the investment" (Qiu et al., 2021, p. 9). Further, the focus of the CSR investments is essential, and they show that community-related CSR is more compelling from an abnormal return perspective on customer or employee-related CSR.

Chiu et al. (2020) study the disclosure of CSR reports for Taiwanese listed firms. They show that firms disclosing the reports benefit from positive abnormal returns driven by improved investor confidence. However, it is essential to note that this is not a reaction to CSR, but rather the CSR reporting by the companies.

Over the years, many studies have examined the impact of the appointment of key members of the senior management team. In part, this is of interest, as the business environment changes in the right personnel can be seen as a valuable resource for the enterprise.

In some cases, the rapidly moving and evolving Information Systems area creates challenges in understanding the exact overlap and difference between crucial roles in the organization. For example, despite many firms having had a chief information officer for a long time, the number of firms now reporting a chief digital officer or chief data officer (CDO) is increasing. Using a study of 112 CDO appointment announcements, Zhan et al. (2020) show an overall neutral reaction to the position announcement. However, for firms with higher growth prospects, particularly digitally focused firms and growth-oriented firms, the appointment of the CDO appears to suggest significant opportunities for the advancement and use of data analytics to drive new revenue. Where there is more clarity around the role, such as when there was no overlapping role, such as the CIO, the market reacts more positively. Further, if there is no CIO and the appointment of an outsider bringing fresh insight into the organization is more positive, which is an important finding from the perspective and institutional entrepreneurship theory, showing how they cannot conform to traditional expectations and instead take the role of the institutional entrepreneur by introducing more transformational approaches.

Using a broader study of supply chain and operations management executives (SCOMEs) appointments, Hendricks et al. (2014) identify a positive stock market reaction on the day of the announcement. Like Zhan et al. (2020), the market reaction is stronger when an outsider is appointed. In particular, when an outsider is appointed to a newly created position, the stock market reaction will be mostly positive. The appointments' importance is increased due to poor stock price and operating performance prior to appointments. While there are some papers with a solid theoretical basis for the hypothesis development, Hendricks et al. (2014, p. 1564) show an exception, where they note: "[t]o the best of our knowledge, there does not exist any literature that provides theory and evidence directly related to SCOMEs that we could use to develop this hypothesis."

Additionally, to establish whether the appointment led to positive changes in stock returns, they also undertook an additional analysis:

We estimate CARs over a 250-day postannouncement period that starts on day 21 and ends on day 272, which spans a year that starts one month after the announcement and ends 13 months after the announcement. The reason we start one month after the announcement is to reflect the possibility that the new SCOME may join sometime after the announcement. We use day 282 to day 481 as the estimation period to compute the CAR. The reason for using a forward estimation period is that the appointment of a SCOME may cause a shift in the parameter estimates, and the forward estimation period will better reflect any such shift. (Hendricks et al., 2014, p. 1576)

In both Zhan et al. (2020) and Hendricks et al. (2014), the announcements in the sample include much information appointee's background that can be used to develop the hypotheses (such as whether the appointment is of an outsider); however, additional investigations may be required, as:

[i]n cases where such information is not available from the announcement, we examine 10-K filings, annual report, and other filings with the Securities and Exchange Commission (SEC) to determine whether appointees are part of TMTs or report to a member of TMTs. (Hendricks et al., 2014, p. 1567)

This shows the additional work and efforts required depending on the circumstances and availability of data. Therefore, it is not sufficient to simply say "there was no data," but instead, we must devise alternate strategies to fill in the gaps in the data as much as possible.

Scott et al. (2011) examine downsizing announcements. During periods of corporate restructuring, there is often an announcement about downsizing and laying off staff. This can often be done to enhance productivity and profitability, but questions have also been raised about whether firms downsize to reach the desired outcomes. For example, the company may be left with insufficient staff to meet demand or experience low morale from those remaining (Cascio, 1993). In a study of events from 1990 to 1992, the sample avoids meta-events associated with the Worker Adjustment and Retraining Notification Act 1998. They find a negative stock market reaction to the announcement that no evidence it is statistically different from zero. However, subsequent long-horizon tests indicate higher returns from the firms announcing downsizing relative to the market portfolios used as a reference.

We can see the investment in human capital as an expansion of resources for the firm that may lead to greater competitiveness. Consequently, Riley et al. (2017) expect to observe a positive stock market reaction to the investments in human capital. In addition, firms with greater research and development investments will experience greater stock-market reactions. In contrast, firms with the more intense physical capital investment will experience less positive stock-market reactions. They also hypothesize an interaction between the R&D intensity and physical capital intensity and also that firms are great advertising intensity would experience a greater stock-market reaction. This study can conclude the signaling or the surrounding messaging about investments in human capital. The insights can be used to advise middle managers and PR personnel.

Modi et al. (2015) use three methods to study service failure from customer information security breaches. The first primary method they use is the short-horizon event study to establish whether there is a stock market reaction and response to the security breaches. However, they supplement this with a long-horizon study designed to confirm the findings. Finally, to further provide evidence supporting the theoretical framework, they employ a small experiment as a third study. While the short-horizon event study is the primary method and takes most of the limelight, supplementary studies within the paper strengthen the message and make the findings more compelling. Further, these do not necessarily need to be incredibly extensive or robust studies as supplements. For instance, while there are few methodological details and rationale provided for the long-horizon event study design in the experiment, the long-horizon event study follows standard protocols due to the brevity and length of the paper. The experiment appears relatively straightforward, with details in the appendix of two newswire excerpts used in the experiment and survey scales adapted from Sia et al. (2009). In this way, sufficient details are provided to assess the study design and be sure it provides additional and valuable information.

We can also examine sustainability issues through event studies. The long-term consequences of resource extraction and use have been well understood, even though they are fundamental to the current industrial era (Bag et al., 2020). The study by Oh et al. (2020) uses several hypotheses and different sources of information and data. The primary hypothesis is based on the distance between the mine site in the nearest water source; proximity leads to more significant discounting of the news of output expansions. A geographic information system was used to compute the variable to use and the subsequent analyses. Two of the moderator variables used for hypotheses two and three were dummy variables. A third moderator was a sum of three standardized variables joined from different sources to reflect the likelihood of collective action being taken by the nearby communities.

While we have made increasingly essential improvements in our sustainability outputs and performance over time, the Dow Jones Sustainability Index was one of the early substantive measures to encourage, evaluate, and promote sustainability. Hawn et al. (2018) note how earlier studies on inclusion in the index, such as Robinson et al. (2011) and Cheung (2011), focused only on U.S. firms, while Cheung and Roca (2013) investigated Asia-Pacific firms. Hawn et al., in contrast, used a sample comprising observations from 27 countries and a more extended period and, consequentially, has more events included. Hawn et al. (2018) find that the events have limited significance when relevant controls and equivalent firms have been used.

DISTINCTIONS AND POINTS TO CONSIDER

Given the range of articles that we have provided a preview to, it is clear that several research design considerations need to be considered further.

First, as we noted in earlier chapters, creating the sample and the event list is crucial. In some cases, authors provide a complete list of events in the paper, such as Kajander et al. (2012), with a small sample size. However, it is impractical in most cases to include a complete sample, where this may be many hundreds of observations. It may now be practical to include a complete list of observations in the sample, perhaps as an online supplement, an appendix, or even a CSV file. If an author provides this level of detail, it will enhance the reproducibility of their research work. Similarly, there is a range of reporting in the search used. While most articles provide some insight into the search string they use in the database they search, as we can see in earlier chapters, even small changes in the parameters might cause substantial differences in the final sample of observations. Finally, of course, there are middle-ground cases; for example, Jacobs and Singhal (2014) provide a complete and extensive list of keywords used during the search in table 1. However, most authors only provide an example of some of the significant keywords or synonyms they are using, such as Hendricks and Singhal (2008) or Kajander et al. (2012). Indeed, providing more details makes it easier for a reader or an evaluator of the research to determine whether the sample is satisfactorily complete.

McWilliams and Siegel (1997) highlighted that wide event windows and confounding events often go poorly together with many early research works containing few details about how they dealt with confounding events. They noticed that when they tried to reproduce the research with a wide event window, a comprehensive search for confounding events, and elimination of the events from consideration as to when the confounding events were found, the number of them meant that the sample disappeared entirely; all observations were affected by confounding events. Indeed, McWilliams and Siegel (1997, p. 646; emphasis in original) note how when they "controlled for confounding events, the magnitudes of the abnormal re- turns were greatly diminished for all windows. More importantly, after controlling for confounding events, we found that the abnormal returns for all three studies were *all* statistically insignificant." That is, with a wide event window, every single event of interest had other confounding events making it impossible to determine whether the stock market reaction was because of the event of interest or the confounding event. Most times, the articles we review do note that they check for confounding events. In most cases, however, there are very few details on that confounding event check. For example, did they consider confounding events within the entire event window or only a day on either side of the event day for each event? Did they only seek events on the EDGAR database, or did they use a more liberal interpretation of which events may be significant? Given that in many management and supply chain studies, the abnormal returns reported are relatively small, if only a few events and stock market reactions were caused by confounding events, this might influence results. Including the confounding events in the sample could make an otherwise insignificant reaction (caused by the observations that should be included) instead of a significant reaction due to the confounding events included in the analysis.

We can also see that there is a range of different abnormal return estimation techniques that are used in these articles. Different methods can estimate abnormal returns, so it becomes important to ensure that the author is not simply reporting the results from the one estimation procedure that provides them with the most publishable results. As noted in earlier chapters, it is ideal to see the authors report on various estimations of abnormal returns with consistency between them. In most cases, it is becoming increasingly important to see a three- or four-factor model used with supporting analysis results also reported for the market model. However, it would also be interesting to see more justification used for the estimation procedure, such as provided by Bose and Leung (2014), noting that out of the various indices selected in the estimation process, one was used that gave the best possible R^2 value for use in the subsequent cross-sectional regression analysis.

Many management issues are global, and indeed, when considering global trade and supply chains, many operations management problems are also of global significance. Therefore, it seems apparent that there is a significant opportunity to conduct further multi-country event studies. In most cases, there are straightforward approaches to conducting U.S.-only studies, which may explain the predominance of research publications using a U.S.-based sample. In addition, while it is easy to identify an appropriate market index use of the market model, sophisticated models such as poor factor models with non-U.S. firms in the sample become very challenging. In addition, other approaches are gaining credibility, such as that outlined in Bose and Leung (2014). The difficulties in calculating the abnormal returns for firms domiciled in other countries should not discourage researchers. If necessary, an aspiring researcher should contact more experienced researchers in the area and discuss the opportunities to collaborate with them if this is one barrier preventing the research from progressing further.

Many of these issues are not isolated to studies published in management or supply chain journals; they are generally more common to event studies. Bouzzine (2021) provided an example of this and shows that many studies mainly use poor checks on compounding events and a wide range of estimation procedures, windows, and test statistics. The review results suggest that we should carefully use the event study method in different disciplines.

ISSUES, CONTROVERSIES, PROBLEMS

There are still many ongoing regulatory and legislative changes that influence different management and supply chain management areas and disciplines. Policymakers need to understand the overall impact of changes in what elements of the glittery changes may cause positive or negative abnormal returns on the terms of the industry. There are still issues with regulatory studies when conducting an event study, particularly given time clustering. However, when accounting for this clustering, researchers can take appropriate measures when calculating abnormal returns and testing for the significance of these returns. There are several early studies and regulations in highly regulated markets, such as the utility markets (Dnes et al., 1998; Dnes & Seaton, 1999; Sawkins, 1995), and these might suggest comparative research into logistics and transport industries. More recently, a range of maritime-focused transport studies have demonstrated the importance of regulatory changes to firms in an industry (Homan, 2006, 2007, 2009a, 2009b).

Many of the studies within operations and supply chain journals present a reasonably basic event study design comprising the first step, calculating abnormal returns, followed by using abnormal turns in a cross-sectional regression study. There is little use of two-way interactions or moderator analysis within the studies, particularly in supply chain studies. However, there are other examples from management journals where more complex event study designs are used. Understanding the interaction between two variables in the regression analysis can allow managers to understand the circumstances where an adverse event may be partially mitigated, providing suggestions for management actions and with more strategic responses for investments in the company.

The choice of variables within the model appears to grow and diminish with time. For example, from 2010 to 2020, several articles focused on capacity slack or buffers, such as examining how inventory slack, capacity slack, and supply chain slack can benefit firms facing a significant event. For the last 30 years, many studies have focused on technology applications, such as Ba et al. (2013) in manufacturing or other studies on corporate information technology systems. This has been partly driven by the information systems community focusing on ERP, planning information systems, and information systems integration (Konchitchki & O'Leary, 2011; Roztocki & Weistroffer, 2008. The basic premise is that implementing these systems should enable a firm to react more positively in the marketplace, capture more value, and reduce their costs by improving operational efficiencies. Indeed, Hendricks et al. (2007) identified that adopting an enterprise resource planning system focusing on the supply chain focus systems generates a positive abnormal return. In this thread, we would also expect to examine further the implementation of new systems based on big data and analytics. One challenge here is that we often consider them a subset of a more comprehensive ERP system with the implementation of a new module, and thus they may not be as widely publicized as an entire ERP system was. However, there are indications that such a big data analytics solution will provide significant operational benefits (Wood et al., 2017).

There is also increasingly a trend towards event studies that take a 'related firms' approach. That is, examining how the impact of one firm influences other firms in the supply chain. There has certainly been an increased professional discourse on how strategic options exercised by one firm can influence others (Lieb & Lieb, 2016), and this may influence future studies and increasingly competitive and crowded logistics marketplaces. As firms implement new services (Shi et al., 2017) or new technologies (Wood et al., 2017), there will increasingly be the opportunity to examine how this influences the structure of the competitive marketplace and whether there are any stock market reactions at the related firm studies might include factors such as power or market dominance. The level of investment or research and development are critical factors that might influence stock market reactions.

Increasingly, I expect we will see a rise of mixed-method approaches where a single research publication reports on several studies that provide additional insight into the one issue or phenomenon of interest. Raithel and Hock provided one such pairing (2021) and examined the crisis response literature on the issues of conformity, under conformity, and over conformity. There are two study designs. The first study is an experiment that enables them to understand the impact on customers. The other study is an event study that allows them to understand the impact perceived by investors. This event study enables them to examine the issue from different perspectives and generates some fascinating insight that we do not find in other study types. For example, they counterintuitively identify that the application of an over confirming strategy reduces stock returns and reputation in the eyes of the customer when compared to the application of conforming strategies. The finding suggests that managers should be careful to identify stakeholder expectations during the crisis and be wary of exceeding those expectations for fear of generating unintended negative consequences for themselves and the employees.

Many of the most exciting management or supply chain issues and challenges facing society now require a range of perspectives to understand. As a result, more management, particularly operations and supply chain research, needs to integrate different methods and perspectives to address these needs (Singhal & Singhal, 2012a, 2012b). through increasing the methodological mix, research should increasingly become relevant and address real needs while generating more interesting insight (MacCarthy et al., 2013).

CONCLUSIONS

This chapter summarizes some supply chain studies and some from the broader management area. Through looking at similarities and differences between the studies, the chapter can provide some insight into the range of types of topics that might be studied and some pertinent points that the reader may find interesting if they go back and read the original studies. Finally, the chapter's conclusion analyzes some of the critical lessons we can learn by examining some studies, suggesting opportunities for improving future event studies.

As this is the book's final chapter, gaining some insight from the studies listed requires understanding many of the methodological issues and factors addressed elsewhere in the volume. When reading the studies noted in the chapter, it is helpful to consider their study design. Consequently, a full coverage of the previous chapters will develop an appreciation of some differences in commentary provided in this chapter. It is worth looking at the original articles and many of the articles that are distinct or provide interesting methodological design considerations that might illuminate how to address particular phenomena or design challenges in future studies.

REFERENCES

Argote, L., & Miron-Spektor, E. (2011). Organizational Learning: From Experience to Knowledge. *Organization Science, 22*(5), 1123–1137. doi:10.1287/orsc.1100.0621

Ba, S., Lisic, L. L., Liu, Q., & Stallaert, J. (2013). Stock market reaction to green vehicle innovation. *Production and Operations Management, 22*(4), 976–990. doi:10.1111/j.1937-5956.2012.01387.x

Barney, J. B. (2012). Purchasing, supply chain management and sustained competitive advantage: The relevance of resource-based theory. *The Journal of Supply Chain Management, 48*(2), 3–6. doi:10.1111/j.1745-493X.2012.03265.x

Bharadwaj, A. S. (2000). A Resource-Based Perspective on Information Technology Capability and Firm Performance: An Empirical Investigation. *Management Information Systems Quarterly, 24*(1), 169–196. doi:10.2307/3250983

Bilgili, H., Tochman Campbell, J., Ellstrand, A. E., & Johnson, J. L. (2017). Riding off into the sunset: Organizational sensegiving, shareholder sensemaking, and reactions to CEO retirement. *Journal of Management Studies, 54*(7), 1019–1049. doi:10.1111/joms.12264

Bose, I., & Leung, A. C. M. (2014). Do phishing alerts impact global corporations? A firm value analysis. *Decision Support Systems, 64*(Supplement C), 67–78. doi:10.1016/j.dss.2014.04.006

Bouzzine, Y. D. (2021). Stock price reactions to environmental pollution events: A systematic literature review of direct and indirect effects and a research agenda. *Journal of Cleaner Production, 316*, 128305. doi:10.1016/j.jclepro.2021.128305

Cascio, W. F. (1993). Downsizing: What do we know? What have we learned? *The Executive, 7*(1), 95–104. doi:10.5465/ame.1993.9409142062

Cheung, A., & Roca, E. (2013). The effect on price, liquidity and risk when stocks are added to and deleted from a sustainability index: Evidence from the Asia Pacific context. *Journal of Asian Economics, 24*, 51–65. doi:10.1016/j.asieco.2012.08.002

Cheung, A. W. K. (2011). Do stock investors value corporate sustainability? Evidence from an event study. *Journal of Business Ethics, 99*(2), 145–165. doi:10.100710551-010-0646-3

Chi, L.-C. (2012). Price reactions to the announcement of the cross-strait Economic Cooperation Framework Agreement. *Applied Economics Quarterly, 58*(3), 213–221. http://dx.doi.org.ezproxy.otago.ac.nz/10.3790/aeq.58.3.213

Chiu, A.-A., Chen, L.-N., & Hu, J.-C. (2020). A study of the relationship between corporate social responsibility report and the stock market. *Sustainability, 12*(21), 9200. doi:10.3390u12219200

Chowdhury, J., & Sarkar, S. (2017). The financial impact of retail store closure announcements. *International Journal of Physical Distribution & Logistics Management, 47*(6), 536–556. Advance online publication. doi:10.1108/IJPDLM-04-2016-0117

Connelly, B. L., Certo, S. T., Ireland, R. D., & Reutzel, C. R. (2011). Signaling Theory: A Review and Assessment. *Journal of Management, 37*(1), 39–67. doi:10.1177/0149206310388419

Deitz, G., Hansen, J., & Richey, R. G. (2009). Coerced integration: The effects of retailer supply chain technology mandates on supplier stock returns. *International Journal of Physical Distribution & Logistics Management, 39*(10), 814–825. doi:10.1108/09600030911011423

Dnes, A. W., Kodwani, D. G., Seaton, J. S., & Wood, D. (1998). The regulation of the United Kingdom electricity industry: An event study of price-capping measures. *Journal of Regulatory Economics, 13*(3), 207–226. doi:10.1023/A:1008027419553

Dnes, A. W., & Seaton, J. S. (1999). The regulation of electricity: Results from an event study. *Applied Economics, 31*(5), 609–618. doi:10.1080/000368499324057

Ellis, K. M., Reus, T. H., Lamont, B. T., & Ranft, A. L. (2011). Transfer Effects in Large Acquisitions: How Size-Specific Experience Matters. *Academy of Management Journal, 54*(6), 1261–1276. doi:10.5465/amj.2009.0122

Ellram, L. M., Tate, W. L., & Billington, C. (2008). Offshore outsourcing of professional services: A transaction cost economics perspective. *Journal of Operations Management, 26*(2), 148–163. doi:10.1016/j.jom.2007.02.008

Eroglu, C., Kurt, A. C., & Elwakil, O. S. (2016). Stock market reaction to quality, safety, and sustainability awards in logistics. *Journal of Business Logistics, 37*(4), 329–345. doi:10.1111/jbl.12145

Filbeck, G., Kumar, S., Liu, J., & Zhao, X. (2016). Supply chain finance and financial contagion from disruptions: Evidence from the automobile industry. *International Journal of Physical Distribution & Logistics Management, 46*(4), 414–438. doi:10.1108/IJPDLM-04-2014-0082

Gibbons, R. (2010). Transaction-cost economics: Past, present, and future? *The Scandinavian Journal of Economics, 112*(2), 263–288. doi:10.1111/j.1467-9442.2010.01609.x

Gong, S. X. H., Firth, M., & Cullinane, K. (2008). International oligopoly and stock market linkages: The case of global airlines. *Transportation Research Part E, Logistics and Transportation Review, 44*(4), 621–636. doi:10.1016/j.tre.2007.05.008

Hawn, O., Chatterji, A. K., & Mitchell, W. (2018). Do investors actually value sustainability? New evidence from investor reactions to the Dow Jones Sustainability Index (DJSI). *Strategic Management Journal, 39*(4), 949–976. doi:10.1002mj.2752

Hendricks, K. B., Hora, M., & Singhal, V. R. (2014). An empirical investigation on the appointments of supply chain and operations management executives. *Management Science, 61*(7), 1562–1583. doi:10.1287/mnsc.2014.1987

Hendricks, K. B., & Singhal, V. R. (2005). An empirical analysis of the effect of supply chain disruptions on long-run stock price performance and equity risk of the firm. *Production and Operations Management, 14*(1), 35–52. doi:10.1111/j.1937-5956.2005.tb00008.x

Hendricks, K. B., & Singhal, V. R. (2008). The effect of product introduction delays on operating performance. *Management Science, 54*(5), 878–892. doi:10.1287/mnsc.1070.0805

Hendricks, K. B., Singhal, V. R., & Stratman, J. K. (2007). The impact of enterprise systems on corporate performance: A study of ERP, SCM, and CRM system implementations. *Journal of Operations Management, 25*(1), 65–82. doi:10.1016/j.jom.2006.02.002

Hendricks, K. B., Singhal, V. R., & Wiedman, C. I. (1995). The impact of capacity expansion on the market value of the firm. *Journal of Operations Management, 12*(3–4), 259–272. doi:10.1016/0272-6963(94)00016-8

Hendricks, K. B., Singhal, V. R., & Zhang, R. (2009). The effect of operational slack, diversification, and vertical relatedness on the stock market reaction to supply chain disruptions. *Journal of Operations Management, 27*(3), 233–246. doi:10.1016/j.jom.2008.09.001

Homan, A. C. (2006). The impact of 9/11 on financial risk, volatility and returns of marine firms. *Maritime Economics & Logistics, 8*(4), 387–401. doi:10.1057/palgrave.mel.9100165

Homan, A. C. (2007). The impact of MTSA on financial risk and volatility of marine firms. *Maritime Policy & Management, 34*(1), 69–79. doi:10.1080/03088830601103459

Homan, A. C. (2009a). The impact of 9/11 on the persistence of financial return volatility of marine firms. *Eastern Economic Journal, 35*(1), 71–83. doi:10.1057/palgrave.eej.9050044

Homan, A. C. (2009b). The impact of MTSA on investment uncertainty and the persistence of financial return volatility of marine firms. *Maritime Policy & Management*, *36*(2), 105–115. doi:10.1080/03088830902868008

House, R. J., Hanges, P. J., Javidan, M., Dorfman, P. W., & Gupta, V. (2004). *Culture, Leadership, and Organizations: The GLOBE Study of 62 Societies*. SAGE Publications.

Jacobs, B. W., & Singhal, V. R. (2014). The effect of product development restructuring on shareholder value. *Production and Operations Management*, *23*(5), 728–743. doi:10.1111/poms.12074

Jacobs, B. W., & Singhal, V. R. (2020). Shareholder value effects of the Volkswagen emissions scandal on the automotive ecosystem. *Production and Operations Management*, *29*(10), 2230–2251. doi:10.1111/poms.13228

Jory, S. R., Ngo, T. N., Wang, D., & Saha, A. (2015). The market response to corporate scandals involving CEOs. *Applied Economics*, *47*(17), 1723–1738. doi:10.1080/00036846.2014.995361

Kajander, J.-K., Sivunen, M., Vimpari, J., Pulkka, L., & Junnila, S. (2012). Market value of sustainability business innovations in the construction sector. *Building Research and Information*, *40*(6), 665–678. doi:10.1080/09613218.2012.703893

Konchitchki, Y., & O'Leary, D. E. (2011). Event study methodologies in information systems research. *International Journal of Accounting Information Systems*, *12*(2), 99–115. doi:10.1016/j.accinf.2011.01.002

Kumar, S., Liu, J., & Scutella, J. (2015). The impact of supply chain disruptions on stockholder wealth in India. *International Journal of Physical Distribution & Logistics Management*, *45*(9/10), 938–958. doi:10.1108/IJPDLM-09-2013-0247

Lieb, R. C., & Lieb, K. J. (2016). 3PL CEO perspectives on the current status and future prospects of the third-party logistics Industry in North America: The 2014 Survey. *Transportation Journal*, *55*(1), 78–92. doi:10.5325/transportationj.55.1.0078

MacCarthy, B. L., Lewis, M., Voss, C., & Narasimhan, R. (2013). The same old methodologies? Perspectives on OM research in the post-lean age. *International Journal of Operations & Production Management*, *33*(7), 934–956. doi:10.1108/IJOPM-08-2013-0373

McWilliams, A., & Siegel, D. (1997). Event studies in management research: Theoretical and empirical issues. *Academy of Management Journal*, *40*(3), 626–657. doi:10.2307/257056

Modi, S. B., Wiles, M. A., & Mishra, S. (2015). Shareholder value implications of service failures in triads: The case of customer information security breaches. *Journal of Operations Management*, *35*(1), 21–39. doi:10.1016/j.jom.2014.10.003

Oh, C. H., Shapiro, D., Ho, S. S. H., & Shin, J. (2020). Location matters: Valuing firm-specific nonmarket risk in the global mining industry. *Strategic Management Journal*, *41*(7), 1210–1244. doi:10.1002mj.3153

Qiao, T., Han, L., & Liu, Y. (2021). Does targeted poverty alleviation disclosure improve stock performance? *Economics Letters*, *201*, 109805. doi:10.1016/j.econlet.2021.109805

Qiu, S., Jiang, J., Liu, X., Chen, M.-H., & Yuan, X. (2021). Can corporate social responsibility protect firm value during the COVID-19 pandemic? *International Journal of Hospitality Management, 93*, 102759. doi:10.1016/j.ijhm.2020.102759

Raithel, S., & Hock, S. J. (2021). The crisis-response match: An empirical investigation. *Strategic Management Journal, 42*(1), 170–184. doi:10.1002mj.3213

Riley, S. M., Michael, S. C., & Mahoney, J. T. (2017). Human capital matters: Market valuation of firm investments in training and the role of complementary assets. *Strategic Management Journal, 38*(9), 1895–1914. doi:10.1002mj.2631

Robinson, M., Kleffner, A., & Bertels, S. (2011). Signaling sustainability leadership: Empirical evidence of the value of DJSI membership. *Journal of Business Ethics, 101*(3), 493–505. doi:10.100710551-011-0735-y

Roztocki, N., & Weistroffer, H. R. (2008). Stock price reactions to investments in EAI and ERP: A comparative event study. *Hawaii International Conference on System Sciences, Proceedings of the 41st Annual*, 403–403. 10.1109/HICSS.2008.411

Roztocki, N., & Weistroffer, H. R. (2015). Investments in enterprise integration technology: An event study. *Information Systems Frontiers, 17*(3), 659–672. http://dx.doi.org.ezproxy.otago.ac.nz/10.1007/s10796-013-9451-8. doi:10.100710796-013-9451-8

Sawkins, J. W. (1995). Measuring the effects of regulation: An event study of the English and Welsh water industry. *Applied Economics Letters, 2*(10), 359–362. doi:10.1080/758518989

Scott, B. G., Ueng, J., Ramaswamy, V., & Chang, C. L. (2011). Layoff and firm long-term performance. *Academy of Strategic Management Journal, 10*(2), 1–10.

Shi, Y., Arthanari, T., & Wood, L. (2017). Developing third-party purchase (3PP) services: New Zealand third-party logistics providers' perspectives. *Supply Chain Management, 22*(1), 40–57. doi:10.1108/SCM-06-2016-0189

Sia, C. L., Lim, K. H., Leung, K., Lee, M. K. O., Huang, W. W., & Benbasat, I. (2009). Web strategies to promote internet shopping: Is cultural-customization needed? *Management Information Systems Quarterly, 33*(3), 491–512. doi:10.2307/20650306

Singhal, K., & Singhal, J. (2012a). Imperatives of the science of operations and supply-chain management. *Journal of Operations Management, 30*(3), 237–244. doi:10.1016/j.jom.2011.11.003

Singhal, K., & Singhal, J. (2012b). Opportunities for developing the science of operations and supply-chain management. *Journal of Operations Management, 30*(3), 245–252. doi:10.1016/j.jom.2011.11.002

Wassmer, U., & Dussauge, P. (2012). Network resource stocks and flows: How do alliance portfolios affect the value of new alliance formations? *Strategic Management Journal, 33*(7), 871–883. doi:10.1002mj.973

Williamson, O. E. (2008). Outsourcing: Transaction cost economics and supply chain management. *The Journal of Supply Chain Management, 44*(2), 5–16. doi:10.1111/j.1745-493X.2008.00051.x

Wood, L. C., Reiners, T., & Srivastava, H. S. (2017). Think exogenous to excel: Alternative supply chain data to improve transparency and decisions. *International Journal of Logistics Research and Applications*, *20*(5), 426–443. doi:10.1080/13675567.2016.1267126

Wood, L. C., & Wang, J. X. (2018). The event study method in logistics research: Overview and a critical analysis. *International Journal of Applied Logistics*, *8*(1), 57–79. doi:10.4018/IJAL.2018010104

Zhan, X., Mu, Y., Nishant, R., & Singhal, V. R. (2020). When do appointments of Chief Digital or Data Officers (CDOs) affect stock prices? *IEEE Transactions on Engineering Management*, 1–14. doi:10.1109/TEM.2020.2984619

ADDITIONAL READING

Arora, P., Hora, M., Singhal, V., & Subramanian, R. (2020). When do appointments of corporate sustainability executives affect shareholder value? *Journal of Operations Management*, *66*(4), 464–487. doi:10.1002/joom.1074

Binder, J. (1998). The event study methodology since 1969. *Review of Quantitative Finance and Accounting*, *11*(2), 111–137. doi:10.1023/A:1008295500105

Binder, J. J. (1985). On the use of the multivariate regression model in event studies. *Journal of Accounting Research*, *23*(1), 370–383. doi:10.2307/2490925

Brown, S. J., & Warner, J. B. (1980). Measuring security price performance. *Journal of Financial Economics*, *8*(3), 205–258. doi:10.1016/0304-405X(80)90002-1

Brown, S. J., & Warner, J. B. (1985). Using daily stock returns: The case of event studies. *Journal of Financial Economics*, *14*(1), 3–31. doi:10.1016/0304-405X(85)90042-X

Duan, C., Grover, V., & Balakrishnan, N. (2009). Business process outsourcing: An event study on the nature of processes and firm valuation. *European Journal of Information Systems*, *18*(5), 442–457. doi:10.1057/ejis.2009.38

Duan, C., Grover, V., Roberts, N., & Balakrishnan, N. (2014). Firm valuation effects of the decision to adopt relationally governed business process outsourcing arrangements. *International Journal of Production Research*, *52*(15), 4673–4694. doi:10.1080/00207543.2014.884289

Fama, E. F. (1970). Efficient capital markets: A review of theory and empirical work. *The Journal of Finance*, *25*(2), 383–417. doi:10.2307/2325486

Fama, E. F. (1991). Efficient capital markets: II. *The Journal of Finance*, *46*(5), 1575–1617. doi:10.1111/j.1540-6261.1991.tb04636.x

Fama, E. F. (1998). Market efficiency, long-term returns, and behavioral finance. *Journal of Financial Economics*, *49*(3), 283–306. doi:10.1016/S0304-405X(98)00026-9

Fama, E. F., & French, K. R. (1993). Common risk factors in the returns on stocks and bonds. *Journal of Financial Economics*, *33*(1), 3–56. doi:10.1016/0304-405X(93)90023-5

Kothari, S. P., & Warner, J. B. (2007). Econometrics of event studies. In B. E. Eckbo (Ed.), *Handbook of Corporate Finance: Empirical Corporate Finance* (Vol. 1, pp. 3–36). North-Holland/Elsevier. doi:10.1016/B978-0-444-53265-7.50015-9

Mitchell, M., & Stafford, E. (2000). Managerial decisions and long-term stock price performance. *The Journal of Business*, *73*(3), 287–329. doi:10.1086/209645

Wood, L. C., Wang, J. X., Duong, L. N. K., Reiners, T., & Smith, R. (2018). Stock market reactions to auto manufacturers' environmental failures. *Journal of Macromarketing*, *38*(4), 364–382. doi:10.1177/0276146718781915

Wood, L. C., Wang, J. X., Olesen, K., & Reiners, T. (2017). The effect of slack, diversification, and time to recall on stock market reaction to toy recalls. *International Journal of Production Economics*, *193*, 244–258. doi:10.1016/j.ijpe.2017.07.021

KEY TERMS AND DEFINITIONS

Abnormal Return: The difference between an observed movement in stock returns that is clearly different or greater than an expected normal or expected return.

Crisis Response: The range of actions taken to plan for and manage a disruptive event to reduce or mitigate the harm to the firm and stakeholders.

Managerial Action: The actions that a manager can take to influence the performance they desire or target.

Resource-Based View (RBV): The theory that resources are fundamental to the success and performance of a firm.

Signalling Theory: The study of how information is provided between two parties who have access to different information. The sender must decide on how to signal or communicate information, such as how the firm decides the information encoded in announcements and press releases.

Stock Market Reaction: A sudden and fast change in the stock prices in reaction to the event, capturing the unbiased estimate of the consequences of the news on the stock's long-term prospects. The stock market reaction, measured by the abnormal returns, is usually the focus of the main hypothesis in the event study project.

Strategic Response: The shared response of the firm's components, given their context, to achieve the desired objective.

Transaction Cost Economics (TCE): The study of the costs of running an economic system, often used to analyze the outsourcing activities and when activities are best outsourced given the new costs that may arise.

Related References

To continue our tradition of advancing media and communications research, we have compiled a list of recommended IGI Global readings. These references will provide additional information and guidance to further enrich your knowledge and assist you with your own research and future publications.

Abashian, N., & Fisher, S. (2018). Intercultural Effectiveness in Libraries: Supporting Success Through Collaboration With Co-Curricular Programs. In B. Blummer, J. Kenton, & M. Wiatrowski (Eds.), *Promoting Ethnic Diversity and Multiculturalism in Higher Education* (pp. 219–236). Hershey, PA: IGI Global. doi:10.4018/978-1-5225-4097-7.ch012

Adebayo, O., Fagbohun, M. O., Esse, U. C., & Nwokeoma, N. M. (2018). Change Management in the Academic Library: Transition From Print to Digital Collections. In R. Bhardwaj (Ed.), *Digitizing the Modern Library and the Transition From Print to Electronic* (pp. 1–28). Hershey, PA: IGI Global. doi:10.4018/978-1-5225-2119-8.ch001

Adegbore, A. M., Quadri, M. O., & Oyewo, O. R. (2018). A Theoretical Approach to the Adoption of Electronic Resource Management Systems (ERMS) in Nigerian University Libraries. In A. Tella & T. Kwanya (Eds.), *Handbook of Research on Managing Intellectual Property in Digital Libraries* (pp. 292–311). Hershey, PA: IGI Global. doi:10.4018/978-1-5225-3093-0.ch015

Adesola, A. P., & Olla, G. O. (2018). Unlocking the Unlimited Potentials of Koha OSS/ILS for Library House-Keeping Functions: A Global View. In M. Khosrow-Pour (Ed.), *Optimizing Contemporary Application and Processes in Open Source Software* (pp. 124–163). Hershey, PA: IGI Global. doi:10.4018/978-1-5225-5314-4.ch006

Adesola, A. P., & Olla, G. O. (2019). Bridging the Digital Divide in Nigerian Information Landscape: The Role of the Library. *International Journal of Digital Literacy and Digital Competence*, *10*(3), 10–31. doi:10.4018/IJDLDC.2019070102

Adetayo, A. J. (2021). Fake News and Social Media Censorship: Examining the Librarian Role. In R. Blankenship (Ed.), *Deep Fakes, Fake News, and Misinformation in Online Teaching and Learning Technologies* (pp. 69–92). IGI Global. https://doi.org/10.4018/978-1-7998-6474-5.ch004

Adetayo, A. J. (2022). Building Civic Engagement in Smart Cities: Role of Smart Libraries. In M. Taher (Ed.), *Handbook of Research on the Role of Libraries, Archives, and Museums in Achieving Civic Engagement and Social Justice in Smart Cities* (pp. 314–333). IGI Global. https://doi.org/10.4018/978-1-7998-8363-0.ch017

Adigun, G. O., Sobalaje, A. J., & Salau, S. A. (2018). Social Media and Copyright in Digital Libraries. In A. Tella & T. Kwanya (Eds.), *Handbook of Research on Managing Intellectual Property in Digital Libraries* (pp. 19–36). Hershey, PA: IGI Global. doi:10.4018/978-1-5225-3093-0.ch002

Adriyana, L., & Fitrina Cahyaningtyas, D. (2022). The Importance of Rural Library Services Based on Social Inclusion in Indonesia. In M. Taher (Ed.), *Handbook of Research on the Role of Libraries, Archives, and Museums in Achieving Civic Engagement and Social Justice in Smart Cities* (pp. 201–218). IGI Global. https://doi.org/10.4018/978-1-7998-8363-0.ch010

Afolabi, O. A. (2018). Myths and Challenges of Building an Effective Digital Library in Developing Nations: An African Perspective. In A. Tella & T. Kwanya (Eds.), *Handbook of Research on Managing Intellectual Property in Digital Libraries* (pp. 51–79). Hershey, PA: IGI Global. doi:10.4018/978-1-5225-3093-0.ch004

Ahuja, Y., & Kumar, P. (2017). Web 2.0 Tools and Application: Knowledge Management and Sharing in Libraries. In B. Gunjal (Ed.), *Managing Knowledge and Scholarly Assets in Academic Libraries* (pp. 218–234). Hershey, PA: IGI Global. doi:10.4018/978-1-5225-1741-2.ch010

Ajmi, A. (2018). Developing In-House Digital Tools: Case Studies From the UMKC School of Law Library. In L. Costello & M. Powers (Eds.), *Developing In-House Digital Tools in Library Spaces* (pp. 117–139). Hershey, PA: IGI Global. doi:10.4018/978-1-5225-2676-6.ch006

Al-Kharousi, R., Al-Harrasi, N. H., Jabur, N. H., & Bouazza, A. (2018). Soft Systems Methodology (SSM) as an Interdisciplinary Approach: Reflection on the Use of SSM in Adoption of Web 2.0 Applications in Omani Academic Libraries. In M. Al-Suqri, A. Al-Kindi, S. AlKindi, & N. Saleem (Eds.), *Promoting Interdisciplinarity in Knowledge Generation and Problem Solving* (pp. 243–257). Hershey, PA: IGI Global. doi:10.4018/978-1-5225-3878-3.ch016

Alenzuela, R. (2017). Research, Leadership, and Resource-Sharing Initiatives: The Role of Local Library Consortia in Access to Medical Information. In S. Ram (Ed.), *Library and Information Services for Bioinformatics Education and Research* (pp. 199–211). Hershey, PA: IGI Global. doi:10.4018/978-1-5225-1871-6.ch012

Alenzuela, R., & Terry, M. A. (2020). Diversity, Indigenous Knowledge, and LIS Pedagogy: Conceptualizing Formal Education in Library and Information Studies in Vanuatu. In R. Alenzuela, H. Kim, & D. Baylen (Eds.), *Internationalization of Library and Information Science Education in the Asia-Pacific Region* (pp. 50–77). IGI Global. doi:10.4018/978-1-7998-2273-8.ch003

Allison, D. (2017). When Sales Talk Meets Reality: Implementing a Self-Checkout Kiosk. In E. Iglesias (Ed.), *Library Technology Funding, Planning, and Deployment* (pp. 36–54). Hershey, PA: IGI Global. doi:10.4018/978-1-5225-1735-1.ch003

Anglim, C. T., & Rusk, F. (2018). Empowering DC's Future Through Information Access. In A. Burtin, J. Fleming, & P. Hampton-Garland (Eds.), *Changing Urban Landscapes Through Public Higher Education* (pp. 57–77). Hershey, PA: IGI Global. doi:10.4018/978-1-5225-3454-9.ch003

Asmi, N. A. (2017). Social Media and Library Services. *International Journal of Library and Information Services*, 6(2), 23–36. doi:10.4018/IJLIS.2017070103

Attademo, G., & Maccaro, A. (2022). Research Ethics in the Social Sciences. In G. Punziano & A. Delli Paoli (Eds.), *Handbook of Research on Advanced Research Methodologies for a Digital Society* (pp. 54–64). IGI Global. https://doi.org/10.4018/978-1-7998-8473-6.ch005

Awoyemi, R. A. (2018). Adoption and Use of Innovative Mobile Technologies in Nigerian Academic Libraries. In J. Keengwe (Ed.), *Handbook of Research on Digital Content, Mobile Learning, and Technology Integration Models in Teacher Education* (pp. 354–389). Hershey, PA: IGI Global. doi:10.4018/978-1-5225-2953-8.ch019

Awoyemi, R. A. (2018). Adoption and Use of Innovative Mobile Technologies in Nigerian Academic Libraries. In J. Keengwe (Ed.), *Handbook of Research on Digital Content, Mobile Learning, and Technology Integration Models in Teacher Education* (pp. 354–389). Hershey, PA: IGI Global. doi:10.4018/978-1-5225-2953-8.ch019

Awoyemi, R. A., & Awoyemi, R. O. (2021). Beyond the Physical Library Space: Creating a 21st Century Digitally-Oriented Library Environment. In C. Chisita, R. Enakrire, O. Durodolu, V. Tsabedze, & J. Ngoaketsi (Eds.), *Handbook of Research on Records and Information Management Strategies for Enhanced Knowledge Coordination* (pp. 189–203). IGI Global. https://doi.org/10.4018/978-1-7998-6618-3.ch012

Babatope, I. S. (2018). Social Media Applications as Effective Service Delivery Tools for Librarians. In M. Khosrow-Pour, D.B.A. (Ed.), Encyclopedia of Information Science and Technology, Fourth Edition (pp. 5252-5261). Hershey, PA: IGI Global. doi:10.4018/978-1-5225-2255-3.ch456

Bakare, A. A. (2018). Digital Libraries and Copyright of Intellectual Property: An Ethical Practice Management. In A. Tella & T. Kwanya (Eds.), *Handbook of Research on Managing Intellectual Property in Digital Libraries* (pp. 377–395). Hershey, PA: IGI Global. doi:10.4018/978-1-5225-3093-0.ch019

Baker, A. A. (2020). To Whose Benefit? At What Cost?: Consideration for Ethical Issues in Social Science Research. In M. Baran & J. Jones (Eds.), *Applied Social Science Approaches to Mixed Methods Research* (pp. 251–260). IGI Global. https://doi.org/10.4018/978-1-7998-1025-4.ch011

Baker-Gardner, R., & Smart, C. (2017). Ignorance or Intent?: A Case Study of Plagiarism in Higher Education among LIS Students in the Caribbean. In D. Velliaris (Ed.), *Handbook of Research on Academic Misconduct in Higher Education* (pp. 182–205). Hershey, PA: IGI Global. doi:10.4018/978-1-5225-1610-1.ch008

Baker-Gardner, R., & Stewart, P. (2018). Educating Caribbean Librarians to Provide Library Education in a Dynamic Information Environment. In S. Bhattacharyya & K. Patnaik (Eds.), *Changing the Scope of Library Instruction in the Digital Age* (pp. 187–226). Hershey, PA: IGI Global. doi:10.4018/978-1-5225-2802-9.ch008

Baran, M. L., & Jones, J. E. (2020). Developing the Research Study: A Step-by-Step Approach. In M. Baran & J. Jones (Eds.), *Applied Social Science Approaches to Mixed Methods Research* (pp. 262–274). IGI Global. https://doi.org/10.4018/978-1-7998-1025-4.ch012

Baskaran, C. (2020). Altmetircs Research: An Impact and Tools. In C. Baskaran (Ed.), *Measuring and Implementing Altmetrics in Library and Information Science Research* (pp. 1–10). IGI Global. https://doi.org/10.4018/978-1-7998-1309-5.ch001

Bengtson, J. (2017). Funding a Gamification Machine. In E. Iglesias (Ed.), *Library Technology Funding, Planning, and Deployment* (pp. 99–112). Hershey, PA: IGI Global. doi:10.4018/978-1-5225-1735-1.ch006

Bhuda, M., & Koitsiwe, M. (2022). The Importance of Underpinning Indigenous Research Using African Indigenous Philosophies: Perspectives From Indigenous Scholars. In R. Tshifhumulo & T. Makhanikhe (Eds.), *Handbook of Research on Protecting and Managing Global Indigenous Knowledge Systems* (pp. 223–248). IGI Global. https://doi.org/10.4018/978-1-7998-7492-8.ch013

Blummer, B., & Kenton, J. M. (2017). Access and Accessibility of Academic Libraries' Electronic Resources and Services: Identifying Themes in the Literature From 2000 to the Present. In H. Alphin Jr, J. Lavine, & R. Chan (Eds.), *Disability and Equity in Higher Education Accessibility* (pp. 242–267). Hershey, PA: IGI Global. doi:10.4018/978-1-5225-2665-0.ch011

Blummer, B., & Kenton, J. M. (2018). Academic and Research Libraries' Portals: A Literature Review From 2003 to the Present. In R. Bhardwaj (Ed.), *Digitizing the Modern Library and the Transition From Print to Electronic* (pp. 29–63). Hershey, PA: IGI Global. doi:10.4018/978-1-5225-2119-8.ch002

Blummer, B., & Kenton, J. M. (2018). International Students and Academic Libraries: Identifying Themes in the Literature From 2001 to the Present. In B. Blummer, J. Kenton, & M. Wiatrowski (Eds.), *Promoting Ethnic Diversity and Multiculturalism in Higher Education* (pp. 237–263). Hershey, PA: IGI Global. doi:10.4018/978-1-5225-4097-7.ch013

Bohuski, L. (2020). What If Your Library Can't Go Green?: Promoting Wellness in Libraries. In A. Kaushik, A. Kumar, & P. Biswas (Eds.), *Handbook of Research on Emerging Trends and Technologies in Library and Information Science* (pp. 13–26). IGI Global. doi:10.4018/978-1-5225-9825-1.ch002

Boom, D. (2017). The Embedded Librarian: Do More With less. In B. Gunjal (Ed.), *Managing Knowledge and Scholarly Assets in Academic Libraries* (pp. 76–97). Hershey, PA: IGI Global. doi:10.4018/978-1-5225-1741-2.ch004

Bosire-Ogechi, E. (2018). Social Media, Social Networking, Copyright, and Digital Libraries. In A. Tella & T. Kwanya (Eds.), *Handbook of Research on Managing Intellectual Property in Digital Libraries* (pp. 37–50). Hershey, PA: IGI Global. doi:10.4018/978-1-5225-3093-0.ch003

Bradley-Sanders, C., & Rudshteyn, A. (2018). MyLibrary at Brooklyn College: Developing a Suite of Digital Tools. In L. Costello & M. Powers (Eds.), *Developing In-House Digital Tools in Library Spaces* (pp. 140–167). Hershey, PA: IGI Global. doi:10.4018/978-1-5225-2676-6.ch007

Brown, V. (2018). Technology Access Gap for Postsecondary Education: A Statewide Case Study. In M. Yildiz, S. Funk, & B. De Abreu (Eds.), *Promoting Global Competencies Through Media Literacy* (pp. 20–40). Hershey, PA: IGI Global. doi:10.4018/978-1-5225-3082-4.ch002

Browne, N. (2021). The IHS Library and Its Response to the COVID-19 Pandemic. In B. Holland (Eds.), *Handbook of Research on Library Response to the COVID-19 Pandemic* (pp. 298-320). IGI Global. https://doi.org/10.4018/978-1-7998-6449-3.ch016

Chaiyasoonthorn, W., & Suksa-ngiam, W. (2018). Users' Acceptance of Online Literature Databases in a Thai University: A Test of UTAUT2. *International Journal of Information Systems in the Service Sector*, *10*(1), 54–70. doi:10.4018/IJISSS.2018010104

Chaudron, G. (2018). Burst Pipes and Leaky Roofs: Small Emergencies Are a Challenge for Libraries. In K. Strang, M. Korstanje, & N. Vajjhala (Eds.), *Research, Practices, and Innovations in Global Risk and Contingency Management* (pp. 211–231). Hershey, PA: IGI Global. doi:10.4018/978-1-5225-4754-9.ch012

Chemulwo, M. J. (2018). Managing Intellectual Property in Digital Libraries and Copyright Challenges. In A. Tella & T. Kwanya (Eds.), *Handbook of Research on Managing Intellectual Property in Digital Libraries* (pp. 165–183). Hershey, PA: IGI Global. doi:10.4018/978-1-5225-3093-0.ch009

Chen, J., Lan, X., Huang, Q., Dong, J., & Chen, C. (2017). Scholarly Learning Commons. In L. Ruan, Q. Zhu, & Y. Ye (Eds.), *Academic Library Development and Administration in China* (pp. 90–109). Hershey, PA: IGI Global. doi:10.4018/978-1-5225-0550-1.ch006

Chigwada, J. P. (2018). Adoption of Open Source Software in Libraries in Developing Countries. *International Journal of Library and Information Services*, *7*(1), 15–29. doi:10.4018/IJLIS.2018010102

Chigwada, J. P. (2020). Librarian Skillsets in the 21st Century: The Changing Role of Librarians in the Digital Era. In N. Osuigwe (Ed.), *Managing and Adapting Library Information Services for Future Users* (pp. 41–58). IGI Global. https://doi.org/10.4018/978-1-7998-1116-9.ch003

Chigwada, J. P. (2020). The Role of the Librarian in the Research Life Cycle: Research Collaboration Among the Library and Faculty. In C. Chisita (Ed.), *Cooperation and Collaboration Initiatives for Libraries and Related Institutions* (pp. 335–346). IGI Global. https://doi.org/10.4018/978-1-7998-0043-9.ch017

Chigwada, J. P. (2021). Research Data Management Services in Tertiary Institutions in Zimbabwe. In B. Holland (Eds.), *Handbook of Research on Knowledge and Organization Systems in Library and Information Science* (pp. 419-437). IGI Global. https://doi.org/10.4018/978-1-7998-7258-0.ch022

Chigwada, J. P., & Maturure, R. (2019). Advocating for Library and Information Services by National Library Associations of Africa in the Context of Sustainable Development Goals. In P. Ngulube (Ed.), *Handbook of Research on Advocacy, Promotion, and Public Programming for Memory Institutions* (pp. 219–237). IGI Global. doi:10.4018/978-1-5225-7429-3.ch012

Chiparausha, B., & Chigwada, J. P. (2019). Promoting Library Services in a Digital Environment in Zimbabwe. In P. Ngulube (Ed.), *Handbook of Research on Advocacy, Promotion, and Public Programming for Memory Institutions* (pp. 284–296). IGI Global. https://doi.org/10.4018/978-1-5225-7429-3.ch015

Chisita, C. T., & Chinyemba, F. (2017). Utilising ICTs for Resource Sharing Initiatives in Academic Institutions in Zimbabwe: Towards a New Trajectory. In B. Gunjal (Ed.), *Managing Knowledge and Scholarly Assets in Academic Libraries* (pp. 174–187). Hershey, PA: IGI Global. doi:10.4018/978-1-5225-1741-2.ch008

Chu, S., Tu, S., Wang, N., & Zhang, W. (2020). Information Equity and Cultural Sharing: The Service for Migrant Workers in Hangzhou Public Library. *International Journal of Library and Information Services*, 9(1), 10–24. https://doi.org/10.4018/IJLIS.2020010102

Clarance, M. M., & Angeline, X. M. (2019). User Opinion on Library Collections and Services: A Case Study of Branch Library in Karaikudi. In S. Thanuskodi (Ed.), *Literacy Skill Development for Library Science Professionals* (pp. 343–375). IGI Global. https://doi.org/10.4018/978-1-5225-7125-4.ch015

Costello, L., & Fazal, S. (2018). Developing Unique Study Room Reservation Systems: Examples From Teachers College and Stony Brook University. In L. Costello & M. Powers (Eds.), *Developing In-House Digital Tools in Library Spaces* (pp. 168–176). Hershey, PA: IGI Global. doi:10.4018/978-1-5225-2676-6.ch008

Cui, Y. (2017). Research Data Management: Models, Challenges, and Actions. In L. Ruan, Q. Zhu, & Y. Ye (Eds.), *Academic Library Development and Administration in China* (pp. 184–195). Hershey, PA: IGI Global. doi:10.4018/978-1-5225-0550-1.ch011

Dhamdhere, S. N., De Smet, E., & Lihitkar, R. (2017). Web-Based Bibliographic Services Offered by Top World and Indian University Libraries: A Comparative Study. *International Journal of Library and Information Services*, 6(1), 53–72. doi:10.4018/IJLIS.2017010104

Eiriemiokhale, K. A. (2018). Copyright Issues in a Digital Library Environment. In A. Tella & T. Kwanya (Eds.), *Handbook of Research on Managing Intellectual Property in Digital Libraries* (pp. 142–164). Hershey, PA: IGI Global. doi:10.4018/978-1-5225-3093-0.ch008

El Mimouni, H., Anderson, J., Tempelman-Kluit, N. F., & Dolan-Mescal, A. (2018). UX Work in Libraries: How (and Why) to Do It. In L. Costello & M. Powers (Eds.), *Developing In-House Digital Tools in Library Spaces* (pp. 1–36). Hershey, PA: IGI Global. doi:10.4018/978-1-5225-2676-6.ch001

Emiri, O. T. (2017). Digital Literacy Skills Among Librarians in University Libraries In the 21st Century in Edo And Delta States, Nigeria. *International Journal of Library and Information Services*, 6(1), 37–52. doi:10.4018/IJLIS.2017010103

Emmelhainz, C. (2020). Educating the Central Asian Librarian: Considering the International MLIS in Kazakhstan. In R. Alenzuela, H. Kim, & D. Baylen (Eds.), *Internationalization of Library and Information Science Education in the Asia-Pacific Region* (pp. 1–32). IGI Global. https://doi.org/10.4018/978-1-7998-2273-8.ch001

Esguerra, A. C. (2020). Library Education and Librarianship in Japan and the Philippines. In R. Alenzuela, H. Kim, & D. Baylen (Eds.), *Internationalization of Library and Information Science Education in the Asia-Pacific Region* (pp. 131–157). IGI Global. https://doi.org/10.4018/978-1-7998-2273-8.ch006

Esposito, T. (2018). Exploring Opportunities in Health Science Information Instructional Outreach: A Case Study Highlighting One Academic Library's Experience. In S. Bhattacharyya & K. Patnaik (Eds.), *Changing the Scope of Library Instruction in the Digital Age* (pp. 118–135). Hershey, PA: IGI Global. doi:10.4018/978-1-5225-2802-9.ch005

Fagbola, O. O., Smart, A. E., & Oluwaseun, B. O. (2020). Application of Cloud Computing Technologies in Academic Library Management: The National Open University of Nigeria Library in Perspective. In A. Tella (Ed.), *Handbook of Research on Digital Devices for Inclusivity and Engagement in Libraries* (pp. 135–159). IGI Global. https://doi.org/10.4018/978-1-5225-9034-7.ch007

Fan, Y., Zhang, X., & Li, G. (2017). Research Initiatives and Projects in Academic Libraries. In L. Ruan, Q. Zhu, & Y. Ye (Eds.), *Academic Library Development and Administration in China* (pp. 230–252). Hershey, PA: IGI Global. doi:10.4018/978-1-5225-0550-1.ch014

Farmer, L. S. (2017). ICT Literacy Integration: Issues and Sample Efforts. In J. Keengwe & P. Bull (Eds.), *Handbook of Research on Transformative Digital Content and Learning Technologies* (pp. 59–80). Hershey, PA: IGI Global. doi:10.4018/978-1-5225-2000-9.ch004

Farmer, L. S. (2017). Data Analytics for Strategic Management: Getting the Right Data. In V. Wang (Ed.), *Encyclopedia of Strategic Leadership and Management* (pp. 810–822). Hershey, PA: IGI Global. doi:10.4018/978-1-5225-1049-9.ch056

Farmer, L. S. (2017). Managing Portable Technologies for Special Education. In V. Wang (Ed.), *Encyclopedia of Strategic Leadership and Management* (pp. 977–987). Hershey, PA: IGI Global. doi:10.4018/978-1-5225-1049-9.ch068

Fujishima, D., & Kamada, T. (2017). Collective Relocation for Associative Distributed Collections of Objects. *International Journal of Software Innovation*, 5(2), 55–69. doi:10.4018/IJSI.2017040104

Ghani, S. R. (2017). Ontology: Advancing Flawless Library Services. In T. Ashraf & N. Kumar (Eds.), *Interdisciplinary Digital Preservation Tools and Technologies* (pp. 79–102). Hershey, PA: IGI Global. doi:10.4018/978-1-5225-1653-8.ch005

Gu, J. (2017). Library Buildings on New Campuses. In L. Ruan, Q. Zhu, & Y. Ye (Eds.), *Academic Library Development and Administration in China* (pp. 110–124). Hershey, PA: IGI Global. doi:10.4018/978-1-5225-0550-1.ch007

Guan, Z., & Wang, J. (2017). The China Academic Social Sciences and Humanities Library (CASHL). In L. Ruan, Q. Zhu, & Y. Ye (Eds.), *Academic Library Development and Administration in China* (pp. 31–54). Hershey, PA: IGI Global. doi:10.4018/978-1-5225-0550-1.ch003

Gul, S., & Shueb, S. (2018). Confronting/Managing the Crisis of Indian Libraries: E-Consortia Initiatives in India - A Way Forward. In R. Bhardwaj (Ed.), *Digitizing the Modern Library and the Transition From Print to Electronic* (pp. 129–163). Hershey, PA: IGI Global. doi:10.4018/978-1-5225-2119-8.ch006

Gunjal, B. (2017). Managing Knowledge and Scholarly Assets in Academic Libraries: Issues and Challenges. In B. Gunjal (Ed.), *Managing Knowledge and Scholarly Assets in Academic Libraries* (pp. 270–279). Hershey, PA: IGI Global. doi:10.4018/978-1-5225-1741-2.ch013

Guo, J., Zhang, H., & Zong, Y. (2017). Leadership Development and Career Planning. In L. Ruan, Q. Zhu, & Y. Ye (Eds.), *Academic Library Development and Administration in China* (pp. 264–279). Hershey, PA: IGI Global. doi:10.4018/978-1-5225-0550-1.ch016

Hahn, J. (2020). Student Engagement and Smart Spaces: Library Browsing and Internet of Things Technology. In B. Holland (Eds.), *Emerging Trends and Impacts of the Internet of Things in Libraries* (pp. 52-70). IGI Global. https://doi.org/10.4018/978-1-7998-4742-7.ch003

Halder, D. (2020). A Transitional Shift From Traditional Library to Digital Library. In A. Kaushik, A. Kumar, & P. Biswas (Eds.), *Handbook of Research on Emerging Trends and Technologies in Library and Information Science* (pp. 147–155). IGI Global. https://doi.org/10.4018/978-1-5225-9825-1.ch011

Hallis, R. (2018). Leveraging Library Instruction in a Digital Age. In S. Bhattacharyya & K. Patnaik (Eds.), *Changing the Scope of Library Instruction in the Digital Age* (pp. 1–23). Hershey, PA: IGI Global. doi:10.4018/978-1-5225-2802-9.ch001

Halupa, C. (2022). An Introduction to Survey Research. In A. Zimmerman (Ed.), *Methodological Innovations in Research and Academic Writing* (pp. 41–62). IGI Global. https://doi.org/10.4018/978-1-7998-8283-1.ch003

Hartsock, R., & Alemneh, D. G. (2018). Electronic Theses and Dissertations (ETDs). In M. Khosrow-Pour, D.B.A. (Ed.), Encyclopedia of Information Science and Technology, Fourth Edition (pp. 6748-6755). Hershey, PA: IGI Global. https://doi.org/ doi:10.4018/978-1-5225-2255-3.ch584

Haugh, D. (2018). Mobile Applications for Libraries. In L. Costello & M. Powers (Eds.), *Developing In-House Digital Tools in Library Spaces* (pp. 76–90). Hershey, PA: IGI Global. doi:10.4018/978-1-5225-2676-6.ch004

Hayes, C. (2022). Methodology and Method in Case Study Research: Framing Research Design in Practice. In S. Watson, S. Austin, & J. Bell (Eds.), *Conceptual Analyses of Curriculum Inquiry Methodologies* (pp. 138-154). IGI Global. https://doi.org/10.4018/978-1-7998-8848-2.ch007

Hayes, C., & Graham, Y. N. (2022). Phenomenology: Conceptually Framing Phenomenological Research Design and Methodology. In S. Watson, S. Austin, & J. Bell (Eds.), *Conceptual Analyses of Curriculum Inquiry Methodologies* (pp. 28-50). IGI Global. https://doi.org/10.4018/978-1-7998-8848-2.ch002

Hill, V. (2017). Digital Citizens as Writers: New Literacies and New Responsibilities. In E. Monske & K. Blair (Eds.), *Handbook of Research on Writing and Composing in the Age of MOOCs* (pp. 56–74). Hershey, PA: IGI Global. doi:10.4018/978-1-5225-1718-4.ch004

Hoh, A. (2019). Expanding the Awareness and Use of Library Collections Through Social Media: A Case Study of the Library of Congress International Collections Social Media Program. In J. Joe & E. Knight (Eds.), *Social Media for Communication and Instruction in Academic Libraries* (pp. 212–236). IGI Global. doi:10.4018/978-1-5225-8097-3.ch013

Holland, B. (2020). Emerging Technology and Today's Libraries. In B. Holland (Eds.), *Emerging Trends and Impacts of the Internet of Things in Libraries* (pp. 1-33). IGI Global. https://doi.org/10.4018/978-1-7998-4742-7.ch001

Homza, A., & Fontno, T. J. (2021). Supporting Teacher Candidates as Social Justice Change-Makers: A Faculty-Librarian Collaboration for Building and Using Diverse Youth Collections. In D. Hartsfield (Ed.), *Handbook of Research on Teaching Diverse Youth Literature to Pre-Service Professionals* (pp. 398–421). IGI Global. https://doi.org/10.4018/978-1-7998-7375-4.ch020

Horne-Popp, L. M., Tessone, E. B., & Welker, J. (2018). If You Build It, They Will Come: Creating a Library Statistics Dashboard for Decision-Making. In L. Costello & M. Powers (Eds.), *Developing In-House Digital Tools in Library Spaces* (pp. 177–203). Hershey, PA: IGI Global. doi:10.4018/978-1-5225-2676-6.ch009

Huang, C., & Xue, H. F. (2017). The China Academic Digital Associative Library (CADAL). In L. Ruan, Q. Zhu, & Y. Ye (Eds.), *Academic Library Development and Administration in China* (pp. 20–30). Hershey, PA: IGI Global. doi:10.4018/978-1-5225-0550-1.ch002

Huang, J., & Vedantham, A. (2019). Cabot Science Library: Creating Transformative Learning Environments in Library Spaces. In A. Darshan Singh, S. Raghunathan, E. Robeck, & B. Sharma (Eds.), *Cases on Smart Learning Environments* (pp. 284–298). IGI Global. doi:10.4018/978-1-5225-6136-1.ch016

Hunsaker, A. J., Majewski, N., & Rocke, L. E. (2018). Pulling Content out the Back Door: Creating an Interactive Digital Collections Experience. In L. Costello & M. Powers (Eds.), *Developing In-House Digital Tools in Library Spaces* (pp. 205–226). Hershey, PA: IGI Global. doi:10.4018/978-1-5225-2676-6.ch010

Hussain, A. (2020). Cutting Edge: Technology's Impact on Library Services. In J. Jesubright & P. Saravanan (Eds.), *Innovations in the Designing and Marketing of Information Services* (pp. 16–27). IGI Global. https://doi.org/10.4018/978-1-7998-1482-5.ch002

Idiegbeyan-ose, J., Owolabi, S. E., Ayooluwa, A., Foluke, O., Toluwani, E., & Sunday, O. (2019). Digital Library and Distance Learning in Developing Countries: Benefits and Challenges. In R. Bhardwaj & P. Banks (Eds.), *Research Data Access and Management in Modern Libraries* (pp. 220–245). IGI Global. https://doi.org/10.4018/978-1-5225-8437-7.ch011

Ifijeh, G., Adebayo, O., Izuagbe, R., & Olawoyin, O. (2018). Institutional Repositories and Libraries in Nigeria: Interrogating the Nexus. *Journal of Cases on Information Technology*, *20*(2), 16–29. doi:10.4018/JCIT.2018040102

Igbinovia, M. O., Solanke, E. O., & Obinyan, O. O. (2020). Building Influence: Strategising for Library Advocacy. In N. Osuigwe (Ed.), *Managing and Adapting Library Information Services for Future Users* (pp. 221–241). IGI Global. https://doi.org/10.4018/978-1-7998-1116-9.ch013

Iglesias, E. (2017). Insourcing and Outsourcing of Library Technology. In E. Iglesias (Ed.), *Library Technology Funding, Planning, and Deployment* (pp. 113–123). Hershey, PA: IGI Global. doi:10.4018/978-1-5225-1735-1.ch007

Ikolo, V. E. (2018). Transformational Leadership for Academic Libraries in Nigeria. In M. Khosrow-Pour, D.B.A. (Ed.), Encyclopedia of Information Science and Technology, Fourth Edition (pp. 5726-5735). Hershey, PA: IGI Global. doi:10.4018/978-1-5225-2255-3.ch497

Ikolo, V. E. (2020). Doctor's Awareness and Perception of Medical Library Resources and Services: A Case Study of Delta State University Teaching Hospital (Delsuth), Nigeria. *International Journal of Library and Information Services*, *9*(2), 58–71. https://doi.org/10.4018/IJLIS.2020070104

Joe, J. A. (2018). Changing Expectations of Academic Libraries. In M. Khosrow-Pour, D.B.A. (Ed.), Encyclopedia of Information Science and Technology, Fourth Edition (pp. 5204-5212). Hershey, PA: IGI Global. doi:10.4018/978-1-5225-2255-3.ch452

Juliana, I., Izuagbe, R., Itsekor, V., Fagbohun, M. O., Asaolu, A., & Nwokeoma, M. N. (2018). The Role of the School Library in Empowering Visually Impaired Children With Lifelong Information Literacy Skills. In P. Epler (Ed.), *Instructional Strategies in General Education and Putting the Individuals With Disabilities Act (IDEA) Into Practice* (pp. 245–271). Hershey, PA: IGI Global. doi:10.4018/978-1-5225-3111-1.ch009

Kalu, C. O., Chidi-Kalu, E. I., & Mafe, T. A. (2021). Research Data Management in an Academic Library. In J. Chigwada & G. Tsvuura (Eds.), *Handbook of Research on Information and Records Management in the Fourth Industrial Revolution* (pp. 38–55). IGI Global. https://doi.org/10.4018/978-1-7998-7740-0.ch003

Kalusopa, T. (2018). Preservation and Access to Digital Materials: Strategic Policy Options for Africa. In P. Ngulube (Ed.), *Handbook of Research on Heritage Management and Preservation* (pp. 150–174). Hershey, PA: IGI Global. doi:10.4018/978-1-5225-3137-1.ch008

Kamau, G. W. (2018). Copyright Challenges in Digital Libraries in Kenya From the Lens of a Librarian. In A. Tella & T. Kwanya (Eds.), *Handbook of Research on Managing Intellectual Property in Digital Libraries* (pp. 312–336). Hershey, PA: IGI Global. doi:10.4018/978-1-5225-3093-0.ch016

Karagöz, E., Güney, L. Ö., & Baran, B. (2022). The Collaborative Digital Content Library Fostering Faculty Members' Collaboratively Building Learning Sources. In G. Durak & S. Çankaya (Eds.), *Handbook of Research on Managing and Designing Online Courses in Synchronous and Asynchronous Environments* (pp. 196–213). IGI Global. doi:10.4018/978-1-7998-8701-0.ch010

Karmakar, R. (2018). Development and Management of Digital Libraries in the Regime of IPR Paradigm. *International Journal of Library and Information Services*, 7(1), 44–57. doi:10.4018/IJLIS.2018010104

Kasemsap, K. (2017). Mastering Knowledge Management in Academic Libraries. In B. Gunjal (Ed.), *Managing Knowledge and Scholarly Assets in Academic Libraries* (pp. 27–55). Hershey, PA: IGI Global. doi:10.4018/978-1-5225-1741-2.ch002

Kehinde, A. (2018). Digital Libraries and the Role of Digital Librarians. In A. Tella & T. Kwanya (Eds.), *Handbook of Research on Managing Intellectual Property in Digital Libraries* (pp. 98–119). Hershey, PA: IGI Global. doi:10.4018/978-1-5225-3093-0.ch006

Kenausis, V., & Herman, D. (2017). Don't Make Us Use the "Get Along Shirt": Communication and Consensus Building in an RFP Process. In E. Iglesias (Ed.), *Library Technology Funding, Planning, and Deployment* (pp. 1–22). Hershey, PA: IGI Global. doi:10.4018/978-1-5225-1735-1.ch001

Kohl, L. E., Lombardi, P., & Moroney, M. (2017). Moving from Local to Global via the Integrated Library System: Cost-Savings, ILS Management, Teams, and End-Users. In E. Iglesias (Ed.), *Library Technology Funding, Planning, and Deployment* (pp. 23–35). Hershey, PA: IGI Global. doi:10.4018/978-1-5225-1735-1.ch002

Kowalsky, M. (2020). School Librarian Experiences of Learning Management Implementation. In A. Tella (Ed.), *Handbook of Research on Digital Devices for Inclusivity and Engagement in Libraries* (pp. 160–184). IGI Global. https://doi.org/10.4018/978-1-5225-9034-7.ch008

Kumar, K. (2018). Library in Your Pocket Delivery of Instruction Service Through Library Mobile Apps: A World in Your Pocket. In S. Bhattacharyya & K. Patnaik (Eds.), *Changing the Scope of Library Instruction in the Digital Age* (pp. 228–249). Hershey, PA: IGI Global. doi:10.4018/978-1-5225-2802-9.ch009

Kwanya, T. (2018). Social Bookmarking in Digital Libraries: Intellectual Property Rights Implications. In A. Tella & T. Kwanya (Eds.), *Handbook of Research on Managing Intellectual Property in Digital Libraries* (pp. 1–18). Hershey, PA: IGI Global. doi:10.4018/978-1-5225-3093-0.ch001

Lapo, P., Makhmudov, G., & Rakhmatullaev, M. (2020). Internationalization of Library and Information Science Education in Tajikistan and Uzbekistan: Implications in Central Asia. In R. Alenzuela, H. Kim, & D. Baylen (Eds.), *Internationalization of Library and Information Science Education in the Asia-Pacific Region* (pp. 225–245). IGI Global. https://doi.org/10.4018/978-1-7998-2273-8.ch010

Lewis, J. K. (2018). Change Leadership Styles and Behaviors in Academic Libraries. In M. Khosrow-Pour, D.B.A. (Ed.), Encyclopedia of Information Science and Technology, Fourth Edition (pp. 5194-5203). Hershey, PA: IGI Global. doi:10.4018/978-1-5225-2255-3.ch451

Lillard, L. L. (2018). Is Interdisciplinary Collaboration in Academia an Elusive Dream?: Can the Institutional Barriers Be Broken Down? A Review of the Literature and the Case of Library Science. In M. Al-Suqri, A. Al-Kindi, S. AlKindi, & N. Saleem (Eds.), *Promoting Interdisciplinarity in Knowledge Generation and Problem Solving* (pp. 139–147). Hershey, PA: IGI Global. doi:10.4018/978-1-5225-3878-3.ch010

Liu, C., Dou, T., Zhou, H., Zhang, B., & Zhang, C. (2021). Library Service Innovation Based on New Information Technology: Taking the Interactive Experience Space "Tsinghua Impression" as an Example. *International Journal of Library and Information Services*, *10*(1), 71–81. https://doi.org/10.4018/IJLIS.2021010106

Long, X., & Yao, B. (2017). The Construction and Development of the Academic Digital Library of Chinese Ancient Collections. In L. Ruan, Q. Zhu, & Y. Ye (Eds.), *Academic Library Development and Administration in China* (pp. 126–135). Hershey, PA: IGI Global. doi:10.4018/978-1-5225-0550-1.ch008

Long, X., & Yao, B. (2020). The Construction and Development of the Academic Digital Library of Chinese Ancient Collections. In I. Management Association (Ed.), *Digital Libraries and Institutional Repositories: Breakthroughs in Research and Practice* (pp. 78-87). IGI Global. https://doi.org/10.4018/978-1-7998-2463-3.ch006

Lowe, M., & Reno, L. M. (2018). Academic Librarianship and Burnout. In *Examining the Emotional Dimensions of Academic Librarianship: Emerging Research and Opportunities* (pp. 72–89). Hershey, PA: IGI Global. doi:10.4018/978-1-5225-3761-8.ch005

Lowe, M., & Reno, L. M. (2018). Emotional Dimensions of Academic Librarianship. In *Examining the Emotional Dimensions of Academic Librarianship: Emerging Research and Opportunities* (pp. 54–71). Hershey, PA: IGI Global. doi:10.4018/978-1-5225-3761-8.ch004

Lowe, M., & Reno, L. M. (2018). Why Isn't This Being Studied? In *Examining the Emotional Dimensions of Academic Librarianship: Emerging Research and Opportunities* (pp. 90–108). Hershey, PA: IGI Global. doi:10.4018/978-1-5225-3761-8.ch006

Lowe, M., & Reno, L. M. (2018). Research Agenda: Research Ideas and Recommendations. In *Examining the Emotional Dimensions of Academic Librarianship: Emerging Research and Opportunities* (pp. 109–125). Hershey, PA: IGI Global. doi:10.4018/978-1-5225-3761-8.ch007

Luyombya, D., Kiyingi, G. W., & Naluwooza, M. (2018). The Nature and Utilisation of Archival Records Deposited in Makerere University Library, Uganda. In P. Ngulube (Ed.), *Handbook of Research on Heritage Management and Preservation* (pp. 96–113). Hershey, PA: IGI Global. doi:10.4018/978-1-5225-3137-1.ch005

Ma, W. Y. (2022). Supporting Indigenous Education From a Distance: Adjusting Strategies to Maintain Access to a Rare Library Collection During a Global Crisis. In P. Pangelinan & T. McVey (Eds.), *Learning and Reconciliation Through Indigenous Education in Oceania* (pp. 197–209). IGI Global. https://doi.org/10.4018/978-1-7998-7736-3.ch012

Mabe, M., & Ashley, E. A. (2017). The Natural Role of the Public Library. In *The Developing Role of Public Libraries in Emergency Management: Emerging Research and Opportunities* (pp. 25–43). Hershey, PA: IGI Global. doi:10.4018/978-1-5225-2196-9.ch003

Mabe, M., & Ashley, E. A. (2017). I'm Trained, Now What? In *The Developing Role of Public Libraries in Emergency Management: Emerging Research and Opportunities* (pp. 87–95). Hershey, PA: IGI Global. doi:10.4018/978-1-5225-2196-9.ch007

Mabe, M., & Ashley, E. A. (2017). Emergency Preparation for the Library and Librarian. In *The Developing Role of Public Libraries in Emergency Management: Emerging Research and Opportunities* (pp. 61–78). Hershey, PA: IGI Global. doi:10.4018/978-1-5225-2196-9.ch005

Mabe, M., & Ashley, E. A. (2017). The CCPL Model. In *The Developing Role of Public Libraries in Emergency Management: Emerging Research and Opportunities* (pp. 15–24). Hershey, PA: IGI Global. doi:10.4018/978-1-5225-2196-9.ch002

Mabe, M., & Ashley, E. A. (2017). The Local Command Structure and How the Library Fits. In *In The Developing Role of Public Libraries in Emergency Management: Emerging Research and Opportunities* (pp. 44–60). Hershey, PA: IGI Global. doi:10.4018/978-1-5225-2196-9.ch004

Mafube, M. A., & Keakopa, S. M. (2019). Customer Services at the Library Archives of the National University of Lesotho. In P. Ngulube (Ed.), *Handbook of Research on Advocacy, Promotion, and Public Programming for Memory Institutions* (pp. 62–76). IGI Global. doi:10.4018/978-1-5225-7429-3.ch004

Majumdar, S. (2022). Community Engagement Through Extension and Outreach Activities: Scope of a College Library. In M. Taher (Ed.), *Handbook of Research on the Role of Libraries, Archives, and Museums in Achieving Civic Engagement and Social Justice in Smart Cities* (pp. 121–138). IGI Global. https://doi.org/10.4018/978-1-7998-8363-0.ch006

Mangone, E. (2022). The Difficult Joining of Theory and Empirical Research: Strengths and Weaknesses of Digital Research Methods. In G. Punziano & A. Delli Paoli (Eds.), *Handbook of Research on Advanced Research Methodologies for a Digital Society* (pp. 11–23). IGI Global. https://doi.org/10.4018/978-1-7998-8473-6.ch002

Manzoor, A. (2018). Social Media: A Librarian's Tool for Instant and Direct Interaction With Library Users. In R. Bhardwaj (Ed.), *Digitizing the Modern Library and the Transition From Print to Electronic* (pp. 112–128). Hershey, PA: IGI Global. doi:10.4018/978-1-5225-2119-8.ch005

Maringanti, H. (2018). A Decision Making Paradigm for Software Development in Libraries. In L. Costello & M. Powers (Eds.), *Developing In-House Digital Tools in Library Spaces* (pp. 59–75). Hershey, PA: IGI Global. doi:10.4018/978-1-5225-2676-6.ch003

Markman, K. M., Ferrarini, M., & Deschenes, A. H. (2018). User Testing and Iterative Design in the Academic Library: A Case Study. In R. Roscoe, S. Craig, & I. Douglas (Eds.), *End-User Considerations in Educational Technology Design* (pp. 160–183). Hershey, PA: IGI Global. doi:10.4018/978-1-5225-2639-1.ch008

Marrazzo, F. (2022). Doing Research With Online Platforms: An Emerging Issue Network. In G. Punziano & A. Delli Paoli (Eds.), *Handbook of Research on Advanced Research Methodologies for a Digital Society* (pp. 65–86). IGI Global. https://doi.org/10.4018/978-1-7998-8473-6.ch006

Mertens, D. (2022). Designing Mixed Methods Studies to Contribute to Social, Economic, and Environmental Justice: Implications for Library and Information Sciences. In P. Ngulube (Ed.), *Handbook of Research on Mixed Methods Research in Information Science* (pp. 173–189). IGI Global. https://doi.org/10.4018/978-1-7998-8844-4.ch009

Moahi, K. H. (2020). The Research Process and Indigenous Epistemologies. In P. Ngulube (Ed.), *Handbook of Research on Connecting Research Methods for Information Science Research* (pp. 245–265). IGI Global. https://doi.org/10.4018/978-1-7998-1471-9.ch013

Mohapatra, N. (2021). Webrarian: A Librarian on the Web. In C. Chisita, R. Enakrire, O. Durodolu, V. Tsabedze, & J. Ngoaketsi (Eds.), *Handbook of Research on Records and Information Management Strategies for Enhanced Knowledge Coordination* (pp. 458–470). IGI Global. https://doi.org/10.4018/978-1-7998-6618-3.ch027

Munatsi, R. (2020). National Research and Knowledge Systems: Role of Libraries. In C. Chisita (Ed.), *Cooperation and Collaboration Initiatives for Libraries and Related Institutions* (pp. 273–293). IGI Global. https://doi.org/10.4018/978-1-7998-0043-9.ch014

Musimbi, W. L., & Mutuku, P. K. (2019). The Future of LIS and Media Training in the Global Era: Challenges and Prospects. In C. Chisita & A. Rusero (Eds.), *Exploring the Relationship Between Media, Libraries, and Archives* (pp. 82–101). IGI Global. doi:10.4018/978-1-5225-5840-8.ch006

Mwanzu, A. (2019). Economics of Resource Sharing via Library Consortia. In C. Chisita & A. Rusero (Eds.), *Exploring the Relationship Between Media, Libraries, and Archives* (pp. 19–34). IGI Global. https://doi.org/10.4018/978-1-5225-5840-8.ch002

Na, L. (2017). Library and Information Science Education and Graduate Programs in Academic Libraries. In L. Ruan, Q. Zhu, & Y. Ye (Eds.), *Academic Library Development and Administration in China* (pp. 218–229). Hershey, PA: IGI Global. doi:10.4018/978-1-5225-0550-1.ch013

Nagarkar, S. P. (2017). Biomedical Librarianship in the Post-Genomic Era. In S. Ram (Ed.), *Library and Information Services for Bioinformatics Education and Research* (pp. 1–17). Hershey, PA: IGI Global. doi:10.4018/978-1-5225-1871-6.ch001

Natarajan, M. (2017). Exploring Knowledge Sharing over Social Media. In R. Chugh (Ed.), *Harnessing Social Media as a Knowledge Management Tool* (pp. 55–73). Hershey, PA: IGI Global. doi:10.4018/978-1-5225-0495-5.ch003

Nazir, T. (2017). Preservation Initiatives in E-Environment to Protect Information Assets. In T. Ashraf & N. Kumar (Eds.), *Interdisciplinary Digital Preservation Tools and Technologies* (pp. 193–208). Hershey, PA: IGI Global. doi:10.4018/978-1-5225-1653-8.ch010

Ngulube, P. (2017). Embedding Indigenous Knowledge in Library and Information Science Education in Anglophone Eastern and Southern Africa. In P. Ngulube (Ed.), *Handbook of Research on Social, Cultural, and Educational Considerations of Indigenous Knowledge in Developing Countries* (pp. 92–115). Hershey, PA: IGI Global. doi:10.4018/978-1-5225-0838-0.ch006

Ngulube, P. (2022). Using Simple and Complex Mixed Methods Research Designs to Understand Research in Information Science. In P. Ngulube (Ed.), *Handbook of Research on Mixed Methods Research in Information Science* (pp. 20–46). IGI Global. doi:10.4018/978-1-7998-8844-4.ch002

Nicolajsen, H. W., Sorensen, F., & Scupola, A. (2018). User Involvement in Service Innovation Processes. In M. Khosrow-Pour (Ed.), *Optimizing Current Practices in E-Services and Mobile Applications* (pp. 42–61). Hershey, PA: IGI Global. doi:10.4018/978-1-5225-5026-6.ch003

Ocholla, D. N. (2022). A Research Dashboard for Aligning Research Components in Research Proposals, Theses, and Dissertations in Library and Information Science. In P. Ngulube (Ed.), *Handbook of Research on Mixed Methods Research in Information Science* (pp. 629–640). IGI Global. https://doi.org/10.4018/978-1-7998-8844-4.ch029

Ochonogor, W. C., & Okite-Amughoro, F. A. (2018). Building an Effective Digital Library in a University Teaching Hospital (UTH) in Nigeria. In A. Tella & T. Kwanya (Eds.), *Handbook of Research on Managing Intellectual Property in Digital Libraries* (pp. 184–204). Hershey, PA: IGI Global. doi:10.4018/978-1-5225-3093-0.ch010

Okada, D. (2020). 10,000 Newly Certified Librarians, 100 Secure Jobs. In R. Alenzuela, H. Kim, & D. Baylen (Eds.), *Internationalization of Library and Information Science Education in the Asia-Pacific Region* (pp. 78–101). IGI Global. https://doi.org/10.4018/978-1-7998-2273-8.ch004

Oladapo, Y. O. (2018). Open Access to Knowledge and Challenges in Digital Libraries. In A. Tella & T. Kwanya (Eds.), *Handbook of Research on Managing Intellectual Property in Digital Libraries* (pp. 260–291). Hershey, PA: IGI Global. doi:10.4018/978-1-5225-3093-0.ch014

Oladokun, O., & Zulu, S. F. (2017). Document Description and Coding as Key Elements in Knowledge, Records, and Information Management. In P. Jain & N. Mnjama (Eds.), *Managing Knowledge Resources and Records in Modern Organizations* (pp. 179–197). Hershey, PA: IGI Global. doi:10.4018/978-1-5225-1965-2.ch011

Olubodun, O. J., & Oye, P. O. (2019). Library: A Tool for Information Dissemination and Creating Awareness in Conflict-Induced Situations. In E. Nyam & F. Idoko (Eds.), *Examining the Social and Economic Impacts of Conflict-Induced Migration* (pp. 55–63). IGI Global. https://doi.org/10.4018/978-1-5225-7615-0.ch003

Omeluzor, S. U., Abayomi, I., & Gbemi-Ogunleye, P. (2018). Contemporary Media for Library Users' Instruction in Academic Libraries in South-West Nigeria: Contemporary Library Instruction in the Digital Age. In S. Bhattacharyya & K. Patnaik (Eds.), *Changing the Scope of Library Instruction in the Digital Age* (pp. 162–185). Hershey, PA: IGI Global. doi:10.4018/978-1-5225-2802-9.ch007

Onwuchekwa, E. O. (2020). Library Signage and Information Graphics: A Communication Tool for Library Users. In A. Tella (Ed.), *Handbook of Research on Digital Devices for Inclusivity and Engagement in Libraries* (pp. 231–237). IGI Global. https://doi.org/10.4018/978-1-5225-9034-7.ch011

Onyancha, O. B. (2020). Informetrics Research Methods Outlined. In P. Ngulube (Ed.), *Handbook of Research on Connecting Research Methods for Information Science Research* (pp. 320–348). IGI Global. https://doi.org/10.4018/978-1-7998-1471-9.ch017

Oshilalu, A. H., & Ogochukwu, E. T. (2017). Modeling a Software for Library and Information Centers. *International Journal of Library and Information Services*, 6(2), 1–10. doi:10.4018/IJLIS.2017070101

Oswal, S. K. (2017). Institutional, Legal, and Attitudinal Barriers to the Accessibility of University Digital Libraries: Implications for Retention of Disabled Students. In H. Alphin Jr, J. Lavine, & R. Chan (Eds.), *Disability and Equity in Higher Education Accessibility* (pp. 223–241). Hershey, PA: IGI Global. doi:10.4018/978-1-5225-2665-0.ch010

Oukrich, J., & Bouikhalene, B. (2017). A Survey of Users' Satisfaction in the University Library by Using a Pareto Analysis and the Automatic Classification Methods. *International Journal of Library and Information Services*, 6(1), 17–36. doi:10.4018/IJLIS.2017010102

Oyelude, A. A., & Oluwaniyi, S. A. (2020). Managing Future Library Services for the Medical Sciences: A Pharmacy Library Experience. In N. Osuigwe (Ed.), *Managing and Adapting Library Information Services for Future Users* (pp. 200–220). IGI Global. https://doi.org/10.4018/978-1-7998-1116-9.ch012

Özel, N. (2018). Developing Visual Literacy Skills Through Library Instructions. In V. Osinska & G. Osinski (Eds.), *Information Visualization Techniques in the Social Sciences and Humanities* (pp. 32–48). Hershey, PA: IGI Global. doi:10.4018/978-1-5225-4990-1.ch003

Paganelli, A. L., & Paganelli, A. L. (2021). Blockchain and the Research Libraries: Expanding Interlibrary Loan and Protecting Privacy. In D. Gunter (Ed.), *Transforming Scholarly Publishing With Blockchain Technologies and AI* (pp. 232–250). IGI Global. https://doi.org/10.4018/978-1-7998-5589-7.ch012

Patel, D., & Thakur, D. (2017). Managing Open Access (OA) Scholarly Information Resources in a University. In A. Munigal (Ed.), *Scholarly Communication and the Publish or Perish Pressures of Academia* (pp. 224–255). Hershey, PA: IGI Global. doi:10.4018/978-1-5225-1697-2.ch011

Patnaik, K. R. (2018). Crafting a Framework for Copyright Literacy and Licensed Content: A Case Study at an Advanced Management Education and Research Library. In S. Bhattacharyya & K. Patnaik (Eds.), *Changing the Scope of Library Instruction in the Digital Age* (pp. 136–160). Hershey, PA: IGI Global. doi:10.4018/978-1-5225-2802-9.ch006

Paynter, K. (2017). Elementary Library Media Specialists' Roles in the Implementation of the Common Core State Standards. In M. Grassetti & S. Brookby (Eds.), *Advancing Next-Generation Teacher Education through Digital Tools and Applications* (pp. 262–283). Hershey, PA: IGI Global. doi:10.4018/978-1-5225-0965-3.ch014

Perry, S. C., & Waggoner, J. (2018). Processes for User-Centered Design and Development: The Omeka Curator Dashboard Project. In L. Costello & M. Powers (Eds.), *Developing In-House Digital Tools in Library Spaces* (pp. 37–58). Hershey, PA: IGI Global. doi:10.4018/978-1-5225-2676-6.ch002

Perumalsamy, R., & Kannan, S. P. (2019). User Information Needs in the Public Libraries in India. In S. Thanuskodi (Ed.), *Literacy Skill Development for Library Science Professionals* (pp. 25–53). IGI Global. https://doi.org/10.4018/978-1-5225-7125-4.ch002

Phuritsabam, B., & Devi, A. B. (2017). Information Seeking Behavior of Medical Scientists at Jawaharlal Nehru Institute of Medical Science: A Study. In S. Ram (Ed.), *Library and Information Services for Bioinformatics Education and Research* (pp. 177–187). Hershey, PA: IGI Global. doi:10.4018/978-1-5225-1871-6.ch010

Quadri, R. F., & Sodiq, O. A. (2018). Managing Intellectual Property in Digital Libraries: The Roles of Digital Librarians. In A. Tella & T. Kwanya (Eds.), *Handbook of Research on Managing Intellectual Property in Digital Libraries* (pp. 337–355). Hershey, PA: IGI Global. doi:10.4018/978-1-5225-3093-0.ch017

Quintana, A. J. (2021). Ensuring Research Integrity. In K. Elufiede & C. Barker Stucky (Eds.), *Strategies and Tactics for Multidisciplinary Writing* (pp. 192–201). IGI Global. https://doi.org/10.4018/978-1-7998-4477-8.ch015

Qutab, S., Adil, S. A., Gardner, L. A., & Ullah, F. S. (2022). The Role of Libraries, Archives, and Museums for Metaliteracy in Smart Cities: Implications, Challenges, and Opportunities. In M. Taher (Ed.), *Handbook of Research on the Role of Libraries, Archives, and Museums in Achieving Civic Engagement and Social Justice in Smart Cities* (pp. 355–375). IGI Global. https://doi.org/10.4018/978-1-7998-8363-0.ch019

Raj, S. K., & De, K. (2020). Electronic Resource Management and Digitisation: Library System of the University of Calcutta. In A. Kaushik, A. Kumar, & P. Biswas (Eds.), *Handbook of Research on Emerging Trends and Technologies in Library and Information Science* (pp. 231–265). IGI Global. https://doi.org/10.4018/978-1-5225-9825-1.ch017

Ram, S. (2017). Library Services for Bioinformatics: Establishing Synergy Data Information and Knowledge. In S. Ram (Ed.), *Library and Information Services for Bioinformatics Education and Research* (pp. 18–33). Hershey, PA: IGI Global. doi:10.4018/978-1-5225-1871-6.ch002

Rao, M. (2017). Use of Institutional Repository for Information Dissemination and Knowledge Management. In B. Gunjal (Ed.), *Managing Knowledge and Scholarly Assets in Academic Libraries* (pp. 156–173). Hershey, PA: IGI Global. doi:10.4018/978-1-5225-1741-2.ch007

Rao, Y., & Zhang, Y. (2017). The Construction and Development of Academic Library Digital Special Subject Databases. In L. Ruan, Q. Zhu, & Y. Ye (Eds.), *Academic Library Development and Administration in China* (pp. 163–183). Hershey, PA: IGI Global. doi:10.4018/978-1-5225-0550-1.ch010

Rao, Y., & Zhang, Y. (2020). The Construction and Development of Academic Library Digital Special Subject Databases. In I. Management Association (Ed.), *Digital Libraries and Institutional Repositories: Breakthroughs in Research and Practice* (pp. 24-44). IGI Global. https://doi.org/10.4018/978-1-7998-2463-3.ch002

Razip, S. N., Kadir, S. F., Saim, S. N., Dolhan, F. N., Jarmil, N., Salleh, N. H., & Rajin, G. (2017). Predicting Users' Intention towards Using Library Self-Issue and Return Systems. In N. Suki (Ed.), *Handbook of Research on Leveraging Consumer Psychology for Effective Customer Engagement* (pp. 102–115). Hershey, PA: IGI Global. doi:10.4018/978-1-5225-0746-8.ch007

Rothwell, S. L. (2018). Librarians and Instructional Design Challenges: Concepts, Examples, and a Flexible Design Framework. In S. Bhattacharyya & K. Patnaik (Eds.), *Changing the Scope of Library Instruction in the Digital Age* (pp. 24–59). Hershey, PA: IGI Global. doi:10.4018/978-1-5225-2802-9.ch002

Roy, L., & Frydman, A. (2018). Community Outreach. In M. Khosrow-Pour, D.B.A. (Ed.), Encyclopedia of Information Science and Technology, Fourth Edition (pp. 6685-6694). Hershey, PA: IGI Global. doi:10.4018/978-1-5225-2255-3.ch579

Rutto, D., & Yudah, O. (2018). E-Books in University Libraries in Kenya: Trends, Usage, and Intellectual Property Issues. In A. Tella & T. Kwanya (Eds.), *Handbook of Research on Managing Intellectual Property in Digital Libraries* (pp. 120–141). Hershey, PA: IGI Global. doi:10.4018/978-1-5225-3093-0.ch007

Sabharwal, A. (2017). The Transformative Role of Institutional Repositories in Academic Knowledge Management. In B. Gunjal (Ed.), *Managing Knowledge and Scholarly Assets in Academic Libraries* (pp. 127–155). Hershey, PA: IGI Global. doi:10.4018/978-1-5225-1741-2.ch006

Sadiku, S. A., Kpakiko, M. M., & Tsafe, A. G. (2018). Institutional Digital Repository and the Challenges of Global Visibility in Nigeria. In A. Tella & T. Kwanya (Eds.), *Handbook of Research on Managing Intellectual Property in Digital Libraries* (pp. 356–376). Hershey, PA: IGI Global. doi:10.4018/978-1-5225-3093-0.ch018

Sahu, M. K. (2018). Web-Scale Discovery Service in Academic Library Environment: A Birds Eye View. *International Journal of Library and Information Services*, 7(1), 1–14. doi:10.4018/IJLIS.2018010101

Salim, F., Saigar, B., Armoham, P. K., Gobalakrishnan, S., Jap, M. Y., & Lim, N. A. (2017). Students' Information-Seeking Intention in Academic Digital Libraries. In N. Suki (Ed.), *Handbook of Research on Leveraging Consumer Psychology for Effective Customer Engagement* (pp. 259–273). Hershey, PA: IGI Global. doi:10.4018/978-1-5225-0746-8.ch017

Saroja, G. (2017). Changing Face of Scholarly Communication and Its Impact on Library and Information Centres. In A. Munigal (Ed.), *Scholarly Communication and the Publish or Perish Pressures of Academia* (pp. 100–117). Hershey, PA: IGI Global. doi:10.4018/978-1-5225-1697-2.ch006

Sauti, L. (2020). Social Media and Library Collaboration: Analysis of Government Libraries (Kaguvi Building). In C. Chisita (Ed.), *Cooperation and Collaboration Initiatives for Libraries and Related Institutions* (pp. 312–334). IGI Global. https://doi.org/10.4018/978-1-7998-0043-9.ch016

Schuster, D. W. (2017). Selection Process for Free Open Source Software. In E. Iglesias (Ed.), *Library Technology Funding, Planning, and Deployment* (pp. 55–71). Hershey, PA: IGI Global. doi:10.4018/978-1-5225-1735-1.ch004

Seagraves, K., & Weyand, L. (2021). From Bake-Alongs to Tech Talks: How One Public Library System Pivoted to Virtual Programming. In B. Holland (Ed.), *Handbook of Research on Library Response to the COVID-19 Pandemic* (pp. 447-480). IGI Global. https://doi.org/10.4018/978-1-7998-6449-3.ch023

Segaetsho, T. (2018). Environmental Consideration in the Preservation of Paper Materials in Heritage Institutions in the East and Southern African Region. In P. Ngulube (Ed.), *Handbook of Research on Heritage Management and Preservation* (pp. 183–212). Hershey, PA: IGI Global. doi:10.4018/978-1-5225-3137-1.ch010

Shakhsi, L. (2017). Cataloging Images in Library, Archive, and Museum. In T. Ashraf & N. Kumar (Eds.), *Interdisciplinary Digital Preservation Tools and Technologies* (pp. 119–141). Hershey, PA: IGI Global. doi:10.4018/978-1-5225-1653-8.ch007

Sharma, C. (2017). Digital Initiatives of the Indian Council of World Affairs' Library. In T. Ashraf & N. Kumar (Eds.), *Interdisciplinary Digital Preservation Tools and Technologies* (pp. 231–241). Hershey, PA: IGI Global. doi:10.4018/978-1-5225-1653-8.ch012

Shook, R. (2022). Achieving Balance Through Fundamentals of Digital Librarianship. In P. Pangelinan & T. McVey (Eds.), *Learning and Reconciliation Through Indigenous Education in Oceania* (pp. 185–196). IGI Global. https://doi.org/10.4018/978-1-7998-7736-3.ch011

Shukla, P., & Das, C. (2020). Plagiarism: The Role of Librarian and Teachers in Combating It. In J. Jesubright & P. Saravanan (Eds.), *Innovations in the Designing and Marketing of Information Services* (pp. 148–158). IGI Global. https://doi.org/10.4018/978-1-7998-1482-5.ch011

Siddaiah, D. K. (2018). Commonwealth Professional Fellowship: A Gateway for the Strategic Development of Libraries in India. In R. Bhardwaj (Ed.), *Digitizing the Modern Library and the Transition From Print to Electronic* (pp. 270–286). Hershey, PA: IGI Global. doi:10.4018/978-1-5225-2119-8.ch012

Silvana de Rosa, A. (2018). Mission, Tools, and Ongoing Developments in the So.Re.Com. "A.S. de Rosa" @-library. In M. Khosrow-Pour, D.B.A. (Ed.), Encyclopedia of Information Science and Technology, Fourth Edition (pp. 5237-5251). Hershey, PA: IGI Global. https://doi.org/ doi:10.4018/978-1-5225-2255-3.ch455

Smolenski, N., Kostic, M., & Sofronijevic, A. M. (2018). Intrapreneurship and Enterprise 2.0 as Grounds for Developing In-House Digital Tools for Handling METS/ALTO Files at the University Library Belgrade. In L. Costello & M. Powers (Eds.), *Developing In-House Digital Tools in Library Spaces* (pp. 92–116). Hershey, PA: IGI Global. doi:10.4018/978-1-5225-2676-6.ch005

Sochay, L., & Junus, R. (2017). From Summon to SearchPlus: The RFP Process for a Discovery Tool at the MSU Libraries. In E. Iglesias (Ed.), *Library Technology Funding, Planning, and Deployment* (pp. 72–98). Hershey, PA: IGI Global. doi:10.4018/978-1-5225-1735-1.ch005

Soliudeen, M. J. (2021). The Relevance of Feedback Mechanisms to Library Databases in Academic Libraries. In A. Maake, B. Maake, & F. Awuor (Eds.), *Digital Solutions and the Case for Africa's Sustainable Development* (pp. 116–130). IGI Global. doi:10.4018/978-1-7998-2967-6.ch008

Sonawane, C. S. (2018). Library Catalogue in the Internet Age. In R. Bhardwaj (Ed.), *Digitizing the Modern Library and the Transition From Print to Electronic* (pp. 204–223). Hershey, PA: IGI Global. doi:10.4018/978-1-5225-2119-8.ch009

Sorokhaibam, S. D., & Mathabela, N. N. (2017). Information Needs and Assessment of Bioinformatics Students at the University of Swaziland: Librarian View. In S. Ram (Ed.), *Library and Information Services for Bioinformatics Education and Research* (pp. 188–198). IGI Global. https://doi.org/10.4018/978-1-5225-1871-6.ch011

Staley, C., Kenyon, R. S., & Marcovitz, D. M. (2018). Embedded Services: Going Beyond the Field of Dreams Model for Online Programs. In D. Polly, M. Putman, T. Petty, & A. Good (Eds.), *Innovative Practices in Teacher Preparation and Graduate-Level Teacher Education Programs* (pp. 368–381). Hershey, PA: IGI Global. doi:10.4018/978-1-5225-3068-8.ch020

Stevenson, C. N. (2020). Data Speaks: Use of Poems and Photography in Qualitative Research. In M. Baran & J. Jones (Eds.), *Applied Social Science Approaches to Mixed Methods Research* (pp. 119–144). IGI Global. doi:10.4018/978-1-7998-1025-4.ch006

Stewart, M. C., Atilano, M., & Arnold, C. L. (2017). Improving Customer Relations with Social Listening: A Case Study of an American Academic Library. *International Journal of Customer Relationship Marketing and Management*, 8(1), 49–63. doi:10.4018/IJCRMM.2017010104

Sukula, S. K., & Bhardwaj, R. K. (2018). An Extensive Discussion on Transition of Libraries: The Panoramic View of Library Resources, Services, and Evolved Librarianship. In R. Bhardwaj (Ed.), *Digitizing the Modern Library and the Transition From Print to Electronic* (pp. 255–269). Hershey, PA: IGI Global. doi:10.4018/978-1-5225-2119-8.ch011

Surendran, B., & Kumar, K. (2020). Implementing Information Literacy Skills and Soft Skills for Better Use of Library Resources and Services. In S. Thanuskodi (Ed.), *Handbook of Research on Digital Content Management and Development in Modern Libraries* (pp. 214–224). IGI Global. doi:10.4018/978-1-7998-2201-1.ch012

Suresh, M., & Ravi, S. (2020). Online Database Use by Science Research Scholars of Alagappa University, Karaikudi: A Study. In S. Thanuskodi (Ed.), *Handbook of Research on Digital Content Management and Development in Modern Libraries* (pp. 86-102). IGI Global. https://doi.org/10.4018/978-1-7998-2201-1.ch006

Tella, A., & Babatunde, B. J. (2017). Determinants of Continuance Intention of Facebook Usage Among Library and Information Science Female Undergraduates in Selected Nigerian Universities. *International Journal of E-Adoption*, 9(2), 59–76. doi:10.4018/IJEA.2017070104

Tella, A., Okojie, V., & Olaniyi, O. T. (2018). Social Bookmarking Tools and Digital Libraries. In A. Tella & T. Kwanya (Eds.), *Handbook of Research on Managing Intellectual Property in Digital Libraries* (pp. 396–409). Hershey, PA: IGI Global. doi:10.4018/978-1-5225-3093-0.ch020

Thobane, M. S., & Jansen van Rensburg, S. K. (2022). Transforming Methods for Research With Indigenous Communities: An African Social Sciences Perspective. In P. Ngulube (Ed.), *Handbook of Research on Mixed Methods Research in Information Science* (pp. 190–203). IGI Global. doi:10.4018/978-1-7998-8844-4.ch010

Thull, J. J. (2018). Librarians and the Evolving Research Needs of Distance Students. In I. Oncioiu (Ed.), *Ethics and Decision-Making for Sustainable Business Practices* (pp. 203–216). Hershey, PA: IGI Global. doi:10.4018/978-1-5225-3773-1.ch012

Titilope, A. O. (2017). Ethical Issues in Library and Information Science Profession in Nigeria: An Appraisal. *International Journal of Library and Information Services*, 6(2), 11–22. doi:10.4018/IJLIS.2017070102

Tutu, J. M. (2018). Intellectual Property Challenges in Digital Library Environments. In A. Tella & T. Kwanya (Eds.), *Handbook of Research on Managing Intellectual Property in Digital Libraries* (pp. 225–240). Hershey, PA: IGI Global. doi:10.4018/978-1-5225-3093-0.ch012

Udo-Anyanwu, A. J., & Alor, A. R. (2020). Library Associations, Leadership, and Programmes: IFLA, AfLIA, and NLA. In N. Osuigwe (Ed.), *Managing and Adapting Library Information Services for Future Users* (pp. 89–102). IGI Global. https://doi.org/10.4018/978-1-7998-1116-9.ch006

Wallace, D., & Hemment, M. (2018). Enabling Scholarship in the Digital Age: A Case for Libraries Creating Value at HBS. In S. Bhattacharyya & K. Patnaik (Eds.), *Changing the Scope of Library Instruction in the Digital Age* (pp. 86–117). Hershey, PA: IGI Global. doi:10.4018/978-1-5225-2802-9.ch004

Wang, W., & Wei, Z. (2021). Tongwei County Library: Practices of Social Cooperation in Grassroots Libraries in Western China. *International Journal of Library and Information Services*, 10(1), 48–60. https://doi.org/10.4018/IJLIS.2021010104

Wani, Z. A., Zainab, T., & Hussain, S. (2018). Web 2.0 From Evolution to Revolutionary Impact in Library and Information Centers. In M. Khosrow-Pour, D.B.A. (Ed.), Encyclopedia of Information Science and Technology, Fourth Edition (pp. 5262-5271). Hershey, PA: IGI Global. https://doi.org/ doi:10.4018/978-1-5225-2255-3.ch457

Watkins, K. E., Nicolaides, A., & Marsick, V. J. (2021). Action Research Approaches. In V. Wang (Ed.), *Promoting Qualitative Research Methods for Critical Reflection and Change* (pp. 119–139). IGI Global. https://doi.org/10.4018/978-1-7998-7600-7.ch007

Weiss, A. P. (2018). Massive Digital Libraries (MDLs). In M. Khosrow-Pour, D.B.A. (Ed.), Encyclopedia of Information Science and Technology, Fourth Edition (pp. 5226-5236). Hershey, PA: IGI Global. https://doi.org/ doi:10.4018/978-1-5225-2255-3.ch454

Wu, S. K., Bess, M., & Price, B. R. (2018). Digitizing Library Outreach: Leveraging Bluetooth Beacons and Mobile Applications to Expand Library Outreach. In R. Bhardwaj (Ed.), *Digitizing the Modern Library and the Transition From Print to Electronic* (pp. 193–203). Hershey, PA: IGI Global. doi:10.4018/978-1-5225-2119-8.ch008

Wulff, E. (2018). Evaluation of Digital Collections and Political Visibility of the Library. In R. Bhardwaj (Ed.), *Digitizing the Modern Library and the Transition From Print to Electronic* (pp. 64–89). Hershey, PA: IGI Global. doi:10.4018/978-1-5225-2119-8.ch003

Wulff, E. (2019). Research Data Access and Management in National Libraries. In R. Bhardwaj & P. Banks (Eds.), *Research Data Access and Management in Modern Libraries* (pp. 1–28). IGI Global. https://doi.org/10.4018/978-1-5225-8437-7.ch001

Xiao, L., & Liu, Y. (2017). Development of Innovative User Services. In L. Ruan, Q. Zhu, & Y. Ye (Eds.), *Academic Library Development and Administration in China* (pp. 56–73). Hershey, PA: IGI Global. doi:10.4018/978-1-5225-0550-1.ch004

Xin, X., & Wu, X. (2017). The Practice of Outreach Services in Chinese Special Libraries. In L. Ruan, Q. Zhu, & Y. Ye (Eds.), *Academic Library Development and Administration in China* (pp. 74–89). Hershey, PA: IGI Global. doi:10.4018/978-1-5225-0550-1.ch005

Yao, X., Zhu, Q., & Liu, J. (2017). The China Academic Library and Information System (CALIS). In L. Ruan, Q. Zhu, & Y. Ye (Eds.), *Academic Library Development and Administration in China* (pp. 1–19). Hershey, PA: IGI Global. doi:10.4018/978-1-5225-0550-1.ch001

Yin, Q., Yingying, W., Yan, Z., & Xiaojia, M. (2017). Resource Sharing and Mutually Beneficial Co-operation: A Look at the New United Model in Public and College Libraries. In L. Ruan, Q. Zhu, & Y. Ye (Eds.), *Academic Library Development and Administration in China* (pp. 334–352). Hershey, PA: IGI Global. doi:10.4018/978-1-5225-0550-1.ch019

Yuhua, F. (2018). Computer Information Library Clusters. In M. Khosrow-Pour, D.B.A. (Ed.), Encyclopedia of Information Science and Technology, Fourth Edition (pp. 4399-4403). Hershey, PA: IGI Global. doi:10.4018/978-1-5225-2255-3.ch382

Yusuf, F., & Owolabi, S. E. (2018). Open Access to Knowledge and Challenges in Digital Libraries: Nigeria's Peculiarity. In A. Tella & T. Kwanya (Eds.), *Handbook of Research on Managing Intellectual Property in Digital Libraries* (pp. 241–259). Hershey, PA: IGI Global. doi:10.4018/978-1-5225-3093-0. ch013

Zhang, Q., Zhang, C., & Zhang, Z. (2021). Open Data Services in the Library: Case Study of the Shanghai Library. *International Journal of Library and Information Services*, *10*(1), 1–17. https://doi. org/10.4018/IJLIS.2021010101

Zhang, W., Zou, W., & Qiu, X. (2019). A Unique Development Road of Urban Public Libraries of China: Practice and Exploration of Pudong Library. *International Journal of Library and Information Services*, *8*(2), 51–71. https://doi.org/10.4018/IJLIS.2019070104

Zhu, S., & Shi, W. (2017). A Bibliometric Analysis of Research and Services in Chinese Academic Libraries. In L. Ruan, Q. Zhu, & Y. Ye (Eds.), *Academic Library Development and Administration in China* (pp. 253–262). Hershey, PA: IGI Global. doi:10.4018/978-1-5225-0550-1.ch015

About the Author

Lincoln C. Wood teaches and researches at the University of Otago (New Zealand) and is an Adjunct Research Fellow at Curtin University (Western Australia). He has previously worked at Curtin University, the Auckland University of Technology, and the University of Auckland. His research investigates the design of sustainable operational systems, improving sustainable and social outcomes through operations and supply chain management practices. His work has particular applications in the construction and logistics sectors and healthcare delivery systems, particularly interested in multi-stakeholder environments. A stream of his research examines managing and lifting operational performance while balancing social consequences, such as ethical and privacy considerations for users in the systems. There are two fundamental approaches he investigates for this. First, technology is often used to enhance capabilities and open new market opportunities. Second is the study of preparing for, recovering from disruptions, and developing resilience. Much of his earlier research work employed qualitative methods, but his focus has turned to mixed methods and quantitative approaches. He has edited several volumes of work on supply chain management and operations management research, focusing on presenting chapters with a strong practical application providing value to business professionals, researchers, and postgraduate students.

Dr Wood is an Associate Editor at the *Journal Supply Chain Management* and is Editor of the *International Journal of Applied Logistics* and the *International Journal of Sociotechnology and Knowledge Development*. In addition, he is active on the boards of other supply chain journals. Publons.com recognized his review work with the award for one of the top 10 ten excellent reviewers (2019) based on editor feedback from Web of Science indexed journals. He has published over sixty articles in leading journals, including *Transportation Research Part B: Methodological, International Journal of Operations & Production Management, Supply Chain Management: An International Journal, International Journal of Production Economics, International Journal of Logistics Management, Annals of Operations Research, Journal of Cleaner Production, Total Quality Management & Business Excellence, Resources, Conservation, and Recycling, International Journal of Project Management, Production Planning & Control,* and the *Journal of Business Research.*

Dr Wood's research and connections with business have led to working closely with several industry associations, including the Chartered Institute of Logistics and Transport (CILT). In addition, his expertise has led to invitations to present and lead workshops and present at several international, industry-focused conferences. Over the years, he has supervised many operations and supply chain students in various topics for their masters and doctoral study and has received recognition from the Otago University Students' Association for his supervision work. He currently teaches courses on operations and supply chain strategy and business and society and teaches courses spanning first-year and final year undergraduate courses and postgraduate classes.

Index

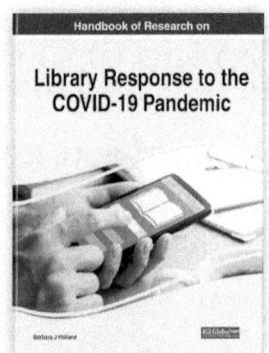

Ensure Quality Research is Introduced to the Academic Community

Become an Evaluator for IGI Global Authored Book Projects

Premier Reference Source

Stabilizing Currency and Preserving Economic Sovereignty Using the Grondona System

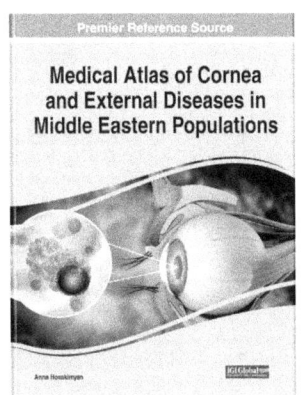

Premier Reference Source

Medical Atlas of Cornea and External Diseases in Middle Eastern Populations

Premier Reference Source

Examining Biophilia and Societal Indifference to Environmental Protection

Premier Reference Source

Using Narratives and Storytelling to Promote Cultural Diversity on College Campuses

The overall success of an authored book project is dependent on quality and timely manuscript evaluations.

Applications and Inquiries may be sent to:
development@igi-global.com

Applicants must have a doctorate (or equivalent degree) as well as publishing, research, and reviewing experience. Authored Book Evaluators are appointed for one-year terms and are expected to complete at least three evaluations per term. Upon successful completion of this term, evaluators can be considered for an additional term.

If you have a colleague that may be interested in this opportunity, we encourage you to share this information with them.

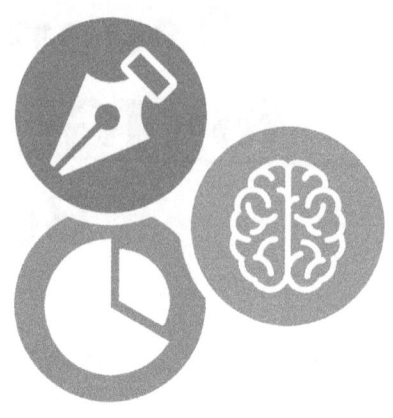

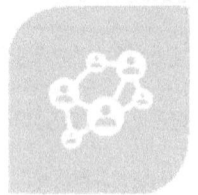

CPSIA information can be obtained
at www.ICGtesting.com
Printed in the USA
BVHW011437230622
640492BV00004B/73

9 781799 889694